MAKE WORK FAIR

ALSO BY IRIS BOHNET

What Works: Gender Equality by Design

MAKE WORK FAIR

Data-Driven Design for Real Results

Iris Bohnet and Siri Chilazi

HARPER
BUSINESS

An Imprint of HarperCollins*Publishers*

First HarperBusiness hardcover published 2025

FIRST EDITION

Designed by Michele Cameron

Library of Congress Cataloging-in-Publication Data

Names: Bohnet, Iris, author. | Chilazi, Siri, author.
Title: Make work fair: data-driven design for real results / Iris Bohnet and Siri Chilazi.
Description: First edition. | New York, NY: Harper Business, an imprint of HarperCollins Publishers, 2025. | Includes bibliographical references and index.
Identifiers: LCCN 2024029286 (print) | LCCN 2024029287 (ebook) | ISBN 9780063374416 (hardcover) | ISBN 9780063374409 (ebook)
Subjects: LCSH: Sex discrimination in employment. | Gender mainstreaming. | Organizational behavior. | Equal pay for equal work.
Classification: LCC HD6060 .B63 2025 (print) | LCC HD6060 (ebook) | DDC 331.4/133—dc23/eng/20240822
LC record available at https://lccn.loc.gov/2024029286
LC ebook record available at https://lccn.loc.gov/2024029287

ISBN 978-0-06-337441-6

24 25 26 27 28 LBC 5 4 3 2 1

To Michael, Dominik, and Luca
and
Paul, Ruth, and Brigitte

To my One, JP
and
Mommy, Daddy, and Suvi
and
George, Sylvia, Lea, and Michael

CONTENTS

CONTENTS

Design for Fairness

In the nineteenth century, the first car was patented in Germany. In the twentieth century, cars started to be mass-produced around the world, and thanks to American inventor Samuel W. Alderson, were made safer when he introduced the first crash test dummy to simulate the impact of car accidents on humans. But we would have to wait until the twenty-first century for cars to become safer for *all*: a few years ago, Swedish engineer Astrid Linder developed the first female* crash test dummy.

Around the world, traffic accidents claim the lives of around 1.3 million people every year. For every person killed, another ten are severely injured and another hundred are slightly injured. While men drive more than women, and therefore are more likely to be involved in car accidents, women are more likely to be injured.

As the research director of traffic safety at the Swedish National Road and Transport Research Institute (VTI), Astrid Linder aims, in her own words, "to make everyone in cars as well protected as possible."

---

* For readability reasons, we use the terms "woman/female" and "man/male" interchangeably to refer to people who identify as women and men, respectively. However, biological sex (often associated with the term "female/male") and socially constructed gender (often associated with the term "woman/man") are distinct concepts. In most social science research studies, participants self-identify their gender.

And to truly include *everyone*, she knows that testing cars exclusively on male dummies isn't enough. Women are not only lighter and shorter than men, on average. Women also have a different body mass distribution, different torso shape, and different joint stiffness than men—and they sit closer to the steering wheel while driving.

All of these differences turn out to matter significantly. When we design cars for the average male body, they keep men meaningfully safer than women. But while many auto manufacturers have voluntarily used scaled-up and scaled-down versions of the average male dummy in their internal tests, regulations around the world continue to specify that only the average adult male dummy needs to be used to represent the entire adult population in safety tests.

Astrid Linder didn't have the power to change these regulations. But far from letting that deter her, she focused on what she could do to make her own work fair. Linder and her team have now developed two female crash test dummies: one to represent an average female body in all types of crashes and one to specifically evaluate car seat safety in rear-impact collisions, where women are up to three times more likely than men to experience a neck injury. There might be some movement on the regulatory front, too: In March 2023, the United States Government Accountability Office recommended in a report to Congress that the National Highway Traffic Safety Administration "develop a plan to address limitations in the information provided by dummies." NHTSA agreed with the recommendation.

Much as the design of the car safety testing process led to greater safety for men than women, our organizations have implicit and explicit structures that advantage some people over others. And much like Astrid Linder, you can make changes in how you deal with such unfairness. We wrote this book to show you how. To cut to the chase: build fairness into everything you do.

You make work fair when you improve how you are doing the things you are already doing. Your daily job. Your core business. If you design safety features for cars, build them so that they work for bodies of all shapes and sizes. If you hire or promote, employ practices that have been proven to give everyone a fair shot. If you create presentations, ensure the images you select are representative of your employees, customers, and the communities you serve. And if you chair a meeting, run it so that you can benefit from everyone's wisdom.

We know that in today's fast-paced workplaces, most of us are being asked to do more with less and it can sometimes feel like there aren't enough hours in the day. So we are not going to pile another one-off training, add-on program, or networking reception onto your plate. We are not going to ask you to do additional "diversity, equity, and inclusion (DEI) work." Instead, we are proposing a paradigm shift. When you make your work fair, it becomes part of what you already do—you are simply doing things better and smarter.

For us, making work fair means designing workplaces where everyone can thrive and perform at their best. This means giving all people—regardless of gender, race, ethnicity, sexual orientation, or any other aspect of their identity or background—access to a playing field where some people are not unfairly advantaged in a way they didn't earn. One where everyone receives support to succeed to their fullest potential through equal access to benefits and opportunities. And one where barriers, visible or invisible, do not stand in the way of some people but not others.

As researchers and behavioral designers, our passion is using evidence to understand what works and what doesn't to dismantle such barriers. Thankfully, our understanding of their nature and impacts has grown tremendously. As a result, our preferred approach is to design fair processes and structures that put everyone on an equal footing when decisions are made, such as when we anonymize résumés and application materials so that people's gender is not a factor in hiring, or when we standardize performance appraisal processes to prevent bias from creeping in. However, sometimes the effects of long-standing barriers are so persistent that treating everyone the same way results in unfair outcomes.

And it starts early. Whether or not children happen to grow up in a high- or low-opportunity neighborhood in the US is crucial for how well they fare as adults. Similarly, whether or not they have the good fortune of being inspired by role models who look like they do has nothing to do with "merit" but instead with who is featured in films, books, and social and other media—and in what roles. Women don't have to be damsels in distress awaiting rescue by a male hero, and men can be nurses and teachers who take great care of their patients and students. Seeing is believing: women in India were more likely to run for public office when they saw other women in political leadership, and girls in France were more likely to study a STEM (science, technology, engineering, and mathematics) subject when they were exposed to female scientists and engineers. On the flip side, to increase the fraction of male primary school teachers, a 40 percent quota for men was in place in university admissions for primary school teacher studies in Finland for a few years; both girls and boys benefited from their presence in classrooms. So, to truly represent everyone—and thus, treat everyone the same—we sometimes have to treat people differently for a while to make up for systemic exclusion in the past.

The good news is that making work fair is possible because every physical environment (such as your office building or manufacturing plant), every formal process (such as hiring or performance management), and every informal way of working (such as meetings or networking) was designed—intentionally or unintentionally—by someone somewhere. While no process design is neutral, *any* process can be redesigned for the better.

That is exactly what Astrid Linder did. Instead of settling for the prevailing wisdom that women are "out-of-position drivers" and therefore more at risk in collisions, she recognized that the real issue was that cars are not designed to take the safety of all occupants into equal consideration. So she did what she could in her role to redesign how cars are safety tested.

Following Linder's example, our book is about changing behaviors, not attitudes. The approach we are using, behavioral design, is rooted in insights into how our minds work. It helps us move from virtuous intentions to action. It allows us to create processes, systems, policies, and environments that help our inherently biased brains nonetheless make fairer and more objective decisions. And it allows us to change outcomes without trying to tackle people's deeply held beliefs. By making these insights widely available and actionable, our hope is to help you design high-performing organizations that tap unprecedented potential and provide unparalleled opportunity—and allow you to spend your resources and time on things that have been shown to be effective.

This book is filled with data-driven solutions—and we wrote it for you. The employee. The junior manager. The senior manager. The human resources (HR) professional. The DEI expert. The C-suite leader. The consultant. The entrepreneur. The policymaker. The investor. The board director. The student in our classroom. And the activist working to advance DEI—as well as the activist working to limit DEI.

While this might sound paradoxical, we actually mean it. Whatever you may think about the current DEI approaches being used in organizations, or however you feel about the current tenor of the public debate around DEI, we hope you share our ultimate goal: making work fair for everyone. Very few people are against fairness but we don't all agree on what it entails. If the definition we offered a couple of pages ago—true equal access and opportunity to thrive—resonates with you, we are good to go. If this is either too little or too much fairness for you, we encourage you to write down your specific concerns now so that you can engage with the data we are going to share with an open mind. At the end, go back to your list. Surely, not all of the insights will resonate with you, but we bet that some will.

Regardless of where you are coming from, we are not here to judge but instead to invite you to join us in discovering how we can (re)design work for real results based on the best evidence social science has to offer. To get to these results, we echo Jamie Dimon, CEO of the world's largest bank, JPMorgan Chase, who at the World Economic Forum meetings in Davos, Switzerland, in January 2024 reminded us that we have to treat fairness like any other line of business, with the same attention to "details, facts, and analysis."

We are thrilled to be your partners in making work fair—because it is both the smart and the right thing to do, and because it is a genuinely game-changing opportunity. No matter your role, no matter your seniority, no matter your scope of responsibilities, no matter where you are in the world, you belong on this quest because merely believing in equal opportunity does not mean that we are building fair organizations.

You have a part to play in making work fair, and in so doing, changing the world, one small step at a time. We are taking these steps ourselves at Harvard University, where our core business is teaching and research. In many courses, faculty use an application called Teachly to help them ensure that their classroom is as level a playing field as possible in terms of student participation. The software tracks which students faculty call on, and after each class session, sends a report of how we are measuring up against the overall composition of the class. Are we giving men more airtime than women? Unintentionally ignoring students whose first language is not English? Calling on the same eager beavers every class while overlooking the tentative hands that occasionally go up in the back row? As much as we consciously believe in fairness, our unconscious tendencies sometimes get in the way.

Iris, for example, learned that she was more likely to call on students who sat on the left side of the room. This was not a political statement, but instead due to a hearing impairment in her right ear. Unconsciously, she favored students whom she expected to hear better. She now tends to stand further to the right in a classroom so that her unconscious mind can be at ease knowing that she will be able to hear everyone. She also shares this "bias" and its root cause with her students so that they can help her manage it. But most importantly, the smart Teachly technology helps Iris live up to her virtuous intentions.

Siri relies on a lower-tech solution when she teaches group exercise classes (in her other beloved "classroom"). She once realized halfway through a workout that while she had been gleefully referring to participants as "ladies," there were, in fact, two gentlemen in the back of the class. As soon as she got home, she wrote out a list of gender-neutral words—"friends," "everyone," "folks," "rock stars," "beautiful people," and so on—that would work to address any crowd and make everyone feel welcome in her class. For Siri, it took several months of focused effort and practice to change her go-to speech patterns, but the inclusive language has since become built into how she addresses people in all contexts.

These are small steps—but steps in the right direction.

Many organizations of all shapes and sizes are, in fact, taking such steps and succeeding. When pop megastar Rihanna's Fenty Beauty launched in 2017 with forty (today, more than fifty) shades of foundation, the idea of serving customers with all skin tones was so embedded into the company's business that they did not even call it out. "Our approach to inclusion marketing has always been about 'showing, not telling,'" explained Sandy Saputo, then chief marketing officer of Fenty Beauty's parent company. "In fact, we never once used the word 'inclusive' in our messaging. 'Inclusive' is how we were defined by the press and consumers."

In Colombia, the country's largest brewery, Bavaria, took its own steps to create a more inclusive workplace when it designed around a national law that restricts women to lifting a maximum of 12.5 kilograms (around 28 pounds) at work. The company reengineered the production line at one of its plants to accommodate the restrictions. It was such a success that Bavaria is now expanding its inclusive production line concept to all of its breweries and making sure that manufacturing occupations are accessible not only to women, but also to people with disabilities.

Including more talent and more customers beats any other talent optimization or sales strategy any day. Encouragingly, Fenty Beauty and Bavaria are not alone. In a massive nationwide experiment with 108 of the largest US companies between 2019 and 2021, the worst gender and race discrimination was concentrated among a small subset of firms. Most companies still had issues to address on gender and race, as well as on age discrimination, but the fact that some firms did decidedly better than others means that we can move the needle toward greater fairness at work.

Whether you are seeking to make your own work fair or are a manager, policymaker, or consultant aiming to change a broader organization, our book will offer you an evidence-based blueprint for how to serve as an agent for meaningful structural change without making it your full-time job. This blueprint is about fixing our systems and empowering everyone in our organizations to do their everyday work smarter. When we make work fair, we view it as essential to the fulfillment of our mission. We recognize that striving will no longer suffice—that only real, measurable results will do.

We begin by debunking key myths to understand why our current efforts are not as effective as they should be (Chapter 1). Spoiler alert: making work fair comes down to treating fairness like you treat all other aspects of your job or business. Then we get to solutions. In Part I (Chapters 2–5), we discover how we can motivate action by making fairness count. In Part II (Chapters 6–9), we discuss how to make fairness stick through smart process design. In Part III (Chapters 10–12), we learn how to make fairness normal by building an environment we want to work in. In our conclusion, we send you off with a final few encouraging examples of how we can transform our behaviors and organizations for good—with real results.

We are building on Iris's earlier book, *What Works: Gender Equality by Design*. Thankfully, not only has our knowledge base grown over the past ten years since *What Works*, but so has the number of success stories we can share to equip you with the inspiration, insights, and tools you need to make your work fair. They include Mia Perdomo, a Colombian entrepreneur who cofounded Latin America's first equity ranking system together with Andrea de la Piedra; Ros Atkins, a British BBC journalist who designed a simple data-tracking system to overhaul gender representation in the media; and Tarana Burke, a pioneering American activist who changed social norms around sexual violence and founded the #MeToo movement.

We will also encounter a host of organizations ranging from the US tech giant Google to Swiss pharmaceutical company Novartis and China's largest travel agency, Trip.com, and from the New York City Fire Department to the European Central Bank and the Indian government. Some of them we have worked with personally, and others we are familiar with through research and published accounts. We present these individuals and organizations as examples of how specific solutions have been implemented, but we are not endorsing any one organization: Nobody has "nailed it" completely when it comes to fairness at work. However, by learning from each other we can start a virtuous cycle: try out new approaches, evaluate what works, inspire others, and get further faster.

The two of us have dedicated our professional lives to making workplaces fair for women, which is also the core expertise of the Women and Public Policy Program, our home base at Harvard Kennedy School. Gender is therefore our primary lens for discussing fairness in this book, and we will consider its intersections with race, sexual orientation, parental status, age, disability, geography, and nationality wherever possible.* Since many of the solutions we share

---

* We should note that social categorizations are highly contextual. In the US context, we use the terms "Black" and "African American" interchangeably even though they are not always considered synonymous, and we use the terms "Hispanic" and "Latina/o" to refer to people with Spanish-speaking, Latin American, and/or Brazilian origins. When we refer to "underrepresented" (or "underestimated," a term venture capitalist Arlan Hamilton encourages to indicate that these groups have historically been shut out from opportunities) groups, we mean people who have been historically underrepresented in employment and leadership relative to their representation in the general population in a given context. In the United States, this means primarily people who identify as Black, Latina/o, Native American, Pacific Islander, and/or Asian American, as well as women, LGBTQ+ people, veterans, people with disabilities, or those from socioeconomically disadvantaged backgrounds.

with you can be used to make work fair along numerous dimensions, not only with respect to gender, we hope you will be inspired to use them to achieve a level playing field for *all*.

Our main focus is people who identify as women and men because we typically don't have enough data to tell you what works for transgender and gender-nonconforming people. Fortunately, change is happening. While the 2020 US Census only asked if people were female or male, in its Household Pulse Survey in 2021, the Census Bureau introduced questions about gender identity for the first time. Moving forward, it is important to generate and study data beyond the binary.

Even though our book focuses on closing gaps where it is women that are currently behind, gender equity is a two-way street. There are certainly areas, such as HEAL (health, education, administration, and literacy) occupations, where men are underrepresented. Just like getting more women into STEM occupations, getting more men engaged in HEAL will require us to "build a pipeline in the education system, provide financial incentives, and reduce the social stigma faced by men," as Richard V. Reeves outlines in his timely book *Of Boys and Men*. As a society, we need to rethink our systems and how we value all types of work, including care.

Systems can transform in both big, top-down ways, as well as small, bottom-up ones. If you are a senior leader reading this, you likely have the power to do the former. Change a company-wide policy overnight. Institute ambitious new goals. Direct the people who report to you to follow a different process for hiring or promotions. And if you do not currently hold organization-wide formal authority, you have the power to do the latter. Use less stereotypical language in your communications. Suggest a new way of conducting meetings. Role-model desired behaviors for your peers and use your voice to influence leaders. You can serve as an agent for structural change because it is these small and big steps that will add up to massive shifts.

And guess what? It's easier than you might think.

Let's get to work.

MAKE WORK FAIR

CHAPTER 1

The Myths We Need to Debunk

"When I think about my experience with diversity, equity, and inclusion in the workplace, my first thought goes to mandatory online training sessions to be completed within the first week of starting a new role. A checkbox for new employees, rarely to be revisited again. And I will fully admit to taking those training sessions much more with a mindset of 'something that has to be done' rather than taking the opportunity to reflect on my own biases. I have to believe that I am not alone in approaching those training sessions in that regard."

The graduate student who gave us permission to share her experience is not alone. Corporate diversity training has existed since the 1960s, when it was born out of the civil rights movement in the United States, and trainings to de-bias our minds have exploded in popularity over the last decade. A focus on de-biasing individuals through training instead of de-biasing systems through larger-scale changes is not altogether surprising because we humans tend to gravitate toward framing problems in individual rather than systemic terms. A people problem, we think, calls for a people solution.

Organizations' focus on individual solutions can have important real-world consequences because it can reduce support for systemic solutions. For example, when messages about gender equality emphasized women's empowerment (i.e., women's potential to overcome gender inequality through self-improvement) as opposed to structural challenges (organizational barriers to women's advancement), people were more likely to support solutions that required women to change themselves rather than solutions that required the organization to change its systems. The study's authors concluded: "When society points to how women *can* change—they can dream bigger, talk louder—it also points to who and what *should* change."

Although empowering women (and all people) to reach their full potential is certainly a goal we endorse, such empowerment can only go so far. Giving a sprinter a better pair of sneakers might make them marginally faster—but if their starting line is, say, 20 meters behind their competitor's for the 100-meter dash, they will still finish second. Efforts to fix individuals are akin to giving them better sneakers without considering the starting line. You will be better off moving everyone to the same starting line and allowing them to compete fairly. Change the playing field, not the players.

Despite our best intentions, this is not how many of us have tried to make workplaces fair. Instead of changing systems, we have focused on changing mindsets. We have invested in short-term programmatic solutions instead of addressing unfair organizational processes that govern how we work every day. We have siloed fairness instead of involving everyone in embedding it.

If we are serious about leveling the playing field and giving everyone a chance to succeed instead of keeping some people out, merely raising awareness won't do. Trainings alone won't do. Nor will the many one-off efforts that companies have focused on. Why?

Because making work fair is not a program but a way of doing things.

Consider what has happened in the last decade. The awareness of the concepts related to fairness has skyrocketed, both in workplaces and among the general public. Terms like "unconscious bias," "microaggressions," and "allyship" have entered the mainstream lexicon as well as companies' onboarding manuals, employee trainings, and marketing materials. Unconscious bias trainings, affinity group events, and empathy-building workshops have become standard fare. Underlying these changes is the belief that increasing people's awareness of their biases will make organizations more fair.

The focus on "corporate DEI," already underway before the COVID-19 pandemic hit, was massively accelerated by the racial reckoning of 2020 that followed the killing of George Floyd and too many others. Organizations made more public statements and commitments than ever indicating their intentions to tackle inequity in earnest. They brought in more consultants and speakers than ever to provide inspiration, training, and technical assistance. And they hired more and more in-house DEI professionals—without necessarily setting them up for success with clear goals, leadership support, or robust budgets. The prevailing approach to workplace fairness became all about intentionality, or the idea that paying more attention to it (and talking and posting about it more) would lead to meaningful progress.

Yet, something was—and is—missing. Siri witnessed this personally a few years ago when she was part of a research team investigating why the most senior ranks in one of the world's largest companies had so few women. The firm's top leaders were more than happy to write sizable checks to fund the research project as well as all of the firm's DEI activities. They even cleared their busy schedules to personally meet and discuss gender equity and came to events to show their support to employee groups. But when it came time to implement the researchers' data-driven recommendations, which centered on redesigning processes that created demonstrable disadvantages for women, the executives balked. The project ended. The company tucked Siri's team's insights neatly into a drawer and continued business as usual.

The firm was not ready for a systemic approach. Like many firms today, it viewed fairness as a nice-to-have on the side, not as a core feature of its business intertwined with everything else it does in product development, sales, marketing, finance, corporate social responsibility, and HR. Unfortunately, as a result, the firm has faced numerous high-profile lawsuits and scandals in recent years, as have many of its peers.

To achieve better results, we need to understand what is going wrong and why our well-intentioned efforts—often based on "best practices" rather than the "best evidence"—have not moved the needle enough. In this chapter, we debunk seven common myths about fairness to clear the way for more effective solutions that truly work.

Myth 1: We Need to De-bias Individuals

A few years ago, when some of the world's largest firms visited the campus of the University of Pennsylvania to recruit graduating seniors for full-time jobs, 90 percent of the recruiters reported that increasing gender and racial diversity was an important consideration in their hiring (as were students' grades and their past summer internship experiences). But the recruiters fell way short of their aspirations to hire fairly. Among STEM majors, women and people of color needed a higher grade point average (GPA) to be considered on par with white men. In addition, white men received 50 percent more credit for their prestigious summer internships than women and people of color with the same internship experiences.

While the recruiters presumably wanted to find more diverse candidates, they were unable to deliver. They faced an "intention-action gap." The results suggest that their evaluation procedures did not protect the recruiters from being influenced by stereotypes of what, say, a typical engineer looks like, or from succumbing to in-group preferences (sometimes also referred to as affinity bias or homophily) whereby they were tempted to hire people similar to them. The firms ended up selecting "those who looked the part" instead of "the best people"—and did not give everyone a fair shot.

All of us fall prey to these types of biases daily. In the face of a constant deluge of information, our brains rely heavily on heuristics—

rules of thumb that help us make sense of the world quickly and mostly subconsciously—to generate judgments and make decisions. Sometimes heuristics serve us well: if you are crossing a street and see from the corner of your eye an object coming at you, the best move is not to stop, ascertain the nature of the object, estimate its speed, and determine how fast you could reach the curb. The best move is to follow your instinct and immediately jump out of the way, per the unconscious pattern that fast-moving objects on streets generally equal dangerous cars.

However, our instincts can also lead us astray. Stereotypes, or generalized beliefs about a particular group of people, can lead to bias—conscious and unconscious—where we make inaccurate judgments about people, as well as prejudice and discrimination where we act on our beliefs and treat people differently because of the group they belong to.

One time when Siri entered her dermatologist's office, she was told to walk down a hallway and wait at the end for the nurse to call her into her appointment. Upon reaching the waiting area, she saw a man dressed in everyday clothes typing on a computer in what looked like the doctor's office. She instantly thought, "Oh, this must be the IT guy. The nurse is surely on her way." Siri was thoroughly shocked (and embarrassed!) when about two minutes later the man got up and walked out to greet her: "Hi, I'm John. I'm the dermatology nurse."

Like every one of us every single day, Siri fell into a classic stereotype trap. She did not act on it but could not help her thoughts being influenced by it. The majority of nurses are women whereas the majority of IT professionals are men, so our brains have learned to associate women with nursing and men with computers and technology. When Siri saw the man in the dermatologist's office, his presence was so counter-stereotypical that it did not even occur to her that he could be the nurse, and her brain came up with a somewhat far-fetched—not to mention stereotypical—explanation for what he was doing at the computer.

This type of unconscious (otherwise known as implicit) bias is different from consciously held (or explicit) attitudes and beliefs. By definition, we are not aware of how our brains unconsciously process information. We are, however, fully aware of the things we consciously believe. When a (female) venture capitalist told us, "Children need their mothers, and mothers are more important, in many ways, than fathers," and when a (male) superior told a humanitarian practitioner, "Women shouldn't be deployed to field sites during humanitarian crises because there are no places for them to wash their hair," they were expressing conscious beliefs about the different roles women and men should play at home and at work. Sometimes these beliefs lead to prejudice and discrimination. When Wall Street's top private banker Jane Heller was told by her male boss earlier in her career, "I don't like women and I don't like women who work. I'm gonna call you 'Henry,'" he aired a clear prejudice against women in the workplace. Conscious beliefs, especially when followed by actions or when encoded into laws and policies that treat women and men differently, remain the source of much gender inequality around the globe. But even if all conscious bias disappeared, we would continue to harbor unconscious biases that influence how we view the world.

When it comes to stereotypes, seeing is believing: What often matters more than who we are is what we see around us. For instance, women and men by and large hold similar gender heuristics—at least in substance, though not always in magnitude—since we have all grown up surrounded by the same social conditioning through role models, movies, toys, textbooks, and so on. Members of traditionally disadvantaged groups are therefore no more immune than those traditionally advantaged.

However, in-group bias, which leads us to favor people we perceive to be in our group—whether based on gender, race, the school we went to, or simply by having the same hobbies—plays out differently depending on the group we identify with. If a group you belong to holds more power than others in society, you will benefit more from being favored by your in-group members. Case in point: In a Canadian study of nearly 40 million outpatient referrals to surgeons between 1997 and 2016, male physicians were more likely to show in-group favoritism and refer patients to male surgeons, disadvantaging female surgeons. Male surgeons received 87 percent of all the referrals made by male physicians (and 79 percent of the referrals made by female physicians), despite making up 78 percent of all surgeons. In-group bias makes it harder for women to break into key networks in professional spaces traditionally dominated by men—and harder for men to be welcomed into the circles of parents on playgrounds, nurses in hospitals, or teachers in elementary schools.

Our biases have far-reaching consequences for others, and when constantly reinforced, they can turn into a self-fulfilling prophecy. By age six, research suggests, American children have absorbed the association of intellectual brilliance and genius with men more than women. Heartbreakingly, six-year-old girls are already less likely than boys to believe that members of their gender are "really, really smart." These stereotypes have a direct influence on children's behavior: girls are less likely than boys to express interest in novel games that are intended for children "who are really, really smart."

In a similar vein, economist Michela Carlana showed that in Italian middle schools, girls underperformed in math when they were assigned a math teacher with strong unconscious beliefs that boys are better at math than girls (as measured by the most widely used tool, the Implicit Association Test*). Furthermore, these girls ended up self-selecting into less demanding high schools, which influenced their career options going forward. The gender stereotypes of the teachers induced the girls—especially those whose math skills were lower to begin with—to doubt themselves, leading them to fail to reach their full potential. One

---

* The IAT, which was developed in the mid-1990s, measures the strength of our unconscious associations, such as that between women and home on the one hand and men and work on the other hand, by tracking how long it takes us to connect words related to these concepts. The IAT is available for free at https://implicit.harvard.edu/.

can only wonder how much talent we collectively are missing in the world when we start to lose out on it at such a young age.

The pernicious effects of bias also play out in the workplace—with negative consequences for individuals and organizations. In grocery stores, female managers were found to allocate disproportionately more time to tasks that allowed them to disprove negative gender stereotypes about their lack of commitment or competence. This meant spending more time on the grocery store floor on tasks they could do visibly in front of subordinates. Unfortunately, it resulted in the female managers spending less time on more invisible, yet equally important, office tasks, which in turn hurt their and their departments' performance. In medicine, where female surgeons were not afforded the same respect and authority as their male counterparts due to gender stereotypes, they behaved more deferentially toward the female nurses they worked with, such as by helping the nurses with their tasks and befriending them outside the operating room. This "managing down" hurt female surgeons' performance.

If you are now thinking that eliminating bias from human brains is necessary to create fairer workplaces, you are not alone. Unfortunately, that approach is hardly feasible because unconscious bias at the individual level is extremely difficult to change. At best, some programmatic interventions have managed to temporarily affect people's attitudes and/or their awareness of bias. But there is little indication that any change in unconscious bias awareness has led to sustainable changes in behavior, according to the most comprehensive meta-analyses* synthesizing evidence from hundreds of studies over the last two decades. Simply put, de-biasing humans is incredibly hard, and might well be impossible.

What we *can* do is de-bias the organizational processes, environ-

---

* A meta-analysis is a type of statistical analysis combining the quantitative results of multiple scientific studies. Meta-analyses help us to evaluate the overall effects of interventions, such as those for bias reduction, that have been documented in a variety of studies and settings across time.

ments, and policies that we have created and that contain built-in bias. Consider the commercial facial recognition software that can accurately identify the gender of a white man in a photo, getting it wrong only 1 percent of the time, but that fails to recognize darker-skinned women up to 35 percent of the time. This software was built and tested by mostly white, mostly male engineers at several of the world's leading tech companies—but it can be reprogrammed to work better for all humans. Or the policy that gives women 26 times more parental leave than men to take care of a child, reinforcing gender stereotypes of women as carers and men as earners. That policy was created by legislators in the UK—but it can be changed to give everyone an equal opportunity to contribute at work and at home. Or the hiring practices used in nearly 1,500 German companies that resulted in a woman with a Turkish-sounding name and a headscarf needing to send almost five times as many applications as an otherwise identical candidate with a German-sounding name and no headscarf to receive the same number of interview invitations. These hiring practices, too, can be redesigned to eliminate bias.

People's actions change when the systems surrounding them change—even if their unconscious or conscious biases do not. Not to mention that a single process or policy is much easier to tackle than dozens, hundreds, or thousands of individual minds. By designing smart systems, we can help ourselves live up to our best intentions and perform even better than we could if left to our own devices.

While it would be wonderful to get everyone to change their hearts and minds and shed their unconscious and conscious biases, evidence simply doesn't suggest that this is a realistic aspiration. Fortunately, we do not need to de-bias ourselves or others to design workplaces that are less biased and more fair.

Myth 2: We Can Train Our Way to Fairness

Trainings—diversity trainings, unconscious bias trainings, how-to-succeed-in-business-as-a-woman trainings—are easy to love because they signal to employees and other stakeholders that leaders care about fairness. In fact, in many workplaces it is employees at all levels who are demanding training. It is a neat way of making everyone feel like they are doing something tangible to make the workplace fair while also allowing business to go on as usual. After all, a check-the-box training session doesn't require us to change what we do day-to-day. It does, however, give organizations something simple to measure and report on so that they can point to improvement on "metrics," such as participation. It also doesn't hurt that in the United States, the existence of a training can be used as a defense in possible lawsuits related to discrimination. And since the impact of trainings on behavior is generally not measured, no one's head is on the chopping block if (or when) there is no improvement in actual outcomes.

However, there is one incredibly compelling reason to *not* love trainings.

The evidence indicates that diversity trainings generally do not work to change behaviors or improve measurable outcomes. An analysis of more than 40 years of personnel and administrative data from over 800 American companies showed that providing diversity training to all employees was not correlated with the likelihood that women or people of color would become managers (except for Latinas, whose chances of making it into management were lower when training was offered). Providing diversity training with legal content—which was the case in three-quarters of all training programs—was associated with a *decrease* in the share of white women, Black women and men, and Asian American women and men in management.

The most rigorous examination to date of a specific real-world unconscious bias training measured the effects of a voluntary one-hour online module in a global organization. Behavioral scientist Edward Chang and collaborators assigned more than 3,000 participating employees in 63 countries to a version of the training that focused on gender bias; a version that focused on all types of biases; or a control version that did not discuss bias but focused on psychological safety in teams. Both versions of the bias-focused training had a positive effect on attitudes toward women in the workplace among those employees who were least supportive of women before the training. That's the good news. The bad news is that over the next twenty weeks, the research team did not find evidence of any behavior change (selecting a woman for informal mentoring, recognizing a woman's work internally, or volunteering to speak with a female over a male new hire) among men or white employees. As the authors point out, these two groups are typically the targets of bias trainings because they hold the majority of leadership positions in organizations.

The one group that did change its behavior was junior female employees in the United States. While managers were not inclined to offer more mentorship after the training, the program made junior women—that is, those who could benefit from receiving mentorship—aware of the opportunity and therefore more likely to seek it out. This is not bad news, even if it's not what the authors had originally expected.

This study is one of very few to examine concrete behavior change as an outcome of bias training. Numerous other studies have examined the impacts of various training interventions on people's awareness of bias, their concern about it, and/or their intention to discuss or confront it. Some show promising effects. For instance, US college students who participated in a twelve-week training curriculum to reduce racial bias showed both significant reductions in unconscious bias and increased concern about discrimination. However, what people say they will do is often very different from what they actually do, which is why more research is needed into the behavior change effects of bias training.

In workplaces, we are most optimistic about targeted, context-specific trainings that make fairness considerations salient in the moment of consequential decisions. For example, at the University of Wisconsin–Madison, STEM and medicine departments whose members had taken and debriefed the IAT, as well as participated in a two-and-a-half-hour workshop about bias, hired more new female faculty than control departments. And for college-aged psychology students, undergoing an interactive simulation about gender bias in academia and debriefing it with a facilitator increased their ability to detect subtle expressions of sexism when evaluating a professor's promotion case a week later. If you are going to invest in training, tailor it to the organizational context and time it to coincide with specific behaviors in specific situations. Choose the moments that matter.

Even more important is to *embed* training as part of a holistic strategy to level the playing field. If you are redesigning your interview process, for example, in line with our recommendations in Chapter 8, it makes sense to get the whole interview team together to explain the rationale for the changes and to train them on the new procedures. In this case, the training supports a structural change and helps to ingrain it even further into how people behave by giving them the tools to deliver. The UK government went the embedding route in 2020 when it decided that unconscious bias training would be phased out in its Civil Service. Instead, the Civil Service vowed to "integrate principles for inclusion and diversity into mainstream core training and leadership modules in a manner which facilitates positive behavior change . . . with a stronger focus on engaging measurable action."

Most workplace bias trainings, however, do not follow this playbook. They are often structured as one-offs and not part of an embedded system change. They are rather generic and delivered on a predetermined cadence, such as once a year or as part of new employee onboarding, instead of in the moments that matter. And the content generally focuses on trying to de-bias individuals and change mindsets instead of providing tools to change behavior or tangible information on how best to operate. James Elfer, founder of behavioral science consultancy MoreThanNow, said it well: "Diversity training, in general terms, is wildly overvalued in comparison to more promising tools and structural changes."

We should also be careful with trainings because they can be harmful to the end goal of making real progress on fairness. Besides backlash from some groups—such as unconscious and conscious bias increasing when people feel pressured to exhibit less of it or feel "morally licensed" to compensate for their good training effort—one of the dangers of diversity training is the window-dressing effect, whereby the mere existence of training leads people to believe that problems have been solved. In a set of experiments, organizations that offered training to promote diversity were perceived to be fairer to underrepresented groups (in this case, women and people of color). This led majority group members (in this case, men and white people) to become less sensitive to discrimination in hiring, promotions, and compensation decisions. They also reacted less favorably to underrepresented group members who claimed discrimination. Women themselves have been shown to perceive organizations to be fairer when they offer diversity training, even when evidence showed that existing hiring practices disadvantaged women. The window-dressing effect can make it harder for us to detect and tackle real discrimination.

The bottom line is clear: The evidence to date says that we cannot simply train ourselves out of bias, nor can we train our way to fairness through random programs. For real results, we need an embedded strategy—one that context-specific and timely trainings that equip people with the tools to act can be a part of.

Myth 3: Programmatic Approaches Are Enough to Yield Sustainable Progress

Beyond training, many of the other approaches that organizations use to promote fairness suffer from a programmatic nature. Instead of being built into core activities like hiring, performance evaluation, and meetings that happen no matter what, many traditional "DEI initiatives" are separate from core work and can be canceled anytime without a direct impact on everyday operations.

Programmatic approaches, even when well-intentioned, can send the message that making work fair is an optional add-on that only matters when other, more pressing priorities don't get in the way. A talk, networking session, or affinity group meeting is easy to skip when "real work" overwhelms your calendar. A one-off workshop series is all too easy to cut when budgets get tight—and this is exactly what has happened in many organizations. There's also the investment of hours, effort, and resources that go into organizing all of this programming, often by members of traditionally disadvantaged groups themselves. Even in the best of times, unless it's part of your core role, it entails extra work that typically takes you away from your "promotable" tasks in the zero-sum game of time (most organizations do not reward and promote people for engaging in such programs). At worst, a focus on organizing one-off programs can shift attention away from more impactful system changes. A splashy International Women's Day event might be easier to envision and execute than a company-wide policy change around flexible work— but the latter is much more likely to produce sustainable, measurable improvement in the metrics that matter (beyond survey feedback saying "that was a great session").

Programs tend not to be evaluated by the organizations that implement them, which is why we know much too little about their impact. But they are popular, and in a world filled with "best practices," it can be enticing to simply copy what another company is doing. With a few exceptions, organizations do not deploy the analytical rigor they use in other contexts to evaluate their efforts. For example, A/B testing—or, more formally, randomized controlled trials—is much more prevalent in marketing departments than in HR. The concept of an A/B test is straightforward: Some people (employees, customers, the general public, etc.) are randomly exposed to version A of a program, product, or message, and others to version B (perhaps, what you are currently doing). We then compare the outcomes of the two (or more) experimental conditions to see which one yields more desirable results. We strongly encourage you to measure the effects of all your

efforts this way to establish whether they are accomplishing anything.

Ericsson, a multinational telecommunications company headquartered in Sweden, did this when it came across one factor potentially
hampering women's career advancement: a gender gap in internal
mobility, whereby fewer women than men moved around the company
in different roles, functions, and geographies. To address the gap, the
company first determined a clear and measurable goal to increase the
number of women applying to internal job openings. In partnership
with researchers, Ericsson then decided that its intervention would
be a message to encourage employees to apply for internal roles. They
designed four different messages to test, one of which was a neutral
"control" that simply asked people about their interest in internal job
opportunities.

In a critical step of the A/B testing process, Ericsson then randomized
roughly 13,000 employees to receive one of the four communications.
Randomization is so important because it allows us to determine the
causal effect of the different messages on people's subsequent actions
among statistically identical groups. Otherwise—if, for example, each
message was sent to a different division—other factors, such as the
idiosyncrasies of each division, could confound the results. Likewise, if
you roll out a new initiative to everyone at the same time, you will not
have a control group against which to measure any possible change.
You will only be able to compare outcomes before and after, and such
comparisons suffer from time trends whereby other changes in your
context, like falling interest rates or the introduction of a new law, actually account for what is happening.

Lastly, Ericsson tracked whether employees in each group actually
visited the company's internal mobility site. Compared with the control,
only the message that told employees "You don't have to be 100 percent qualified to explore these opportunities" closed the gender gap
in interest. The other two messages, which featured a senior female
leader encouraging people to apply and a social norms message telling

employees to join thousands of colleagues in exploring internal opportunities, resulted in more interest from men, exacerbating the gender gap. This is precisely why we urge you to evaluate the impact of your efforts: well-meaning great ideas don't always work or can even backfire unexpectedly.

Employee resource groups (ERGs, sometimes also called business resource groups or affinity groups) are an example of a ubiquitous programmatic practice whose impact has not been evaluated on a large scale. The little evidence we have on their effectiveness is mixed. The presence of ERGs is linked to increases in the shares of white women and Latino men (but decreases in white and Black men) in management, with no statistically significant effects for members of other groups.

Programmatic initiatives like ERGs have traditionally been introduced to manage the symptoms of underlying inequities, such as the isolation people feel when they are "the few" or "the only" due to underrepresentation. While ERGs might offer a much-needed reprieve from inequity to their members—including by making role models and support available and by making people from underrepresented groups feel more heard and seen—they are typically unable to change the organizational systems that generate the inequity to begin with, such as biased evaluation processes. Indeed, based on a 2022 McKinsey & Company report building on insights from nearly 25,000 employees across the United States, ERGs were rated highest on community building. Employees were less optimistic about their ERG's role in the other dimensions explored: external engagement, allyship, leadership connection, and career advancement.

Many programs are designed to help women and members of other traditionally underrepresented groups navigate the existing system more successfully instead of changing the system so that everyone can thrive. Since the latter is essential to make work fair, we expect that organizations choosing to have programs, including ERGs, will make more progress when they "are no longer just social networks but are groups of individuals that strategically impact business," in the words of Sudhakar Chintharlapalli, former India Network chair at pharmaceutical company Lilly.

Myth 4: Fairness Is the Responsibility of DEI Professionals Alone

Even though most companies have corporate communications or public relations departments that specialize in conveying information, most of us need to regularly write emails, create slide decks, and speak up in meetings. Everyone needs at least a base level of communication skills for an organization to function.

So it is with fairness as well. While experts like DEI officers or specialist external consultants can be a valuable resource, true progress requires all of us to have the skills to do our work in fairer ways. The key operative word here is "all."

Many of us have bought into the fallacy that a few dedicated DEI professionals can "fix unfairness" for a whole workplace of hundreds or thousands of individuals. However, "The actual job of delivering real progress on DEI outcomes does not reside in a central chief diversity officer or small DEI team alone," as Julie Coffman, the chief diversity officer at consulting firm Bain & Co., reminds us. Decisions affecting whom to hire, promote, advance, and develop in an organization are made by numerous people across functions and departments.

When making work fair is viewed as its own silo, we cannot make the systemic changes that are required to see measurable results. Leveling the playing field is part of every single person's job. No matter your job description or function, you are a "fairness officer." This doesn't mean that you need to take on additional responsibilities (or attend more trainings or programs!). Rather, you make fairness happen when you make it (your) work and improve how you are doing your job. Much like we cannot delegate financial or people decisions to the finance or HR department alone, we cannot delegate making the workplace fair to DEI experts alone.

This is not to say that DEI professionals don't have an important role to play in embedding fairness. In an ideal world, a company's DEI team would be a resource coordinating knowledge-sharing and skill-building for the rest of the organization. With their subject matter expertise, DEI professionals are uniquely positioned to spot areas of improvement; guide teams in redesigning their work practices; and galvanize culture change. This obviously requires not only adequate resources but also leadership's backing—things that have been too often missing in recent years. And even the best-supported DEI teams can only do so much. Unless all employees are striving to make their work more fair, we won't truly embed fairness into our organizations.

Myth 5: Fairness Is Not Compatible with Meritocracy

The evidence is overwhelming that people's different life outcomes are not purely a function of their personal choices and preferences, though it is true that everyone is not born with the same inherent preferences, nor do—or should—we all aspire to the same goals in life. People are also dealt a drastically different set of cards to start with.

Consider what happened in the program for gifted students in the sixth-largest school district in the United States, Broward County in Florida, which serves more than a quarter-million learners. The process for identifying unusually intelligent students—who get placed in special classrooms and receive extra academic stimulation—used to begin in the first or second grade when either teachers or parents would refer promising students to psychologists for IQ testing. Under this system, 12 percent of the students in the programs were Black and 16 percent Hispanic, despite students of color making up the majority of students in the school district.

But then Broward administrators made what turned out to be a life-changing decision for many of their students. In 2005, the district moved to a universal screening system where all second graders were screened with standardized tests to identify potentially gifted students. This system redesign uncovered large numbers of students of color who had previously been overlooked for the gifted program, and with no changes in eligibility requirements, the participation of Black and Hispanic students increased by 80 and 130 percent, respectively. Nobel laureate David Card and economist Laura Giuliano concluded that "Blacks and Hispanics, free/reduced-price lunch participants [i.e., low-income students], English language learners [students with a non-English first language], and girls were all systematically 'underreferred' in the traditional parent/teacher referral system." In other words, giftedness is unrelated to gender, race, language background, and socioeconomic status, but opportunities are not—and members of underappreciated groups fare better when fairness is built in. More systematic and objective assessments trump subjective referrals.

The world is not a meritocracy where the best people rise to the top purely based on their superior capabilities. It turns out that having someone see and recognize your potential, and then having a system in place for nurturing it, is a big piece of the puzzle. As the parents and teachers in Broward County—and, on the flip side, the middle school teachers in Italy—have shown us, competence and potential is often in the eye of the beholder and we tend to have an easier time spotting it in the usual suspects.

Given that, as of this writing, every single US president throughout history has been a man, it is no surprise that it's difficult for a woman to be perceived as "presidential" in the United States since the word is quite literally defined in a male image. Remember this the next time you hear someone say that they only look for, hire, or promote the "best people." Who gets to decide what "best" looks like?

We have encountered our fair share of senior executives who express concern that bringing more traditionally underrepresented people into their organization, especially into the leadership ranks, will entail "lowering the bar." We take this concern seriously, particularly in situations where the available pool—or the proverbial pipeline—is too small to fill existing leadership roles. However, the evidence is overwhelming that the pipeline is a legitimate issue only in a small number of cases. The much bigger deal is that we currently do not benefit from all the best people available—that is, from 100 percent of the talent pool.

Take the example of the European Central Bank (ECB), the central bank for the member countries of the euro area. In 2013, the ECB introduced gender targets for managerial positions as part of its diversity action plan, and in 2019, it exceeded its goal for senior managers with 30 percent women. Along the way, the ECB was able to close the gender gap in promotions, advancing women on par with men. The promoted women ended up having even better salary trajectories than their male counterparts, dispelling any concerns of "lowering the bar" and suggesting that before the intervention, some of the best talent had not made it through.

This is also what economist Nava Ashraf and coauthors found when they analyzed the data of a large multinational company with one hundred thousand employees working in more than one hundred countries. Women tended to outperform men precisely in situations where the barriers to entry were high, as only the very best made it through. Put differently, the firm was not only leaving talent but also productivity gains on the proverbial table because it did not have a meritocracy. The authors conclude that "without these barriers, productivity would be 32 percent higher for the same level of employment and wage bill."

The myth of meritocracy is just that: a myth. Making work fair is not about giving anyone an unfair advantage, nor is it about getting everyone to the same endpoint. It is about finally leveling a playing field that has been unfairly holding some people back for way too long so that they have an equal shot at succeeding to their full potential.

Myth 6: Your Gain Equals My Loss

Another fairness myth we frequently encounter is what one of the leading decision-making and negotiation scholars, Max Bazerman, calls the "mythical-fixed-pie mindset": the often-incorrect assumption (also called zero-sum thinking) that one person's gain has to equal another person's loss, or that there is only a finite amount of resources to go around. In some cases, this is, of course, true. The number of people who can win in the Olympics is finite; the number of spots available in most legislatures is fixed; and when haggling with a merchant, a lower price for you equals less money for them. But in most workplace situations, more issues are at play, allowing for creative solutions where all parties end up being better off. The more we are stuck in the fixed-pie mentality, the harder it is to spot the opportunities to expand the pie for everyone's benefit.

While genuine zero-sum situations are relatively rare, zero-sum beliefs are not, and much research suggests that our zero-sum beliefs can be limiting. Unsurprisingly, people with zero-sum beliefs are less likely to want to help their colleagues and be an ally to members of underrepresented groups. In three studies, men's zero-sum thinking increased when they were exposed to information highlighting the gains women have made in education, politics, and the workplace over the last century. This, in turn, increased sexism and lowered men's support for workplace policies promoting gender equity. Another study supporting these findings showed that people's zero-sum beliefs about gender at work tend to be reflective of broader zero-sum beliefs about women's gains coming at the expense of men across different domains, including politics and family life; such beliefs were more pronounced among men than women.

And yet the US economy has benefited tremendously from being able to draw from a larger talent pool today than, say, in the 1960s, when 94 percent of all doctors and lawyers were white men. Up to 40 percent of economic growth per person post-1960 is due to a better allocation of talent. It is an unequivocally good thing that today, all law school graduates can go on to practice law—in contrast to Sandra Day O'Connor, who would go on to become the first female justice on the US Supreme Court but who could only get a job as a legal secretary when she graduated from Stanford Law School at the top of her class in 1952. As US commerce secretary Gina Raimondo stated in the context of America's infrastructure workforce, "It's an economic necessity to figure out how to attract, train, and retain women into these fields if we're going to get the job done."

As another example of how fairness is not about taking away from one group and giving to another, consider the Americans with Disabilities Act of 1990, which prohibits discrimination on the basis of disability and aims to ensure that people with disabilities have the same opportunities as anyone else to participate in everyday life. Among many provisions, the law includes regulations about making public spaces more accessible for people with mobility challenges, such as by having elevators, installing access ramps, and lowering curbs. At the time of the law's introduction, approximately 4 percent of the US adult population—over 8 million people—had a mobility disability and directly benefited from these changes. Today that share has grown to more than 12 percent, or approximately 30 million people. But actually, everyone benefited. Have you ever taken public transportation with a suitcase in tow? Pushed a child in a stroller or wheeled your groceries in a cart? Walked your bike while out and about? A redesign of the physical environment that was inspired by the experiences of people who differed in their ability turned out to make life better for everyone because it built fairness into how we do things.

There is extensive evidence in behavioral economics and social psychology on the positive impact fairness has on cooperation, trust, performance, and many more desirable outcomes. So if we finally figure out what a truly fair employee experience looks like and if we move from lamenting the lack of progress on fairness to actually making some, it will be a win-win for the world: a world where talent—no matter what it looks like or where it comes from—can flourish; a world where each of us can interact with and learn from more interesting fellow humans; and a world where organizations can benefit from a historical wealth of previously overlooked talent. Making work fair can expand the pie for all of our benefit.

Note that while we want to debunk the myth of a zero-sum world, this is not a call for making the business case for fairness. As organizational behavior scholars Robin Ely and David Thomas write in a *Harvard Business Review* article aptly titled "Enough Already with the Business Case," the business case sends the message to traditionally underrepresented colleagues that they are only valuable if they improve the organization's bottom line. It also raises a disconcerting question: If data ever emerged suggesting that including women and people of color harmed a company's profitability, could that be used as an excuse to exclude them even further from the workplace?

More practically, the business case can be counterproductive. Examining Fortune 500 companies' public-facing communications, social psychologists Oriane Georgeac and Aneeta Rattan found that 80 percent used a business case to justify their focus on diversity while less than 5 percent used a fairness case, justifying diversity based on equal opportunity or a moral imperative (the remaining companies did not explicitly address their focus on diversity). However, subsequent studies showed that the business case—and, to a much lesser extent, the fairness case—caused underrepresented groups to anticipate a lower sense of belonging in the companies. As a result, LGBTQ+ individuals, women in STEM, and African Americans were less interested in joining those organizations. The authors summarize: "Don't justify your commitment to diversity at all. . . . If you don't need an explanation for the presence of well-represented groups in the workplace beyond their expertise, then you don't need a justification for the presence of underrepresented groups either."

We had an epiphany about this while watching the documentary *RBG*, in which the second woman on the US Supreme Court, the late justice Ruth Bader Ginsburg, describes her experience of starting Harvard Law School as one of only nine women in a class of over five hundred men in 1956. At a dinner the dean hosted for these nine women, recalled Ginsburg, "He asked each of us to stand up and tell him what we were doing taking a seat that could be occupied by a man."

The realization hit us like a lightning bolt: Men have never been asked to justify their presence in any position of power. It is only the people not in power today—including women and members of other underestimated groups—who are asked to make the business case for why they deserve to be there. This is fundamentally unfair and fundamentally wrong. Until the day that someone makes the business case for why white men, who in the United States constitute 30 percent of the population, should occupy nearly 90 percent of Fortune 500 CEO positions and approximately 60 percent of both the US Congress and corporate leadership, we will take the rationale for fairness as a given. As scholars Sonia Kang and Sarah Kaplan powerfully note: "To make progress in achieving gender equality, we must declare the discussion on whether and why we should pursue equality to be over."

We could not agree more. Making work fair is unequivocally the right and smart thing to do—and a win-win for us all.

Myth 7: Fairness Requires a Different Approach than Other Business Imperatives

We are not lawyers, but some of the most common concerns we encounter when we work with organizations relate to the legal landscape around fairness. Laws are obviously different—and evolving—everywhere, so first and foremost, we encourage you to consult legal counsel to understand your context and get input on the design and implementation of your efforts. While we cannot provide legal advice, let us share with you a guiding principle:

Treat fairness with the same seriousness and commitment as you treat any other aspect of your work or business that you care about.

On numerous issues, organizations have to manage compliance considerations, make decisions about risk appetite, and consult legal counsel for advice. Likewise, the regulations governing things like privacy and intellectual property depend on jurisdiction, and we somehow navigate that complexity. The General Data Protection Regulation (GDPR), for example, which came into effect in the European Union in 2018, dramatically changed how companies around the world deal with personal data since it applies to any entity doing business with people located in the EU.

Making work fair comes with a side of legal considerations, just like accounting, mergers and acquisitions, and talent management, so collaborate closely with your legal advisors to identify mutually workable solutions. Instead of asking your legal department, "Can we do this?" (to which the likely answer is no), ask, "How can we do this in a legally compliant way that avoids unnecessary risk?" In our experience, when organizational leaders signal a strong commitment to design for fairness, lawyers will work with them to do just that. But legal experts are trained to focus on what can go wrong, so business leaders need to maintain a focus on what can and needs to go right.

There are also meaningful risks involved in *not* tackling unfairness. Would you rather not conduct cybersecurity audits and wait until a hacker disrupts your operations and embarrasses your organization publicly? Or would you prefer to opt for continuous monitoring of potential security threats and nip them in the bud? Negative publicity, scandals, discrimination lawsuits, missing out on key talent, dips in performance, and employee turnover all have costs associated with them, and they are just some of the very real risks that come with not working proactively to make your workplace fair. Social media company Pinterest knows this all too well: in 2020, it paid $22.5 million to its former COO, Françoise Brougher, in the largest public individual gender discrimination settlement at the time.

We should note that the legal landscape in the United States is complex and may even differ across states. On the one hand, organizations are legally prohibited from setting diversity-related *quotas* and from considering "protected classes" (race; color; religion; sex, including pregnancy, sexual orientation, or gender identity; national origin; age; disability; and genetic information, including family medical history) in employment decisions. On the other hand, a large swath of US companies, including all federal (sub)contractors, are subject to equal opportunity and antidiscrimination executive orders, which prohibit them from discriminating on the basis of most or all of these characteristics. Furthermore, these companies are required to take affirmative action to ensure equal employment opportunity, including by developing written affirmative action plans (AAPs) that set out specific aspirations; making good-faith efforts to recruit from diverse sources; and by filing an annual disclosure form summarizing their workforce composition. To navigate these legal nuances, you need legal counsel. As social scientists, however, we want to point out that research has found AAP goals to be effective at increasing workforce diversity, especially for underrepresented racial and ethnic groups.

* * *

At the end of a recent unconscious bias webinar we attended, the speakers were asked how we should think about tackling unconscious and conscious biases and minimizing their harmful effects. The speakers acknowledged that eliminating bias from our minds is likely impossible, so they instead invited participants to "raise awareness."

We are not asking you to merely raise awareness. Our book is an invitation for you to act. Act to change your and your organization's systems, not people's minds. Act to build fairness into how you do things. The concept of DEI as it currently exists is ripe for a rethink because the way we are doing it is not working as well as we need it to. In this world of limited time, attention, money, and goodwill, it is imperative that we spend our valuable resources on the tools that have been shown to work instead of copy-paste practices for which there is no convincing evidence of effectiveness.

Having liberated ourselves from common myths, the solution to the problem of unfairness now lies at our collective fingertips: we need to replace bias with built-in fairness. Once we leverage systems to make work fair on a larger scale, seeing real results will become easier and faster. And every single one of us can do this in our own work.

PART I

MAKE IT COUNT: MOTIVATING ACTION

CHAPTER 2

Data as an Engine for Change

"We measure what we treasure."

"What gets measured gets done."

"What doesn't get measured doesn't count."

Truisms about the importance of data and measurement abound. While we agree with all of them, here is what we really want you to know about data when it comes to fairness at work:

Data becomes a powerful engine for change when we harness it as a tool, not as an end in itself.

Measuring fairness is merely the first step, as BBC journalist Ros Atkins knows. In late 2016, he was feeling galvanized and stumped at the same time. Atkins was flying home to London from a one-week executive education opportunity involving Stanford University, which had thoroughly sold him on the power of data to drive transformational change in organizations. The only problem was that Atkins realized he did not have data available on an issue he cared deeply about in his own work as the presenter of a nightly prime-time BBC news program: the number of women and men featured on his show. Atkins knew that his journalism would be more powerful if it represented the communities it serves, but like numerous well-intentioned people, he lacked the numbers to determine what that representation looked like.

Instead of throwing in the towel, Atkins decided to generate the data himself. In early 2017, he convinced the editors and producers on his team to spend two minutes after each show tallying up—by hand on Post-it notes, as Siri witnessed in person—the number of women and men who had appeared as contributors during his sixty minutes on-air. Right off the bat, the team made an important decision: As the presenter of the show, Ros Atkins himself would not be included in the count since the team had no control over his presence. Likewise, key protagonists in the day's stories without whom the news couldn't be reported, such as the prime minister making a speech or the eyewitness to an event, would not be counted since the editorial team could not influence the day's stories. However, everyone else—correspondents, interviewees, commentators, and experts invited to shed light on the day's news— would be counted since the team selected them. In other words, Atkins and his colleagues decided to focus their measurement on the things they could control.

The first results shocked everyone. After a month of counting, only an average of 39 percent of the contributors featured on Atkins's program, *Outside Source*, were women. The number was lower than anyone had expected. Jolted and determined, Atkins and his team resolved to improve their performance and set a specific goal: reaching a 50–50 gender balance in contributors. For them, choosing this goal was straightforward because they saw it as their mission to accurately reflect the overall population's gender balance. With an increased focus and daily tallying of data, the team hit an average monthly share of 51 percent women contributors for the first time three months later. That was in April 2017, and the *Outside Source* team consistently remained at or above 50 percent women contributors until the program's conclusion in April 2023.

Atkins's story would already be impressive if it ended here. But this was merely the first chapter in what has evolved into a global movement to make news and the media more representative of the communities they cover—50:50 The Equality Project. Started by Atkins in 2017, the project reached 750 participating teams within the BBC globally across TV, radio, and digital content. In addition, more than 150 external partner organizations joined in. They span the world from South Africa to Finland and Indonesia to the United States and range from other news outlets (like the *Financial Times*) and corporations (like Unilever and PwC) to journalism schools.

What all of these BBC teams and partner organizations have in common is that they have embedded a simple counting and data-tracking methodology to move the needle toward fairness while profoundly shifting who is seen and heard. In accordance with Ros Atkins's original vision, they are using the act of collecting and sharing data as a tool to make a bigger, more consequential shift toward "fairly representing our world," as the BBC describes it. The results are real and measurable: At the BBC, on average 60–70 percent of participating teams reach gender parity in contributors each month. Audiences have discerned a change, too, with 69 percent reporting in 2022 that they noticed more women in content. As Matthew Napier, series producer for the BBC's *Songs of Praise*, noted: "We have managed to keep it going [even] during COVID-19 because it has become part of the furniture here and just the way we do things."

Data is how we make sense of the world around us. It is therefore essential to our understanding of what is fair and what isn't. Without data, we don't truly know how we are doing or whether we are moving in the right direction. Yet, on a recent call, we heard the CEO of a midsize American professional services firm express great confidence in his firm: "We don't have pay gaps here," said the CEO. When we gently asked, "How do you know?," his response was "Believe me, I've been at this firm for nearly forty years. I just know." This may sound extreme, but you'd be surprised to hear how often we encounter similar sentiments. People "know" things without seemingly any evidence, which begs our go-to question: "Based on what data?"

When you see a doctor and tell them you're feeling unwell, that is only the starting point for the visit. Any doctor worth their salt will ask a series of specific questions to gather more data on your symptoms as well as your medical history and baseline health in order to identify the root cause of your symptoms. It is only after a thorough diagnosis like this that your doctor can prescribe the proper treatment (and a really good doctor will schedule a follow-up to gather more data on whether the treatment is working as intended). Data is, therefore, the essential first step to diagnose how well we are doing and reveal where our pain points lie. As Oona King, chief diversity and inclusion officer at Uber, says, "Data is like an X-ray. You live in fear about the pain in your chest until you finally do the medical tests to figure out exactly what's going on."

We don't want you to live in fear. Rather, we want you to feel empowered to use data to understand your and your organization's baseline around workplace fairness; uncover opportunities for improvement; and allow you to know, at any point in time, whether your efforts are moving the needle. Given that we tend to measure what matters (as John Doerr explains beautifully in his eponymous book), we want you to take a rigorously data-driven approach to fairness at work—both because it works and because treating fairness with the same seriousness as we treat the other things that matter is required for real results.

Indeed, data-driven decision-making is an effective tool to improve organizational performance. A study looking at 179 American publicly traded companies found that firms that had data available for business decision-making—and that actually used it for this purpose—had significantly higher output and productivity. Google, one of the pioneers in using data to drive decision-making, put this into practice when it examined more than 10,000 performance evaluations in conjunction with employee retention rates. The analysis allowed the company to pinpoint effective supervisor behaviors and then train managers on those specific skills. As a result, median favorability scores for managers increased.

In the pages that follow, we will answer questions like what data we should collect; who should collect the data and when; and how data should be presented and analyzed to motivate behavior change. Our advice is based on the best evidence available, but you will invariably have to adjust it to your legal context. Numerous, specific regulations around the world require the collection and disclosure of some data related to fairness, and you should know the rules that govern the region(s) where you operate. Furthermore, in some jurisdictions, it is illegal to collect certain demographic information, and we certainly don't want you to run afoul of the law where you are. But, fundamentally, you should *want* to collect data on how fair your workplace is whenever regulations allow it, and even if they don't require it, because it is impossible to measure improvement without a baseline.

Collect Data You Care About

In 2004, when Oscar-winning actor Geena Davis's daughter was two years old, the pair started watching children's TV and movies together. Davis immediately noticed that there were far more male than female characters on-screen. In the documentary *This Changes Everything*, Davis recalls: "Whenever I had a meeting in Hollywood, I'd say, 'Have you ever noticed how few female characters there are in movies made for kids?' Every single person said, 'Oh, no, no, no, that's not true anymore. That's been fixed.' Nobody I talked to was seeing the problem I was seeing." Just like Ros Atkins at the BBC, Davis realized that the first step toward making change was to gather the data to understand the scope of the problem and prove that it was real.

And she did. That same year, Davis founded the Geena Davis Institute on Gender in Media to generate research and work collaboratively with the entertainment industry to promote gender balance and reduce stereotyping. To do this, the institute has developed two unique software tools: The first quantifies screen and speaking time in audio and video content, and the second scans preproduction scripts for stereotypical portrayals of characters and identifies opportunities for greater representation. Besides gender, the institute tracks data for race/ethnicity, LGBTQIA+, disability, age (fifty and up), and body type. Across two decades, the institute's annual reports reveal that some important progress has been made: For example, the one hundred top-grossing family films have reached gender parity in lead characters. Still, much more work remains to be done. Male characters continue to outnumber female ones by a two-to-one margin across advertising, film, and TV, and female characters are substantially more likely to be objectified and shown in revealing clothing.

This disparity is also what the MaLisa Foundation, established in 2016, found for German films. Women on-screen tend to be "young, thin, and in relationships." Women with disabilities are missing almost completely, and women with a migration background are substantially underrepresented compared to their proportion in the German population. Perhaps most concerningly, a study examining the year 2020 found that gender-based violence against women and children occurred in one-third of programs shown on German television between 6:00 and 10:00 p.m. Survivors were rarely the focus of the attention, and prevention or support were not topics typically discussed. Maria Furtwängler, a physician and actor who founded the MaLisa Foundation with her daughter Elisabeth, explained: "Media shape[s] our perception of reality. As media professionals, we have a special responsibility, especially when it comes to an urgent societal issue such as violence against women. If we present it in a distorted way, we tend to become part of the problem, whereas we can and should be part of the solution."

We concur. Data like this matters because it reflects whose voices are heard, how knowledge and collective intelligence is created, and who is available as a role model for others. To put it bluntly, data related to fairness is often missing because we haven't cared enough to collect or analyze it—or because we are too afraid to confront what the X-ray will reveal about the cause of our chest pain. We are here to tell you that real progress on workplace fairness is measurable progress, which means that the sooner you get the X-ray, the better.

The first step is to understand what data you should collect. While some of us will need to generate our data from scratch like Ros Atkins (by manual counting) or Geena Davis (by developing software to do the job), most of us will be able to rely on at least some existing data as a starting point, though it might not currently be organized in the most accessible or user-friendly way. In the United States, Title VII of the Civil Rights Act of 1964 requires employers with 100 or more employees (or federal contractors with at least 50 employees and contracts worth at least $50,000 per year) to annually report key workforce data to the EEO-1 Commission.* Firms have to disclose the raw number of employees by gender and race/ethnicity across ten standardized occupational categories. However, even in smaller organizations that are not subject to these requirements, there is some kind of record of when employees were hired, what they get paid, and so on. Start with whatever data you have and build from there.

The exact set of metrics you can and should collect will vary from context to context. If you are an individual contributor, start with data that pertains directly to your own work, like Ros Atkins did. Who is talking in your work group meetings? What is the makeup of your team? Whom do you mentor or sponsor? Even without sophisticated databases or an army of people analytics experts, a single resourceful individual can begin to create measurable change.

If you have the ability to influence a larger portion of your organization, we encourage you to push for more systematic data

---

* The EEO-1 Commission is a collaboration between the Equal Employment Opportunity Commission (EEOC) and the Office of Federal Contract Compliance Programs (OFCCP), which are two entities charged with enforcing nondiscrimination in employment laws in the United States.

collection by gender and other relevant characteristics. This could cover representation (e.g., number of employees by function and level; number of employees reporting up to each senior leader), developmental opportunities (e.g., promotion rates by role and function; number and share of employees moving laterally in the organization), performance assessment (e.g., performance evaluation scores by level, function, tenure, and manager; correlation between performance score and time to promotion), compensation (e.g., total compensation controlling for level, function, tenure, geography, and education; starting compensation for new hires; employees in each pay quartile/quintile/decile of the organization), uptake of policies (e.g., number and share of employees utilizing flexible work arrangements and taking parental leave), and employee satisfaction and well-being (e.g., employee survey results and satisfaction scores; number of internal and external complaints). At a high level, our advice boils down to this:

Measure what you actually care about—and in so doing, treat data related to fairness the same way you treat data related to all your other business priorities.

This, however, turns out to require a bit more thoughtfulness than one might first imagine. In the realm of fairness, many organizations track things like the number of ERGs or the percentage of employees that have completed a voluntary unconscious bias training. But are these metrics indicative of actual progress? Does the mere existence of an ERG, or the fact that someone sat (or multitasked) their way through a one-hour online module, mean that your organization is less biased? In the realm of sales, tracking the number of customer interactions or completed sales calls would never suffice since actual realized revenue is what companies truly aim for.

Measuring workplace fairness with the same seriousness means tracking metrics that monitor not only effort, but also the results you care about—and the things that drive those results. Representation, for example, is the sum of hiring and promotion, minus attrition. A dearth of women at the top of an organization could be caused by low rates of external hiring for women at different levels, and/or low rates of promotion for women anywhere in the hierarchy, and/or high rates of attrition for women at any level.

Each of these drivers of representation breaks down into several subcomponents that are also worth unpacking. Take hiring, for which you should look at data at each stage of the process: who applies compared to the available pool; who makes it through the screening and interview stages compared to who was in the pool at the preceding stage; and who ends up getting selected compared to the short list at the final stage (we will discuss recruitment, screening, and hiring in greater depth in Chapters 6–8). And let us not forget the offer stage: reviewing the ultimately agreed-upon employment terms (salary, other compensation, seniority, etc.) by gender ensures that women are not systematically underpaid or "downleveled" into more junior positions than their qualifications would merit.

Tracking all of this data by gender—and, ideally, many other characteristics, as we explain in a moment—is essential to pinpoint areas of potential bias and more precisely diagnose what is broken before we prescribe the medicine. There is no point in, say, buying software to anonymize all candidates' résumés if your data indicates that the group of applicants that makes it through the résumé review stage is gender representative but the drop-off in women actually occurs at the final decision stage long after résumés have been reviewed.

Beyond representation, it is important to track data on whether everyone has an equal chance to succeed on a level playing field. For example, you could compare the rates at which women and men are promoted (i.e., how much time they spend at a given rank before advancing to the next one) or examine how performance scores are correlated with promotions to see if the same scores translate into equal career advancement for women and men (newsflash: research suggests they don't, with men reaping higher rewards than women for the same scores).

Another critical aspect of data collection and analysis is using an intersectional lens where possible (by "possible" we mean if your sample size is large enough to protect people's identities while drawing meaningful inferences). Legal scholar Kimberlé Crenshaw coined the term "intersectionality" in 1989 to describe the fact that multiple social identities interact to create overlapping (dis)advantages. A queer Black woman might have a very different experience of her workplace compared to a straight, white, female colleague, even though both identify as women. As a consequence, aggregate statistics can mask vastly different outcomes for various subgroups.

Consider the gender pay gap. In 2022, all American women earned, on average, 82 cents to a white, non-Hispanic man's dollar. But beyond the average, an intersectional perspective reveals a more nuanced picture: Latinas made only 65 cents to a white, non-Hispanic man's dollar, Native Hawaiian and Pacific Islander women only 68 cents, Black women only 70 cents, white women 83 cents, and Asian American women 93 cents. The pay gap also varied substantially among different groups of Asian Americans. Taiwanese and Indian women's average pay was slightly higher than that of white, non-Hispanic men, while Nepalese and Bangladeshi women's pay was only about half that.* Generally, straight women earn less than lesbian or bisexual women, although the pattern is less consistent than the one for men where straight men have systematically been found to be paid more than gay or bisexual men.

For any outcome of interest, such as pay, it is therefore essential to collect other data points beyond gender (such as race, ethnicity, sexual orientation, age, parental status, full- or part-time work status, nationality, or socioeconomic background) and analyze them intersectionally to reveal potential differences across subgroups. Since this can quickly

---

* It is important to note that these statistics underreport the earnings gap between women and men because they are typically calculated based on people who work full-time, year-round and substantially fewer women than men work that way (women are more likely to work part-time, for example).

get overwhelming because there are infinite possible intersections, we remind you of our starting advice: measure what you care about. In the United States, the intersections of gender, race, and sexual orientation are currently among the most salient and most tracked. McKinsey & Company and LeanIn.Org's annual *Women in the Workplace* report, for example, collects and presents all data by binary gender and binary race, breaking it down for white women, women of color, white men, and men of color. In other contexts, different intersections, such as those of gender and disability or gender and indigeneity, might be more relevant.

Our advice is to start by measuring one or a few metrics that are important to you, knowing that you can add more with time (and keeping in mind that additional intersectional dimensions will add more nuance to your analyses and may even change your conclusions). 50:50 The Equality Project started by focusing only on the number of female and male contributors because Ros Atkins's strong instinct was that asking people to measure too many things from the outset would result in them not measuring anything at all. To build momentum for the novel concept of data-driven representational change—and to accommodate the daily realities of busy newsrooms where journalists were skeptical about finding time to count gender—he consciously simplified the data tracking approach. With the concept proven and hundreds of teams successfully monitoring and improving their gender data, in 2021, 50:50 expanded to track disability and ethnicity among on-air contributors, with plans to expand further into socioeconomic diversity. The data thus far has revealed that as teams start to monitor disability and ethnicity, their gender numbers often dip in the short term. While 50:50 The Equality Project doesn't yet track data intersectionally (results for gender, ethnicity, and disability are all reported separately), all participating teams are encouraged to think in intersectional terms when selecting contributors to help mitigate such dips.

The inherently sensitive nature of social identity data raises the important issue of how it should be collected, and the right answer will vary by organization, country, and context. We need to remain vigilant about not collecting identifiable data and invite people to self-disclose whatever data they are prepared to share voluntarily. At the same time, we also have to guard against selection bias where only a subset of employees is willing to provide information. Sometimes, those who volunteer to participate are not representative of the full population of interest, which can potentially skew results. This is why every survey is trying to maximize the response rate—and why attaining a high response rate matters for organizations to ensure the accuracy of the data they are collecting. But how employees are asked to provide their personal data can make a difference.

In an experiment that behavioral science consultancy MoreThan-Now conducted with Transport for London (TfL), two thousand TfL employees were asked to provide their demographic data via one of five similarly worded emails. The only difference was the motive for the request. The control condition, in which employees were simply asked to "Please give us your demographic data," yielded a 42 percent response rate, on average. Those who were asked to share their data because TfL is "committed to reflecting the city we serve" were about equally as likely to respond, whereas messages around social norms, loss aversion, and prosocial behavior yielded overall lower response rates. Moreover, the messages affected members of different groups differently. For example, while the control version worked fine for most respondents, the social norms message was the clear winner for "people from a minority background," increasing their response rates by more than 50 percent compared to the control. If you are struggling to collect self-identification data from your employees, consider following TfL's example: test your own messaging and compare different groups' response rates to their respective underlying baselines.

Google tracks its employees' gender, race, sexual orientation, disability status, military service, and national identity with more than 80 percent of its workforce voluntarily sharing this information as of 2023. Over many years, the company has built a culture of transparency and data-driven decision-making in all domains, including people operations, which has contributed to high employee engagement in surveys. In parallel, the company has expanded its data tracking from looking only at representation a decade ago to now tracking hiring, attrition, leadership composition, and its tech and non-tech workforces separately, in addition to company-wide representation. James Heighington, chief of staff for diversity, equity, and inclusion at Google, shared that the data from Google's annual employee pulse survey was analyzed by fourteen categories of identity, including gender and race intersectionally, to understand employees' workplace experiences and identify pain points. These analyses have inspired tangible improvements that employees can see, such as sponsorship and mentorship opportunities.

The lesson for organizations large enough to guarantee respondents' anonymity is to invest effort in building trust so that employees feel comfortable to voluntarily share their personal data, and to solidify that trust by using the collected data to drive visible positive change. To share this and other learnings with the tech sector, Iris and Siri recently served on a task force together with James Heighington, Oona King, and others. We include the resulting Action to Catalyze Tech (ACT) Report as a resource for you in our endnotes.

Using an external specialist vendor to collect and track employee data and administer surveys can be helpful to ensure privacy and confidentiality and thereby encourage broad participation. Besides, many organizations do not have the expertise internally to design effective surveys or conduct complex data analyses. Australian retail bank Police & Nurses Limited (P&N Group) worked with analytics and survey platform Culture Amp to include an option for employees to share their personal data as part of regular engagement surveys. At the same time, they also raised awareness about the privacy safeguards around the surveys. As a result, the share of employees voluntarily self-disclosing their demographic details increased by nearly 25 percentage points to 85 percent of the workforce, allowing P&N Group to analyze the data by gender and identify major gaps in women's and men's experiences around career development and flexible working. Beyond Culture Amp (and while not an exhaustive list), companies like Aleria, Diversio, Kanarys, and Pulsely offer surveys whose results are analyzed and aggregated on user-friendly dashboards, while OrganizationView allows companies to glean insights from open-text survey responses by using artificial intelligence (AI) to analyze key themes.

Small numbers present a special data collection challenge. Employees who work for a smaller organization, are members of an underrepresented group, or are in the numerical minority may be concerned about maintaining anonymity and therefore not share their data. In a 2022 study by the Pew Research Center, for example, 1.6 percent of adults identified as nonbinary or transgender in the United States, which means that many (smaller) organizations won't be able to collect gender identity information safely without jeopardizing people's privacy—an issue the United Nations recently called attention to.

From a data analysis point of view, small samples are inherently challenging because they have higher variability than larger samples, leading them to be less accurate and useful for inferences. Simply put, a sample of 500 Latinas is much more informative and representative regarding their workplace experiences than a sample of 5. Yet, being in a numerical minority doesn't render anyone's data less important.

Whenever a group's data is purposefully not reported due to privacy concerns, or missing due to lack of representation in your organization, note that fact explicitly. Always track and report both actual, raw numbers as well as percentages, since in small groups, for example, losing a single queer woman can lead the representation of both women and members of the LGBTQ+ community to fluctuate wildly. And supplement quantitative analyses with qualitative data (such as interviews, focus groups, and free-text comments in surveys), which can be especially helpful in shedding light on the experiences of smaller groups of employees and explaining patterns observed in quantitative data. As organizational behavior scholars Laura Morgan Roberts and Melissa Thomas-Hunt potently note: "When it comes to [fairness], not everything that counts can be counted. . . . People's narratives offer a valuable lens into organizational culture, climate, and experiences of inclusion and exclusion."

Using data as a tool to improve fairness applies not only to the workforce-related topics we have discussed so far, but also to your organization's business activities. In the museum world, that includes art collections. While women make up approximately half of American artists and a majority of art school students, they represent only a small fraction of art museum holdings in the United States. The Museum of Fine Arts, Boston (MFA) has accepted female artists' works into its collection since it was founded more than 150 years ago, but as of 2019, women made up only 8 percent of the artists in its collections by one estimate.

Even though tracking data on the gender and racial composition of the MFA's collections can be challenging—for example, the gender or race of the creators of historic works cannot always be definitively identified—the museum has resolved to use data to educate and drive progress. Nonie Gadsden, curator of the 2019 Women Take the Floor exhibition, which shed light on gender inequity in the art world, explained: "At first, I didn't believe in the premise of the show [exhibiting women artists separately on their own] as I thought we were past that. Didn't the Feminist Art Movement of the 1970s change that? But curating the exhibition forced me to look at what is still happening today in the art world: the statistics of here and now are as appalling as those from 45–50 years ago. We need to highlight this so more people are aware of the continued inequity for women working in the arts."

This data-driven focus is starting to yield measurable results. Under chair Frederick Ilchman's direction, the MFA's Art of Europe department acquired more paintings by women in three years than in the preceding three decades. In 2019, the contemporary department quietly reinstalled its collections to reach gender parity in shown works; in 2023, they increased that ratio to 60 percent female and 40 percent male artists. And through a new form, the museum is asking living artists to self-identify their gender to enable more accurate data tracking going forward.

Make Data Simple, Salient, and Accessible

How data is collected and by whom, and how it is presented, plays a huge role in determining whether it can empower people to level the playing field. Data related to workplace fairness is typically gathered, tracked, and shared by (and among) select individuals in HR, DEI, or people analytics teams such that frontline employees have little access to it. Ironically, it is those exact employees whose daily decisions about whom to hire, staff on a team, or sponsor will shape what the data looks like. While it is not always possible to give access to such data—for legal, privacy, or confidentiality reasons—ownership over the numbers was seen to be important at the BBC. Nina Goswami, who led 50:50 The Equality Project after Ros Atkins from 2020 to 2022, explained the logic: "When a content-creating team joins 50:50, I want the participating journalists to be using a piece of paper and manually doing monitoring, because it really changes your mindset. The physical action of pen to paper is so powerful and so simple, but it helps journalists to see the bigger picture."

Similar to 50:50, EqualVoice, an initiative by Ringier, a Swiss media company, also makes gender representation data available to its journalists, but it has opted for an automated approach to collect it. At the heart of the initiative is the EqualVoice Factor, a scientifically evaluated measurement tool that uses a semantic algorithm to analyze print, digital, and video content. A total of 32 media brands in seven European countries reaching about 50 million readers analyzed their publications using the EqualVoice Factor in 2023. The goal is to reach 100 million users by 2025. In its annual report, EqualVoice shows progress toward equal representation in almost all the media covered, with some outlets taking bigger and some smaller steps.

Once collected, data is more likely to move us into action—or help us choose the right action—when it is simple (i.e., easy to grasp) and salient (i.e., relevant and in-the-moment). Take the famous example of nutrition guidelines. For decades, the US Department of Agriculture used a pyramid diagram to communicate to Americans what foods they should consume, and how much, with the aim of enabling them to make healthier dietary choices. The only problem, of course, is that we don't eat off pyramids. The pyramid made it very difficult to translate into practice how much grilled chicken, rice with beans, or roasted vegetables to pile onto our plates at the moment of consumption. In other words, it wasn't simple or salient. In 2011, the pyramid was retired in favor of a much more intuitive and easy-to-understand diagram: an actual plate, which shows exactly how much of the surface area should be covered by proteins, grains, fruits, and vegetables.

In our busy daily lives, we often process information using mental shortcuts. Complicated or detailed information that requires us to tap into a slower, more deliberative mode of thinking doesn't align with these shortcuts, so we often ignore it. Therefore, data presented simply and saliently helps us to draw the right conclusions and act accordingly—and, in many cases, better. Traffic light labeling that marks foods as red, yellow, or green depending on their healthfulness has a greater impact on people's food choices than exact calorie counts on menus, since the traffic light system is easier to grasp (and most of us don't know how many calories we should aim to consume daily anyway). Placing a relatively healthier, sugar-free Coke Zero first in a lineup of drink choices on a touchscreen increases its consumption vis-à-vis regular Coca-Cola because it becomes more salient, and because as the first icon to select, it is easier to go for. And expressing a vehicle's fuel efficiency in gallons per 100 miles driven, rather than in miles per gallon, leads consumers to a more accurate understanding because the former metric is more directly related to costs and fuel consumption.

The message in all of these examples is that in order to be actionable and to influence behavior, data needs to be available, relevant, and easy to grasp for the right people. Employee information that languishes in obscure HR databases that are accessible to only a handful of people is the opposite, even though it's common. Similarly, high-level company-wide metrics are not helpful to the individual manager who is trying to understand how to hire and promote more fairly.

50:50 The Equality Project is an illuminating example of how gathering the right data and presenting it in ways that promote action can create data-driven change. All participating content-creating teams collect and track their own data on simple spreadsheets that allow them to know the gender split of contributors in their content at any time. Once a month, teams submit their data to the 50:50 Project team, which collects and shares it among all participants on a dashboard. Importantly, the combination of the spreadsheet and dashboard allows teams to track their progress over time, as well as in comparison to others.

Social comparisons are a key component of salience because they trigger our competitive instincts. We humans care about what others think of us and no one wants to be at the bottom of the heap. "Upward comparisons," where we compare ourselves against others who are performing better, tend to lead to "upward drive." For 50:50 Project teams, knowing that everyone else can see their results is a powerful motivator. Even though the project's communications are relentlessly positive and never call out underperformers, lagging teams don't want to remain at the back of the pack. At the other end of the spectrum, top-performing teams take pride in seeing their achievements widely recognized, which only serves to motivate them further given that everyone is aligned on the importance of the goal.

To make comparisons across time more salient and tracking of actual progress easier, share the same data points consistently and keep your definitions of things like "leadership levels" or "tech versus non-tech roles" the same as much as possible. Too many organizations report random or inconsistent data points from year to year, such as the total share of women in the workforce one year and the share of women at certain leadership levels the next. We are sympathetic to people's desire to present their efforts in the best light, but obscuring the numbers in the short term will only delay the inevitable. Also, resist the temptation to make the picture look better by aggregating data for multiple groups (as in, "five of the eleven board members are *women or minorities*" or "Black women make up a record 11 percent of *managers and directors*"). Ideally, we recommend presenting data on the same categories that you collect it on, barring confidentiality concerns, to create accountability and build trust. At JPMorgan Chase, CEO Jamie Dimon drove this point home when the HR department showed him data on the firm's workforce: "Don't lump it together," he responded. "Come back and show me the numbers by VPs, EDs [executive directors], MDs [managing directors], and hiring and retention."

We challenge you to think about how you might be able to bring these principles to life in your own work. At the individual or team level, could you, for example, track and report the intersectional gender split of the funding requests you reviewed (if you are a loan officer) or entrepreneurs you brought in to pitch for you and decided to fund (if you are an investor) in the last month? Or track and report the intersectional gender split of people you engaged for user interface testing over the last year (if you are a product designer)? Sometimes, all it takes is one person to start counting and sharing their numbers for others to follow suit. And at the organizational level, if legally permissible in your context, could you provide managers real-time access to their team composition and hiring and promotion data, perhaps with comparative information on how their team's results stack up against those of their peers? Or rank all your senior leaders quarterly by the share of women (again, intersectionally, if possible) in their leadership pipelines? Once you have identified what data you will collect and on what cadence, institute a simple method for sharing it with the relevant people to enable the data to drive measurable results.

Analyze Your Data

Data can only move the needle when it is analyzed to generate actionable insights. Take pay gaps as an example. Senior leaders at American restaurant chain Denny's, which runs annual pay equity checks designed to ensure equal compensation across characteristics like gender, race, and sexual orientation, put it well: "We strive to judge progress through data, not anecdotes."

The power of data analyses lies both in pinpointing the factors that are causing any observed differences and in motivating people to erase them. While collecting raw data and comparing averages on pay or representation (or any other variable of interest) across groups is a step in the right direction, if you want to uncover the drivers of your numbers, you can't stop there. You need data scientists, statisticians, or econometricians to dig deeper and unpack what is going on. When Google did this, for example, it learned that what superficially looked like a gender gap in turnover was actually a "parent gap." It was not women on the whole who were more likely to leave, but specifically new mothers, calling for a different kind of intervention.

In terms of pay equity, analyzing whether women and men receive equal pay for equal work—and if not, why this might be the case—is a necessary but insufficient condition for fairness in remuneration. To achieve the latter, we need to go beyond equal work and analyze equal pay for work of equal value, which we will turn to in Chapter 4. But first, let's focus on the "necessary." If you are in a position to pay people, or if you have access to compensation data (whether for a whole organization or just a handful of individuals), you must make sure that equal work is compensated equally independent of employees' social identities. Here is how to follow in Denny's footsteps and conduct your own pay gap analysis.

The first step is deciding whether you want the analysis to be confidential. This may not be necessary if you're reviewing pay data for contractors in your home, for example. But larger organizations may wish to consult a lawyer for advice to ensure proper data protection. The next step is collecting or compiling data on employees' work details (e.g., role, title, responsibilities, location, tenure) as well as their characteristics of interest (e.g., gender, race, caregiver status). To determine "pay," be sure to include all components of compensation, including base salary, (performance) bonuses, commissions, equity awards, and any additional discretionary monies paid. Then compare the total pay (or, if you want to get granular, all the different components) across employees doing similar work to detect gaps and understand what may be driving them. Statistical analyses such as multiple regressions can control for variables like occupation, education, experience, seniority, or job performance to reveal any "unexplained" gaps that do not arise from these discernible factors. Finally, make any adjustments to close the gaps—for example, using the "structured approach" included in the endnotes—and repeat the analysis at least annually.

If this type of diagnosis is beyond your current data analysis capabilities, there are specialist vendors that can help. EDGE, Equality Check, Gapsquare, and Syndio, for example, offer organizations software to structure and examine their compensation data and run all the necessary statistical analyses to determine whether and why pay gaps exist. In addition, they help companies report on pay equity and comply with specific disclosure requirements, such as those for gender pay gap reporting in countries like Iceland, Norway, and the United Kingdom, as well as—starting in 2024—all of the EU.

The Organisation for Economic Co-operation and Development (OECD) recommends using the simple and freely available regression-based tool Logib, which Switzerland introduced in 2006 to help companies better understand what drives their gender pay gaps. Research suggests that the tool is working and, in particular, has shrunk the part of the gender pay gap that cannot be explained by observable factors. This is important because in today's world, measurable variables like education or work experience can no longer explain gender differences in pay: in the United States as well as in most other OECD countries, women receive the majority of degrees at every level and are therefore better educated than men across the board. To put this into perspective, the US Department of Labor concluded in 2023 that "women must complete one additional degree in order to be paid the same wages as a man with less education."

Using big data to inform people decisions is increasingly popular in larger organizations that benefit from a data-rich environment. In Chapter 7, we will take a closer look at some of these practices, including predictive analytics and artificial intelligence. For now, know that people analytics can be extremely useful in your data-driven fairness practices. It helps you discover what is going on (to go with the Google example, notice that women were more likely to leave), diagnose why you see a particular pattern (because some women became mothers and tended to have more care responsibilities), predict what will happen going forward (based on a given employee's characteristics and circumstances, the likelihood that they would leave increased by X percent), and, often through A/B testing of potential courses of action, prescribe a path forward (e.g., if care leave were increased, the gender gap in turnover could be closed—which is what Google found and implemented).

Of course, not everyone has a large data set at their disposal, which is why we need to learn from the evidence provided by others on potential pain points and the medicine prescribed to address them. If you are part of a SME (a small and medium-sized enterprise), we have included in the endnotes a report focused on how SMEs can make work fair that you might find useful.

Share Data in Real Time

To maximize the potential of data as a tool to drive change, it must be available to the right people in time to influence relevant decisions (as legally permissible). Details about the composition of a particular candidate pool, for instance, are useful to inform whether the job requisition should be closed or kept open longer to cast a wider net for candidates. On the flip side, a year-end look-back that reveals that aspirational goals were missed does nothing to help people take action to meet those goals, at least until next year—although we do recommend compiling and sharing such annual reports to track progress over the long term, as discussed in Chapter 5.

At the BBC, Ros Atkins and his colleagues tally up the number of female and male contributors after every night's program when journalists are paying attention, and immediately enter the data into their tracking spreadsheet, where they can see it day-to-day, week-to-week, and month-to-month. While results are shared monthly among all participating teams to sustain motivation and momentum, teams monitor their numbers constantly and often make midmonth course corrections if they see themselves slipping behind. This is only possible because they have the real-time data on hand.

The important takeaway for all of us who care about real results is that building fairness into our work means making it a proactive consideration for decisions. Take the case of layoffs. Too many organizations have realized the impact of their downsizing decisions only after it was too late. In 2015, Microsoft, for example, reported that the percentage of women at the company worldwide had decreased from 29 percent in September 2014 to 26.8 percent a year later. The change was attributed to "a strategic business decision made in the longer-term interests of the company," which was the restructuring of its phone hardware business and the closure of factories outside the United States upon its recent acquisition of Nokia. Nokia turned out to have employed a larger share of women compared with

Microsoft, and the layoffs disproportionately affected former Nokia employees.

The fortunate part of this story is that Microsoft was able to identify the exact cause of the dip because it collected and reported data by business unit. The unfortunate part is that the impacts of the decision continued to reverberate the following year, when Microsoft shared that the representation of women had declined one more percentage point to 25.8 percent in 2015 (for context, by 2022, women made up 32.7 percent of Microsoft's global workforce). While we are not suggesting that Microsoft should have made "strategic business decisions" based on gender, we *are* suggesting that all organizations should take the fairness implications of such decisions into account to guard against unintended disparate impact before plans are finalized. For example, a proactive fairness analysis could identify unintended bias in the company's layoff criteria in time for it to reexamine them and potentially shift to different considerations.

This is exactly what VICE Media did in the early 2020s. Its former chief people officer, Daisy Auger-Domínguez, explained that before layoffs, the company assessed potential negative consequences for different groups of employees, such as women and people of color, and made sure managers were aware of the fairness implications of eliminating specific roles: "We took that analysis back to leaders and asked: 'What kind of organization do you want to have on the other side of this?'"

Formal decision rules like "last hired/first fired" can disproportionately impact women and people of color (or members of other historically underrepresented groups who have often been hired more recently) and lead to unintended reductions in diversity. Indeed, early data from a wave of US tech industry layoffs in late 2022 showed that women as well as Black and Hispanic employees accounted for a larger share of layoffs than their representation in the industry would have warranted, as Reboot Representation and McKinsey & Company reported. And a study of more than 300 US firms that downsized between 1971 and 2002 showed that when organizations did not consider fairness in their decision-making and layoffs were based solely on tenure or position, the share of female and Black managers declined by around 20 percent. Organizations that did track representation were able to prevent such losses.

* * *

To circle back to where we started: We choose to measure the things that we truly care about. Data is critical to our efforts to embed fairness and drive meaningful progress because it enables us to establish a baseline, to evaluate whether what we are doing is working, to mark milestones and celebrate wins, to keep gut instincts and overconfidence in check, and to sustain momentum. As Daniella Foster, senior vice president at global pharmaceutical and biotechnology firm Bayer's Consumer Health Division, told us: "It's a totally different conversation when you have the data."

Let us leave you with what we think is the most profound takeaway of this chapter. That is to treat data related to fairness with the same rigor and seriousness as you treat all other business data. Collect, analyze, and share it to improve how you work with the same targeted persistence that you use sales data to improve sales and customer acquisition data to increase profit margins. And use it as the starting point to tap into an even more powerful tool for change: goals, which are our next topic.

1. Collect data you care about
2. Make data simple, salient, and accessible
3. Analyze your data
4. Share data in real time

CHAPTER 3

Goals That Promote
Desirable Behavior

In 2009, Helena Morrissey, then CEO of Newton Investment Management and long one of the most influential people in the British financial services sector, attended a lunch for women in finance in London. The finance industry is notoriously male-dominated and Morrissey herself had suffered some experiences early in her career that had made it clear that finance wasn't a world of equal opportunity for women. But after more than two decades, Morrissey was keenly aware that the many efforts to advance women had not been successful. "At this lunch, I realized that everybody was stuck. No one was getting anywhere despite lots of efforts. It dawned on me that we just must be doing something wrong. So much effort, so little to show for it," she shared during a visit to Harvard a few years later.

This realization became the start of the 30% Club, a campaign to boost the number of women on boards and in the executive leadership of companies. In 2010, Morrissey founded the coalition with seven "initial and enlightened" chairmen of some of the largest companies in the UK who—like her—recognized that having more diverse, modern, and effective boardrooms would be critical for future success. They set out to convince their peers that appointing more women to boards and into senior leadership was both necessary and good business. And they had their work cut out for them: in 2011, women occupied an abysmal 12.5 percent share of the board seats of the 100 largest companies by market value listed on the UK Financial Times Stock Exchange (the FTSE 100).

The 30% Club was named for its initial goal of reaching a minimum of 30 percent women on boards and in senior leadership in the United Kingdom. While some felt the goal should have been 50 percent, Morrissey was mindful of the prevailing reality: starting from 12 percent, 50 percent felt a long way off. But 30 percent could be doable. Regardless of the specific number, choosing a goal against which progress or lack thereof could be measured felt essential. Morrissey reflected: "In the past, we would talk about, 'How many [women's] events are we holding a year? How many people are coming to the events? What is the feedback around the events?' It was very easy to confuse talk with action and action with results. Whereas running a business, I was very conscious that I had metrics. I had ways of measuring whether I was any good." Now she was determined to bring the same data-driven rigor to promoting fairness in business.

Around the same time, gender balance in corporate governance was becoming a top priority for the UK government. In 2011 it established a commission, known as the Davies Review, led by Lord Davies of Abersoch and chief executive Denise Wilson, to develop recommendations for increasing women's presence on boards. Among the ten recommendations the commission released was a suggested target of 25 percent women on FTSE 100 boards by 2015—that is, *doubling* the share of women in four years—with interim annual public reporting on the proportion of women in corporate leadership.

Considering the historical trends of women's presence in boardrooms in the UK, the goal was very ambitious (and though it fell five percentage points short of Morrissey's own, she supported it enthusiastically). The coalition that came together to nudge companies forward was equally ambitious. In addition to pressure from the government and peer outreach and public agitation from the 30% Club, researchers and journalists raised the public profile of the issue by sharing evidence on the current state of women's representation on boards as well as barriers to progress. Executive search firms, a key stakeholder in helping companies fill vacant board seats, started competing against each other on who could place the most women. The board chairs and FTSE 100 chairmen (99 of the 100 were men at the time) started shifting social norms in their peer group through behind-the-scenes cajoling, spurred on by the 30% Club.

As a result, in 2015, the Davies Review reported that FTSE 100 companies as a whole had exceeded the 25 percent goal. A successor commission—the Hampton-Alexander Review—was promptly established to build on the initial success and continue the work of diversifying Britain's top corporate ranks. In 2016, the Hampton-Alexander Review issued a new set of five recommendations aimed at CEOs, the UK government, investors, and executive search firms, which included an updated goal of 33 percent women on FTSE 350 boards by 2020. Importantly, this new goal not only raised the numerical bar and included many more companies in its scope, but it also extended the target to cover executive committees and their direct reports (i.e., senior corporate leadership, not only board members).

Yet again, the goal "appeared ambitious and stretching"—and yet again, it was achieved. At the end of 2020, FTSE 350 companies reached 34.3 percent women on their boards, on average, and all-male boards had disappeared. Following the proven model, a third phase of the UK's voluntary, business-led effort to increase the number of women in corporate leadership was inaugurated in 2021, with a new minimum target of 40 percent women on both FTSE 350 boards and leadership teams by 2025. As of 2024, the FTSE 350 had already exceeded the board target. Progress in diversifying senior executive roles, where women's representation stood at 35 percent, has been slower.

In the meantime, the 30% Club has grown into a global movement to continue increasing the representation of women in corporate leadership with chapters in more than twenty countries. The Club encourages board chairs and CEOs to appoint women to senior positions; shares information to help organizations improve their diversity at all levels; utilizes media and social media to promote its cause; and commissions relevant research.

Reflecting on the key takeaways from the journey, Ruth Sealy, who at the time was the lead researcher of the annual UK Female FTSE Report at Cranfield School of Management, remarked: "One of the fascinating changes in organizations has been the acceptance of the use of targets. Five years ago, there was uproar about the Davies target: 'How dare people interfere with our business!' Now, the number of companies that have publicly stated diversity targets is increasing. . . . It's not rocket science. You wouldn't make any other organizational change without a measurable target or some timeframe."

When we humans feel strongly about accomplishing something, we often turn to goals. Simply put, a goal is a desirable outcome that we have difficulty achieving, even when we know it is theoretically doable. We set goals to move ourselves from good intentions to action, and to make ourselves do things—often, novel and different things— that we wouldn't otherwise do if left to our own devices. Whether it's losing weight, generating high sales, or saving money to buy a home, we instinctively know that having a clear target in sight increases our odds of success. And with good reason: research over more than five decades has consistently shown that goals are one of the best tools to motivate us *and* help us achieve our aims. In fact, when Oona King, then the VP of diversity, equity, and inclusion at technology company Snap Inc., reached out to us in 2019 and asked what single thing could move the needle on workplace fairness the most, we suggested goals (though we feel compelled to be clear that there is no silver bullet when it comes to making work fair).

Although goals are not a new tool in organizational management, they are relatively new in this arena. While 87 percent of Fortune 500 companies share generic statements about valuing diversity on their websites, and 97 percent of Fortune 100 companies publicly highlight their diversity initiatives (such as bias trainings, affinity groups, and internships for members of traditionally underrepresented groups), as of January 2021, only 16 percent of Fortune 100 companies publicized concrete diversity goals related to interviewing, hiring, or promotion. Happily, a number of organizations, including Airbnb, PwC, Snap Inc., Starbucks, The Home Depot, and Xerox, have been using goals as a key part of a systemic strategy to make work fair.

Goals sometimes scare us for the same reasons that they have been proven to work so effectively: they provide an indisputable benchmark against which to evaluate progress; they introduce time pressure; and they focus attention on the topic of the goal. Most managers are already accountable for various specific, measurable, and time-bound performance targets, including sales, customer acquisition, cost cutting, product launches, and budgets. Goals related to fairness at work should be no different: if you want to make your organization more fair, you need to tackle the challenge with the same seriousness as any other business issue. Reaching fairness goals requires no more—and no less—than deploying the same approaches that we use to achieve goals in other areas. Indeed, examining US companies between 1971 and 2002, sociologists Alexandra Kalev and Frank Dobbin found that companies that set diversity goals had 3 to 8 percent greater representation of several traditionally underrepresented groups (white and Latina women as well as Black, Latino, and Asian American men) compared to what they would have had without those goals.

Importantly, goals are distinct from quotas. While goals are voluntary and set by people or organizations themselves, quotas are requirements that demand certain benchmarks be met, such as having a particular share of board seats occupied by women. In jurisdictions where quotas are legal, they are typically instituted by legislative or regulatory bodies that also have the authority to impose sanctions when organizations fail to comply.

Despite being unlawful in some countries, like the United States, quotas have been used extensively around the world to advance the participation of members of historically underrepresented groups in political and business leadership. Approximately 120 countries have some form of legislative gender quota, and dozens of countries have gender quotas for corporate boards. And they produce results. In Rwanda, a new 2003 constitution granted at least 30 percent of positions in all political decision-making bodies to women, and the country has been the world leader in women's parliamentary representation with more than 60 percent female legislators for many years. In France, a law that became effective in 2017 phased in a 40 percent quota for women on the boards of its largest companies; as of 2023, the country topped the global ranking of women's representation on corporate boards at over 43 percent (up from a mere 26 percent in 2013). Incidentally, with its voluntary, goal-based approach, the UK ranked a close second at just over 40 percent in 2023.

Quotas also work in other contexts. In the domain of chess, the introduction of a quota in the highly male-dominated French Club Championship in 1990 led to more and better female chess players, with no large negative effects on men. And in India, quotas have long been used to increase the representation of members of lower castes in educational institutions and government jobs.

Our focus in this chapter is voluntary, self-set goals for individuals and organizations. However, in the fairness domain, the effects of quotas have been studied more comprehensively than those of goals to date. We will therefore draw on some lessons learned from the implementation of quotas—such as how to mitigate the backlash that they sometimes generate—to inform productive goal-setting practices.

As our expertise is in behavioral science and not law, we do not provide legal advice but rather draw on the best available social science evidence to inspire you to set effective fairness goals at work. Depending on your jurisdiction, representational goals (such as attaining a particular percentage of women in senior leadership) may be allowed and may even be the norm—or they may carry some legal risk such that setting *aspirational* targets based on efforts rather than outcomes might be more advisable. As of this writing, fairness goals are increasingly endorsed in Europe and other parts of the world, whereas in the United States, the Supreme Court's June 2023 ruling that deemed race-conscious college admissions policies to be unlawful gave some companies pause (though the ruling did not apply to workplace contexts). We always encourage you to consult legal counsel on the specifics of your context.

Even though goals are an important component of a holistic approach to fairness, they are just that—a component. While data is critical to pinpoint areas for improvement, and goals are a powerful tool to help us move into action, know that even in the absence of data-driven targets, you can act to level the playing field and build fairness into your work. If goals just seem too risky for you, keep reading and implement some of the other strategies we share with you in the forthcoming chapters (especially in Parts II and III). These strategies are designed to de-bias the workplace and remove barriers for everyone—without singling out any particular group—to make work fair and lift all proverbial boats together.

Make Your Outcome Goals Stretching and Specific

In 2020, global professional services firm Accenture published a series of goals, committing to increase the representation of Black employees in its US workforce from 9 percent to 12 percent and the share of Hispanic American employees from 9.5 percent to 13 percent by 2025. Before formalizing these goals, the company had pressure-tested them to ensure their feasibility. Accenture weighed the goals against external benchmarks; consulted legal advisors as well as its African American board members; and ran the numbers against its existing racial/ethnic representation, attrition rates, and recruitment data. Its calculations showed that to reach the targets, the company would have to achieve a roughly 60 percent increase in the number of Black and Hispanic American employees, something Accenture deemed realistic.

We encourage you to follow Accenture's example of a thoughtful approach in setting specific goals for the outcomes you care about. Ask yourself the same questions you would ask with respect to other strategic aspirations: What is our vision for where we want to be three (or five) years from now? Is that vision based on general impressions or specific data? What stands between our current state and that vision, and what goals can help us get there?

The first step in setting stretching, yet feasible, goals is to analyze your organization's data to determine which areas might benefit from them. As discussed in Chapter 2, a general rule of thumb is that any gender gaps warrant further examination. For example, are men significantly overrepresented in external hiring at senior levels? Do women spend more time in a given role than men before they get promoted? What is the gender breakdown of the users of your product, and are certain groups underrepresented?

The next step is to review relevant benchmarks to determine what targets would be realistic, yet stretching. Goals that challenge us have been shown to stimulate more behavior change than easy ones, but for maximum effectiveness, the level of challenge must be well calibrated. Per the classic Goldilocks principle, it needs to be not too much, not too little, but just right. Overly challenging—or worse, impossible-to-attain—goals can backfire because people get demotivated when they realize how far behind they are. This effect was observed in retirement savings, where some employees were less likely to set aside money for retirement when informed of their colleagues' higher savings levels. In a similar vein, when managers have less confidence in their ability to reach assigned goals or cannot envision the concrete steps to get there, they are less likely to remain committed to the goals.

On the flip side, goals that are not ambitious enough are also problematic. They can undermine the whole enterprise of goal setting by sending the signal that no striving or extra effort is required to reach the target. We should therefore compare ourselves slightly upward against benchmarks that make us want to do and be better—but not so far up that we lose all hope of getting there.

So how to ensure your goals are "just right"? Calculate what actual behaviors are needed to attain the target, and then determine if it's feasible. If doubling the number of female engineers in three years would require filling nine out of ten vacancies with women (and the job market's availability or your historical hiring average is closer to one in ten), you are likely setting yourself up for failure with a goal that is overly stretching. But if reaching your target generally requires more of the same, such as continuing to recruit candidate pools that are around 10 percent female engineers, then you are not being sufficiently ambitious. Amazon, for example, reported in 2021 that it aims to double the number of Black directors and vice presidents in the United States year-over-year and increase the number of women in senior tech and science roles by 30 percent year-over-year, which is doable but challenging in its context.

Amazon was comparing itself against its past performance, which is one common approach to benchmarks. Other useful benchmarks include the general population or the local labor market; the projected future labor market, which in most places will invariably be more diverse than the current one; and peer organizations. The Coca-Cola Company benchmarks itself against the census of the full US population, and its goal, announced in 2021, is to align the racial and ethnic composition of its US employees with the census across all levels of the company by 2030.

Sometimes benchmarks are implicit rather than explicit. Among the boards of S&P 1500 companies (which cover approximately 90 percent of the market capitalization of US stocks and which have, on average, ten board members), boards with exactly two women are statistically overrepresented. This "twokenism" phenomenon stems from the fact that boards are likely comparing themselves to each other and inferring the desirable number of women from the prevailing descriptive social norm, that is, what they see most everyone else doing. Having fewer than two women on a board makes a large US company an outlier, but once it joins the herd and meets the lowest socially acceptable threshold with two female board members, it does not feel compelled to go beyond the status quo and add more. Individuals as well as organizations strive to match the level of diversity in their peer groups, but not go beyond it. The lesson here is to beware benchmarks that conveniently make you feel good about yourself.

The final step in effective goal setting is to determine the specific targets you will commit to. Sports apparel maker Adidas, for example, stated that it aims to increase the proportion of women in management positions globally to at least 40 percent by 2025 and fill a minimum of 30 percent of all newly open positions in the United States with Black and Latina/o candidates. These are specific, measurable, and time-bound targets that in Adidas's context are also stretching.

One goal you may wish to consider is proportionality, which we conceptualized with our collaborator, Oliver Hauser. Many organizations have higher numbers of women and members of other traditionally underrepresented groups at lower levels, with their proportions gradually dwindling at more senior levels. The goal of gender proportionality stipulates that a given level in an organization should aim to reflect the gender composition of the level immediately below it. If women make up 41 percent of managers in an organization, and 50 percent of entry-level employees (the level immediately below manager), the gender proportionality goal for the organization would be to reach 50 percent women at the manager level in a reasonable yet challenging timeframe, depending on its promotion frequency and criteria, rate of external hiring, and attrition. Similarly, the goal for the director level (the level above manager) could be set at 41 percent women, since that is where the feeder level (manager) currently stands. In this way, over time, a simple proportionality goal will help organizations increase the number of women throughout the entire hierarchy. Besides overall representation, gender proportionality can be applied specifically to promotions, in which case the goal would be to promote women in proportion to their representation at the feeder level (e.g., at least 41 percent of people promoted from manager to director should be women).

American television network CBS is an example of taking goals a step further by building them into its core business. In 2020, CBS introduced targets to have at least a quarter of its annual unscripted development budget go toward creators and producers who are Black, Indigenous, or People of Color (BIPOC), and to have half of the casts in those shows be BIPOC. In 2023, the California Public Employees' Retirement System (CalPERS), the largest public pension fund in the United States, put its money to work for fairness through a $1 billion investment in two new funds that focus on backing small and up-and-coming private equity firms helmed by "talent that is chronically underrepresented in alternative asset management." CalPERS chief investment officer Nicole Musicco emphasized the business rationale of the investment, noting that by directing its money to younger private equity managers, CalPERS would be one of the first investors to be invited to participate in new, emerging deals. These are powerful illustrations of treating fairness as a core part of all of your activities.

Lastly, consider setting outcome goals not only for the top-level results you care about, such as representation, but also their drivers. The overall number of women (or any group) in an organization is the outcome resulting from various activities like sourcing, recruitment, hiring, promotion, performance evaluations, allocation of stretch opportunities, visibility in front of key leaders, and selection into high-potential programs. In addition to an overall company-wide representation goal, all of these components could have their own outcome goals (where allowed by law), such as having both women and men make up at least 40 percent of the people identified as high-potential talent.

Deploy Process Goals to Support Your Outcome Goals

Successful goals should be based on outcomes, not intentions. Recently, a global professional services firm that Siri worked with reached out to get her feedback on their draft goals. They included a deadline for making diversity, equity, and inclusion training available to all staff, as well as a target date by which DEI-related key performance indicators (KPIs) would be included on all staff scorecards. Yet Siri couldn't help but focus on what was *not* included in the goals: any desired, measurable outcomes from the training, or the expected levels of the KPIs.

Like this firm, many organizations gravitate toward setting goals around processes (such as training 100 percent of the staff) rather than outcomes (such as turnover) because process goals seem more achievable and less risky. Both types of goals can be effective at changing behavior, and they benefit from each other when used in tandem. For example, an outcome goal to achieve gender parity in some set of well-defined senior positions could be combined with a process goal to use evidence-based hiring techniques in 100 percent of appointment processes for those positions. Once you have settled on your top-level outcome goals, we recommend that you consider supporting their attainment with relevant process goals.

Some of the most popular process goals in use today are so-called slate goals that relate to the composition of candidate pools and interview panels. For example, in 2020, the US division of global pharmaceutical firm Novartis implemented "guidelines" requiring gender and racial/ethnic diversity on its candidate slates and among the groups of employees interviewing candidates. By 2021, more than 90 percent of candidate slates were considered gender-diverse and more than 80 percent racially/ethnically diverse (though Novartis

US does not publicly specify what exactly "diverse" means). While (largely) meeting the process goal is an accomplishment in itself, it does beg the question: Did the change in the composition of the candidate and interviewer slates change who ultimately got hired? Novartis's assessment that its commitment "is having a direct impact on the number of women joining the company" makes us hopeful, but more broadly, the evidence on the effects of slate goals is only beginning to emerge—and the final verdict is still out.

Perhaps the most famous slate goal is the Rooney Rule, instituted by the National Football League (NFL) in 2002 and named after legendary Pittsburgh Steelers owner Dan Rooney, who chaired the committee that created it. In its first iteration, the rule required NFL teams to interview at least one (racial) minority candidate for each head coach opening. The intention behind the rule was to increase the number of Black head coaches in a league where 60–70 percent of players were—and are—Black, but at the time, only 2 out of 32 head coaches were Black. However, the rule said nothing about outcomes, only the process. It did not spell out any accountability mechanism, including potential penalties (only once ever, in 2003, has the NFL fined a team president for filling a position without interviewing candidates of color). And it did not redesign the underlying structures and incentives that govern the league and its teams' operations. In other words, the Rooney Rule did very little to embed fairness into the NFL.

The Rooney Rule's more than twenty-year track record is generally underwhelming. Initially, there was some promise: a nonwhite candidate was about 20 percent more likely to be hired as a head coach in the first ten years with the Rooney Rule compared to the pre-Rooney era. In 2007, the Super Bowl featured two Black head coaches for the first time, and during the 2011 season, seven teams were coached by Black men. However, this increase in diversity was not sustained. By 2013 there were only three Black coaches left, and all of the eight open coaching spots were given to white candidates.

In the four years up to and including 2022, at most 3 of 32 NFL coaches were Black.

In light of these outcomes, DeMaurice Smith, executive director of the NFL Players Association from 2009 to 2023, dubbed the Rooney Rule a "tokenism tool." Research helps to explain why that might be the case. Between 2013 and 2017 when 6 Black and 29 white coaches were hired, a Black coach was significantly more likely to be selected if they were one of two Black coaches interviewed, as opposed to the only one. More generally, much evidence suggests that individuals who differ from the numerical majority in one salient attribute, such as gender or race, tend to be disproportionately scrutinized and their differences exaggerated. As a result, being different from everyone else in a finalist pool markedly decreases one's chances of getting selected. Such tokenism is more severe when the numerical proportions are extremely skewed, so one "different" candidate in a pool of finalists faces greater scrutiny and stereotypical judgment than several. Case in point: in one study, when people evaluated a three-person finalist pool where two candidates were the same gender or race and one was different, they tended to recommend hiring one of the two candidates in the majority (more than would have been statistically warranted) whether they were women, men, Black, or white. In other words, it takes more than one counter-stereotypical individual for us to overcome our stereotypes—and interviewing just one candidate who is different from the rest doesn't cut it.

In 2020, the NFL took these learnings to heart and announced that more than one racial minority candidate would have to be interviewed in head coach searches. It also expanded the Rooney Rule to cover other coaching positions, which are often feeders into the head coach position, and implemented an incentive in the form of additional draft picks to teams that cultivate underrepresented talent. The impact of these changes is yet to be evaluated.

In the meantime, variations of the Rooney Rule have spread across the American business community with companies like Bank of America, Dollar General, Groupon, Hilton, JPMorgan Chase, and Meta committing at different points to using it internally. The New York City Police Department also announced that it would interview at least one applicant of color for positions above captain. While proponents tout slate goals as effective, as far as we are aware they have not been rigorously (or publicly) evaluated in the corporate contexts where they have been deployed, nor have their parameters been clearly established in the legal realm.

Anecdotal evidence on the drawbacks should give us pause. As the *Washington Post* and *New York Times* have reported, in some cases underrepresented candidates were invited to "fake interviews" to check the box on a slate requirement even though the positions had already been promised to majority candidates. In other organizations, the absence of clear enforcement mechanisms has led to low compliance with slate goals. In yet others, employees have been disillusioned to realize that a single quick fix cannot immediately remedy the long-standing, systemic problem of underrepresentation.

Other sectors are also experimenting with slate goals. An interesting example of how they can be built into HR practices is the Mansfield Rule, which was launched in 2017 by Diversity Lab, an organization working to advance gender, racial, disability, and LGBTQ+ diversity in the legal sector. The Mansfield Rule directs voluntarily participating entities—as of 2023, more than 360 American, Canadian, and British law firms, and more than 75 legal departments—to consider a broad slate of 30–50 percent underrepresented talent for key leadership and governance roles. Companies are also asked to track more than a dozen leadership-related talent processes, such as how people are selected for pitch teams, promoted to equity partner, or appointed as practice group leaders, as well as the outcomes of those processes. To gain Mansfield certification on an annual basis, companies need to share their data with Diversity Lab.

Just like the goals set for women's representation on corporate boards in the UK, the Mansfield Rule certification process has become progressively more ambitious. In its first iteration, companies were asked to consider 30 percent women and lawyers from historically underrepresented racial and ethnic groups for all high-level leadership roles. The goal has been expanded in scope to now also include the consideration of LGBTQ+ lawyers and lawyers with disabilities, as well as more roles and activities that impact the leadership pipeline. By requiring annual recertification and by constantly raising the bar, Diversity Lab wants to help companies stay on track and avoid the pitfall of complacency once the first milestone has been reached.

The precise effect of the Mansfield Rule on diversifying the leadership ranks of the legal profession is difficult to evaluate because participation in it is voluntary, meaning that the set of firms seeking certification may well be systematically different from those not involved. Thus we don't have the typical control group of an A/B test available to assess impact. In any case, the good news is that law firms and legal departments have become more diverse in recent years.

It is worth noting that both Diversity Lab and the UK boards deployed goals as one component of a more holistic approach to drive workplace fairness. Diversity Lab offers participating firms assistance with the implementation of the Mansfield Rule by, for example, setting up tracking systems for the relevant data and coordinating monthly knowledge-sharing calls among participants. Law firms report that new ways of making decisions tend to outlast individual leaders since they are built into the structures and broader culture. Similarly, in the UK, the 30% Club, the government, academics, and the media worked in concert to shine a light on changes in women's representation on boards. In fact, how to talk about these changes was one of the recommendations Iris made when meeting with government representatives early in the process. Rather than focusing on the lack of women, she advised highlighting progress made to signal that the proverbial train had left the station and a movement was underway. This well-tested behavioral science approach, which we will discuss in more detail in Chapter 11, was complemented by individual outreach to the laggards. As Sue Vinnicombe, lead author of Cranfield University's annual Female FTSE Board Report, noted: "There were a lot of pushes and pinches, including [then–prime minister] David Cameron writing to companies when they consistently did not have a woman on the board."

The bottom line is that despite their challenges, process goals, including slate goals, can play a role in promoting fairness, especially when used in tandem with outcome goals.

Frame Goals Productively

How goals are introduced, framed, and justified makes a big difference in how they are received. Well-framed goals can yield significant performance-enhancing benefits, while poorly framed ones can lead to backlash, unintended negative consequences, or false progress. Here are four key things to watch out for to ensure your goals have the intended effects.

The first is backlash. If goals are seen to advantage one group (say, women) at the expense of another (men), they can be rejected on grounds of unfairness, especially if people perceive the workplace as a zero-sum game where one person's gain is another person's loss. This backlash can occur even if the goals intend to level a playing field that was previously unfairly disadvantaging women—or as the unattributed saying goes, "When you're accustomed to privilege, equality feels like oppression."

In a series of laboratory experiments, Iris along with colleagues showed that male employers hired fewer female candidates when they were informed that other employers had hired more women. Male employers did not "correct" for the behavior of others this way when it was men who had been previously hired at greater rates, and female employers hired women and men in roughly equal proportions regardless of what others did. This reactance phenomenon seems most likely to occur when members of a historically advantaged group (e.g., men, racial/ethnic majorities, straight people, able-bodied individuals) perceive their group and status as being threatened, like when goals are introduced to increase the presence of other groups.

One strategy to reduce the likelihood of such backlash is to set and communicate goals inclusively. The gender proportionality principle is an example: it is gender-neutral since it encourages proportional representation of all genders, considering who is qualified and available, and it helps to frame fairness as a collective effort. Making work fair should be everyone's job and those currently in the majority are not exempt. Global food and facilities management company Sodexo followed this playbook when it started to frame its representation goals as achieving balance between women and men, instead of focusing only on increasing women's representation. Sodexo's former global chief diversity officer, Rohini Anand, writes that this framing "appeared less threatening and helped garner support."

These framing strategies can also help with the second challenge with goals, which is potential negative outcomes for their targets. Diversity goals in hiring, for example, can lead newly recruited colleagues from traditionally underrepresented groups to be branded as "diversity hires," undermining their credibility and competence in the eyes of peers. Siri recently heard a senior male finance leader express—in front of the whole division—his delight at the arrival of a new female colleague because "we really needed to hire a woman." Similarly, when a senior male venture capitalist proudly told us that "we haven't lowered the bar for women at our firm," the unspoken underlying assumption was that normally, women would only be hired if standards were relaxed.

Anticipating this type of stigma, underrepresented candidates may be less likely to seek or accept positions in the first place. Indeed, laboratory evidence shows that in competitive settings with gender quotas, women became targets of sabotage by their peers. Such negative interpersonal repercussions can be mitigated when employees feel solidarity with each other and realize that everyone's contributions matter for collective success. In French chess clubs, for example, "quota women" contributed to Club Championship points in the same way as men, making them feel equally important and preventing worries about whether they belonged. The clubs themselves were incentivized to support and coach the female players because their overall performance depended on the performance of the women as much as the men. Other organizations can foster such team spirit by purposefully emphasizing that *everyone* plays a part in the organization's collective success.

The third thing to be mindful of as you craft your goals is false progress, or surface-level changes without real underlying change. For example, a goal to increase women's representation in top management might lead to more women having leadership-level titles but not the associated organizational scope, clout, or job responsibilities. Tracking various outcome measures is therefore necessary to ensure that meeting goals doesn't come at the expense of actually leveling the playing field. In an academic workplace, this could entail tracking not only the number of underrepresented faculty in a department (i.e., pure representation), but also research support, teaching assignments, and service responsibilities. The Massachusetts Institute of Technology (MIT) did this a few years ago and learned that its female faculty were not institutionally set up for success in the same way as their male colleagues—an example of a broader phenomenon known as performance-support bias, which we will return to later.

Lastly, watch out for tunnel vision, or the downside of the "what does not get measured, does not count" phenomenon. Simply put, you get what you pay for. A goal to increase women's representation in management is likely to do just that, but unlikely to magically also increase the representation of, say, people of color. Focusing exclusively on numerical representation goals can lead to the neglect of other important and relevant considerations. At worst, goals can backfire, or have the opposite of the intended effect, such as if they bring increasingly more women into a toxic work environment that does not foster their success. Therefore, frame goals as one essential component of a holistic strategy to become a better-functioning workplace or team, and make sure they address fairness along multiple balanced dimensions. Monitoring both goal-related and (seemingly) goal-unrelated data closely, as we detailed earlier, will allow you to spot potential signs of unintended consequences.

Support Goal Attainment

Whether you've tried to spend less time on social media, drink less alcohol, or read more books, you probably know from personal experience that attaining goals is hard (even when you're motivated!). Fortunately, research points us to several tried-and-tested ways we can help ourselves achieve our aims.

Making a plan for how you will achieve your goal is a simple yet highly effective strategy to follow through on your intentions. Thinking through where, when, and how you will take steps to meet your goal has been shown to increase voting, recycling, test preparation, and healthy eating, among many other beneficial behaviors. You can put this inexpensive nudge into practice immediately to make your work more fair. Set aside scheduled time to sponsor or mentor colleagues to increase the likelihood that it happens. Plan how you would intervene in the face of an offensive remark to be ready should the situation arise. Build a new step into your regular workflow, such as a prompt to review the representativeness of short-listed speakers before you invite them to an event.

Once you have a goal—and, ideally, a plan—monitoring progress is key to staying motivated, and one effective approach involves scorecards and dashboards. Accenture's top five hundred leaders globally are measured on a scorecard that puts the extent to which they advance the company's diversity and inclusion goals on par with their achievement of sales, revenue, and profitability goals and retention of key talent. Germany-based global pharmaceutical company Bayer also uses integrated scorecards as an accountability tool. The company has set a public goal of achieving gender parity across all management levels by 2025, and parity at each individual level by 2030. Leaders' performance on fairness metrics is regularly tracked and reported to the board as part of quarterly earnings reports.

While we do not know the optimal cadence of progress monitoring, it has to happen with some frequency—but not so often that it limits people's ability to act. One paper on goal attainment, for example, shows that setting a two-week goal can be more effective than setting a weekly goal, as the latter can limit flexibility too much. At the same time, both of these shorter-term goals were better at changing behavior than one long-term (annual) goal. As always, context matters. At the BBC's 50:50 The Equality Project, the 50–50 gender parity goal is set at the monthly level in recognition of the unpredictable nature of news: On any given day, journalists may be required to feature specific subject matter experts who tip the gender scales one way or the other. But over the course of a month, they have enough flexibility to be able to meet the goal.

Monitoring progress goes hand in hand with another highly effective strategy to support goal attainment: social accountability. We humans inherently care about what other people think, and so do organizations. The mere prospect of being asked to explain or justify our actions to others has been shown to lead us to invest more effort in problem solving and to make less biased decisions. For example, the "comply-or-explain" approach, where people are asked to either comply with a directive or explain why they did not follow it, has been used in the UK, Australia, and many other countries with great success to drive change in companies' diversity policies, women's representation on corporate boards, and corporate governance.

We are more likely to achieve organization-wide goals when we hold specific people or entities, such as a senior leader or a task force, accountable for them. A chief diversity officer or board member who asks C-suite colleagues about their promotion track records and representation numbers—even without formal power to change anything—activates social accountability by reminding them that their actions are "being watched." This expectation of visibility is one key driver of behavior change, both for individuals and organizations.

Making goals relevant and salient, that is, pertinent to one's job and regularly top-of-mind, is yet another way to increase the likelihood that people will follow through on them. Consider translating big, company-wide goals to the level of individual employees (where permitted by law) and support aggregate goals with subgoals. For example, while an individual leader may not have it within their control to equalize women's and men's advancement rates across the whole firm, they certainly can aim for improvement within their own group of direct and indirect reports. Indeed, breaking long or complicated tasks into bite-sized pieces has been shown to increase people's interest, tenacity, and enjoyment in pursuing them.

Global consumer goods giant Unilever did exactly this in 2010 when it announced a company-wide goal of increasing women's representation in managerial ranks from 38 percent to 50 percent in ten years. This ambitious, high-level goal—which Unilever met ahead of schedule in March 2020—was accompanied by more granular internal targets for each market and function. They were tracked by an executive council monthly and reported to the Global Diversity Board three times a year. In Unilever's experience, breaking the company-wide goal into smaller, actionable pieces relevant to individual leaders increased awareness of what was fair at key decision moments around hiring, promotion, and retention, which in turn helped leaders make more goal-aligned decisions.

Gaining the buy-in of the people whose actions will determine whether fairness goals are reached is crucial. Employees often ignore newly instituted goals and continue with old practices, especially when there is no progress monitoring or accountability. In one financial services company we worked with, employees involved in recruitment continued to tap their networks for leads even after a formal policy change discontinued the use of internal referrals in hiring. Thus, overcoming employees' resistance to new goals and associated processes is critical. One way to do that is to engage managers directly in making work fair. Research has shown that when managers personally participate in recruiting, training, and developing women, they are less resistant toward fairness goals (and their firms are more gender diverse).

Asking people to set their own goals can also work. Travel company Expedia and healthcare giant Johnson & Johnson have reported asking employees to self-select diversity, equity, and inclusion goals, which are subsequently tracked as part of the performance evaluation process. They are onto something: among marathon runners and economics students, individuals who self-set and disclosed a specific performance goal did better than those who either did not set a goal or did not publicize it.

Lastly, incentives are another important lever to support goal attainment. So important, in fact, that we have dedicated the next chapter entirely to them.

* * *

Goals are a powerful tool to make real, measurable progress on fairness, and the good news is we already know how to use them. In our personal lives as well as in many aspects of our work, we regularly set goals to clarify what we want to achieve, motivate ourselves to act, and establish a benchmark against which to track progress. A company preparing to launch a new product would never embark on the journey without first setting internal deadlines for project completion and instituting specific targets for things like revenue, number of units sold, and market share. An executive would never say, "We care deeply about our new product and building it to be as successful as it can be. So we are going to do our best, launch it when it's ready, and see how sales go from there." If the company encountered problems in the product design phase, it wouldn't fix them by celebrating a "Product Development Day" or by organizing a series of conversations about the value of product design. You get the point: we need to approach fairness in the same goal-driven way we approach the rest of our business.

---

1. Make your outcome goals stretching and specific
2. Deploy process goals to support your outcome goals
3. Frame goals productively
4. Support goal attainment

CHAPTER 4

Incentives to Drive Results

In September 2021, one of the largest hotels in our hometown—the Omni Boston Hotel at the Seaport—opened its doors. The first project developed under the "Massport Model" set a new standard for how to make public/private development projects more fair. When the Massachusetts Port Authority (Massport), the owner of the land, solicited bids for a luxury hotel development in Boston's Seaport District, one of the hottest real estate markets in the US, it informed developers that their bids would be evaluated based on four equally weighted criteria: building design, construction experience, financial capabilities, and diversity and inclusion plans. Giving diversity and inclusion so much weight was unprecedented. In the winning bid from Omni Hotels/New Boston Hospitality, 30 percent of the total construction and architectural fees went to women or minority-owned businesses; people of color comprised about 28 percent of total equity ownership; and Omni Hotels committed to a goal of at least 20 percent of goods and services being purchased from women or minority-owned companies.

Without the high-powered incentives, it is unlikely that this would have been the outcome of the project. Jonathan Davis, CEO of the Davis Companies, a real estate development company part of the team of winning bidders, explained that developers generally seek the fastest and simplest way to get a job done. They are likely to stay within their networks, working with people and organizations they have known and collaborated with for a long time. Massport's incentives changed their considerations: "Had Massport not set these rules of engagement, this is not the most cost-effective way to get the job done," remarked Davis.

L. Duane Jackson, a member of Massport's board, was a longtime advocate for the participation of underrepresented businesses in publicly owned real estate development in Boston. He understood that this large-scale project presented a unique chance to propel equal opportunity, and that to make it happen, one would have to design the incentives just right: "I did not rely on the private sector to accomplish my goals," Jackson explained. "Instead, I promoted a policy that altered the rules, leveled the playing field, and provided a pathway forward to a more equitable solution to a problem of diversity and inclusion in the real estate ecosystem in Boston." In May 2023, Boston mayor Michelle Wu was joined by leaders from four additional Massachusetts cities in subscribing to the "Massport model" and pledging that 25 percent of evaluation criteria in private and public real estate projects would be assigned to DEI.

Incentives, including financial ones, are an important tool in a behavioral designer's toolbox. They are a legally permissible means to advance fairness in many jurisdictions but not in all, so we again advise you to consult legal counsel. Incentives steer our actions in a particular direction and motivate us to do things that we might not have otherwise done, either because we simply were too used to doing things our usual way, or because the benefits of a new approach did not outweigh the (real or perceived) costs involved. To make things fair, an additional nudge is sometimes necessary.

When companies tie things like compensation or promotions to goals, they signal that they take these objectives seriously. For people to know whether they did a good job, they need to understand what they are managing towards—including which goals—and be rewarded accordingly. The 2022 *Women in the Workplace* report reveals that 34 percent of companies factored the achievement of goals related to workplace fairness into managers' performance reviews.

Mastercard, for example, introduced new performance metrics for its senior leaders when it tied their bonuses to the company's track record on carbon emissions, financial inclusion, and the gender pay gap. The new compensation model was rolled out to cover all employees in 2022. "Tying DEI and environment, social, and governance (ESG) to the business is an important way to ensure those efforts are sustainable and business critical, and tying executive and even employee compensation to ESG goals is one clear way to do it," Randall Tucker, Mastercard's executive vice president and chief inclusion officer, said.

Tech giant Intel made public in 2018 that it ties 7 percent of all employee bonuses to internal hiring and retention goals, and starting in 2022, to increased representation of women in technical roles. Telecommunications conglomerate Verizon reported in 2021 that an ESG metric makes up 10 percent of the short-term incentive award for corporate employees, including the CEO. Verizon went one step further than most companies and publicly specified what that metric entails: a US workforce with at least 60 percent minority and female employees, and at least $5.2 billion of overall supplier spending on minority- and female-owned firms. Other companies that have tied executive pay to the degree to which specific representation targets are met include American Express, McDonald's, and Nike.

Incentive schemes raise important design questions, such as how large an incentive has to be to bite. This is something Massport did not have to worry about: a project worth $500 million speaks for itself. But do the typical incentives to make progress on ESG considerations have enough teeth to drive behavior change? Companies are hoping that with the appropriate training and information sharing, they might.

But change—any change—is hard. Many people don't change their diets even though it would improve their health. As it turns out, only a small fraction of our inertia is due to a lack of information. Most of us are aware that salads tend to have fewer calories than burgers. Even in more complex settings, information matters surprisingly little. Research trying to understand why large textile firms in India were not adopting advanced management practices that would increase productivity found that only 15 percent of the non-adoption was due to a lack of information. Almost half of the inaction came down to firms not believing that the new practices were worth introducing. Typically, firms preferred working their machines until they failed instead of preventing premature breakdown through improved maintenance.

This is a more general problem. We tend to underinvest in preventive care. For instance, people still smoke tobacco, and obesity is spreading from high-income to low-income countries despite increased attention to the health risks posed by smoking and obesity. These intertemporal choice problems, where we incur costs today to reap benefits tomorrow (or later), are incredibly thorny. They also affect investments in workplace fairness. Much like maintaining a machine today so that it does not break down tomorrow, taking care of our workforce today so that it does not burn out, quit, or sue the company for discrimination tomorrow is costly. What makes the trade-off between today and tomorrow more tricky is that the costs of today are pretty much certain while we know much less about whether or not the benefits will in fact kick in as hoped tomorrow.

Incentives help us stack the deck in favor of change. Keeping things the way they are is often safer and cheaper, at least in the short term. In 1988, economists William Samuelson and Richard Zeckhauser coined the term "status quo bias" to capture this phenomenon: clinging on to what we know and what we have makes us worse decision-makers because we do not judge alternative options accurately and therefore tend to forgo valuable opportunities.

What worked for the Indian textile firms might also help us make work more fair: for them, showing instead of telling went a long way. When the firms got to experience what a difference a few new trial machines made, they were substantially more inclined to switch from old to new ways of doing things. Proof of concept is one of the most useful strategies in change management, as Ros Atkins demonstrated when he proved the power of his counting methodology on his own show at the BBC before inviting other teams to join him. Proof of concept not only provides the data necessary for decision-making; it also builds trust between those recommending change and those having to adopt it—and, possibly most importantly, helps us focus on solutions.

So, when we work with organizations, we often recommend starting small and running a pilot that does not threaten the status quo but demonstrates that something new can be done. Given our inherent change aversion and our creativity in coming up with excuses for why inaction or procrastination is the right strategy, asking someone to take a look at something we have already tried out is much less threatening than requesting someone to switch to a completely new way of operating.

This is also why the high-level incentives provided by the traditional macroeconomic case for gender equity won't be enough. Take Japan as an example. The realization that increasing women's labor force participation would boost gross domestic product (GDP) led to "Womenomics," a term coined by Kathy Matsui and colleagues of Goldman Sachs in a 1999 research paper on economic growth in Japan. It became a pillar of the late prime minister Shinzo Abe's economic policy—and indeed helped to increase women's labor force participation. However, women tended to be stuck in lower-paying and less senior roles that lacked the job security men enjoyed. In the end, Womenomics did not have a transformative impact on gender equity. A macro case for women's empowerment did not automatically bring about the micro-incentives necessary for organizations and society to adjust policies, procedures, and cultural norms to create a level playing field. In 2023, Japan ranked 104th in the World Bank's survey on women's economic opportunity and 123rd in the World Economic Forum's Economic Participation and Opportunity Index, slightly below the rank it had in 2016 when data was first collected in the Forum's annual Global Gender Gap Report.

Beyond Japan, women's labor force participation is low in many countries, including in other large economies like India. According to the International Monetary Fund, the GDP boost provided by women's increased participation would be substantial in Japan, in India, and around the world, and GDP per capita would also increase as a larger talent pool would lead to better matches between job seekers and employers. At the individual level, benefits of working for pay also abound, including health improvements for mothers and children due to delayed childbirth; increased investments in children's education; reductions in poverty at all ages; and an equalization of decision-making power at home. Yet none of these incentives are strong enough to truly move the needle. For more women to join the labor force, employers need to help counteract the many forces that work against increased participation. Meaningful, individual-level incentives are required.

This also applies to organizations. Even incentives within a manager's remit—say, the belief that diversity improves team performance—do not automatically propel team leaders to seek out team members who are different from each other or invest in inclusive practices that help everyone thrive. Normally there are too many competing "business cases" in a manager's life: produce more, at higher quality and speed; increase customer satisfaction; comply with safety and other regulations; decrease risk; nurture creativity and innovation; and maximize quarterly earnings, to name but a few. Fairness will only rise to the top of this list if we build it into the manager's priorities—and this is what individual-level incentives are for. However, when companies add ever more goals to an employee's KPIs, this invariably decreases the relative weight of each metric. While getting incentives right is no easy feat, this chapter will share how we can design them for increased impact.

Put Incentives into the Right Bucket

Incentive pay for executives is prevalent. According to the 2023 Compensation Best Practices Report by Payscale, close to 80 percent of about 5,000 surveyed organizations, mostly from North America and Europe, offer a combination of a fixed base salary and incentive pay to their executives. In these schemes, the overall payout is based on meeting quantifiable performance metrics that are often largely financial.

For better or—in this case—worse, this means that the weight any given non-financial metric receives is tiny. Imagine a two-thirds/one-third pay mix where 67 percent of total compensation is fixed and 33 percent is variable (i.e., given as a bonus). Most investors expect a large share of the variable bonus to be tied to financial performance conditions. Assuming another two-thirds/one-third split of the bonus, this leaves 11 percent of total compensation for all non-financial considerations combined, including environmental, social, and governance factors. In all likelihood, we end up with little more than a couple of percentage points for social considerations such as the diversity of the workforce, pay equity, human rights, community outreach, inclusion survey results, supplier policies, and the like. So, if an executive's total compensation is $300,000, this might imply that about $3,000 is at risk if they violate a proportional promotion goal or do not meet a specific hiring target in a given year.

Among S&P 500 companies in 2022, only about a quarter used an incentive structure with discrete, weighted metrics with a specific goal attached, as in our example above. Most firms employed a scorecard approach where a certain fraction of an incentive plan is designated to a bundle of goals, leaving more discretion to the evaluators (e.g., a board compensation committee) to interpret and adjust. Another quarter did not rely on quantified metrics at all but applied a fully discretionary approach. Maybe, after all, companies are not putting all that much money where their mouth is?

It is unlikely that companies will shift to larger fairness incentives anytime soon—but maybe we can make them more meaningful. For starters, to drive fairer behaviors with smaller incentives, you can seek help in the behavioral designer's toolbox and "shape the story your incentives tell." A better understanding of the psychology behind incentives will help you make them more effective.

Consider what happened when Iris recently asked her seventeen-year-old son whether he would be willing to bike eight miles to downtown Boston to take advantage of a $100 discount on a computer that a particular store offered. Alternatively, he could go to a nearby store and save himself the hassle and the additional hour or two that the Boston trip would involve. And yes, he would be the beneficiary of the $100 saved. Without hesitation, he decided to ride his bike into town. A 10 percent discount on a $1,000 computer was too good to pass up. A few days later, when Iris sat in the passenger seat of their car while her son was practicing his driving, she asked him another question. Would he be willing to bike to Boston for a $100 discount on a new car that cost, say, $20,000 (and he could keep the saved money again)? "No way," he responded. "Why would I do that?"

"Because it would be the rational thing to do," Iris said. "A hundred dollars saved out of $20,000 (a 0.5 percent discount) should not be worth less than $100 saved out of $1,000."

If you now side with Iris's son, you are not alone. People care about the size of their savings relative to the total price. Saving 10 percent compared to half a percent feels more significant. In an actual car shopping experiment, a savings of $450 was about twice as powerful at motivating vehicle purchases when described as a prepaid gas card instead of a discount on the vehicle price. Imagine the feeling of getting gas, not just once but multiple times, completely for free, or at a discount of 100 percent each time!

Behavioral economist Richard Thaler was awarded the Nobel Prize in Economics in 2017 for what is known as "mental accounting" and related behavioral insights. He posited that the human brain

organizes financial activities in different buckets, often with their individual budgets, leading to money not being fungible. While saving
$100 should have the same value to us independent of which "bucket"
the savings comes from, Iris's son (and much research) shows that it
doesn't. So, if you can find the right bucket for your incentive, it will
be more effective.

Xylem Inc., a large American water technology company, must
have understood this behavioral tendency when it made the unusual
move to create its own bucket for ESG and introduce an award that
focused 100 percent on ESG priorities in its long-term incentive plan.
With clear performance conditions, the plan benefits from the psychology behind incentives. It might well be more effective at aligning
executives' behavior with ESG goals than the typical short-term
incentive plan where ESG metrics are part of a bucket of several
other considerations that—in addition to accounting for a small
fraction of the overall incentive—are often unhelpfully referred to as
"non-financial performance measures" (and include things like risk,
compliance, and other governance topics).

If you want to maximize the effectiveness of your incentives for
fairness, follow Xylem's example and consider making them a bucket
of their own—or assign them to an existing bucket where they will be
a sizable contributor.

Employ a Loss Frame

In addition to mental accounting, behavioral designers should be
aware of another behavioral phenomenon—loss aversion—described
in a famous 1979 paper by psychologists Daniel Kahneman and
Amos Tversky. "Losses tend to loom larger than gains," they said—in
fact, about twice as large. While we hope that you have never lost
any money, if you have, try to remember what it felt like. The pain of
losing, say $100, tends to be much bigger than the joy we experience
when gaining the same amount. This is why people are more likely to
pay their dues on time when there is a penalty for late payments but

are less responsive to benefit from the same savings when discounts for early payments are offered. A penalty is a loss and also signals that a wrong has been committed; a savings is a gain without any moral connotations. Loss aversion is one of the reasons pay cuts are particularly painful, and companies try to avoid them at all costs. They are, rightly, concerned about their impact on morale and motivation.

The question before us is whether we can frame a given incentive as a loss instead of a gain to enhance its motivational power. Deducting money from some initially granted award is not common—and can be legally complicated—but a field experiment with a Chinese high-tech firm is illustrative. Here is what the company said to some of its employees (the loss frame group): "The company is rewarding productivity. We will grant you a provisional bonus of RMB 80 [around $11] before the start of every work week. For every week in which your team's weekly production average is below 20 units/hour, the bonus will be taken away." Another group of workers was in the gain frame where they were promised a same-sized reward as a bonus at the end of the week if they met the same performance conditions.

It turns out the workers conformed to the predictions of loss aversion. Both groups outperformed the baseline where they did not receive any incentives, but the group that feared losing their already awarded bonus (loss frame) significantly outperformed the workers who were hoping to receive the reward at the end of the week (gain frame). The effect persisted over the four-month time frame of the experiment, suggesting that how you frame incentives can make a big difference. People will work hard to win a promised reward—but they will work even harder to keep an existing reward from disappearing.

If applying these insights to the advancement of fairness sounds unseemly, take a look at what personal computer company HP did in 2017. Its general counsel, Kim Rivera, introduced a new program that cut legal fees to outside counsel by 10 percent if the legal team did not include at least one relationship partner or attorney managing at least 10 percent of billable hours who was from an underrepresented group in terms of gender, race, ethnicity, sexual orientation, or disability status. All law firms with more than ten attorneys in the United States that wanted to do business with HP needed to meet this minimum standard. HP added that this staffing requirement was a minimum and more diversity on the legal teams would be viewed favorably. "Our initiative is meant to make sure that opportunity at that business is spread more evenly to folks," Rivera said in 2020. She also reported that in just three years, HP had moved from 46 percent of law firms meeting these requirements to 95 percent complying.

Reward Without Delay

Many companies have an employee referral program where current employees receive a bonus for successful referrals. Firms perceive a job candidate that someone has vouched for as better, taking the referral as an additional positive signal in the hiring process. Not only do referrals lower recruitment costs but referred employees have also been found to be more likely to perform better, stay longer, and be more satisfied with the employer. Accordingly, referred job applicants end up being more likely to be hired than nonreferred ones.

Referrals tend to be even more important for women and people of color seeking a job. The additional signal a referral provides can make all the difference for someone who has to contend with biases in the hiring process. The problem is that employees often recommend people they know—friends, former colleagues and schoolmates, people in their social circles—who tend to look like they do.

Intel decided to tackle this challenge by offering twice the referral reward for candidates from underrepresented groups. Companies like Accenture and Pinterest followed suit. After a six-week experiment prompting its engineers to identify candidates underrepresented in tech roles (that is, women and people of color), Pinterest reported a dramatic increase in the referrals of those candidates. As long as white men are in the majority in an organization, it is unlikely that referred candidates will be representative of the broader working population—unless we can increase the prize that awaits referrers at the end.

Note that it is not irrelevant that referring employees receive a bonus immediately after a successful hire. People tend to be more willing to go the extra mile if they are compensated for it right then and there. We tend to discount the future much more than is traditionally assumed in economic models, a tendency sometimes referred to as "present bias." You not only have to increase the benefits but also move them up. Benefits accrued far in the future will give you much less bang for your buck.

An experiment to raise young children's immunization rates in India drove this home for us. In rural Rajasthan, many mothers had to travel quite far to take their small children to an immunization camp. Thus immunization was not only a slightly unpleasant experience for the children but also quite costly for the mothers. To make matters worse, there was no guarantee that the clinic would be able to administer the shots once they arrived due to several logistical and supply chain challenges. Overcoming this uncertainty already helped a lot: when mothers were assured in advance that their children would receive their shots, immunization rates increased by about 10 percentage points. What was more surprising was that two pounds of lentils and some metal plates as a reward for a completed immunization drove the change even further, with a more than 30 percentage point (or sixfold) increase in immunizations compared to the baseline with no incentives.

So, immediate gratification is what we have to go for. When we create enjoyable experiences to counterbalance the costs associated with something unpleasant or difficult, we engage in what Katherine Milkman, Julia Minson, and Kevin Volpp have coined "temptation bundling." Another evidence-based example we love is watching your favorite show or listening to a fun podcast or audiobook while exercising. Although equating fairness with exercise would be too simple, there are some parallels. Finding a successful candidate to refer outside of our go-to network requires effort—and that effort can be counterbalanced by immediate rewards.

Signal Your Values

A few years ago, people who had previously self-disclosed their political leanings participated in a simple experiment where they were
asked to stuff campaign mailings for either the Democratic or Republican candidate in a US presidential election. The letters were then
sent to independent voters in Ohio, an important swing state. The
researchers behind the experiment were interested in the following
questions: Did the workers' political leanings affect their effort in
this task, that is, the number of envelopes they stuffed in the time
available, and what would happen if people were paid for their performance, that is, for the number of envelopes stuffed?

Perhaps not surprisingly, ideologically aligned workers who were
asked to stuff envelopes for a candidate from their preferred party
stuffed 72 percent more envelopes than those who were misaligned.
Incentives also mattered. When these workers were paid for performance, the aligned workers' productivity grew only a little bit but
nonaligned workers were motivated to substantially increase their
effort.

This experiment illustrates an important point about incentives
that goes far beyond stuffing envelopes. People who feel aligned with
an organization's values do not primarily work for the money. Sure,
they also care about financial incentives, but compared to their nonaligned colleagues, such incentives play a smaller role in their overall
motivation and productivity.

To what degree financial and nonfinancial incentives complement
each other is an empirical question that we have yet to fully answer.
While financial incentives typically increase performance, there are
cases where they don't, and even cases where they have the opposite
effect. We have to make sure financial incentives do not inadvertently
crowd out a person's intrinsic motivation—something daycare centers
in Israel had to learn the hard way when they introduced penalties
for parents who picked their children up late. Instead of decreasing

the likelihood that parents arrived late, the monetary penalties increased it. The penalty changed the social contract between parents and teachers. Beforehand, parents felt bad about keeping teachers late and tried to be on time whenever possible. Once the penalty was introduced, instead of seeing it as the fine it was supposed to be, parents interpreted it as a price that entitled them to an extra half hour of childcare if they were willing to pay for it.

In other cases, financial incentives just do not make a difference either way. When a textile factory in China tried to keep its employees from throwing waste scraps of cloth on the floor by offering financial incentives to dispose of waste in the appropriate bins, it failed. Despite the slipping hazards the cloths created, employees could not be bothered. Maybe the incentives were too small, or maybe the managers could have come up with something more powerful that did not involve money at all? Two researchers, Sherry Jueyu Wu and Betsy Levy Paluck, had an idea. They sprinkled the factory floors with decals depicting golden coins, which are a symbol of good fortune in China— and their instincts were proven right. Employees were significantly less likely to throw their leftovers on the floor because covering good luck symbols with trash was not a culturally appropriate thing to do.

Understanding what motivates behavior is thus key to designing effective incentives. Generally, younger people tend to care more about ESG than older cohorts. A 2022 survey by the Hoover Institute and partners found that millennials and Gen Zers (born between 1981 and 2012) are more than twice as likely as baby boomers (born between 1946 and 1964) to indicate that they are very concerned "about social issues (e.g., workplace diversity, income inequality, and workplace conditions)." According to the Deloitte Global Human Capital Trends surveys of more than 10,000 business and HR leaders in over 100 countries between 2018 and 2023, organizations are increasingly judged not only based on their financial performance but also on their relationships with their employees, customers, and society at large. These surveys also report that Gen Z and millennial employees are more likely to stay with their employers for more than five years if they are satisfied with their employers' social and environmental impact. So the primary function of ESG incentives might not be to drive accountability internally but instead to send a signal about a company's values to employees and job seekers. An extensive review of the literature on the (nonfinancial) meaning of work finds that such signaling is indeed happening, including by firms like General Motors, IBM, and Microsoft, which rely on their corporate social responsibility strategies to attract job candidates.

It is not just employees who care. Media and investor interest in topics like a company's ecological footprint or its treatment of workers has increased dramatically. ESG health has become an indicator of a company's health more generally, influencing shareholders' assessments of risk and potential growth. BlackRock, the world's largest asset manager, was one of the first investors to act on this information. It stated in its 2020 Investment Stewardship Report that it had voted more than 1,500 times against board directors for lack of diversity and would continue to do so. BlackRock then expanded its diversity expectations beyond boards to include all employees, asking companies in the US to disclose the gender, racial, and ethnic composition of their workforce (data they typically already collect and report on an EEO-1 form).

We encourage you to think expansively about all the spheres in which you might use incentives to push for fairness and signal your values. The Academy of Motion Picture Arts and Sciences did just this when it announced that beginning in 2024, films must meet specific representation benchmarks to be considered for the Academy Award for Best Picture. Movies need to satisfy at least two of four criteria, all of which have to do with having more women and members of underrepresented racial and ethnic groups featured in story lines and involved in production teams as actors, interns, leaders, and executives. According to the Academy, the goal behind the incentive was to "encourage equitable representation on and off screen in order to better reflect the diversity of the movie-going audience." Similar standards are already in place for receiving funding for film projects in the United Kingdom.

Given the enormous heterogeneity in the degree to which people care, sorting based on values certainly has benefits for those involved: Democrats get to stuff campaign envelopes for Democratic candidates and Republicans for Republican candidates, and those who care about fairness get to work in organizations that share this value and those who don't find employment elsewhere. The bad news is that we will likely see even more polarization and politicization going forward.

Provide Meaningful Incentives to Work

People care about many attributes of a job, compensation being one of them. More precisely, people care about the money they get to take home at the end of the day, that is, their pay plus benefits, minus taxes. Pay, and to some degree benefits, are most directly under the control of employers. While companies can do little about taxes once they have set up shop in a particular jurisdiction, knowing how different tax regimes can disincentivize their employees might influence their location decisions. For example, if part-time employees are not interested in expanding their work hours, this may be due not to the conditions at work or their responsibilities outside of work, but instead to the additional income being taxed so heavily that it simply does not pay for them to work more.

To make work pay, employers should start with what is under their control, including the compensation (and benefits) people receive. The largest chunk of the earnings gap between similarly skilled women and men is due to *within-firm* gender differences in responsibilities and seniority, which are caused by bias and discrimination as well as how work is structured. Parts II and III of our book focus on addressing these inequities in organizations.

Much of the remainder of the earnings gap is due to differences *across firms*: women are more likely to work in lower-quality and lower-paying jobs with fewer benefits than men. According to the US Department of Labor, in 2023, two-thirds of full-time workers in occupations that paid less than $30,000 per year were women, but fewer than one-third of full-time workers in occupations that paid $100,000 or more were women. In addition, women were significantly less likely to receive variable pay (such as bonuses), and when they did, they made 20 percent less than otherwise similar men. With the gender gap in earnings generally increasing with age, women end up with lower pension benefits, which makes them more vulnerable than men to poverty in retirement. In OECD countries, the old-age poverty rate is about 50 percent higher for women than for men, on average, due to a combination of lower earnings and higher life expectancy.

We subscribe to the Equal Pay International Coalition's (EPIC) definition of equal pay: "Equal pay means that women and men have the right to receive equal remuneration for work of equal value." This includes, of course, equal pay for equal work, which we discussed earlier. But this definition goes further because earnings differences across occupations did not come about by happenstance. Rather, our valuation of work is highly gendered such that the occupations in which women are most highly represented, like care work, are systematically undervalued. In the United States, for example, janitors, who are mostly men, make on average 15 percent more than maids and housecleaners, who are mostly women, even though the nature of the job is extremely similar. Moreover, studies examining the US labor market from the mid-1900s to the early 2000s find that when women enter an occupation in greater numbers, pay generally declines. Take recreation workers, who work in parks or lead camp activities. This occupation went from being mostly male in 1950 to mostly female in 2000, and in that time, the median hourly wages in the field dropped by 57 percentage points, accounting for inflation.

Therefore, various countries, including Canada and New Zealand, have started to assess the value of jobs based on gender-neutral criteria related to skills, qualifications, working conditions, effort, and levels of responsibility, and then adapt remuneration policies accordingly. In most OECD countries, job classification systems are common in the public but not in the private sector. Still, six countries (Canada, Finland, France, Iceland, Portugal, and Spain) also mandate their use in private companies and employ the classification systems in their pay audits. The International Labour Organization (ILO) has developed guidelines for employers that we include in the endnotes as a great starting point.

Paying women and men fairly is not only the right thing to do ethically (and legally). It is also a business imperative. Employees who feel that they are underpaid compared to their peers work less hard, perform worse, and are more likely to leave—if firms can attract them in the first place. Evidence from Denmark shows that firms with lower earnings gaps between women and men were able to hire more women, who in turn were more likely to be promoted into higher-paid positions than in other firms.

In addition to pay and benefits, employers need to be aware of how the tax systems in their jurisdictions impact employees' net earnings. Many countries, including Germany and the United States, tend to punish the "second earner" in a household with a higher tax rate. Such tax systems are considered not to be tax neutral as they provide differential incentives to work for the two adults in a dual-earner household.

Realizing that the design of a tax system may impact people's incentives to work, including the number of hours worked, the G20 has included gender equity in tax systems as one of its core priorities. Based on a 2022 report comparing forty-three G20 and OECD countries, the degree to which gender considerations are included in tax codes varies widely. Seven of the forty-three countries reported explicit gender bias in their tax systems. Switzerland was one of them. It indicated gender bias in its personal income tax system because it is based on household taxation of income, where instead of each individual being taxed separately, the family is taxed as one unit. Combined with a progressive income tax schedule, this disincentivizes the labor force participation of the second income earner as their income is subject to higher marginal tax rates than those of the first income earner. Women made up about three-quarters of second earners in the countries studied and, thus, paid the highest price for nonneutral tax schemes. In the US, for example, the marginal tax rate of a typical second-income earner can be as high as in Sweden, a country that has much higher average tax rates but relies on independent taxation of family members.

These tax disincentives also mean that part-time workers find it unattractive to move to full-time work in joint taxation countries. Sometimes referred to as the "part-time work trap," the higher marginal tax rate for second earners working full- rather than part-time heavily incentivizes part-time work. This is evident in the mostly German-speaking countries—Austria, Germany, and Switzerland—which, along with the Netherlands, have the highest gender differences in part-time work: women were up to five times as likely to work part-time as men in 2022.

Unfortunately, analyzing the gender implications of tax policies is not common. A majority of countries do not collect gender-disaggregated data on the impact of tax policies, tax administration, or tax compliance. They should. Two economists, Alexander Bick and Nicola Fuchs-Schündeln, estimated how many more hours women would work if the countries with a joint taxation structure switched to separate taxation (with the average tax levied on married couples being identical). In the US, this would lead to an 8 percent increase—and in Germany, an astounding 25 percent increase—in hours worked, which by all accounts would allow German companies to tap into an unprecedentedly large talent pool. This is exactly what happened in Sweden when it moved from joint to separate taxation

in 1971. It substantially increased the share of married women participating in the labor market.

In the United States, the introduction of the Earned Income Tax
Credit (EITC) had a similarly strong impact on female labor force
participation, although it only benefited mothers. First introduced in
1975, the EITC was a refundable tax credit for low-income working
parents corresponding to a 10 percent earnings subsidy for the poorest
households. Research shows that it increased maternal employment
by 7 percent. Later expansions transformed the EITC into one of the
country's largest antipoverty programs with continuing positive effects
on mothers' workforce participation, earnings, and health as well as
broader impacts on poverty reduction and increases in child welfare.
Financial incentives really do matter.

* * *

If there is one thing you take away from our discussion, let it be that
incentives are all around us whether we have consciously designed
them or not. Choosing to reward employees or leaders for building a
fairer organization is as much a statement as *not* doing so—and, as we
have seen, current and prospective employees, shareholders, and the
media are paying attention. So design your incentives wisely because
they are a powerful tool to drive results and signal what you stand for.

1. Put incentives into the right bucket
2. Employ a loss frame
3. Reward without delay
4. Signal your values
5. Provide meaningful incentives to work

CHAPTER 5

Transparency for Accountability

At age fourteen, Mia Perdomo wrote in her diary that she was a feminist. A decade later, she was thoroughly fed up with the "patriarchal and machismo" way women and girls were treated in Latin America. After she trained as a psychologist, Perdomo's career took a turn in 2014 when she attended a leadership program at Georgetown University and met Peruvian entrepreneur Andrea de la Piedra, an expert in making social enterprises financially sustainable. The two decided to do something to close gender gaps in economic opportunity in Latin America and came up with the idea to cofound a firm specializing in gender equality at work. Very quickly, they realized that companies wouldn't give them the time of day: "We would go up to firms and they would say, 'We don't know what you're talking about. Gender equality is a given; we're fine,'" explained Perdomo. "We decided that we would create a gender equality ranking to get the corporations' attention. Then, we could measure them so that they would realize they really didn't have gender equality the way they thought."

So they did. Perdomo and de la Piedra cofounded Aequales, a consultancy that measures, trains, and certifies organizations in DEI. Since 2015, Aequales has deployed its measurement tool and first-ever gender equality ranking system, Ranking PAR, in over

2,000 companies across 18 Latin American countries. PAR digs into voluntarily participating companies' data, processes, and policies related to intersectional gender equity through more than 60 questions, such as how many women and men were hired in the previous year. The questionnaire also asks about things like whether the company has a gender equity and/or diversity policy, and how it is communicated; what other dimensions of diversity are tracked intersectionally with gender; and how large the budget allocated to gender equity is. For accountability, companies need to attach supporting documentation, and external specialist firms audit the process.

Many companies participate year after year in what has become a "pedagogical" process: the mere act of responding to the questions teaches organizations about evidence-based practices, gives them new ideas, and makes them realize where they are falling short. Companies participating in PAR can also opt to receive detailed benchmarking data for their industry and region (though individual companies' data is always kept confidential). As an added incentive, Aequales hands out highly coveted annual awards for the ten best companies in each industry. Cofounders Perdomo and de la Piedra explain: "The power of the PAR Ranking is to tie gender equality to what organizations care most about: their reputation. Before PAR, corporate gender equality was not a thing at all in Latin America. But lobbying CEOs and C-suite leaders with their own data in hand has gotten them to want to do better than their peers—and look good in front of their teams. Now, organizations of all sorts are proud of their achievements and have a whole conversation and agenda around gender equality."

Organizations like Aequales make data speak. Rankings put outcomes into perspective and move data from an informational tool to an instrument of evaluation. As we have seen, collecting and sharing data internally—among people in the organization who can make a difference in what the data looks like—is an important driver of real results. In this chapter, we will discuss how and why disclosing data externally is helpful to move the needle further. But first, a word of caution: not all transparency is created equal, and passively sharing data is not the panacea for progress that many take it to be.

The story of what has happened in the US tech industry is illuminating. In the early 2010s, interest started to mount regarding the workforce composition of the world's largest and most significant tech companies, mostly headquartered in the United States. Despite many requests from news organizations, the companies (with some exceptions, including Dell, Ingram Micro, and Intel) refused to disclose their numbers until they were compelled to do so in 2014 by a Freedom of Information Act request. The data painted a bleak picture of diversity in tech: on average, women comprised less than a third of the workforces at companies like Apple, Facebook, Google, and Microsoft, while Black and Hispanic employees combined comprised less than a tenth of employees.

The one good thing to come out of these reports was a more sustained movement toward voluntary data disclosure as tech companies started to release annual DEI missives. The industry also began to deploy cutting-edge analytics and often dedicated greater-than-average resources to its efforts. We were initially optimistic about these developments because disclosure requirements have spurred innovation and progress in domains as varied as what and where we eat, how we spend our money, and how much energy we consume. Think of the sanitary inspection grades that restaurants have to display in their windows; the minimum payment warning provided on your monthly credit card statement; or the energy efficiency label on your refrigerator. Information disclosure has been shown to shift behaviors and outcomes—when done well.

Therefore, it is surprising that progress has not been faster in the tech sector. Intel, for example, has been consistent and thorough in publishing its workforce data ever since it released its first corporate responsibility report in 2002. Back then, 24.7 percent of its US workforce was comprised of women. At the end of 2022, two decades later, that number stood at 25.9 percent for the overall workforce and 22.3 percent for technical roles (most other tech companies report very similar numbers). Intel's current goal is to reach 40 percent women in technical roles by 2030.

So, what went wrong? Why didn't data transparency become the silver bullet for fairness that so many hoped it would? We don't know for sure but fear that transparency didn't translate into accountability, nor did it create incentives to change. As noted by the ACT Report, the framework for collective action on DEI in the tech industry mentioned earlier, "Publishing data became the 'end' instead of the 'means,' and simply normalized the status quo."

Given that the annual DEI reports were born out of a compliance exercise, companies typically reported the bare-bones data they already had on hand—in the US, the workforce representation numbers they had to share with the EEO-1 Commission—and might not have done the kinds of detailed analyses we have recommended to understand what factors were driving gaps. Indeed, research examining disclosures in contexts ranging from human rights to securities law has shown that reporting statistical data alone is "unlikely to change corporate behavior." Accountability is crucial, as restaurants know: when their sanitary inspection grade is a B or C, patrons will stop coming. Short of the press writing a few scathing articles each year around the time of the DEI reports' publication, tech companies had no entity to hold them accountable for their slow progress. And since all tech companies' data was bad, nobody *felt* particularly bad about their numbers.

Even though it's not a silver bullet, we are strong advocates of transparency around data, goals, and incentives related to workplace fairness. The key is to think of disclosure as an important step in the journey of data-driven change, not the final destination. Collecting and analyzing data reveals the true state of affairs, as we discussed in Chapter 2, and enables us to focus on the best solutions. Setting goals based on data gives us specific targets to strive for, which helps us stay on track and be strategic in managing our efforts, as we discussed in Chapter 3. Deploying incentives keeps us motivated and allows us to bring people along, as we discussed in Chapter 4. In this chapter, we will share how transparent disclosure enables us to proactively benchmark ourselves against our peers, and also allows external parties—consumers, regulators, shareholders, job seekers, civil society, nonprofits—to hold us accountable, which increases our odds of success. When done right, reporting data helps keep our eyes on the ball that really matters: making work fair.

Disclose to Drive Progress

At its heart, the power of transparency lies in making actions and their consequences observable. A management consulting firm where Siri worked at the start of her career asked all of its employees to follow the so-called red-face test in determining the appropriateness of their actions: "Would you have an embarrassed red face if an article about what you did appeared on the front page of the *New York Times* and all your friends and family read it?" When our actions are visible, we are more likely to be on our best behavior, or as US Supreme Court justice Louis Brandeis quipped more than a century ago: "Sunlight is said to be the best of disinfectants."

This principle has been shown to work in numerous contexts. American taxpayers who had owed taxes for years were more likely to repay their debts when their delinquency was made more visible to their neighbors on online lists of tax delinquents. In Norway, when tax filings became easily accessible online in 2001, business owners reported on average 3 percent higher incomes than they otherwise would have—an effect the authors attribute to tax evasion shaming resulting from public disclosure. And in Major League Baseball, umpires made fewer racially biased calls when they were being monitored by technology and more closely scrutinized by crowds. The knowledge that our actions are being watched drives us toward more virtuous—and fair—behaviors.

We are therefore heartened to see that transparency is demonstrably on the rise. Legal scholar Atinuke Adediran examined nearly 3,500

ESG reports of 1,288 Russell 3000 companies listed on the New York Stock Exchange or the Nasdaq index and found that diversity-related disclosures have become a fixture of the reports in recent years. The number of US public companies sharing ESG reports almost tripled between 2017 and 2021, and 95 percent of companies mentioned gender or racial diversity in their reports. As of 2023, more than three-quarters of Russell 1000 companies were publicly reporting some data points related to their workforce composition by gender and race/ethnicity.

Meanwhile, in the European Union, even more dramatic change is taking place. The Corporate Sustainability Reporting Directive (CSRD) that takes effect between 2024 and 2028 mandates extensive disclosures of fairness-related policies, risks, and results. Some estimate that the directive will reach about 50,000 companies located in (or with subsidiaries in) the EU. The directive requires detailed disclosures related to "own workforce" in three areas: working conditions, including "work-life balance indicators"; access to equal opportunities, including the "pay gap between women and men" and "discrimination incidents related to equal opportunities"; and other work-related rights, including "severe human rights issues and incidents."

Disclosing data publicly is important because it allows stakeholders inside and outside your organization to factor the information into their decisions about where to work, what to buy, and what to invest in. As such, transparency is a type of incentive to promote fairness at work. It is also a design principle to influence behavior at the individual and collective levels. When you know that your actions are being watched and your progress is being tracked, the upside of success—and, conversely, the downside of failure—is greater.

Examining major US technology and financial firms that made gender diversity disclosures between 2014 and 2018, researchers found that investors rewarded public companies with relatively more and punished those with relatively less gender diversity. Announcing relatively high gender diversity numbers led to an increase in a firm's stock price, whereas announcing relatively lower gender diversity statistics led to a negative stock price reaction. Consumers were somewhat more forgiving. In a recent experiment, consumers appreciated transparency around workforce data even when it revealed racial disparities. Their attitudes toward a hypothetical e-commerce company and their perceptions of its commitment to DEI were more favorable when the company shared its workforce diversity data than when consumers knew the company had collected the data but did not share it.

Our advice on how to approach external data disclosure not mandated by regulators is reminiscent of our advice on how to approach internal data presentation for maximum impact:

Disclose what you care (most) about.

To benefit from the motivating effects of transparency, we should report the metrics that we (most) care about making progress on, and thus use the act of disclosure as further motivation for improvement. The "most" is in parentheses because in many cases, reporting on absolutely everything you are doing and tracking is not feasible. Deciding what to disclose can therefore help organizations prioritize areas of focus and align internal resources accordingly. In the realm of environmental impact, for example, Walmart executives discovered as they were filling out a questionnaire for the Carbon Disclosure Project that contrary to intuition, refrigerants in grocery stores made up a larger share of the corporation's greenhouse gas footprint than its transportation fleet. This enabled the company to shift the focus of its emissions reduction efforts.

Disclosure pays off with goals, too, as goals set publicly are particularly effective at promoting progress. Much research, including a recent meta-analysis examining the effects of goal setting (including how publicly it is done) on behavior change in 141 randomized controlled trials, strongly suggests that Accenture had it right when it decided to make its goals public in 2020: "While we had set internal representation goals for many years, we realized that change would come only if we held ourselves publicly accountable, sharing our goals internally and externally," wrote Chief Leadership and Human Resources Officer Ellyn Shook in *Harvard Business Review*. Making goals public encourages people and organizations to work harder to reach them.

Public goals also send a signal internally and externally that an organization is serious about making work fair—which can have surprising positive consequences. In an experiment with nearly 3,000 female employees at multinational telecommunications company Ericsson, women expressed significantly heightened career aspirations when they were informed as part of their annual performance reviews that the company had diversity goals and executives were financially incentivized to meet them. The proportion of women wanting to manage others in the following year increased by 15 percent (closing the gender gap in management aspirations), and the proportion of early-career and low-tenure women wanting to take on a bigger challenge increased by 20 and 56 percent, respectively, compared to the control condition where participants weren't told about Ericsson's diversity goals and incentives. Disclosing goals, therefore, can influence not only the behavior of the goal setters themselves (in this case, Ericsson's senior management) but also that of other stakeholders, such as employees. Research suggests that the more specific the public goals are, the better: numerical, forward-looking targets focusing on workforce composition were most strongly associated with higher degrees of diversity after the disclosure of a goal. Thus, stakeholders who believe that people and organizations that are willing to set specific public goals are more likely to follow through on them are often right.

Many organizations are leading the way in courageously sharing their goals. In its publicly accessible annual diversity report, Snap Inc. tracks its performance against its five-year (2020–25) goals, showing both current numbers as well as year-on-year change. Besides specific goals to increase the presence of members of various underrepresented groups in its workforce, Snap has also set a goal to double its spending with underrepresented suppliers.

In addition to disclosing data, goals, and incentives, we encourage you to share your learnings. Which activities to improve workplace fairness have moved the needle for you? Did you try something that failed to create measurable progress? While we understand that it can seem counterintuitive to offer a peek behind the curtain—and some companies have gone so far as to argue in litigation that diversity data should be treated like trade secrets—increased transparency not just about results but also about processes is a powerful way to facilitate collective learning, experimentation, and ultimately, progress. We have witnessed this ourselves. In a workshop we hosted in March 2024 for companies interested in promoting change, we were heartened to see how much information competitors were willing to share on their learnings. They had realized that making work fair was in everyone's best interest.

Treating data as a public resource in this way can also foster innovation. An interesting precedent exists: In 2001, nine leading US research universities voluntarily came together to push for gender parity on their faculty. Even though the universities were competitors for talent (faculty, staff, and students), they compared policies, processes, and data; shared findings as they conducted deeper data analyses; and traded resources. This kind of collaboration can be especially important in industries like tech and finance that have traditionally played "diversity musical chairs" by swapping a small number of women and employees of color between them. Coming together to expand the pool and fundamentally change how they approach hiring and career development can help firms ensure that the perspectives of women and underrepresented racial groups are duly included.

Transparency around workforce composition data is an important part of making work fair. So is transparency around the fairness standards we apply to how we do things in our organizations. Consider the example of clinical trials, which are an essential component of bringing new medicines to market. In the US, women continue to be underrepresented in trials across all therapeutic areas, in many cases by egregious margins. A 2022 analysis of nearly 1,500 clinical trials with more than 300,000 participants revealed that only 41 percent overall were women. In psychiatry, women are 60 percent of patients but only 42 percent of clinical trial participants. New research further shows that when clinical trials aren't racially representative, Black patients find information on a drug's efficacy less relevant—and physicians caring for Black patients are less likely to prescribe new drugs tested on unrepresentative samples.

Given that clinical trials are a central part of its business, Pfizer, one of the world's largest pharmaceutical companies, did a thorough analysis of its 213 clinical trials conducted between 2011 and 2020 (which included more than 100,000 participants). The analysis examined all clinical trial participants by sex, race, ethnicity, and age in comparison to the general population, and revealed that while women and Black people were included in trials at levels matching the general population overall, Hispanic individuals were under-represented. Besides sharing the data openly and promising to continue to track it, Pfizer is working to build fairness into the design of its clinical trials by, for example, choosing trial sites in more diverse communities and removing barriers to trial access by working with patient advocacy organizations.

Compare to Create Accountability

Transparency can be leveraged to create the kind of true accountability that pushes us toward measurable progress. When we have access to information about our organization and others that enables us to benchmark ourselves against peers, the natural drive toward social comparisons kicks in. Equally importantly, when external parties have access to information that enables them to make consumption, investment, and other decisions accordingly—in other words, hold our feet to the fire—accountability starts to work its magic.

Besides enabling benchmarking against peers and tapping into our inherent competitiveness, transparency creates accountability and promotes behavior change by introducing the potential of being celebrated if we are doing well, or being named and shamed if we are doing poorly. While the fear of what people think can stifle free inquiry and discourse, for better or worse, it matters. Both the carrot and the stick are effective at influencing behavior because we humans have an inherent desire to be part of the herd and an inherent aversion to being shamed. Women, for example, were shown to speak up more on counter-stereotypical topics if they received social recognition for it. The recognition provided a signal that women's contributions were welcome and that they did not need to fear biased reactions. But once again, there is a comparative element: awards mean less when everyone gets one, or when they signal that the expected behavior is so exceptional that it cannot be assumed to be the social norm.

On the flip side, if we are being shamed along with everyone around us, we do not stand out from the herd and the potency of the shaming decreases. This is one of the explanations behind US tech companies' failure to improve their numbers through mere reporting. Since everyone's workforce diversity was lacking, there was no reason to fear "not measuring up" as nearly all firms were in the same boat—and the longer the numbers didn't move, the less acute the imperative to improve became. In the words of Ros Atkins of the BBC: "After a while of not doing well in the eyes of your peers, it inevitably stings less." Besides, it was all too easy for companies to compare themselves downward against peers that were doing even worse and to conclude that, actually, they were not performing that badly.

Around the world, many organizations provide comparative data for companies to benchmark themselves against in order to improve fairness. Similar to Aequales, Switzerland-based EDGE, launched in

2011 at the World Economic Forum and led by Aniela Unguresan, offers companies the opportunity to become EDGE Certified as well as "a holistic framework against which organizations can measure where they stand in terms of gender and intersectional equity." Equileap is a Netherlands-based, independent data provider that ranks several thousand companies on approximately 20 gender equity metrics, with data going back to 2014. JUST Capital, an independent US nonprofit, offers another data-driven benchmarking tool in the form of the JUST Jobs Scorecard. And the Women's Empowerment Principles Gender Gap Analysis Tool, a collaboration between the UN Global Compact, UN Women, and the Inter-American Development Bank, is a free tool for organizations around the world to voluntarily and informally benchmark themselves. Lastly, US-based BlendScore focuses on unsolicited and publicly available, up-to-date data for hundreds of companies based on sources such as firms' own websites and reports, their regulatory filings, public employment websites like LinkedIn and Glassdoor, and donations and political activity. BlendScore's aim, according to its founder Stephanie VanPutten, is to provide a real-time "FICO [credit] score for corporate social responsibility."

While not an exhaustive list of rankings, we want to give you a taste of this global movement toward increased transparency. At the same time, we feel compelled to remind you that transparency doesn't automatically translate into accountability. For that, you need incentives, whether internal or external—and action.

Connect Reporting to Action

In 2007, biotech firm Genentech's then–CEO, Art Levinson, gave a pivotal presentation at a town hall meeting. Using a few simple data points in a table, he made a compelling case that something was going wrong in how the company fostered its talent. While Genentech overall was roughly 50–50 in its representation of women and men, there were enormous differences by level. Women comprised 44 percent of managers and supervisors, 41 percent of directors, and a shocking 16 percent of officers (sadly, such numbers are no surprise to those of us who examine organizations' representation data on a regular basis). Levinson challenged the crowd: "Do people see what's wrong with this? Is there anyone in this room who can tell me that this is okay? Because it's not."

The disclosure of these simple and salient data points inspired a yearslong effort to level the playing field in Genentech's leadership ranks. To start, the company collected more quantitative and qualitative data to better diagnose the sources of the problem. Among other things, they examined potential gender biases in the process of filling open roles by looking at gender differences in who applied and was invited to interview, as well as who received and accepted offers. Surveys and focus groups provided additional insight and revealed that women were often excluded from informal networks; felt they received less actionable feedback than men; and had less access to stretch assignments that would position them for higher-level roles. With a concrete goal of increasing by 50 percent the number of women qualified for senior leadership positions, and with a baseline against which to measure progress, Genentech set out to systematically dismantle the barriers the data had allowed it to identify. As a result, the company more than doubled the share of female officers, meeting its goal in 2017. Importantly, in 2019, Genentech started sharing all of this data with its employees.

The act of transparently reporting on progress, just like the act of collecting data and setting goals in the first place, can be a powerful motivator—but, once again, it needs to be done right. If disclosure is not linked to concrete changes in practices and policies, meaningful improvements are highly unlikely to happen. We should follow Genentech's example and use disclosure strategically to focus our attention on the most critical areas that require improvement, and to galvanize people into action. Even though reporting data is a worthy endeavor, it is also time-consuming and too easy to mistake for the real work that needs to happen to make work fair. "At the BBC, organizing the annual 50:50 Challenge month, for which we report data externally and not only internally, creates more work for the 50:50 team on top of the daily work of counting and tracking women in our programs," explained Ros Atkins. "That's worth doing for the extra focus it brings and the accountability and transparency that it provides. But when taking on that commitment, we must never lose sight of the reason we're doing it: to use that focus, accountability, and transparency to spur us to improve representation in our journalism."

Sometimes the mere request for a specific data analysis can catalyze progress. The Nordic division of a global professional services firm had this exact experience when its HR leaders asked to see the data related to their sales pipeline by gender. Naturally, that data existed: the company had always tracked who was working on which project, proposal, and sales opportunity. But no one had ever thought to aggregate the data across the division and then analyze it by gender to see if there were systematic differences in the types of sales opportunities that women and men worked on. For example, did men tend to work on larger accounts and sales? Or did certain senior partners tend to pick the same junior associates for their sales pitches, leading to more career development and networking opportunities for them? The HR leaders shared with us that even before the data was fully analyzed, simply asking for it raised awareness and motivated new conversations about the allocation of opportunities in the firm. Many firms participating in Aequales's Ranking PAR similarly report that the act of answering thoughtfully crafted questions about what they are currently doing has, in itself, become a nudge to do better.

Design Pay Transparency for Success

A few years ago, Iris and her coauthor, Richard Zeckhauser, ran a simple experiment. Participants in the experiment were assigned either to the role of employer or employee, and each employer was given a pot of real money. They then had to offer a share of that money to their employee, who could either accept or reject the offer. If they rejected, neither of the parties earned anything; if they accepted, both the employer and employee went home with their respective shares of the pot as proposed by the employer.

Then we introduced transparency. In one condition, employees did not know how much money each employer had available but were informed of what employers were offering on average before they had to decide whether they would accept the offer they had received. This information completely changed the game, which we played over several rounds. Fearing that employees would reject offers below the average, employers quickly raised their offers, which consequently converged. Employers did not want to stand out with a lower offer that would be rejected (in fact, employees did reject the few straggling employers who kept making offers below par), nor did they feel the need to be extra generous by offering more than what everyone else offered. As most employers needed to correct their offers upward, transparency led to not only more similar but also higher offers on average.

While the experiment was designed to demonstrate the power of social comparisons and not to examine transparency in pay, in many ways, what happened in our lab gives you a good intuition for what pay transparency proponents have in mind. The hope is that knowing what your peers earn could increase employees' bargaining power and lead to a similar convergence of pay as in our experiment, thereby helping to close gender gaps and increase women's pay.

People hate being paid less than comparable peers. This is why in March 2016, five of the leading soccer players in the US—Carli Lloyd, Alex Morgan, Megan Rapinoe, Becky Sauerbrunn, and Hope Solo— filed a wage discrimination complaint with the Equal Employment Opportunity Commission. The US Women's National Soccer Team had been trying to convince the US Soccer Federation (USSF) for many years that they were grossly underpaid compared to their male colleagues, particularly given that the women's team had won the World Cup four times while the men's team had never made it anywhere close to a World Cup final (and had not even qualified in about half of the tournaments). With the complaint unresolved, in 2019 Rapinoe and teammates filed a gender discrimination lawsuit against the USSF. She explained: "We very much believe it is our responsibility, not only for our team or for the future US players, but for players around the world—and frankly, women around the world—to feel like they have an ally in standing up for themselves, and fighting for what they believe in, and fighting for what they deserve and for what they feel like they have earned."

Disappointingly, a judge ruled against the women and sided almost completely with the USSF in 2020. But thankfully, this was not the end of the story. In a surprising turn of events and after a six-year fight, in the spring of 2022 the painful saga came to an end with a settlement between the women athletes and the USSF. It included back pay for compensation not received in earlier years, something the *New York Times* referred to as "a tacit admission that compensation for the men's and women's teams had been unequal for years." In addition, the USSF agreed to equal pay and equal working conditions for the women's and the men's national soccer teams. The deal came about due to the women players' perseverance, much support from fans and the public, and, in the end, the men's team siding with the women and agreeing to equal pay. In 2023, FIFA, the organization that governs international soccer, followed suit and substantially increased the prize money for the Women's World Cup. It also set a target of equal prize money in the next two World Cups for men and women in 2026 and 2027, respectively.

As this example shows, knowing what a colleague earns can be a game changer in making equal pay for equal work a reality. In fact, pay disclosure is one of the domains in which transparency has produced the most promising results for fairness. In 2023, the European Union introduced new pay transparency rules mandating, among other requirements, that employers provide job seekers with information on the starting salary or the pay range of advertised positions; do not ask about candidates' pay history; and respond to employees' inquiries about average pay levels ("broken down by sex, for categories of employees doing the same work or work of equal value") or the criteria that determine pay and career advancement.

Since 2000, more than 70 percent of OECD countries have introduced pay transparency policies. In her comprehensive overview, economist Zoe Cullen describes eighteen different policies that steer pay transparency in the countries that have enacted some transparency laws. The most common policies focus on creating pay equity within an organization, either by mandating gender pay gap or salary range disclosures or, as is popular in many US states, by guaranteeing employees the right to discuss their compensation with their coworkers. In 2014, President Barack Obama signed an executive order that protects the right of employees working for federal contractors to discuss their pay, and the National Labor Relations Board now generally interprets its mandate as giving most American private sector employees the right to discuss their pay. Unfortunately, these policies can have unintended consequences.

Policies focused on internal comparisons between coworkers are generally successful at decreasing wage gaps between women and men. But they can also lead to pay overall growing more slowly in the presence of transparency compared with in its absence. The Danish experience is illustrative. Denmark was one of the early movers on pay transparency in 2006 when it introduced legislation mandating that companies with more than 35 employees share information on wages by gender and occupation internally. As a result, the gender pay gap decreased by 13 percent compared to pre-legislation levels, but average pay grew by about 3 percent less than in control firms with slightly fewer than 35 employees (which therefore were not subject to the law). Similar dynamics were found in Canada when individual university faculty members' salaries were disclosed, as well as in the United Kingdom, where a 2017 policy requires companies with more than 250 employees to disclose their mean and median gender pay gaps and the representation of women and men in each pay quartile. In all of these cases, transparency helped decrease pay gaps between women and men, but instead of increasing women's pay to catch up with men's, it resulted in organizations slowing down the growth of men's pay.

Why this is happening is not entirely clear. Cullen wonders whether firms might have become more reluctant to grant high-pay exceptions—which tend to be more often requested by men—since they know that in the new world of transparency, these could set precedents for future pay negotiations. Internal pay comparisons also run the risk of demotivating employees as, by definition, half of them will learn that they are paid below the median. When a random set of workers in an Indian manufacturing plant was informed of their peers' salaries, they ended up being less productive and less satisfied with their work. In a similar vein, job satisfaction was hit hard after government employees' salaries were published online in California. We fear that the more pay information is internally focused and the more we can attribute compensation to specific individuals, the more likely we are to see these unwelcome side effects.

If you, like our students, believe that shining the light on pretty much everything must be a good thing, consider salary history bans as a counterexample. These bans prohibit employers from asking job applicants about their prior pay, and they have been introduced by several states and local jurisdictions in the United States since 2017. They explicitly limit the amount of information available—and for good reason: employers tend to anchor their offers on prior pay, exacerbating gender differences in compensation that likely started with the very first salary people received. Fortunately, salary history bans are working and have decreased pay gaps by increasing the pay of women and people of color. So, sometimes, less is more when it comes to information.

The good news doesn't stop there. We don't have to give up on pay transparency. Instead, we have to make it better—and as always, design is key. The evidence looks more promising for policies that require cross-firm, as opposed to within-firm, pay transparency, such as salary information to be included in job advertisements.

In Austria, employers have been required since 2011 to include a minimum wage offer. The policy decreased the gender pay gap and increased average pay with women benefiting most in jobs that needed to be filled with some urgency (which likely indicates that firms had less bargaining power). In Slovakia, where employers are expected to include wage information in all job postings, average pay likewise increased while gender gaps decreased. In the United States, similar laws were passed in New York City, California, and Washington State in 2022–23, but we do not yet have data on their impact. Colorado, however, mandated that expected salary be included in job advertisements slightly earlier, in January 2021, and researchers have noted that posted salaries increased by more than 3 percent. Job seekers are paying attention and the competitive pressure between firms seems to have done the job in narrowing gender pay gaps.

Much research in negotiation has looked at potential gender differences in setting pay. Building on the seminal 2003 book *Women Don't Ask* by Linda Babcock and Sara Laschever, a 2020 study examining teachers' pay negotiations in Wisconsin found that female teachers were much less likely than their male counterparts to ever have negotiated their pay. The researchers were curious to see whether these teachers would benefit from more information because earlier work by organizational behavior scholar Hannah Riley Bowles and coauthors revealed that decreasing ambiguity in pay negotiations can help narrow, and in some cases even erase, the pay gap between women and men. Indeed, Wisconsin teachers who knew someone who had negotiated (and/or knew how much they ended up with) were more likely to negotiate themselves. Additional information empowers women to ask, something we are not always eager to do because we accurately anticipate social backlash. Yet asking can go a long way.

On Hired.com, a recruitment platform for engineers, job seekers are required to indicate the pay they are seeking after they share their résumé. Based on these two pieces of information, companies then respond with an offer. Economist Nina Roussille found that male applicants ask for more and are offered more. The pattern of resulting starting salaries was almost entirely driven by the initial gender gap in asking. But then something interesting happened. In 2018, the platform provided some job seekers with information on the median offers similar candidates had received—and the magic of pay transparency unfolded. The additional information fully closed gender gaps in salary asks and offers. Remarkably, all of this was possible without apparent social backlash for women: Despite their higher asks, female job seekers received the same number of offers as their male counterparts. As it turns out, women seem to be aware of this. In an experiment where an identical job ad either included information on the negotiability of pay or not, women were more likely to apply when explicitly invited to the negotiating table. A recent experiment with experienced MBA students likewise showed that when women and men were given a hypothetical job offer, including comparative salary information successfully reduced gender pay gaps. In some cases, research suggests that the gender gap in salary negotiations is closing and perhaps even reversing.

Just like individuals, we are hopeful that companies will act when transparency provides them with relevant information. Natasha Lamb, cofounder and managing partner of impact investment firm Arjuna Capital, is helping to bring such information to light. Since 2014, Arjuna has leveraged its power as a shareholder to propose resolutions that ask companies to report their pay gaps as well as policies and quantitative targets to close them. Arjuna reports that its proposals have induced more than twenty Fortune 500 companies (including Apple, JPMorgan Chase, Nike, and Starbucks) to publicly disclose and commit to eliminating their gender and racial pay gaps. In an effort to further increase transparency around firms' pay practices, Arjuna publishes an annual scorecard that ranks companies on an A–F scale in terms of their quantitative pay disclosures, commitment to annual reporting, and goals to close pay gaps. At Microsoft's 2021 annual meeting, Arjuna won 78 percent investor support for its proposal to demand more public accountability in response to sexual harassment complaints; the following year, Microsoft published a fifty-page report on its policies and improvement plans. Lamb reflected on these wins: "I think one of the reasons we've been so successful on the activist side is because we're bringing that investor lens. When we engage on issues we're doing so from the perspective of it being accretive to returns."

Cross-firm benchmarking can have many benefits beyond closing gender pay gaps. In most cases, firms have no interest in being an outlier (although some purposely pay above market to attract and retain the best talent). When one of the largest payroll processing firms with access to the pay data of 650,000 US companies made its proprietary salary benchmark available to its clients, Zoe Cullen and coauthors examined how this affected the firms' pay setting. Much like in Iris and Richard's experiment, the pay of new hires rapidly converged and led to a decrease in pay dispersion of over 25 percent. While the researchers did not have any demographic information available, overall wage levels as well as retention rates also increased by a few percentage points, which feels like a win-win for both employers and employees.

To recap our pay transparency conversation: In basically all cases, transparency has helped to decrease gender pay gaps. However, efforts that focus on internal, within-firm comparisons among coworkers appear to have more unintended consequences than those aimed at external, cross-firm comparisons. Thankfully, mandates to include pay (range) information in job postings are on the rise in

Europe with the EU's 2023 rules and in the US with an increasing number of states following in Colorado's footsteps. This allows more people to benefit from the additional information provided—and in this fast-evolving field, us researchers to better understand what works best.

* * *

If you take one thing away from our overall discussion on transparency, let it be this:

Like data, transparency becomes an engine for change when we harness it as a tool, not as an end.

Transparency around workplace fairness is both a principle underpinning organization-wide operations and policies as well as a design choice to influence individual behavior. It allows us to benchmark ourselves against peers to understand how well we are actually doing, and it enables internal and external stakeholders to keep us accountable. Disclosure is particularly potent when we, or those watching us, care about what transparency reveals. This is why a "C" label on a restaurant's door matters or why pay information in job ads works. Restaurantgoers and job seekers care very much about the quality of the food they are about to consume and the compensation they are likely to receive—and it is exactly in those moments when disclosure drives action that transparency becomes a powerful accelerator of change.

---

1. Disclose to drive progress
2. Compare to create accountability
3. Connect reporting to action
4. Design pay transparency for success

PART II

MAKE IT STICK:
FINDING AND
DEVELOPING TALENT

CHAPTER 6

Talent Attraction to Cast a Wide Net

In 2017, the New York City Fire Department (FDNY) reached out to the city's Behavioral Design Team for advice on how to increase the diversity of its workforce. This was not the first time the FDNY was trying to attract more female, Black, and Hispanic candidates, but this time it was committed to doing so using the best evidence available. Examining past recruitment cycles to diagnose where the department was losing candidates, the Behavioral Design Team identified the very first step in the talent attraction process as a potential hurdle. Applicants needed to take a civil service exam before they could be considered—but many prospects who had expressed enthusiasm beforehand failed to do so. Members of the traditionally underrepresented groups that the FDNY was keen to attract were particularly likely to drop off.

The reason for the drop-off was not entirely obvious. Building on insights from behavioral science, the Team proposed a simple theory: What if some applicants were deterred by the $30 fee required to take the test—either because the amount was too high or because the test was an unwelcome nuisance? As we've mentioned, process design is not neutral. Even small barriers to entry can have big impacts, especially for those uncertain about whether they are a good "fit" for the job to begin with. First-generation college students, for example, have been shown to be more deterred by administrative hassles than other students, reporting a lower sense of belonging and an increased likelihood of dropping out. They were more likely to attribute their difficulties to their own shortcomings rather than those of the system. To counteract such differential impacts of process complexity where the most vulnerable are most affected, a little help can make all the difference. A bit of assistance dealing with application procedures dramatically increased the likelihood that low- and moderate-income families availed themselves of government support programs like college financial aid.

So, the FDNY decided to give it a go and test if removing the fee might increase the number of applicants, particularly from underrepresented groups. To be able to compare the filing rates of those exempted from the fee with those who had to pay the standard exam fee, a random sample of potential applicants was notified that their exam fee had been waived. The fee waiver led to an impressive increase in those willing to take the test: 37 percent among all applicants, and even more astonishingly, 83 percent among female and 84 percent among Black candidates.

The fee—a seemingly small process hurdle—affected job seekers differently depending on their identity. People who are less certain about whether they possess the relevant qualifications are more likely to think that they are responsible for the trouble. Much research suggests that women tend to underestimate their abilities, particularly in domains dominated by men (often referred to as "male-typed" domains).

According to economist Raviv Murciano-Goroff, such differences in modesty hurt female job seekers substantially. In the market for software engineers, for example, one of the most important pieces of information recruiters look for when screening an application is the technical skills a candidate reports. Female programmers who had exactly the same technical skills (e.g., knowledge of a programming language) as men, however, were 11 percent less likely to self-report them on their résumés. These women were too pessimistic about their own qualifications and did not mention expertise that their male counterparts were proud to showcase. Recruiters did not adjust for this and were less likely to invite a woman to an interview.

These women might be less likely to apply to begin with, as their higher standards regarding their own qualifications might also lead them to overestimate what it would take to make the cut. Based on a field experiment with more than 10,000 job seekers, men were willing to apply when they met 52 percent of the required qualifications and women when they met 56 percent. The gender gap was driven by less qualified men being more likely to believe that they were "good enough" than similarly qualified women.

These findings are particularly painful as much evidence suggests that some employers are inflating the requirements necessary for a given job, leaving them without the talent they need. For example, in 2015, a college degree was required by 67 percent of job ads looking for production supervisors—when only 16 percent of currently employed production supervisors actually had one. Thankfully, employers have started to respond. Based on one study, almost half of middle-skill and almost one-third of high-skill occupations underwent a significant degree reset between 2017 and 2019. The resets often went hand in hand with a stronger focus on specific skills rather than check-the-box qualifications, a recurring theme in the next three chapters.

This chapter will focus on attracting talent, and the next two on screening job applicants and evaluating the pool of finalists more effectively and fairly. Bias might affect all three stages of the hiring process, and we hope that our detailed coverage will help you diagnose the particular challenges your team or organization is facing.

At the talent attraction stage, several promising pathways to fairness have emerged, sometimes inspired by research in other domains. As discussed in the previous chapter, women are more likely to negotiate the less ambiguous the situation is. This is why, when

Iris served as academic dean at Harvard Kennedy School and had to negotiate with the faculty the school was trying to hire, she was very transparent (and honest) about what was negotiable and what was not. In politics, researchers have documented gender gaps in willingness to run for public office. Women tend to wait for "the ask" legitimizing their candidacy, especially in fields where they are not assumed to belong. Reaching out to potentially suitable candidates can help—even if they had not put themselves forward initially. In this chapter, we suggest that adding more clarity to our job advertisements and actively inviting potential job seekers in holds much promise for recruitment as well.

Clarify Standards and Expectations

Communication is a two-way street. Not everything that is said is heard, and different receivers might interpret the same message differently. This is what one of the largest employers in Australia learned when it selected candidates for leadership positions. Among finalists who did not get the job, men seemed to take the rejection better than women: they were almost twice as likely to reapply to another leadership opportunity later. From the organization's perspective, reapplications were welcome and recruiters wanted high-potential finalists they had already evaluated to remain in the pool. In theory, the strategy could also be appealing to the job candidates. Given that they had already gone through the trouble of putting together an application, why not use it again if a similar position became available in the same organization in the future? Only it did not pan out that way for women.

While we do not know what went through these applicants' minds, Iris and her coauthors had a suspicion: maybe women read more into a rejection than men. Research suggests that women take rejections in domains where they are underrepresented—in this case, leadership positions—as another indication that they are not wanted, and ambiguity does not help. At this organization, about 20 percent of applicants made it into the pool of finalists—but nobody knew. It was left up to the rejected candidates to infer their relative standing compared to other people who had applied, and perhaps women underestimated how well they had done.

To eliminate this ambiguity and find out whether our theory had any bearing, we collaborated with the employer and ran an experiment. We (truthfully) informed a random set of the rejected finalists that they were in the top 20 percent, and then waited to see who reapplied for another position during the next twelve months. The results were rather astonishing. The additional clarity completely closed the gender gap in reapplication rates compared to a control group that did not receive any information after being rejected.

Our study reinforces the fact that process designs are not neutral. Ambiguity invites different interpretations, and these interpretations often have something to do with our personal backgrounds. The comment of one Black female product manager in the US stuck with us: "When I'm navigating the job application process, I don't have people in my corner to help me understand my worth." Knowing your worth, whether in terms of capability, seniority, or salary, is no easy task, and job advertisements don't necessarily make it easier, as they typically leave much room for interpretation. What exactly is the employer looking for? Which qualifications are a "must" and which ones are a "nice-to-have"? How many years of work experience are really needed, and does experience in adjacent job categories count? Am I good enough?

Economist Katherine Baldiga Coffman shared our unease about the ambiguity in job ads, so she and her coauthors set out to do something about it. Partnering with Upwork, the largest global freelancing website, the team posted various job advertisements for actual positions (such as research support) that they needed filled. At the end, they offered jobs to the most qualified freelancers for the advertised pay.

The researchers took advantage of a helpful feature on the online employment platform. It offered standardized tests of skills and aptitudes that the freelancers who signed up with Upwork could take if they wished to add this information to their profiles. Upworkers could take as many tests as they liked for free and were informed of their test scores as well as the scores of others who had already taken the same test (but no information was shared on the types of jobs that test takers had applied to or were recruited for; thus, while the comparison information was helpful, it did not provide insight into the competition an applicant might face).

In order to decrease the ambiguity inherent in most job ads, the researchers then provided a random set of freelancers with specific information on the qualifications their employer of interest was looking for so that they could more easily calibrate whether they were qualified. A typical sentence looked like this: "We invite applicants with an Analytical Skills test score of 4.05 to apply for the expert-level job." In the control condition, Upworkers received no such additional information.

Providing information on the desired qualifications had no impact on male applicants. In contrast, the impact on women was remarkable: while only 6 percent of qualified women applied in the control condition, 29 percent applied when ambiguity was reduced. This led to a larger share of qualified candidates applying overall, a clear win for the hiring company. It was able to attract a larger pool of more diverse and better qualified candidates by making explicit what the bar was for a successful application. Knowledge of the "bar" was key. Female job seekers not only viewed themselves as less capable than equally qualified men, but also differed in their beliefs about how high the bar was. Compared to men, women tended to underestimate their own ability and overestimate what was required to be a competitive applicant. Changing people's beliefs about the bar levels the playing field.

Ideally, the purpose of a well-crafted job ad is to attract the right kinds of applicants, including those who are appropriately qualified.

Generally, companies tend to shy away from underqualified, and in many cases also overqualified, applicants as they fear that the former will underperform and the latter will leave soon. According to research conducted with the ride-sharing company Uber, toned-down job ads focusing on core requirements rather than optional qualifications might help do that. The changes Uber made to its ads for corporate jobs included removing language such as "PhD preferred" and adjectives such as "excellent" (e.g., in combination with "coding skills") and replacing "fluency" in a coding language with "experience."

These changes led to a 7 percent increase in job applications to the over 600 corporate job postings at Uber in the United States in the fall of 2018. It did not affect the gender composition of the applicant pool—but it changed the types of women and men who applied. The traditional job postings led to a gender gap in applicant skill with female applicants being more qualified than their male counterparts. Indeed, much evidence suggests that given the gender differences in perceived ability, women are often overqualified for the jobs they apply to. When the language was toned down to focus only on required skills, the gender gap in applicant skill disappeared.

Reach Out to a Broad Set of Applicants

The COVID-19 pandemic led to many more employees working from home and, in the US in particular, an exodus from big cities. This development has broken down geographic barriers whereby employers in Silicon Valley started to employ workers from Alabama and Tennessee and people no longer had to move to the expensive Bay Area. In addition, many firms in the Valley now recruit through programs that provide training to members of underrepresented groups, such as Hackbright, which focuses on women, and Code2040, which focuses on Black and Hispanic programmers.

Our own employer, Harvard University, has also expanded the number of states it is hiring from. At a recent town hall meeting, the university's chief human resources officer, Manuel Cuevas-Trisán, reported that it has made a big difference in applicant pools. More generally, organizations increasingly go to where the talent is, including historically Black or women's colleges and professional organizations such as the National Association of Asian American Professionals, LGBT Meeting Professionals Association, or Women for Hire. Such a broadening of the pool of potential applicants is welcome for many reasons. It helps alleviate inequities due to location and background, and employers benefit from a larger, more diverse pool to choose from.

Having said this, the identified talent does not always come. For women, specifics of the work environment remain key. Female applicants have been found to shy away from work environments with hypercompetitive compensation schemes, high pay uncertainty, and opaque salary negotiations. In addition, women tend to be more influenced by the actions of other applicants than men. Economist Laura Gee found that female applicants were more likely to apply to jobs when many others did as well. At first this sounds counterintuitive, as more applicants means more competition. But if you are uncertain whether this is the right job for you, perhaps because you do not quite "fit" the norm, you may well take others' behavior as a cue that you should throw your hat in the ring too.

In order to attract more talent, organizations have started to rewrite their hiring criteria. James Heighington of Google shared in a 2023 seminar at Harvard Kennedy School that Google started reducing the number of words in its job ads after an internal analysis discovered a dramatic drop in the number of female applicants when the list of minimum qualifications exceeded 54 words. The new approach helped to increase the fraction of women who applied by 11 percent.

This is also why many universities have moved from searching for faculty in specific subfields of an academic discipline to looking at broader categories. In the fall of 2022, the University of California, Berkeley was looking for an assistant professor with expertise in statistics and data science whose work relates to, well, almost anything of interest: "The Berkeley Statistics Department currently seeks applicants with outstanding records in Statistics and Data Science for a position at the Assistant Professor level. We are particularly interested in candidates working in data science at the interface of statistics with the biological, medical, physical, and social sciences."

Sometimes, unexpected messages can attract a broader pool of applicants. Economist Nava Ashraf and behavioral scientist Elizabeth Linos both wondered about the power of incentives, particularly in environments where doing well financially is not the main driver of people's interest in a job. Perhaps, when public service motivation can be assumed, better career opportunities could make all the difference? This is exactly what they found in two very different contexts. Health sector employers in Zambia and police forces in the United States learned that highly talented job seekers, especially among women and people of color in the US, were particularly attracted by job ads that emphasized doing well instead of doing good. Sending the right messages in your job descriptions can truly pay off, leaving you with more applicants who are also more qualified and more diverse.

Other organizations hire search firms tasked with delivering a deep pool of potential candidates. But do they actually deliver? Despite the fact that most top management jobs are filled by a process that involves search firms, the evidence is incredibly thin. Executive search firms typically guard their data and processes carefully, given that these tend to constitute their comparative advantage in the marketplace. One of the few times researchers have been able to peek behind the curtain yielded a study by management scholar Isabel Fernandez-Mateo and sociologist Roberto Fernandez. They were given access to the records of one of the leading senior executive search firms in the United Kingdom, covering 219 vacancies at the most senior corporate levels (C-suites and boards of directors). The data included both active job candidates who had applied to an opening as well as, importantly, passive candidates who were included on long lists by the search firm without them having applied. Of the more than 13,000 candidates examined in this study, a large majority—86 percent—were passive candidates who were not initially aware that they were being considered for an opening.

Overall, only 11 percent of the candidates were women, and they were more likely to be passive than active candidates. This is a first data point suggesting that search firms are possibly able to broaden applicant pools in a way that standard hiring processes aren't. Passive candidates were mostly identified based on one simple rule: working in a role similar to the job vacancy at hand. For example, if the hiring firm was looking for a chief marketing officer, the search firm would look for chief marketing officers at competitors, at slightly smaller firms, at a level below—or for people in adjacent roles. The latter consideration warrants your particular attention. The world's largest website for job listings, Indeed, found that such breadth, including a stronger focus on skills rather than specific roles (something we will return to in Chapter 8), dramatically increases the number of job seekers who apply.

Alas, even though search firms were able to broaden the pool and increase the share of women on their lists, they were less likely to reach out and interview female passive candidates. And when invited, female passive candidates were less likely to agree to become active candidates than their male counterparts. This may have many reasons, including gender gaps in mobility in dual-career households. Knowing this, search consultants might be less likely to interview a female passive candidate because they expect the returns on their investment to be higher when they call a male candidate.

Once women were in the active candidate pool, though, they were equally as likely to be hired as male candidates, suggesting that in this second hiring stage, gender did not factor in, which therefore did not make up for the gender gaps that had emerged earlier during the recruitment process. As this was not a controlled experiment, we need to be careful with our conclusions. But based on the data presented, more women were placed in senior roles by the executive search firm than through the standard processes, which included both direct external and internal hires by the firms.

Given the limited empirical evidence available, it is too early to render a verdict on search firms. Certainly, the above evidence is encouraging but it is based on one firm only. The more important takeaway is that women are more likely to join if we explicitly invite them in.

De-bias Job Advertisements

In many parts of the world, gendered job advertisements have been in use for quite some time. So much so that Human Rights Watch issued a special report in 2018 titled *"Only Men Need Apply": Gender Discrimination in Job Advertisements in China.* The organization analyzed more than 36,000 job ads posted on Chinese recruitment platforms, including company websites and social media, from 2013 to 2018. It found rather blatant discriminatory practices—or as Sophie Richardson, China director at Human Rights Watch, said: "Nearly one in five job ads for China's national civil service called for 'men only' or 'men preferred,' while major companies like Alibaba have published recruitment ads promising applicants 'beautiful girls' as coworkers."

In India, a 2018 World Bank Report not only found an abundance of gendered words (generally favoring men) in the 800,000 job postings it analyzed, but also discovered that in accordance with occupational segregation, employers tended to use female-typed words for lower-paying and male-typed words for higher-paying jobs. Employers assumed that women would not want to apply to an engineering job and men were not made to be teachers; thus they looked for "determined engineers" and "dedicated teachers."

Thankfully, there are signs that job ads explicitly stating employer gender preference are dying out. In fact, they had been prohibited in China for some time but it took a 2016 regulation threatening online job platforms and employers with hefty fines to initiate change on the ground. In the meantime, most of the largest job boards have discontinued explicitly advertising by gender, and the laggards were forced to do so in 2019 with the ban basically taking effect overnight. Exploiting this fact, economists Peter Kuhn, Kailing Shen, and Shuo Zhang document in a series of studies what a difference the change made. Before the ban, gendered ads were highly successful in attracting the desired gender: 95 percent of applicants invited to a job interview were of the desired gender (with no difference between women and men). This was mostly due to job seekers almost exclusively applying to jobs of "their gender." And they were right to do so. The few women who dared to apply to "men's jobs" were substantially less likely to be considered. Interestingly, job postings without any specific gender preference were more likely to attract male applicants. Women shied away from the gender ambiguity and tended to only apply when their gender was explicitly invited.

The impact of the ban was immediate but not symmetric: men were more likely to apply to jobs previously classified as women's jobs and to be chosen. Women also benefited from the change, just not as much as men. Overall, the ban substantially increased the number of applications and the quality of the applicant pool. With explicit gender segregation out of the way, better matches between employers and job seekers were possible. Chinese firms now enter the second phase of making job advertisements fair. Like their counterparts in other countries that banned explicitly gendered advertisements earlier, they must now go after implicit and often unintentional gender cues, such as gendered language, in their job postings.

When a Spanish-speaking recruitment platform for technology positions in Latin America ran an experiment to see what difference using gender-inclusive language made, it found that the fraction of women who applied to jobs increased (particularly in fields where the share of women was not too low, suggesting that there might be limits to the power of gender-inclusive language in occupations where there are basically no women to start with). In a follow-up experiment where researchers wanted to measure the magnitude of the impact, they found that gender-inclusive language was about as powerful in attracting women as stating that employees could work remotely (and definitely more powerful than explicit diversity statements, a topic we will return to in a couple of pages). Referring to a programmer not just as "programador" (the masculine gender) but instead as "programadora/programador" (the feminine and the masculine gender) strikes us as a rather low-cost investment with a potentially high return.

There are a number of tools to address unhelpful language in job advertisements. Textio, one of the early movers in this space in the US, informs recruiters in real time of how the language in their job ads will likely impact the gender composition of their applicant pool. In earlier research in Canada, stereotypically masculine words such as "assertive," "determined," or "independent" were found to be more likely to attract men while female-typed words such as "responsible," "dedicated," and "sociable" were more appealing to women. In addition, an experimental study by organizational behavior scholars Joyce He and Sonia Kang revealed that removing masculine language from job ads did not just reach more women but also more men, namely those who were less likely to identify with strong traditional norms of masculinity. While some things are hard, this is not one of them. Organizations can design fairer job postings and broaden the applicant pool if they wish to do so.

We suspect that the promise of high impact at relatively low cost is why so many companies are now de-biasing their job ads. It won't solve all problems but it is hard to see how it could hurt. T-Mobile, a telecommunications company, reports that when it used Textio to help make its job ads more fair, it was able to attract 17 percent more women and fill open roles five days faster. The latter finding is important as recruiters are often incentivized mostly on speed. This is a rather short-term perspective that may come to haunt organizations later on. While it did not pose a conflict for T-Mobile, we encourage organizations to review to what extent they prioritize how quickly—as compared to how well—roles are filled.

In her 2018 article in the *Atlantic*, Jessica Nordell reports that communication platform Slack, working with Textio, started using phrases such as "care deeply" or "lasting relationships" to signal to female job seekers that they wanted to invite them in. This is in stark contrast to other technology companies that continue to feature words like "maniacal" and "wickedly" that empirically resonate with men but not women. To follow in Slack's footsteps, you might find useful a free gender decoder based on one of the earliest papers on the topic by psychologist Danielle Gaucher and colleagues. In addition, the Canadian research partnership Engendering Success in STEM has developed a helpful, evidence-based cheat sheet (included in the endnotes) that reminds recruiters of the core features of a gender-debiased job advertisement.

Overall, in English-speaking countries, the impact of gendered words seems to be most pronounced in particularly male-typed environments such as entrepreneurship, where women are heavily underrepresented among founders, employees, and investors. In contrast, recent evidence suggests that gendered language might be losing its importance in some of the more established firms. Why this is the case is not entirely clear. Perhaps some stereotypes have lost their power, particularly in the English language, which is much less gendered than, for example, Romance languages.

If you want to go beyond de-biasing language, you can learn from an intervention that was implemented in Peru to attract women to apply to a five-month training program for coders. In Peru, just 7 percent of coders are women, so economists Lucía Del Carpio and Maria Guadalupe knew that a relatively heavy-handed approach was called for. They introduced what they referred to as an "identity de-biasing" message to counter prevailing stereotypes about women not being welcome and succeeding in tech. They shared that firms were interested in recruiting women, provided a female role model in tech who was also a graduate of the program, and pointed out the value of the network that participants would be part of going forward. The message doubled the fraction of (qualified) female applicants, and a follow-up field experiment in Mexico suggested that this was mostly due to seeing a female role model. We do not know how these messages would have affected men as the training program targeted women only.

While highlighting a counter-stereotypical image in a job posting can work as an aspirational signal of where the organization is heading, we need to be careful about not misrepresenting our workforce. Employers do not want to be accused of what two 2020 articles, one in *Harvard Business Review* and one in *Forbes*, referred to as "woke washing" or "diversity washing," where companies pretend to care about fairness without making any real changes. Tricking women or members of underrepresented groups into a job that pretends to be fair when there is hardly any diversity in the organization is not a viable (let alone ethical) strategy.

Aptly titled "Show, Don't Tell," research from the United States strongly suggests that only evidence-based fairness cues work. Inflating racial diversity increased African Americans' and Latina/os' fears of not fitting in and not being able to perform well at work. Similarly, exaggerating organizational gender diversity in job advertisements tends to backfire, decreasing both women's and men's interest in the employer when the messaging is perceived as insincere. Job applicants only seem to give the company the benefit of the doubt when diversity cues are coupled with clear indications of diversity aspirations going forward or, even better, credible signals of change already taking place.

Send Credible Signals

When we speak with executives to share our research insights, they often ask us whether companies that go one step further and explicitly declare their commitment to fairness in their job ads are successful in attracting more (especially underrepresented) candidates. This typically triggers an interesting discussion. In a recent executive education program at Harvard Kennedy School, a Black woman raised the concern that organizations that are too explicit about their diversity aspirations might undermine the very people they want to support. Such goals might objectify members of traditionally marginalized groups, she argued, reducing them to one specific part of their identity. She is not alone. Job seekers of color have been found to be less attracted to organizations where they fear that they will be tokenized and potentially discriminated against once hired.

Even a possibly well-intended EEO statement (such as this one: "Company X is an equal opportunity employer. All qualified applicants will receive consideration for employment without regard to sex, color, age, or any other protected characteristics") can backfire. According to one field experiment conducted in ten US cities, the addition of an EEO statement to job postings decreased the likelihood that job seekers of color applied, particularly those who were more educated and who lived in cities where a large majority of the population was white. Job seekers either did not want to be symbolic hires or did not believe that the companies would walk the talk. A Canadian study proves them right: companies with diversity statements were not less likely to discriminate.

The more important question, then, is whether we can improve on generic diversity statements, such as the EEO statement that might inadvertently send the wrong signals. A study that gives us hope examined a US financial services firm that was interested in increasing the fraction of undergraduates from underrepresented backgrounds that participated in one of its professional development programs. When the firm explicitly stated that it valued diversity (e.g., by saying that it considered diversity a competitive advantage or a key part of the company's culture), it more than doubled the fraction of Black and Hispanic applicants, which also translated into doubling the likelihood that they were selected. The diversity statements did not depress applications from members of groups that were not underrepresented in this program (whites, Asian Americans, and women).

Explicitly including attributes that people care about can also be a credible fairness signal in job ads. We served as advisors on a randomized controlled trial that the UK Behavioural Insights Team conducted in collaboration with job search platform Indeed, where employers posting a job advertisement were nudged to indicate whether the job came with any flexible working options (including flextime, work from home, job share, and part-time). Previously the platform had not provided employers with a convenient way to indicate flexible work options; now they could simply check boxes while uploading their job ad. Flexibility then became a search term that allowed job seekers to easily find jobs that offered their desired flexible work options. To make flexibility even more salient, Indeed also included a bullet point indicating whether a given job was flexible in the metadata for each job. All this to say that this information was not buried in the job descriptions.

And it showed. Across more than 55,000 employers posting over 200,000 job ads to which more than 5.5 million people applied, the results were remarkable. Jobs with flexible options received 30 percent more applications, and the number of jobs advertised as flexible increased by 20 percent. An even larger follow-up trial in the UK found similar results. And when the British department store John Lewis & Partners and Swiss insurer Zurich Insurance started advertising jobs as flexible by default (i.e., they proactively made all jobs flexible with part-time options), this also increased applications significantly—in the latter case, especially from women.

It looks like UC Berkeley has taken this to heart. In another part of their job posting looking for a statistician/data scientist, we learn the following: "Diversity, equity, inclusion, and belonging are core values of the Department of Statistics. We believe that our excellence can only be fully realized by faculty, students, and staff who share fully our commitment to these values. The Department is committed to addressing the family needs of faculty, including dual-career couples and single parents. We are also interested in candidates who have had non-traditional career paths or who have taken time off for family reasons, or who have achieved excellence in careers outside academia."

This is also what organizational behavior scholars Robin Ely and David Thomas conclude based on dozens of years of research on the topic: only organizations that truly value diversity can succeed. Employers might value diversity for many reasons, one being the preferences of the people they are trying to attract. Indeed, the evidence is mounting that many job seekers care.

Zippia, a job search site and career advice agency in the United States, provides job seekers with interesting sets of data, including the living wages across the country's states and districts (as of the writing of this book, they were highest in Washington, DC, and lowest in Kentucky) as well as a ranking of states based on the number of malpractice lawsuits. If you are not a doctor, you might not care as much about the latter (though in case you are curious, Louisiana had the most and Hawaii the fewest lawsuits). But here is a more broadly relevant piece of information: in a 2021 experiment run with almost 270,000 unique job seekers and job postings from more than 100,000 companies, one random group of participants was informed of how the salaries a company offered compared to its peers from similar locations (the salary score), while a second group was informed of how the employer's workforce diversity fared (the diversity score). These two treatments were compared with a control group that only received the information contained in standard job listings, without salary or diversity scores. So, did job seekers favor companies with higher scores—on salary and/or on diversity? Would *you* care?

Unsurprisingly, job seekers were more likely to click on job postings by companies that offered higher salaries compared to their peers. More importantly for our purposes here, job seekers were *also* more likely to focus on companies with higher diversity scores. This fondness for high-diversity employers was most pronounced among entry-level job seekers, women, and white applicants. In a follow-up survey, job seekers expressed that one of the core reasons they cared about diversity was their personal preferences. They thought diversity was an important value and wanted to work for a company that shared that belief.

How might applicants feel about firms that send more credible signals of their commitment to diversity, such as by setting public diversity goals? Behavioral scientist Erika Kirgios and colleagues ran a field experiment to answer exactly this question. In 2020, they used Craigslist to post job advertisements to fill remote, part-time research analyst positions in 113 US cities. After conducting their study, the academics ended up hiring several research analysts through this process.

In the first stage, more than 5,500 job seekers expressed interest in learning more about the advertised positions (and also provided their résumés as well as information on their demographic characteristics). In the second stage, job seekers were randomly assigned to receive either a generic diversity statement or one coupled with a concrete diversity commitment. Specifically, the first group saw this: "We value diversity. We strive to have an organization where every team member brings a unique perspective and every team member has the opportunity to succeed. **We are committed to diversity and inclusion for all, and we believe this commitment improves our work and our workplace.**" The second group saw the same statement followed by this additional sentence: "**That's why we've set a goal of hiring at least one woman or racial minority for every white man we hire in our organization**" (highlights from original).

As it happens, adding the specific diversity goal significantly increased the likelihood that women and people of color applied. White men were equally likely to apply in both scenarios and applicant "quality" (as judged by educational background) did not differ across groups. If anything, the women and people of color responding to the specific diversity goal were slightly better educated. In a follow-up study focused on female applicants only, women reported that a specific diversity goal sent a more credible signal than a simple diversity statement that they and other traditionally discriminated-against applicants would be seriously considered, evaluated, and potentially offered a job. This is an interesting addendum to our discussion of goals in Chapter 3. We know that concrete, specific goals (as compared to vague ones) increase people's motivation to reach them—and this is exactly why the diversity goals send a credible message to job seekers.

Diversity goals, quotas, and affirmative action (where legal) have generally been successful in attracting highly qualified women of different backgrounds in a number of contexts. In a clever design that allowed researchers to compare who applied with and without affirmative action in Colombia, job seekers were informed that affirmative action would play a role either before or after they applied. Knowing that affirmative action would be implemented increased the likelihood that women applied, closing the gender gap in applications without systematically deterring men, and did not affect the quality of the top 15 percent of the applicant pool that companies typically hire from. Similar effects were found in laboratory experiments in Austria and the United States, suggesting that gender quotas can serve as a sorting device able to attract highly qualified women.

Despite these encouraging findings, hiring managers are often reluctant to push diversity too hard in their job ads. In the United States, legal risk is a primary concern. More generally, a common worry, in addition to the objectification discussed above, is that concrete diversity affirmations could deter white people and men from applying. Based on the evidence to date, these concerns are exaggerated. An applicant pool is not fixed, so it is not a zero-sum game. And as we have seen, men and white job seekers may also value diversity.

* * *

To benefit from 100 percent of the talent pool, organizations need to rethink how they attract talent. You can broaden your applicant pool by providing more precise, more inclusive, and more credible information about what you are looking for and what the job seeker can expect if they decide to join your organization. And to overcome gender differences in people's assessment of their relative standing, consider more active and targeted outreach to the candidates you want to attract.

---

1. Clarify standards and expectations
2. Reach out to a broad set of applicants
3. De-bias job advertisements
4. Send credible signals

CHAPTER 7

Applicant Screening for Accuracy

When recruiters screen applications, they tend to spend less than ten seconds per application on average. In addition, the first application reviewed on Monday morning likely receives different scrutiny than application number 125 that arrives on a manager's desk after they have screened the first 124 résumés. One study conducted with the Swiss recruitment platform Job-Room found that even the time of day when résumés were screened mattered. Recruiters spent less time per applicant during late mornings and late afternoons before leaving for lunch or dinner and were more likely to show a preference for Swiss applicants compared to immigrants. Presumably, a hungry stomach does not help our cognitive prowess.

At the screening stage, rules of thumb—such as stereotypes—help recruiters put people into boxes and make judgments quickly. Our gut tells us that an Anna or Aditi would make for an excellent nurse and an Adam or Anil for a great engineer. The nature of the job people apply to, whether female- or male-dominated, tends to loom large when recruiters screen applicants. Traditionally, women have been found to be less likely to be invited for an interview in male-typed, higher-paying, and more-senior jobs, and men less likely to receive a callback for female-typed jobs. Intersectionality also plays an important role with parenthood and age affecting female and male applicants differentially: Age discrimination tends to be a bigger concern for women than men. Mothers experience substantially more discrimination than childless women or fathers. While fathers sometimes are penalized, employers expect them to be committed to their jobs, something mothers (and women more generally) must first prove.

These findings are the result of audit or correspondence experiments, which have become researchers' favorite tool for testing for potential discrimination at the screening stage. When conducting such studies, researchers respond to job openings by randomly submitting résumés of identical pairs of candidates who differ only along one dimension, such as gender, race, or religion. They then measure whether the likelihood that a given candidate receives a callback differs based on this one characteristic. If among otherwise identical candidates a white applicant, say, receives more callbacks than a Black applicant, this is taken to indicate discrimination. To date, more than 300 audit studies have been conducted mostly in European countries and in the United States, with about 20 percent stemming from countries in Asia, Africa, and Latin America. Most studies focus on entry-level jobs as the approach of an audit study is not feasible for more senior roles or executive positions.

Based on this evidence, bias against members of traditionally underrepresented groups is unfortunately still going strong in most cases. Among various European countries, Canada, and the United States, France was the only country where a small decrease in ethnic or racial discrimination could be detected in recent years. The news for gender is mixed in the high-income countries studied. Stereotypes against women applying to entry-level jobs in male-dominated occupations have significantly weakened and in some cases, disappeared or even reversed in Europe and North America—but the same is not true for men applying to jobs in female-dominated occupations. Similarly, most audit studies continue to find discrimination based on applicants' sexual orientation or gender identity, with some evidence suggesting that employers have a particular preference for straight male applicants when they look for male-typed attributes such as assertiveness, ambition, and aggressiveness. The pattern for women is less clear. Much less is known about transgender people although a majority of survey respondents report having experienced employment discrimination in the US. In 2020, the US Supreme Court confirmed that federal law prohibits discrimination based on sexual orientation and gender identity in employment, much like it prohibits any form of sex discrimination, but these protections are less well-known than many others.

Based on a massive audit study in the US, including more than one hundred Fortune 500 firms, economist Patrick Kline and coauthors construct race and gender discrimination report cards for the firms. Leveraging the power of transparency discussed earlier, the discrimination report cards explicitly name the firms doing well and those doing poorly. This allows job seekers to make more informed choices. We share the authors' hope that this could also induce more cross-firm learning: "To the extent that these differences are driven by HR practices or other firm policies, there may be opportunities for the substantial set of firms that scored poorly to improve their behavior by imitating the practices of those that scored more highly."

One such practice we should scrutinize is the information we use when screening job applicants. To select candidates, employers typically rely on a relatively small number of signals contained in a job seeker's application. Recruiters draw inferences about applicants' capability by looking at their employment history and their educational background. Unfortunately, research evidence suggests that the relationship between either past employment or education and future performance is rather tenuous. In addition, these criteria have undesirable gender effects.

Signals of competence tend to be most important for people who want to join counter-stereotypical professions where their capability is not assumed but must be proven. For example, research shows that only the very best female investment professionals offering investment recommendations received the same kind of attention as their male counterparts. Similarly, only the content posted by women who had already built a reputation on an online platform focused on STEM fields was taken seriously. This is also why female STEM students at Boston University wanted their grades reported to potential future employers even though their university's COVID policies would have allowed them to be hidden. These women, in contrast to their male counterparts and female students in other subjects, feared that employers would be more likely to follow their gut and go with the stereotypical male applicants if they did not make this additional information available.

Sadly, when women can signal their competence, as in the case of grades, thereby overcoming one gendered hurdle, they encounter another: they may be judged to be lacking warmth. High-achieving male math majors were three times more likely to hear back from an employer when they applied for a job than their equally strong female colleagues. High-achieving women in English did not encounter similar penalties. They did not violate any gendered norms, in contrast to the high-performing female math majors who excelled in a domain where they were not considered to belong.

This has been coined the "competence-likability dilemma": women can be perceived as competent *or* likable, but rarely both. Competent women defy social norms of what women "should" be like because the traits associated with competence (e.g., confidence or assertiveness—traits also typically associated with masculinity) clash with those associated with likability (e.g., warmth and kindness—traits also stereotypically associated with femininity). We expect experts to be male, not female (try searching for the image of an "expert" on the internet!).

One of the biggest hurdles for traditionally underrepresented job applicants is that hiring managers want to "like" the people they will be working with. People do not like norm violators and feel more comfortable with others who look and think like they do (recall in-group bias from Chapter 1). In the words of one venture capitalist: "[The way] we all hire people is, 'Do I like that person? Do I have things in common with them?' If you hire people that way, you do not end up with diversity"—or the best talent, we might add.

To at least overcome the first hurdle in the hiring process, members of traditionally disadvantaged groups have started to downplay their identities in the materials used for screening, but this is neither a winning (nor a desirable) strategy. For example, "covering in cover letters," the title of one research paper, can backfire. When female applicants used what Joyce He and Sonia Kang refer to as "identity-based impression-management," whereby they attempted to appear less feminine in their job applications, they were less likely to be hired. Similarly, "whitened résumés," where job candidates removed references to their race or ethnicity when they perceived an employer to not value diversity, have yielded mixed results.

Given the large number of issues related to screening, organizations are increasingly taking action. Some focus on improving human decision-making by redesigning processes, focusing recruiters' attention on what really matters, and/or removing irrelevant information from consideration altogether, such as by hiding applicants' demographic characteristics from recruiters. Advertising and public relations agency Ogilvy, the international organization UNICEF, and one of the world's largest publishing houses, Penguin Random House, have all worked with a recruitment platform, Applied, that helps them do just that. We suspect they fear that knowledge of a job candidate's gender, race, or nationality muddies the waters, decreasing the likelihood that they will be able to identify the best candidates instead of those who look the part.

Others have given up on humans' ability to get this right and have moved on to machine-based assessments. After all, an algorithm is not affected by the time of day it screens a résumé or whether a given résumé is evaluated first or last. But if the algorithm is trained to look for the same information as human recruiters, such as educational background and work experience, it will also fall prey to the biases we have just discussed. Accordingly, algorithms can address some of the problems of human decision-making but not others—and in addition, can create new ones.

Many fear that by relying on algorithms, we will produce bias at scale. Indeed, examples describing allegations of algorithmic bias abound in the popular press. A few years ago, Amazon was reported to have scrapped a screening algorithm that punished female applicants for using such "unusual" words as "women" on their résumés. In 2015, Google had to apologize for and promise to fix one of its products after software engineer Jacky Alciné informed the company that Google Photos classified Black people as gorillas. In 2019, New York State regulators launched an investigation of Apple Card when the algorithm that determined the creditworthiness of applicants was accused of gender discrimination: A husband was dismayed to find out that he was offered twenty times the credit line his wife was even though she had the better credit score of the two. As it turns out, the investigation concluded that there was no evidence of algorithmic bias.

What is clear is that machine learning algorithms built on the past tend to propagate existing patterns, including those regarding gender. As you likely experienced when searching for "experts" online, many internet search algorithms fall prey to this very problem. Among the fifty-two countries included in the World Economic Forum's Global Gender Gap Index, a Google image search for the supposedly gender-neutral term "person" was substantially more likely to yield men in countries with greater gender inequality. Google searches for "person" in Iceland and Finland, for example, yielded about 50 percent male images, but in Turkey and Hungary more than 80 percent of "persons" were male. This may be due to the data the search engine was trained on and/or an updating mechanism such as reinforcement learning where the algorithm learns based on users' behavior. If users are more likely to click on men when searching for "person," the algorithm learns that "persons" tend to be male and will reflect this pattern going forward, in effect reinforcing the way we all are using the product.

The Center for Equity, Gender, and Leadership at UC Berkeley's Haas School of Business started to track publicly available instances of alleged bias in machine learning algorithms in 1988. It reports that almost half of the AI systems examined showed gender bias, with a quarter demonstrating both gender and racial bias. While these are worrisome statistics, we need more data on the impact of algorithmic bias on intersectional identities. The empirical research on AI and intersectionality, as well as gender identity, is in its infancy. In a call to action in *MIT Sloan Management Review*, roboticist Ayanna Howard reminds us not only of the perils but also of the promise: "AI has the ability to improve quality of life and well-being for all individuals when carefully crafted. When developing AI systems through an intersectional framework, the magnification of certain biases can be mitigated."

Five female thought leaders—researchers Joy Buolamwini, Rumman Chowdhury, Seeta Peña Gangadharan, Timnit Gebru, and Safiya Umoja Noble—have been at the forefront of this discussion, warning about bias in AI long before it became fashionable to do so. They have experienced backlash for their work, including some of them losing their jobs, but all now lead efforts to help make AI (both the more traditional predictive AI and generative AI based on large language models) better.

Our message to you is this: as both human *and* algorithmic judgments can be influenced by bias, we need to mitigate against potential discriminatory outcomes regardless of how we screen candidates. Given the increasing relevance of algorithms at the screening stage, we will devote a good chunk of this chapter to better understand how to go about this for predictive AI. While this part will be slightly more technical by necessity, our approach to AI is a bit like driving school: you do not need to know how to build a car in order to drive one, but you need to learn how to operate it and engage safely with others on the road. We will begin by examining what we can do to help humans make better decisions, and then move on to machines.

Randomize the Order in Which You Review Applications

Some decision traps cannot be prevented but their impact can at least be mitigated. Various US states have figured out how. To enhance electoral accuracy and fairness, they rotate candidate names on the ballot. While this would ideally be done across voters, it typically takes place across counties such that, for example, some counties in New Hampshire placed Hillary Clinton and some others Donald Trump at the top of their ballots in the 2016 US presidential election. From a researcher's perspective, the advantage of the scheme is that we can examine whether even within a state—in this particular case, a very prominent one where the first presidential primaries take place and stakes are high—there is a first-place advantage. And there is. So, randomization cannot keep primacy from happening, but it can make sure the primacy advantage, that is, whether or not a name is listed first on a ballot, is balanced among all candidates.

Not all states randomize the order in which candidate names appear on the ballot. In 2016, Trump lost the national popular vote but won the electoral college vote, making him the forty-fifth president of the United States. In four states, he won the electoral college with particularly tiny margins of the popular vote: with a margin of 1.2 percent of the popular vote, he won 29 electoral votes in Florida; with a margin of 0.2 percent, 16 electoral votes in Michigan; with a margin of 0.7 percent, 20 electoral votes in Pennsylvania; and with a margin of 0.8 percent, 10 electoral votes in Wisconsin. In Florida, Michigan, and Wisconsin, Donald Trump was listed first on all ballots, while in Pennsylvania, Hillary Clinton was listed first. Research by political psychologist Jon Krosnick and colleagues suggests that if Florida, Michigan, and Wisconsin had rotated the order in which the candidates' names appeared on the ballot across precincts with Clinton listed first in some and Trump listed first in others (similar to the systems applied in California, New Hampshire, North Dakota, and Ohio), Trump may well have lost the election.

Primacy has been shown to affect a large number of election outcomes across political parties. Whether or not a name appears first on a ballot sends a signal—and while ballots are not meant to be interpreted as rank orders, the data suggests that they too often are.

Not surprisingly, there is a primacy effect in the screening of applications too. In a study conducted by the recruitment platform Applied, reviewers evaluated the first application they saw more positively than the rest of the applications, on average. What is more, order mattered across all applications screened. Reviewers were influenced by the strength or weakness of the application they had seen immediately before.

If more than one reviewer screens applications, randomization can help in the same way it helps in our elections. It will not be able to mitigate order effects completely as, in contrast to voting, randomization takes place across a small number of reviewers only. But it can help increase the chances that a candidate isn't unfairly (dis)advantaged purely based on when they are reviewed.

Screen for Expertise Rather than Career Gaps

In addition to screening for competence, employers look for signals of commitment to infer how dedicated a job applicant might be when hired. For example, employers tend to penalize lapses in employment as people with prolonged leaves—whether due to spells of unemployment or illness, or time taken to care for children or older relatives—are assumed to be less committed to the job. Such gaps on people's résumés have been shown to decrease applicants' chances of being invited to an interview, but there is an additional motherhood (and, in some cases, fatherhood) penalty that only people with childcare responsibilities are subject to. According to a study conducted in the US by sociologist Kate Weisshaar, parents who discontinued work to care for their family experienced higher hiring penalties than otherwise identical mothers and fathers who had been continuously employed (or applicants whose career break was due to a job loss).

Employers might have to adjust their screening processes to younger workers, who are much more likely to move in and out of the workforce. They may also need to respond to new trends related to experiences during COVID-19, when people took career breaks for many different reasons. As it is increasingly difficult for employers to find job candidates without a career break, taking employment gaps as a sign of a lack of commitment is even more questionable today than it was before. Accordingly, LinkedIn now allows job seekers to add commentary to the times they left the workforce. For example, some LinkedIn users describe how caregiving made them more patient and resilient. Recent research suggests that such skills are increasingly in demand. In addition, employers are also trying to keep people who take leave in their orbit through "returnship" programs that aim to bring back former employees who have taken time out during their careers.

What if we could make career break considerations less important altogether? We can use behavioral design to do just that. As it happens, the typical résumé format makes employment gaps particularly salient, so two of our collaborators, Ariella Kristal and Oliver Hauser, saw an opportunity. Along with colleagues, they explored the impact that different ways of framing work experience on résumés would have on employer callback rates. In the winter of 2020, they responded to job postings by more than 9,000 employers in the United Kingdom across eight sectors (including high- and low-skill jobs such as software engineering, call center operations, finance, manufacturing, production management, and care work).

They presented candidates' job history either by the number of years a job was held or, as is commonly done, by indicating the dates during which the applicants had worked in a given job. Specifically, the revised résumés displayed a single number indicating the years worked (e.g., "3 years: Assistant Manager, Operations") instead of listing the exact timeframe during which this occurred (e.g., "July 2015–June 2018: Assistant Manager, Operations").

Before sharing with you what the researchers found, we should note that work experience is neither our favorite nor the most accurate predictor of future success. But we definitely prefer years worked over employment gaps for screening purposes. While still sharing information accurately, the change in framing made the applicants' acquired expertise salient but obfuscated employment gaps—and had quite a remarkable effect. When prior work experience was shown by the number of years worked but without dates, it increased the likelihood that a candidate would be invited to an interview by 15 percent. This finding held for women and men as well as for different levels of total work experience. While this reframing is gender-neutral on its face, it will disproportionately benefit those more likely to have had career breaks: women. We should also note that the current, traditional design most benefits those without career breaks—that is, men—reminding us that we cannot assume existing designs to be neutral.

Remove Irrelevant Information

In the world of venture capital, the lack of women—both as investors and as recipients of venture funding—is a well-known problem. In the United States, around 85 percent of check-writing investors are men, and only around 2 percent of venture funding goes to female founders (or all-female founding teams). Several venture capital firms have taken steps to change these numbers. In 2021, Azolla Ventures redacted names, email addresses, current school and company names, and other personal information (e.g., LinkedIn page, references to a candidate's race/gender) from applicants' résumés and cover letters. They decided not to hide majors, years in school, job titles, past schools and employers, locations, phone numbers, and student group names. There is nothing magical about these choices and some might argue that more information should have been removed given that, for example, student group names might indicate an applicant's gender, race, nationality, religion, or sexual orientation, to name but a few. But given that there is no one right answer to the question of what information should be redacted to successfully de-bias résumé screening, we applaud Azolla for experimenting and learning—and, importantly, for sharing their insights.

They learned that anonymizing résumés substantially increased the fraction of women and applicants with an Asian background who moved ahead to the interview stage. Specifically, the fraction of female applicants who made it through screening increased from 35 percent pre-anonymization to 62 percent post-anonymization, and the fraction of Asian applicants from 29 percent to 48 percent. The process did not raise the fraction of African American or Latina/o interviewees. The firm reports that applicants of these two under-represented groups made up less than 8 percent of the pool, leading it to conclude that "a blind review optimizes for equality but not for equity: it applies the same treatment to all candidates but fails to recognize differences in starting points." With this sentence, Azolla Ventures has identified one of the biggest concerns about anonymized screening processes: they do not address injustices experienced in the past but only level the playing field at a certain moment in time.

Does this mean that we should give up on anonymization? Or can increasing equality also benefit those disadvantaged by larger systems of discrimination? Audit studies on the impact of résumé anonymization in European countries—including Belgium, France, Germany, the Netherlands, Sweden, and Switzerland—have all focused on ethnicity, and mostly found that anonymization worked. It erased differences in callback rates between Caucasian applicants and applicants with other ethnic backgrounds in all countries but France (which we will revisit in a moment). Unfortunately, rather little is known for the United States. An early, now-canonical example of anonymous screening processes stems from American symphony orchestras that started to audition musicians behind a screen in the 1970s. At the time, only about 5 percent of the musicians in these orchestras were women; this fraction has climbed at least sevenfold since.

Being invited to an interview, of course, is not the same as being offered a job. Unfortunately, we rarely know whether equal treatment at the screening stage can be upheld during the evaluation process once hiring managers are aware of the applicant's identity. A participant in an executive education program who found herself in just this situation explained to us that additional hurdles definitely emerged once people realized that their favorite candidate was a Black man—but the anonymized screening process made it much harder to come up with good arguments for why he was not a great fit. The organization ended up making him an offer.

In her illuminating book, *Inclusion Revolution*, Daisy Auger-Domínguez shares that during her time at Google, hiding names during the screening process increased the fraction of female engineers at every stage of the hiring process, resulting in more female engineers being hired. Anonymization did not work for applicants of color, though. Auger-Domínguez reports small increases during the screening process but no success in moving this higher share of African American and Hispanic software engineers through the interview stage. So while anonymization has been shown to be effective in many contexts, the final verdict is still out on exactly for whom it works and when. We urge you to try it out yourself if you can. It is a simple experiment to run, and you might learn a lot.

Many academic journals now rely on double-blind review processes where neither the author nor the peer reviewer is aware of the other's identity. Most researchers support such anonymization. Comparing how likely a research paper was to be accepted by reviewers depending on whether the author was shown to be a Nobel laureate as opposed to an unknown author revealed a dramatic difference: When reviewers thought that the paper was written by a Nobel laureate, they were ten times more likely to directly accept it. An anonymized version of the manuscript hit the middle ground with fewer outright acceptances than with a prominent author and fewer outright rejections than with an unknown author. This might be why NASA introduced a double-blind review to evaluate astronomers' requests for observation time on the Hubble Space Telescope in 2018. In 2021, the journal *Nature* reported a record number of first-time users: 32 percent of successful proposals were submitted by investigators who had not been given access to Hubble before.

One hiring platform's slogan, "Performance over Privilege and Pedigree," might have it right. The platform, GapJumpers, offers anonymized screening to help recruiters overcome their biases. Another one, Antibias, does the same. The one thing that neither GapJumpers nor Antibias nor the blind evaluation processes at NASA can do is address injustices that happened before someone applies. If an organization is already committed to attacking such unfairness through other means or takes such information into account because it values diversity, removing gender or race identifiers might not be the answer. Simply put, if your legal context currently allows you to use the demographic data on a résumé to proactively seek out underrepresented candidates, then taking that demographic data away will eliminate your ability to do so going forward.

This helps explain why the anonymization of résumés reduced the chance that applicants with immigrant backgrounds or from disadvantaged neighborhoods were invited to an interview in the French study mentioned before. The firms that participated in the study were not a representative sample of all French firms. Instead they comprised a subset of firms that had already hired people with disadvantaged backgrounds at higher-than-average rates, likely using information from résumés to help them do that. Organizations must therefore assess whether they are more like these French firms or more like Google and Azolla Ventures. The latter realized that bias had prevented them from giving women and some other underrepresented applicants a fair chance, leaving them with only a fraction of the available talent pool before anonymization. Based on the available evidence, we assume that most organizations fall into this category and would benefit from removing applicant identifiers.

Applied, the hiring platform that did the research on order effects in screening, took these insights one step further. It went beyond redacting applicant names and backgrounds and removed résumés altogether. Kate Glazebrook, Applied's cofounder, took seriously the research showing that education and experience are hardly related to job performance. She also argued against automation as many of the algorithms currently in use scrape résumés focusing on exactly these variables to create shortlists for employers. Instead, Applied decided to home in on applicants' skills directly, something many firms only do in the next step of the hiring process, after having already screened out a large number of applicants. Skills are among the best predictors of on-the-job performance, and we will devote a large portion of our next chapter to better understanding what skills-based assessments look like.

While Applied was ahead of the game with its early focus on skills, it also had to learn that employers were not quite ready to let go of résumés. In Glazebrook's own words: "I had not anticipated that the artifact of the CV itself would be so powerful. It is a piece of paper. It has been around for over 100 years, and when pushed, most people see that it's a deeply flawed, arcane measure of who a person is and what they can do. However, people are very attached to their ways of doing things, and defaults are powerful. CVs are comforting and we are asking companies to get rid of them. We had to get smart—we knew a system where there were no CVs at all would probably not be adopted, at least not in the short term."

Accordingly, Applied introduced a scoring tool that helps recruiters screen résumés more objectively, with more accuracy and less bias. In addition, the platform allows users to immediately learn whether a job ad would be likely to attract talent with the skills and traits they are looking for. Applied also continues to measure and evaluate: Knowing that turnover is one of employers' primary concerns, it analyzed how its platform did in terms of retention. It found that 96 percent of employees hired through Applied were still working in their organizations one year later, comparing favorably to the benchmark of 82 percent.

The lessons Applied learned are instructive. Getting people to change the way they have been doing things is hard. In addition, companies are skeptical of whether a new tool would in fact work for them. Despite our enthusiasm for evidence-based platforms that measure and share their learnings (Iris has served on the board of Applied), we agree that firms themselves have to also keep measuring and evaluating the tools they use, both in terms of their effectiveness and their fairness.

To do just that, we can take inspiration from economist Tatiana Mocanu's research evaluating the impact of a federal provision that required more impartial hiring practices in the Brazilian public sector. Examining data from 1980 to 2020, she found that making screening more impartial (including by removing names from applications) and limiting discretion in hiring practices (including by improving interviews, which we will return to in the next chapter) substantially decreased gender gaps in application rates, evaluation scores, and hiring decisions.

De-bias Your Algorithms

We now turn our attention from human screening to algorithmic screening, focusing on the class of "traditional algorithms" most commonly used at the screening stage to make predictions (not generative AI that creates new content). Much like the evidence on bias in human decision-making, the data that such algorithms can produce biased results is overwhelming—in criminal justice, healthcare, finance, advertising, and many more domains, including hiring.

In 2022, the US Equal Employment Opportunity Commission issued guidance on the use of algorithms in hiring, with a particular focus on their impact on people with disabilities. The EEOC's list of issues that could undermine a fair employment process was long: résumé scanners that prioritize applications using certain keywords; employee-monitoring software that rates employees on the basis of their keystrokes or other factors; virtual assistants or chatbots that ask job candidates about their qualifications and reject those who do not meet predefined requirements; video interviewing software that evaluates candidates based on their facial expressions and speech patterns; and testing software that provides "job fit" scores for applicants or employees regarding their personalities, aptitudes, cognitive skills, or perceived cultural fit based on their performance on a game or on a more traditional test. This is why it is paramount to de-bias the algorithms we use.

Most firms use machine learning to make predictions about applicants' future productivity (or other outcomes of interest) based on observed applicant attributes (or inputs). These attributes are typically gleaned from résumés (e.g., educational background or job experience) but can also include various types of assessment tests. To establish whether they can in fact predict performance, data scientists examine how they are related to existing employees' success in the organization in a historical data set. If, say, educational background has traditionally done a good job predicting retention rates such that graduates from certain universities are more likely to stay in the firm long term, this then feeds into a decision rule assessing current job applicants. So, inputs, outcomes, and data are key:

1. **Input variables.** The information an algorithm incorporates as the basis of its prediction can be problematic in various ways. For example, when educational background is proxied by grades, those in colleges with grade inflation will fare better. In addition, with information on lots of topics increasingly available, some employers have started to rely on data from nonwork domains to predict work performance. Job applicants' credit scores have been used as an input variable for job-screening algorithms, the argument being that people who pay their bills on time are more likely to work hard. Even if true, this could turn into a vicious cycle where those with low credit scores do not get jobs, further worsening their ability to repay their loans, further decreasing their job prospects, and so forth (which is one of the reasons several US states have restricted employers' access to job applicants' credit scores).

2. **Target outcomes.** Choosing which outcome to focus on seems rather obvious: Most organizations would like for their employees to be high performers. Measuring performance is not straightforward, though. Often, performance is not directly observable but depends on subjective evaluations by managers, which can be influenced by lots of factors, including the identities of the evaluator and the evaluated. A low performance score thus could be due to biased assessment, something an algorithm does not recognize.

3. **Data.** When determining how the chosen input variables are related to the outcome(s) of choice, data scientists need to rely on past data to run a training procedure. To state the obvious, history is not always a good predictor of the future. In addition, it is tempting to rely on historical "convenience samples," such as incumbent employees, to establish whether there exists a relationship between the input and outcome variables in question. However, this training set is not representative of job applicants. Such selection bias is a huge challenge for algorithmic assessments. Training samples based

on past data might also not be representative because they include extraordinary events no longer relevant or because they are unable to anticipate extraordinary events relevant today. Skills useful then may no longer help optimize performance today, let alone tomorrow.

The last point merits further exploration. There are many reasons why we might not *want* to replicate the past. Sexism and the many other "isms" we are here to fight should be top-of-mind. What this means for our algorithms is that we are looking for a pattern possibly not yet present in existing data: a new one, a better one, a fairer one that allows everyone to thrive and employers to benefit from 100 percent of the talent pool. This is a hard problem for machine learning, as it is inherently backward-looking. If the data is not there in the training set, well, then it isn't, turning the past into a self-fulfilling prophecy. Take your favorite social media site or streaming service that filters the content you see based on your past choices. Going with such user preferences, often based on reinforcement learning, means supporting our tendency to look for confirming evidence—that is, confirmation bias. Sadly, it can also lead to bias against out-group members. Many fear this contributes to the increased misinformation and polarization we see in the US and in many other countries.

By now you will have realized that algorithms can end up being biased not only because of what we often loosely refer to as "algorithmic bias," but because we humans are biased. It is human designers who choose biased predictors, biased outcomes, and/or biased training sets. In some cases, this happens because they don't look hard enough; in other cases, because unbiased data sets don't exist. But rather than trying to fix all the humans involved in the design of an algorithm, we can try to fix the algorithm itself. If you have access to the input and outcome variables as well as the training data, you can have an internal audit team rerun the analysis to determine whether they can replicate, or even improve on, the initial predictions.

When a group of researchers discovered a few years ago that healthcare services were not allocated fairly in the United States, one specific algorithm stood out—and fixing that one algorithm moved the needle quite dramatically. The designers of the original algorithm wanted to help identify the sickest patients so that care could be better targeted. Unfortunately, they proxied sickness with healthcare expenditures, and given that less money is spent on Black patients than equally sick white ones in the US, the algorithm believed Black Americans to be healthier and less in need of care than their white counterparts.

Once identified, the problem could be addressed quite quickly. Both the researchers and the original designers were keen to eliminate the bias. The fix, a new proxy for health needs, dramatically increased the number of Black patients receiving the care they needed (indeed, more than doubled it!). In our assessment, this is the biggest advantage of algorithms. Sure, they can address more complex problems, can learn from more data, are faster, and are not impacted by some of the heuristics such as order effects that harm human judgment. But most importantly, they can be monitored and either fixed or shut down more easily than millions of individual human minds.

Increase Data and Model Transparency

Access to the data feeding into an algorithm is key to an organization's ability to fix it. Therefore, transparency is the principle most agreed upon in the literature on ethical frameworks for artificial intelligence. But what might this entail? A recent study by researchers from Northeastern University who collaborated with the recruitment platform pymetrics (acquired by Harver in 2022) on an algorithmic audit is instructive. At pymetrics, neither experience nor education nor anything else on an applicant's résumé is considered as an input during the screening phase. CEO and cofounder Frida Polli explains: "Today, 75 percent of applicants are cut based on the résumé, an archaic system that doesn't predict job fit." Instead the platform uses cognitive science–based assessments to recommend to their clients whom they should interview. The company has job applicants participate in a number of exercises that measure behavioral tendencies such as risk tolerance, effort, attention, learning, and fairness.

Alas, pymetrics also had to learn that not every company was ready to give up résumés immediately. But as discussed earlier, showing rather than telling goes a long way. When consumer goods company Unilever started working with pymetrics for its US entry-level hiring, it decided to combine résumé screening with applicants playing twelve behavioral games designed by pymetrics to determine who would move on to the interview stage. After it had implemented this new process, Unilever reported substantial gains in the diversity of interviewed candidates. Offer acceptance rates also increased from 64 percent to 82 percent.

To validate which behavioral input variables to use, pymetrics conducts a local validation examining how behavior in their games is correlated with performance on the job in their training set, using incumbent employees. Recall that using existing employees as the training set, while a common practice, is likely one of the biggest vulnerabilities of the algorithm (and we will return to how pymetrics addresses it in a moment).

Research suggests that it is these historical training sets that should be the focus of your attention if you want to de-bias an algorithm. In a field experiment, about 400 machine learning engineers were tasked with designing an algorithm to predict the math performance of potential applicants based on the typical biographical information supplied in résumés. Every designer was given the exact same set of biographical information as input variables; was instructed to optimize the algorithm for the same outcome variable, math performance; and was told to test their model on the same data set of 20,000 potential applicants (representative of the underlying population).

Here was the difference: One group of engineers was provided with the kind of convenience data set typically used for training purposes where the data suffers from selection bias (only the information of those already hired was included). The engineers in this group were explicitly told that their data was a biased sample and that the data stemmed from those who had historically been hired rather than from a representative sample. This "biased data group" was compared with an "unbiased data group," where the engineers were provided with a representative sample of data from the underlying population.

It turns out representative data is key. The engineers in the "biased data group" were unable to correct for the bias in their data, which led to biased predictions. The engineers' demographic characteristics did not matter—bad data led to bad outcomes and good data to good outcomes independent of who was involved. Nor did the engineers' implicit bias measured through an Implicit Association Test make a difference. Interestingly, however, while women did not make less-biased choices than men, or Black engineers less-biased choices than white engineers, they made different types of errors such that diverse teams of engineers would have outperformed homogeneous ones. The researchers did not actually create teams but looked at how outcomes by demographic group differed from outcomes across groups. Cross-demographic averaging led to better performance than same-demographic averages. This result is intriguing as it suggests that diversity could lead to better outcomes even if the individual members of the various groups all make biased choices—as long as they are not biased in exactly the same way.

Pymetrics avoids the problem of biased training sets leading to biased algorithms by using input variables that, generally speaking, do not systematically differ across genders or races. If the base rates of the variables are the same across groups, one can train an algorithm from relatively homogeneous populations and still produce an algorithm that finds diverse candidates. However, one cannot rely on this technique alone to ensure that algorithms are unbiased. One has to actually test them.

Test the Impact of Your Algorithms

Testing your algorithm is essential both during model building and when the algorithm is deployed to its target audience: actual people applying to actual jobs. The question at this stage is whether the model can generalize to a data set not previously used. Relying on such a testing set, pymetrics makes sure its model has no differential impact based on job seekers' identity (using the US Uniform Guidelines on Employee Selection Procedures as the standard). If pymetrics finds evidence of disparate impact, it recalibrates the weights of input variables correlated with the outcome. This model—"the best-performing predictive model that meets the fairness criteria"—is the one it shares with the hiring firm. Based on job applicants' choices in the cognitive science games, the model then chooses the candidates most likely to succeed in the hiring firm.

Pymetrics also tests the algorithm in action, which is the second test we highly recommend. This version of A/B testing, where the hiring firm uses an algorithm in parallel with its traditional screening process, is becoming increasingly popular. This allows the hiring firm to learn how algorithmic assessments differ from the results of its traditional processes (such as human résumé screens) and answers the question of whom they would have passed through to the interview stage with and without the algorithm.

Working with a large company, researcher Bo Cowgill helped do exactly this and evaluate the impact of the firm's new screening algorithm in a field experiment. Experienced human screeners and a machine learning algorithm had access to identical information on résumés submitted by candidates applying for jobs as software engineers. A random mechanism decided whether the professional screeners or the algorithm determined who was invited to an interview. In the end, candidates selected by the machine learning algorithm were 14 percent more likely to be successful in the interview and receive a job offer, and 18 percent more likely to accept such an offer, than those chosen by humans. Because of the algorithm, the firm ended up hiring more nontraditional candidates, including women, candidates of color, candidates without job referrals or prior work experience, and graduates from non-elite colleges. To top it all off, these nontraditional hires were more productive.

Hiring is not the only domain where algorithms outperform human judgments both in terms of accuracy and in terms of fairness. Examining the prevailing evidence in criminal justice, applied mathematician and computer scientist Sharad Goel concludes that "algorithms typically outperform criminal justice professionals in assessing risk," while computer scientist Jon Kleinberg and colleagues go as far as to suggest that "the algorithm is a force for racial equity," based on their evaluation of algorithms and humans predicting recidivism. Other scholars have focused on lending decisions and document that machine learning can help overcome bias against immigrants and older loan applicants— and increase profits.

To repeat it once more: the beauty of algorithms is that we can scrutinize them and experiment with their behavior. But we must truly follow through and do the testing! A review of US vendors that offer automated screening of job candidates suggests that most do not explain how specifically they have tested and/or de-biased their tools. Many vendors argue that the inputs they use are unbiased and do not need to be adjusted as they do not produce different outcomes by demographic group.

While we hope the vendors in fact do a great job testing, we suggest learning from the formal validation processes employed to test the efficacy of medicines. We have gained confidence in our headache medication not because we understand its molecular structure or because a vendor vouched for it, but because it has gone through clinical trials. Such randomized controlled trials are the gold standard for establishing what works and what doesn't, for whom, and under what circumstances, and it is because of this evidence that the US Food and Drug Administration (FDA) and its counterparts elsewhere in the world feel comfortable allowing new medications on the market (they also had to learn that testing on representative samples is key). Organizations need to do the same for their algorithms and test their impact on the relevant populations before they are unleashed.

As we are writing this book, generative AI, such as ChatGPT, developed by OpenAI and trained on the corpus of text available on the internet, is increasing in importance. Some companies may already use it to create job advertisements or to map desired job skills to recruitment sites. The big difference to traditional AI is that generative AI goes beyond pattern detection, data classification, and predictions to produce new content, write text, develop code, and create imagery (including deepfakes and hallucinations). As such, all the concerns raised above apply also to generative AI, and in a much more pronounced way. Generative AI is more complex and harder to understand, so using unbiased data sets that go beyond what is openly available on the internet and testing them is even more important.

In August 2023, Rumman Chowdhury's nongovernmental organization (NGO), Humane Intelligence, collaborated with the White House on a hackathon where the major large language models in use at the time (developed by Anthropic, Google, Hugging Face, NVIDIA, OpenAI, and Stability AI) were scrutinized. At Harvard, computer scientist Latanya Sweeney teaches a similar class, aptly called "Data Science to Save the World," which is also focused on evaluating the impact of the tools we use. We believe that such enhanced testing and experimenting is the way forward.

* * *

To summarize, both human and algorithmic judgments can lead us astray. Some biases are shared by humans and machines because the latter are programmed by the former. Others are not, and an algorithm's biggest advantage might also be its biggest pitfall: rather than millions of people making decisions, it is one tool that makes those calls. One tool can be fixed more easily than millions of minds—but if we get it wrong, the impact of our mistake is that much greater.

---

1. Randomize the order in which you review applications
2. Screen for expertise rather than career gaps
3. Remove irrelevant information
4. De-bias your algorithms
5. Increase data and model transparency
6. Test the impact of your algorithm

CHAPTER 8

Hiring the Best Person for the Job

When Ginni Rometty was CEO of technology corporation IBM, she introduced "skills-first" hiring, arguing that the filters we typically use, such as education and experience, are not helpful in many jobs. Instead companies should ask themselves what skills are required to succeed in a given role—say, computer programming or selling software—and then find job seekers who either have or want to acquire those skills, even if they don't have a computer science or business degree. By creating on-ramps through internship and apprenticeship opportunities, which are more common in European countries, IBM was able to dramatically broaden its talent pool. A skills-based approach holds the promise of better matches between jobs and employees, Rometty and coauthors suggest.

The Cleveland Clinic, an academic medical center, was so impressed with the approach that after a pilot with 400 roles where it adjusted degree and credential requirements, it rolled out the skills analysis to thousands more roles. Greg Case, CEO of the risk management consulting firm Aon, succinctly summarized the approach: "Asking how we give people access to our companies, that is the wrong question. The real question is, 'How can we equip ourselves to access this talent?'"

Delta Air Lines and Bank of America also use the approach to promote internal career mobility. Alongside Aon, the Cleveland Clinic, and IBM, they are members of the OneTen coalition, which is committed to closing the opportunity gap for Black talent. In contrast to many organizations that focus on inputs only, they measure whether the approach is working by using outcome data that is disaggregated by gender and race. "Measuring how many people go through a development program is one thing, but what you really should be measuring is how many people who went through that program are being promoted to the next level," Brian Moynihan, Bank of America's CEO, explained.

Organizations from all sectors, including various state governments, are increasingly turning to skills-based hiring. By June 2023, at least ten states had instituted a focus on skills. In our home state, Massachusetts governor Maura Healey signed an executive order on skills-based hiring for the state's workforce in January 2024. A recent McKinsey & Company article describes how organizations like Rework America Alliance, the Business Roundtable's Multiple Pathways Initiative, and the Tear the Paper Ceiling campaign produce real results for fairness and efficiency. These efforts are supported by a call to action by former secretary of state Condoleezza Rice, who believes that "America needs to 'make a lot more use' of skills-based hiring."

The question, then, is how to best assess an applicant's skills during this stage of the hiring process. Do the typical techniques used today, such as interviews and assessment tools, enable us to identify the best talent for the job?

Unfortunately, the evidence suggests the answer is likely no. Interviews, for example, are fraught with problems. Numerous biases can lead us astray. To name but a few: in-group bias makes us prefer people who look like we do; stereotypes lead us to prefer candidates who look like the typical employee; halo effects cause us to put too much weight on first impressions; and confirmation bias makes us look for evidence confirming our gut instincts while ignoring contrary information. You can see where this is going. It is hard to come up with unbiased assessments that allow us to hire the best people through interviews.

In-person audit studies measure the degree to which interviewers can be impartial. Unbeknownst to the hiring managers, pairs of comparable applicants who only differ in one attribute under study participate in job interviews. Researchers often work with actors who pose as, say, Jamal Jones and Greg Smith, a Black and a white applicant comparable in physical appearance, age, and demeanor who have been assigned equivalent fictitious employment credentials like education and work experience, and have received training on how to behave in the interview.

For obvious reasons, this research approach is more controversial than the audit studies discussed in the previous chapter. It creates additional work for hiring managers who have to evaluate fictitious job applicants who, if offered the job, will turn them down. Due to this ethical controversy and the complexity of the endeavor, a 2020 meta-analysis identified only 12 such studies with a total sample of 13,000 job applicants. They all focus on ethnicity or race.

Among the candidates invited to an interview, white applicants received about 50 percent more job offers than their otherwise comparable counterparts from underrepresented groups, whether the study looked at bias against job applicants with a Middle Eastern or North African background in countries such as Belgium, Denmark, France, Italy, Spain, and Sweden, or against African Americans and Hispanics in the United States. This 50 percent gap is in addition to the racial bias that candidates encounter at the screening stage before they even make it to the interview. These two stages of discrimination add up to an overall difference in job offers of 150 percent! Put differently, from start to finish, white job candidates were 150 percent more likely to receive an offer than otherwise comparable applicants from underrepresented groups.

Sadly, seeing an actual person and receiving additional information such as demeanor and appearance did not counteract interviewer bias. In some ways, being confronted with another human makes things worse. We cannot help but be influenced by what job applicants wear (our favorite color maybe?), how they speak (with a dialect maybe?), and how they look (attractive maybe?). Based on a large data set from entrepreneurial pitch competitions as well as laboratory experiments in the US, we know that such irrelevant factors affect evaluators. Investors favored pitches delivered by men, especially attractive men, even when the substance of the pitch was identical to the pitches presented by women.

In light of this, we should not be surprised that interviews, particularly unstructured ones, are bad predictors of future performance. It is in these unstructured contexts that unconscious bias flourishes. When people have discretion in their judgments, rules of thumb such as stereotypes are hard to avoid. Judicial decision-making is an interesting case in point as judges typically have some degree of discretion. And the more discretion they have, the more gender and race gaps in sentencing among otherwise similar defendants increase, as research on federal district court judges finds.

What to do? Generally, adding structure to our decision-making helps. An extensive body of research shows that we can improve the quality of our decisions when we rely on good information that is predictive of the outcomes that we care about and, importantly for our purposes, when we combine this information in helpful ways. It is here where our intuition falls short. It has a hard time remembering and processing the information received and consistently weighing it across candidates. Thankfully, help is available. We can employ decision aids and decision rules that assist us in benefiting from the information collected.

Take the Apgar score as an example. The score gives healthcare providers a first indication of how well a newborn is doing right after birth. These experts have learned not to simply trust their gut but instead employ a structured approach where the baby is evaluated based on five dimensions—heart rate, breathing, muscle tone, reflexes, and skin color—and each category receives a score of 0, 1, or 2. We can apply these insights to interviewing candidates. If seasoned healthcare professionals need help, perhaps those of us interviewing job candidates only a couple of times a year could benefit from some decision aids too.

In many ways, skills-based assessment tests are such aids. In this chapter, we will share the best available evidence on how to make interviews and other formal assessment tools more effective and fair. As a reminder, even if you do not control these procedures for your whole organization, you may be able to implement many of our suggestions in your own work. At the end, we will push the boundaries a bit further and examine what hiring would look like if we basically did away with interviews altogether. This last option might not be right for everyone, but we want to at least show you what the frontier of hiring could look like: more like matchmaking in the dating world, which apparently is on the rise again.

Create an Interview Checklist

It all starts with a simple list. What is it that you want to evaluate? Determine the skills, knowledge, and competencies a successful candidate should have and design the questions you want to ask accordingly. Each question should elicit information that allows you to better assess something you care about—and, ideally, focus squarely on the competencies required. We are always astonished to discover that questions like "Please tell us about yourself" or "What are your greatest strengths?" are still beloved by many interviewers. What competencies are these questions testing, exactly?

It is also important to define the criteria you will use to evaluate responses beforehand so that you know what you are looking for when talking to a candidate. It is easy to be swayed by, say, the first candidate's vision but then completely focus on execution when you talk to the second candidate. The list will help you focus and make sure you collect comparable information on all the criteria you care about.

If this feels like an interview checklist, this is exactly what we are building! And you should not shy away from it but join an increasing number of companies that told us they are using one. For example, after a workshop in March 2023, Qualtrics, the global cloud software company, shared with us how our work had helped the company move from unstructured interviews to a more structured process. The 2021 *Women in the Workplace* report applauds the increase in evidence-based hiring practices and suggests that "companies that have made the greatest strides in women's representation are more likely to have these practices in place."

You might want to follow suit. Together with Anisha Asundi, we advised the UK Behavioural Insights Team on evidence-based guidelines for structured interviews (included in the endnotes) that you might find helpful. In contrast to unstructured interviews where you basically go with the flow, structured interviews have been shown to be much more predictive of future performance. You can inform the candidates that you are following a predetermined set of questions that you cannot deviate from (even if they mention that they root for the same sports team that you root for). At the end of the formal, evaluative interview, you can explicitly transition into a more informal conversation where the candidate can ask you some questions and you can provide additional information on what working at your organization might look like.

To conduct a gold standard structured interview, ask all candidates the same set of questions in the same order. Determine a scoring rubric and the weights you want to give to each question beforehand. You might want to weight all of them equally or you may decide that the responses to your first and your fourth question are essential, so they should get more weight. Importantly, do not "redefine merit" for each candidate by weighing the answers differently depending on who gives them.

To calibrate your assessments across all of the candidates you have interviewed for a given role, evaluate responses horizontally, that is, by looking at all candidates' answers to Question 1, then all answers to Question 2, and so forth. An important insight of behavioral science is that it is almost impossible for us to make absolute judgments. Whether or not you like the apple pie served at a dinner party has something to do with the apple pies you are used to. And what informs our assessment of food also matters when we evaluate people. Comparisons help us calibrate our judgments, making them both more accurate and more fair. Without comparators available, our minds tend to revert to what is available to them as a model example.

This is exactly what Iris and her coauthors found when they tested the theory in the laboratory. When presented with one candidate at a time, people were much more likely to stick with the stereotypical candidate even when that candidate had performed worse on the task at hand than what they could expect from another candidate. The stereotypes worked both ways: people preferred inferior male candidates for math and inferior female candidates for verbal tasks. In contrast, when given the opportunity to compare across more than one candidate at a time and calibrate judgments, the stereotypes lost out to competence, leading the team to entitle the resulting article, "When Performance Trumps Gender Bias."

These insights informed the advice Iris gave when the Nobel Prize Foundation invited her to Stockholm, Sweden, in 2018. She recommended that nominators like her be explicitly asked to propose more than one person at a time for the Nobel Prize. Every year, Iris gets a letter from the Nobel Prize Foundation inviting her to nominate someone for the Nobel Prize in Economics, and every year until 2018, Iris had nominated exactly one person. Given our research suggesting that people do a worse job when thinking of only one person at a time, might she (and other nominators) have been influenced by what a typical Nobel laureate looks like? After all, about 95 percent of Nobel Prizes throughout history have been awarded to men (who have been mostly white and mostly from Western countries). With this stereotype in mind, we might not even have thought of candidates who did not fit the norm or, when they did cross our minds, evaluated them more harshly.

In 2019, the Nobel Prize Foundation explicitly invited nominators to "put forward names corresponding to three different discoveries." In theory, this had already been possible beforehand, but it "was not highlighted until now meaning it might have been underused," including by people like Iris. In addition, and also for the first time, nominators were explicitly instructed "to consider diversity in gender, geography, and topic." Göran Hansson, secretary-general of the Royal Swedish Academy of Sciences, told *Nature*: "We don't work in a vacuum. We need the scientific community to see the women scientists, and to nominate those who have made outstanding contributions."

You can apply this insight too. If you normally hire for one open position in February, another one in May, and a third in September, try to run these hiring processes in parallel around the same time as a "batch," if you can. When making just a single hire at a time, we tend to pick someone who aligns with preconceived notions. Behavioral scientist Edward Chang and coauthors termed this problem the "isolated choice effect." They showed that when evaluators hire in batches, they are more likely to choose people who differ from those already in the group, thus ending up with more gender-diverse groups than they started out with.

Protocol does not equal rigidity but instead helps all of us, including doctors and nurses who ended up providing better care for their patients, as surgeon and public health researcher Atul Gawande describes in his book *Checklist Manifesto*. Checklists have also helped financial advisors deliver improved service to their clients and pilots fly us to our destinations more safely. A checklist is a decision aid that helps us be more consistent and comprehensive. It also serves as a reminder to follow through on our virtuous intentions and not be sidetracked by irrelevant information a candidate chooses to share.

Canadian equity strategy firm Tidal Equality used these insights when it built the Equity Sequence®, its decision-making framework for considering fairness in all types of workplace decisions. The Equity Sequence® is a simple, open-ended set of five questions that helps users to discover where bias might lurk in their processes, products, services, or systems—and then guides them toward making fairer redesigns.

In Canada, the University of Manitoba applied the approach to review its admissions procedures for the Master of Physician Assistant Studies program, where prerequisites used to include a four-year science undergraduate degree with a high average GPA. The Equity Sequence® encouraged the university to question who might be unnecessarily excluded under these criteria and who had decided the criteria in the first place. The program shifted to accepting students from all kinds of undergraduate academic backgrounds, not just science, and included new assessment criteria around community service, advocacy efforts, language, and life experiences. It also reduced ambiguity around what GPAs would be accepted and began to consider GPAs both across all four years of undergraduate studies as well as the most recent two (recognizing that some members of traditionally underrepresented groups might end up academically strong but have a slow start). As a result, members of underrepresented racial groups increased from 10 percent to 45 percent of admitted students, and the gender mix of the class went from 10 percent male and 90 percent female to 40 percent male and 60 percent female.

Improve the Interview Process

In addition to designing a set of questions based on what you look for in a candidate and deciding on the scoring of the responses and weighting of the questions, you also need to think about who will be involved in the interview process. Note that while it is helpful for candidates to meet a diverse set of interviewers, diversity on the selection committee does not guarantee unbiased assessments. Most biases—other than in-group preferences—are shared. We all, independent of our own social identity, tend to be impacted by stereotypes, and, for example, tend to associate engineering with men and nursing with women. As such, simply including underrepresented voices in the group of interviewers is not enough to de-bias the process. It may still help you, though, but for a different reason. A candidate might be more likely to accept your offer if they see people like themselves represented in the firm.

In interviews, have candidates meet the evaluators one-on-one. While panel interviews are common, we advise against them. On a panel, interviewers are unable to form truly independent judgments as they will be influenced by each other, increasing the likelihood that they fall prey to groupthink, where the group's judgment is worse than the aggregate of the interviewers' individual assessments. Much of this influence is subtle and unconscious, such as noticing whether a fellow interviewer is leaning forward or back (indicating interest or disinterest in what the candidate is saying); whether their tone of voice is excited or judgmental; and whether they are nodding along and taking prolific notes as the candidate is speaking, or checking the messages on their phone instead.

When interviewing, take notes for each response received and compare candidates' responses horizontally. Submit your scores multiplied by the weight you have assigned to the question to the person leading the recruitment process (often, someone from HR) who can aggregate all final scores received for each candidate. Finally, if part of your process, meet with the other interviewers to discuss possible notable discrepancies in your scores.

Much like you should not meet with a job candidate in a group, you should not discuss your thoughts with other evaluators before you have submitted your scores. It is just too easy to fall right back into what you have successfully averted by meeting with the candidates individually: groupthink. The territory is particularly treacherous if you hear the most senior person's opinion before you have made up your own mind. A good practice is that even in the final calibration meeting, after everyone has submitted their scores, the most senior person speaks last. McKinsey & Company reports that members of the German initiative Chefsache, where the consulting firm collaborates with companies such as Allianz, Bayer, Google, and Siemens, have adopted various of these de-biasing techniques as part of their "advocating equal opportunities for women and men, including in top management positions."

When Iris discussed ways to de-bias the hiring process in an executive education program at Harvard, one participant not only took these insights to heart—he also took them into his own hands. Upon his return to the US government agency where he still serves in a senior role today, he started implementing change. He was particularly struck by the recommendation not to conduct panel interviews, which were ubiquitous in his organization. While he did not work in HR, as a senior executive and hiring manager, he knew he had some control over the practices his office employed and felt compelled to explore ways of reducing bias in the process. So he swiftly proposed and was approved to lead a group effort to design and test a modified hiring system.

Working together with Siri, his cross-functional thirteen-member project team evaluated existing hiring processes against the evidence-based approaches just discussed. While the team could not influence candidate sourcing or where jobs were advertised, once the office received the list of the prescreened candidates who had applied for a job opening, it could decide the structure of the interviews, the questions asked during interviews, and whether or not skills-based tests were included in the process. It was clear that this group wanted to "not just talk but do things," as our senior executive explained. He was supported by a colleague suggesting that "even if you just develop a rubric, that's so much more than we used to do. We would just get a pile of résumés and randomly look through them."

The department ended up anonymizing résumés and evaluating them separately from other assessments; moving from unstructured to structured interviews where criteria and weightings were determined in advance; replacing panel interviews with one-on-one interviews; and introducing more and more skills-based assessments. In an ideal case, at the end they had three independently assessed scores for each candidate, one based on the résumé, one based on the interview, and one based on a work sample test (the topic of the next section)—which is exactly the process we employ when evaluating applicants for jobs at the Women and Public Policy Program and very similar to how Cisco chose its CEO, Chuck Robbins.

If this process strikes you as too labor-intensive, consider using one of the technological tools available. They can make your life easier and lead to better and more diverse hires. In the end, however, the proof is in the pudding—which is why we are intrigued by tools that keep measuring what works and what does not. So, if you do not test and evaluate your hiring practices yourself—either because you don't want to or don't have the sample size or financial resources—using a tool that has been tested and whose impact has been evaluated might be the way to go.

Use an Unbiased Skills-Based Assessment Task

Most technology companies evaluate job seekers applying for a software engineer position not exclusively based on their background or an interview, but also based on a work sample test. Simply put, work sample tests are exercises or tasks that are designed to test for a particular competency and mimic important aspects of the actual job as closely as possible. For many software engineering jobs, applicants are asked to participate in a coding challenge. Intrigued by what held the promise of being a more objective and predictive way of assessing performance, Iris was delighted when the CEO of a platform offering practice assessments for coders reached out to her a couple of years ago. He had heard about our work and wanted to make sure that his platform did not inadvertently disadvantage women through the tools it used.

While software development and computer science still are male-stereotyped fields, we had high hopes that a work sample test could make a difference, especially since these tests are designed to assess candidates' quality of work rather than the candidates themselves. Simulation exercises and situational judgment tests are variants of the same idea where applicants are evaluated based on how they engage with realistic workplace scenarios. A meta-analysis examining workplace decisions in female- and male-typed jobs showed that the degree to which men were favored for male-dominated jobs was substantially reduced when evaluators had information available that clearly indicated a candidate's high competence. Perhaps solving a coding problem successfully could do precisely that.

A variety of platforms are available to prepare prospective programmers for the assessment processes typically used by technology companies, including Coderbyte, CoderPad, Codility, Hacker-Rank, and Pramp. We were given access to all of the data of one of these platforms, including the practice coders' gender, hometown, educational background, work experience, preparation level, and—most importantly—how they performed on the practice test. We found a small but persistent gender gap in objectively measured performance on the coding task, even among equally qualified female and male coders with the same work experience. The gap was made worse when raters subjectively evaluated the coders, suggesting that possibly both stereotype threat—the risk of confirming a negative stereotype about one's group, which can depress one's performance—and rater bias were at play. It was then that it occurred to us that maybe something was wrong with the test. Perhaps we had discovered an example of disparate impact.

In many cases when applicants have to write code, they are observed by an evaluator. In fact, candidates are typically asked to think aloud while working toward a solution so that the evaluator can assess their thought process. Such whiteboarding exercises have recently been criticized. One article compares them to a procedure purposely developed to induce stress—the Trier social stress test—that has been used by psychologists and neuroscientists for research purposes. This stress-inducing test has people give an interview-style presentation and do mental arithmetic in front of an audience. It fulfills its purpose: being watched and evaluated while performing a cognitively demanding task reliably induces stress, possibly even more so among people for whom math problems activate stereotype threat.

This is why what many of us experienced in eighth grade when asked to solve a math problem at the front of class might not be so different from what candidates describe during whiteboarding assessments: "freezing," "bombing," and "choking." Perhaps what the typical tech company is actually measuring when assessing software developers this way is not so much their competence, knowledge, or skills, but instead their ability to handle stress. While everyone might be stressed in such a setting, those experiencing stereotype threat are likely to experience even more performance anxiety.

To dig further, data scientist Mahnaz Behroozi and colleagues ran an experiment where half of the participating computer science students completed a public whiteboarding exercise and the other half a private whiteboarding exercise. The sample was small, so at this point, we only have suggestive evidence available—but the pattern is quite clear. When observed, not a single female computer science student completed the problem correctly; in the private setting, all women were able to do so. Overall, almost twice as many subjects failed when observed, and performance was reduced by more than half in the public as compared to the private setting. In accordance with their performance, students also reported being more at ease and experiencing less cognitive load and stress in the private setting.

Separating test takers from evaluators might have an additional benefit. In follow-up work on our coding platform study, Iris's collaborators tested whether removing the social contact from code writing might improve matters and only shared either people's initials or first names with evaluators. Both interventions worked, closing the gender gap in subjective evaluations completely, suggesting that it was not just the knowledge of a coder's gender (through their first name) that affected raters' assessments. Instead, a context where reviewers and coders directly interact with each other might make stereotypes more salient for both the candidate and the reviewer, inducing stereotype threat in the former and bias in the latter.

Given that the predictive value of public versus private problem solving is unclear, tech companies might be well advised to follow in instant messaging platform Slack's footsteps and do away with public whiteboarding. Slack not only has applicants work on the problem in private, but it also removes all applicant identifiers before it evaluates the outcome of the exercise. In one go, Slack is able to remove both stereotype threat and evaluator bias, helping the company identify the most qualified software engineers unencumbered by what they look like.

Some of our readers might now be reminded of their experiences interviewing for a job in consulting. Case-based interviews are another example of a rather public assessment method about whose predictive validity we know little. A *Harvard Business Review* article by two authors who have been involved in recruiting at most of the top-tier strategy firms advises caution. Laszlo Bock, former senior vice president of people operations at Google, goes as far as to call case interviews "worthless" in his book, *Work Rules!*

Some consulting firms are taking this to heart and now evaluate job applicants more like Slack. One company, for example, asked candidates to read a memorandum and write down the questions they would want to ask before making a decision based on the information provided. Evaluators then also removed the names of the applicants and rated the responses based on predefined criteria, leading them to advance candidates to the final round who had struggled in case-based assessments.

To be clear, skills-based assessment tests are generally highly advisable, but they are not all created equal, and small tweaks like the ones introduced by Slack and the consulting firm just mentioned can make a big difference. Overall, job-related measures such as work sample tests and structured interviews come out on top in meta-analyses comparing how well different indicators fare in predicting future performance. Measures of cognitive ability, integrity, and emotional intelligence also fare relatively well—in contrast to years of experience and generic measures of openness, emotional stability, agreeableness, conscientiousness, or extraversion, which together with the unstructured interview rank at the bottom.

This is why Applied, the hiring platform we discussed in the previous chapter, skips the traditional résumé screening stage altogether and moves directly to skills-based assessments that map on to the tasks employees will have to complete. For example, a question for someone applying for a job as a fundraising manager might look like this: "It's your first week on the job and you've been given a list of fundraising prospects interested in supporting us. How do you spend your week?"

Designing questions that capture the skills an employer is looking for in the most effective and unbiased way is no easy feat, which is why the company keeps testing the impact of its assessment tools. For example, it tested how 700 applicants fared when put through the Applied evaluation as compared to a traditional résumé sift in a consulting firm. The results were thought-provoking: with their usual approach, the firm would never have hired, or even met, 60 percent of the candidates it ended up extending job offers to. Applied also reports that it was able to fill 45 percent of the roles UK technology companies hired for with women or nonbinary candidates, exceeding the industry standard of 30 percent. More generally, while it is too early for a final verdict on the gender impacts of skills-based hiring, the evidence to date looks promising. Based on a 2023 LinkedIn report, the share of women in the talent pool would grow dramatically in jobs where women are underrepresented.

If you want to design your own skills-based assessment tasks, you might want to take inspiration from sample questions shared by Applied and guidelines from the UK's Behavioural Insights Team (both included in the endnotes). Most importantly, though, we urge you to test your tasks for adverse impact. If people of particular backgrounds or specific social identities systematically perform worse, consider adjusting the task. Only an unbiased tool helps you assess job candidates accurately and fairly.

Validate Your Assessment Approaches

In our experience, hiring managers do not leverage available tools enough and instead trust their own judgment too much—even if, on average, employing some basic statistical tools outperforms human assessments. One meta-analysis took a close look at this, comparing how well humans versus statistical tools were able to predict future performance, both at work and at school. The analysis only included studies where an apples-to-apples comparison was possible, that is, where humans and statistical tools were provided with identical pieces of information on a candidate, such as performance on cognitive ability tests, personality tests, or assessment center exercises. The question the researchers asked was simple: Who was better able to turn these different pieces of information into something useful and actually predict future job performance? The statistical tools won—by a lot. The improvement in prediction was greater than 50 percent!

Convincing hiring managers to give more formal assessments a chance is not always easy because most of us tend to hold our own decision-making in high regard. You may want to follow in Unilever's footsteps and have each applicant go through the traditional hiring process—say, an interview—and, in parallel, also through the new assessment tool of choice. Much like the firm that worked with Applied, you can then compare whom you would have hired based on the traditional process and whom you would hire based on the new tool. Such a proof of concept can go a long way with skeptical managers.

In one study, 15 firms were interested in hiring people for relatively standardized data entry jobs. The firms wanted to know whether the introduction of a specific assessment tool would help them combat high turnover, a particular concern in this occupation. Specifically, they were wondering whether informing their hiring managers, who previously had hired candidates based on résumés and interviews, of the test score for each applicant would improve the quality of their hiring decisions. To make it easier for managers to incorporate this information, candidates with the highest test scores were marked in green, those with moderate scores in yellow, and those with the lowest scores in red. The assessment tool consisted of an online survey and included questions on computer/technical skills, personality, cognitive skills, fit for the job, as well as various job scenarios. Hiring managers were nudged to take test scores into consideration in their hiring decisions, although there was no specific requirement.

So, what did the managers end up doing when testing was introduced for 400,000 applicants of whom they hired 91,000? It turns out that those who deviated from the test score by, for example, hiring an applicant who tested red but forgoing one who tested yellow or green, or preferring one who tested yellow when a green one would have been available, did worse. Yellows stayed 20 percent longer than reds, and greens stayed 11 percent longer than yellows. The managers had to learn the hard way that it was better for their firms if they relied on the assessment tool rather than whatever intuition they had formed based on résumé reviews and interviews. This was harder for some than for others. The data showed that some managers were fine trusting the tool while others were not—but unfortunately, the researchers were not given access to any demographic information on managers or applicants, so we cannot pinpoint how they went astray when left to their own devices.

Measuring impact remains key. When a national US retailer with more than 1,300 stores switched from informal to test-based assessments, turnover decreased. But in this case, the researchers had information on demographic characteristics and discovered a bit of a puzzle. The switch did not change the demographic composition of who was hired even though, on average, applicants from under-represented groups performed worse on the test. As it happens, the disparate impact of the test on scores did not translate into disparate impact on the chances of being hired. We do not hire averages but only the best, so also have to take distributions into account.

This is a potentially important point for those of us interested in using formal assessment tests, so let's quickly look at an example. Assume that applicants come from two groups, A and B, and each group has five applicants. The test scores of the five group A applicants (on a scale from 1 to 10) are 1, 2, 3, 9, and 10, respectively, for an average score of 5. The scores of the five group B applicants are 2, 3, 7, 9, and 9, respectively, for an average score of 6. Since an organization does not hire all applicants but only the best, it may have a score cutoff. For example, it may only make job offers to applicants who scored 9 or above, thus making offers to two group A applicants and two group B applicants. Note that if the cutoff were 10, then only one group A applicant would receive an offer—even though, on average, group A members performed worse on the test. Thus a test can have adverse impact on average but not negatively affect those who end up being hired. The test in the research study was better than humans at identifying the best candidates within each demographic subgroup.

For the time being, the preponderance of evidence suggests that statistical assessment typically trumps intuitive assessment. However, as always, this may not apply under all circumstances to all jobs in all firms. Make sure whatever you do works for you by testing and validating! In addition, make sure you include your hiring managers in this discussion. You do not want to demoralize them but instead help them do their jobs more effectively and fairly. Given the work-force analytics available today, it is not hard for your HR team to perform some of the above analyses and check which of the assess-ment tools you use, including interviews and résumés, are actually predictive of future performance without disadvantaging members of specific groups.

You might learn that one of the tools does better than another, or that a combination of various tools is the way to go. This could have another advantage: Research suggests that people are more open to trusting the results of statistical analyses if they have some say in the final outcome. Such human involvement could happen in different ways. Test-based scores could be reviewed side-by-side with human-based scores to make the invisible visible, followed by a discussion about both assessment methodologies to increase accountability through debate. Alternatively, hiring managers could use the statis-tical assessment as an anchor or starting point and justify deviations with a transparent approach, such as comply-or-explain, whereby managers need to either comply with the initial statistical assessment or specifically justify why they are deviating from it.

Go Beyond Evaluation: Matchmaking

Given that accurate evaluation is so hard and implementation is often constrained by managerial resistance, perhaps we should find better ways to attract people with the right skills (including those committed to learning them). If we can come up with designs that motivate job candidates to self-select into the jobs that are right for them, everyone will win. Of course, this is no easy feat as job applicants know them-selves but do not know as much about the job. So, employers have to make it as easy as possible for applicants to predict what working as an accountant, a librarian, or a mechanic is like, and create incentives for the applicants to choose based on their true competencies.

A focus on skills is a promising first step. Imagine your job descriptions did not specify required experience and educational background but focused exclusively on the skills and competencies required for the role. Further, imagine that job seekers who had self-disclosed the skills and competencies they have or would like to acquire and the types of organizations they would be interested in working for would be matched to the roles. In fact, you do not just have to go with your imagination but can learn from what is already out there. To help candidates better understand the skills they have, hiring platforms such as Kalibrr in the Philippines and Job-Room in Switzerland provide job seekers with skills tests and then match them with employers in need of those skills.

Based on these skills and other preferences (say, location) that job seekers and employers (or students and schools/universities) might express, they are then paired with each other. Alvin Roth, a Nobel laureate in economics, has done pioneering work designing algorithms to match supply and demand in various domains, including helping New York City and Boston match the best available students with the best available schools and people in need of an organ with available organ donors. Other canonical examples include the National Resident Matching Program for young doctors in the United States and student matching to universities in Germany, where a clearinghouse allocates all seats in medicine and related subjects.

It certainly seems as if many positions are ripe for a centralized clearinghouse that would match applicants to jobs as, say, analysts in banking or consulting, product managers in technology, research analysts in international organizations, teachers in schools, or administrative officers in government. This is not an exhaustive list but gives a flavor of the kinds of job markets that could benefit: generally, ones where there are many job seekers and many jobs to be filled.

We urge more employers and more job seekers to try out skills-based matchmaking. It might well level the playing field in a way never seen before and prepare us better for the future of work where a twenty-year-old pedigree may no longer be relevant for the jobs of the moment and where reskilling and upskilling will become the new normal.

* * *

The message of this chapter is straightforward: You cannot leave the evaluation of your candidates up to your gut instinct. The more discipline we can add to the evaluation process—by moving from unstructured to structured interviews and from informal to formal skills-based assessment tools—the more likely we will be able to identify the best possible job candidate. And what is even better, in most cases the additional rigor also helps us overcome our biased assessments, particularly if we examine the impacts our tests might have on various groups beforehand.

---

1. Create an interview checklist
2. Improve the interview process
3. Use an unbiased skills-based assessment task
4. Validate your assessment approaches
5. Go beyond evaluation: matchmaking

CHAPTER 9

Career Advancement
That Works for All

In the spring of 2021, Amazon's senior vice president of People eXperience and Technology, Beth Galetti, announced that the company would "inspect any statistically significant demographic differences in Q1 2021 performance ratings . . . to identify root causes and, as necessary, implement action plans." Potential gender or race gaps in performance appraisals are not a challenge specific to Amazon, nor a new problem. They are a well-documented fact. In the United States, employees of color have been found to receive lower ratings than their white counterparts, and in many countries, female employees have been found to be rated more negatively than men, particularly when their "potential" for career advancement was considered. In our research with a multinational financial services firm headquartered in the United States, gender and race dynamics colluded, leaving women of color with the lowest performance ratings of all.

Performance reviews play a huge role in determining promotions. They are also related to compensation and retention, which means making them fair is core to closing the gender gap in career advancement. More generally, we should just make them better. For example, performance assessments of employees of similar ability can vary widely depending on their manager. Sometimes all that matters is how lenient one's manager is. In one service sector firm, otherwise comparable employees who were supervised by generous, generally high-rating managers earned about 10 percent more per year than employees assessed by harsh, generally low-rating managers. In addition, when using performance appraisals to assess an employee's potential for a more senior role, managers often rely on the wrong indicators. A great salesperson does not automatically make for a great supervisor.

Evaluation bias is widespread. For example, male students in France and the Netherlands did not like being taught by female professors as much as they enjoyed being taught by male professors. Even though their learning, as measured by final test scores, did not depend on the gender of their professor, they evaluated female faculty, particularly the more junior ones, more harshly than male instructors. Perhaps female faculty taught differently, explained less intuitively, or differed in other ways that made their teaching less appealing to men? An online teaching experiment conducted in the US suggests otherwise. In this case, the same instructors interacted with students on discussion boards, in some instances identifying themselves as female and in others as male. When the students perceived the (same) instructor to be a woman, they gave her lower teaching ratings than when they perceived the instructor to be a man.

Most women in positions of authority are subject to these dynamics. This is not something that only occurs in the classroom. People tend to respond differently to female leaders, experts, and advisors than to their male counterparts. Backlash against women in positions of authority has been documented for leaders in business, politics, education, health, the military, civil society, and—well—everywhere. Sadly, people tend not to like confident, competent, assertive, and self-promoting women (for short, "agentic" women), and instead prefer women who conform to our stereotypes of what a "good" woman does and looks like: she cares and comforts, supports and nurtures, displaying what social scientists describe as "communal attributes."

To be clear, male nurses also experience backlash as they do not conform to the norm. What is unique to women is that they are punished across domains when they climb up the career ladder. Much like nursing is perceived to be a female domain, leadership is perceived to be a male domain—even more so in male-dominated industries such as finance, tech, and construction or male-dominated disciplines such as economics, physics, and mathematics.

Gendered notions of leadership aptitude, drive, vision, and other highly subjective elements feed into our performance appraisals. All of us should follow in the footsteps of Amazon and take a close look at our data to investigate whether bias could have crept into our performance assessments. Everyone who has ever been tasked with evaluating someone knows how hard this is. Impossible, really. An evaluator needs to first be aware of all components of the work performed and then make correct attributions; that is, give equal credit (or blame) for equal performance (or lack thereof).

Sociologist Shelley Correll and colleagues show that both conditions are easily violated. We do not see equally, nor do we attribute equally. Analyzing the language used by managers at a technology company when describing employees' performance and potential in their annual performance reviews, the research team found that implicit beliefs about gender influenced how managers made sense of what they saw and how they interpreted it. While female and male employees' general performance and technical and business-related skills were viewed similarly by their managers, significant differences emerged in more subjective categories such as communication style. Women were twice as likely to be described as having a communication style that was too aggressive compared to men. They were also perceived as more helpful than men—but unfortunately, helpfulness was not a highly valued behavior.

What managers valued most were people who "took charge" and were seen to be "geniuses" and "visionaries." These leaders were believed to truly make a difference. And they were rewarded for it, or so one would think, as the data analysis revealed that male leaders who were praised for these attributes received the top ratings. However, their female counterparts with the same attributes did not. In contrast, while female and male employees were equally likely to be seen as "needing technical skills or improvement to move forward," this verdict lowered women's ratings more than men's.

Gender differences in our assignment of credit and blame for equal behavior are ubiquitous. In economics, female researchers received less credit when they collaborated with men on a research project. Reviewers believed that the men had contributed more to the success of a study than their female collaborators. This attribution bias substantially decreased these female academics' likelihood of getting tenure, the most important career milestone in an academic's life, similar to making partner in a law or consulting firm (only in academia, tenure typically is for life).

In another male-dominated field—the surgical profession—female surgeons have been found to receive less credit for good and more blame for bad outcomes. Based on US Medicare data, physicians referred significantly more patients to male than to female surgeons after a successful surgery and significantly fewer patients to female than to male surgeons after an unsuccessful one. Joan Williams, legal scholar and founder of Bias Interrupters, aptly refers to this as the "prove-it-again" bias, where the mistakes of counter-stereotypical individuals loom larger as they confirm people's (negative) stereotypes. Only when they outperform, or prove their worth again and again, do they start to be viewed as equal.

Gender punishment gaps may cost women dearly. One study found that female financial advisors were 20 percent more likely to lose their job and 30 percent less likely to find a new one following an incident of misconduct than similar male advisors. The data even suggests that the misconduct women engaged in was less costly to the firm and women were less likely to reoffend. A similar pattern also applied to men of color, who, like women, were subject to harsher penalties. As it turns out, the gender punishment gap was smaller when the share of female managers was larger, and the race gap decreased with a larger share of managers of color. This goes well beyond the financial services sector. Gender punishment gaps have been documented for a wide set of American companies in the S&P 500, S&P MidCap 400, and S&P SmallCap 600. Following negative firm performance, gender gaps in involuntary turnover and pay decreases are still common.

Bias by managers, which we refer to as "bias from above," is complemented by "bias from below." In Ethiopia, employees were less likely to follow identical guidance when it came from female compared to male managers. The consequence was that employees led by women performed worse. In Malawi, farmers were less likely to adopt a new agricultural technology when instructed by female experts; they ended up with lower farm yields. And in India, people were less likely to adhere to a female leader's advice regarding contributions to a public good. In the US, temporary workers disliked being criticized by a female manager more than when the same criticism came from a male superior, leading to a 70 percent larger drop in job satisfaction and a doubling of the fraction of people indicating that they would not want to work for the firm again in the future.

One thing seems to be clear: Humans do not like to be told what to do by women because we associate leadership with men. Even when we accept women as leaders, we tend to have gendered expectations of them. The employees in Ethiopia did not think that female managers were as knowledgeable and the temporary workers in the US did not expect female managers to be as critical as male managers. Our default assumption in countries as different as Ethiopia, France, India, Malawi, the Netherlands, and the United States is that men are competent and therefore entitled to offer guidance and feedback, including criticism. And while the gender gaps in assumed competence are frustrating enough, to make matters worse, we also expect women to simply be nicer.

Research on bias—and in some cases, outright discrimination—from below has garnered increased attention in recent years. If employees are less likely to listen to their female bosses, it is much harder for women to be effective leaders. This could lead to a vicious cycle where women who anticipate discrimination from below are less willing to volunteer or compete for leadership roles and where managers, expressing bias from above, are less likely to select them. This pattern is possible even if women are equally as competent and ambitious as men: It is not gender differences in confidence but rather expectations of gendered treatment that hold women back.

Sadly, this cycle begins early and is difficult to disrupt when an organization starts from a low base rate. One of the largest manufacturing firms in Europe, with more than 200,000 employees, had to learn this the hard way. With only 9 percent of all female employees serving in leadership positions, its junior women did not see a pathway to managerial roles for themselves. They were not interested in being considered for promotion to team leader. Such "broken rungs" on career ladders are commonplace and have been identified as one of the key reasons women are underrepresented in senior management in the annual *Women in the Workplace* reports. Based on the 2023 report, women of color experienced the biggest drop between entry-level positions and the C-suite: while women and men of color each represented about an equal share of entry-level positions, that share dropped only a couple of percentage points for men of color but threefold for women of color. Black and Hispanic women were most severely affected. The gender gap in promotions from entry level to manager was 9 percentage points for white women and 27 percentage points for women of color in North American firms. In the European manufacturer, men were a staggering 90 percent more likely to apply to team leadership positions.

We cannot gloss over the race gap in promotions among junior women in the United States. Analyzing the career prospects of 9,000 entry-level professional hires in a professional services firm between 2014 and 2020, behavioral scientist Elizabeth Linos and collaborators took a closer look at Black and white women's experiences. They found that Black women were less likely to be promoted than white women and less likely to still work in the firm after two years. The gap in promotions and turnover was particularly pronounced when Black women worked in teams with larger shares of white coworkers.

The data did not offer a clear answer as to why the racial composition of the team played such a huge role. It showed, however, that Black women's lower promotion rates were associated with fewer billable hours in teams with higher shares of white coworkers, suggesting that firms have to become more intentional about how they staff their teams. We have known at least since the work of sociologist Rosabeth Moss Kanter in the 1970s that relative numbers matter on teams. Members of heavily underrepresented groups are more likely to be tokenized and Black women are doubly disadvantaged due to their gender and race ("double jeopardy"). On more balanced teams, stereotypes are less salient, and people of different backgrounds are more likely to flourish.

Without intentional design, we should not be surprised to see a gender gap in middle management: it is no fun to be in this sandwich position. The asymmetry with which credit and blame are assigned makes a comparison of the benefits and costs of pursuing career opportunities rather unattractive for many women, and the additional race dynamics on teams make matters even worse. To make work fair, we must ensure that the cost-benefit ratio for all women who want to climb up the career ladder is on par with that for their male colleagues. This chapter offers guidance on how to redesign performance evaluation and promotion processes to assess and reward performance more accurately.

Mitigate Against Bias in Performance Ratings

Ratings are omnipresent. We rate our Uber and Lyft drivers, restaurants, hotel and Airbnb accommodations, sellers on Amazon, books, movies, and user experiences on platforms. We rate at airports, in supermarkets, online, and offline. Five-star rating scales are popular, and so are binary choices: thumbs up or down. We tend to be influenced by ratings independent of the effort that went into them or the trustworthiness of the raters. And we certainly tend to be oblivious to how the design of the rating system might impact our assessments. For example, according to sociologists Lauren Rivera and András Tilcsik, a 10-point rating scale is worse for women than a 6-point scale, especially in male-dominated fields.

Here is why: A rating of 10 conjures up notions of perfection in a way that a rating of 6 does not. As we discussed, women tend to be held to higher standards, particularly in male-dominated fields. For a woman to earn a 10, she must "hit it out of the park," to use a (male-typed) baseball idiom, and be truly extraordinary. Indeed, the researchers found that men were about 50 percent more likely to earn a 10 than women—a gender gap that almost magically vanished when the employer decided to switch from a 10-point to a 6-point scale. Women and men were almost exactly as likely to earn a 6.

People differed in their expectations of what a "perfect 6" looked like as compared to a "perfect 10." The likelihood that an evaluator would use superlative language to describe the highest-rated employees was almost twice as high when the 10-point scale was employed. Put differently, a 6 on a 6-point scale corresponded to an impressive performance; a 10 on a 10-point scale was out-of-this-world genius. Therefore, as long as a rating of 10 is associated with perfection, women won't win, or as Lauren Rivera put it: "The number ten carries this cultural connotation of perfection. . . . Research shows that, due to gender stereotypes of competence, we just don't think women are perfect. We are more likely to scrutinize women and their performance."

The researchers did not find such scale effects in more gender-balanced or female-dominated fields. It is easier for us to imagine that a female psychologist could be brilliant than that female scientists like Marie Curie (1903), Maria Goeppert Mayer (1963), Donna Strickland (2018), Andrea Ghez (2020), or Anne L'Huillier (2023) could win the Nobel Prize in Physics. And while we cannot read a trend into a sample of five (out of 225 laureates who have been awarded the Nobel Prize in Physics between 1901 and 2023), it is encouraging that in contrast to the earlier recipients, Ghez and L'Huillier did not have to wait a half century to be awarded the prize. Perhaps gender stereotypes based on field, industry, or sector are weakening, or maybe the process changes Iris suggested to the Nobel Prize Foundation in 2018 are also helping. When numbers change, beliefs about what the world does and should look like will follow.

In the meantime, you may want to consider revisiting your performance appraisal scales. Generally, you should be wary of any rating scale. They just invite comparisons with stereotypes, or more generally, what we are used to. A normally lit room will seem brighter to people who mostly work underground and warmer to those who mostly work in relatively colder spaces. And a loud female voice might be perceived as aggressive while the same loudness in a man would not.

To illustrate the phenomenon known in psychology as "shifting standards," psychologist Robert Livingston, author of the important book on racial bias *The Conversation*, and Iris used to conduct a little experiment in their executive education programs. They asked participants to guess, on a scale of 1 to 10, how tall Robert and Iris were, with 10 meaning very tall and 1 very short. People typically assigned Robert a 7 and Iris an 8 or a 9. It turns out they are the same height: 5'9" or 1.74 m tall. But people did not give them identical "credit" for their height. Implicitly, people compared Robert to the average man and Iris to the average woman. And while the specific averages vary across countries, the average man tends to be taller than the average woman around the world. In contrast, when asked to estimate their height in feet or meters, people did much better and the gender gap disappeared.

Unfortunately, replacing performance ratings with numeric measures is rarely possible. Very few employees are evaluated based on the number of snow shovels produced or vacuum cleaners sold. But while only a second-best solution, you still can mitigate against rating bias. The financial services company we mentioned at the start of this chapter is using calibration meetings for this purpose. Manager ratings are scrutinized for potential inconsistencies, idiosyncrasies, and bias. Some managers might overall be harsher evaluators than others, disadvantaging members of their teams. Others might value aspects of employee behavior—say, excessive risk-taking—that are not aligned with firm preferences. And yet others might evaluate Asian, Black, or Hispanic employees differently than white employees, or lower female employees' performance ratings more than those of their male counterparts when they need additional support. A heat map can identify which issues arise where. Maybe procurement is struggling with different inconsistencies than sales, requiring different kinds of interventions. Data analysis once again allows firms to correctly diagnose the problem and prescribe the medicine that is really needed. No matter the exact challenge, performance-reward and performance-punishment bias can be addressed.

Use More and More Accurate Performance Data

You may now worry that performance metrics themselves could be biased—and you are right to be concerned. Here are some instances where men have been found to outperform women based on the commonly used performance metrics in the respective professions: male lawyers billing more hours to clients; male real estate agents listing more homes; male physicians seeing more patients; and male academics writing more papers. Accordingly, they should get higher performance ratings, be more likely to be promoted, and receive more pay (which, of course, they do). But consider this: female law-yers have been found to commit fewer ethical violations; female real estate agents to focus on fewer but higher-priced homes; female physicians' patients to be less likely to die or be readmitted to the hospital; and female researchers to write more clearly. The point here is not to argue that these gender differences in outcomes always apply, but rather to raise the possibility that depending on the met-rics we use, we may favor one gender over another.

In 2016, forty years after it was first introduced, multi-industry conglomerate GE replaced its legendary Employee Management System. The company, which under former chairman and CEO Jack Welch's leadership was well-known for its hard-charging an-nual performance appraisal process, decided to basically do away with it and instead focus on more frequent check-ins enabled by an app. Managers could now communicate with their teams more often, offer spontaneous feedback, and develop a sense of shared purpose and accountability. As GE executives Leonardo Baldassarre and Brian Finken described in a *Harvard Business Review* article, the new format enabled managers to "empower and inspire" rather than "command and control." The year-end conversations still took place but benefited from more granular data accumulated over the year that led to a better assessment of an employee's contributions and achievements.

GE's focus on more frequent touchpoints, or "real-time performance development," could be part of a trend. IBM also replaced its annual performance reviews with quarterly check-ins. Its former chief human resources officer, Diane Gherson, had realized that for goals to work in a fast-paced environment, they needed to be constantly reviewed and adjusted. Managers at Google also meet with their employees once per month to discuss performance, development, and any other issues that may arise. In addition, Googlers not only receive feedback from their managers but also from their peers and direct reports, including—importantly—regarding their contributions to specific projects.

Open-ended feedback forms that invite generic commentary on how an employee is doing are the home of bias because the ambiguity involved invites sense-making and filling in the blanks. Social scientist Paola Cecchi-Dimeglio discovered this in a professional services firm where women received less "negative personality-based criticism" with more specific feedback prompts. So here is another trend: more data—more frequent, from more people, and more specific—improves our judgments.

So, "more" can be synonymous with "better" in the case of performance data, particularly if the data is rather specific. Few firms are transparent about the specific set of performance criteria or key performance indicators they focus on, but most use both outcome measures (e.g., business results or customer satisfaction) and behavioral metrics, or how the employee achieved the results (e.g., collaboration or risk management). The more specific and externally verifiable your metrics are, the more often you collect them, and the larger the set of people providing input on them, the more accurate we expect your final judgment to be. In contrast, in-group bias and stereotypes might impact your judgment in more subjective assessments. There is also a plethora of other cognitive biases that might cloud your judgment, such as recency bias, where you overweight what happened more recently, and hindsight bias, where you believe you knew the outcome all along. And of course, when you are the only one to make an assessment, there is also sheer idiosyncrasy, perhaps based on your mood or the time of day. $N=1$ rarely is the optimal sample size.

As you might have noticed, we've avoided using the word "objective," as we fear there are few, if any, truly objective performance criteria. But we can make our subjective assessments more accurate if we ask all our evaluators to explain them, including by providing concrete supporting evidence. For example, why exactly did we think a team member needed more experience before being considered for promotion and how did the lack of experience manifest itself? Or how did we come up with a "needs improvement" rating on vision? What evidence do we have to support this assessment? Such accountability can help. It has been shown to decrease bias in work assessments, particularly when evaluators knew that they would be held publicly accountable and felt like the audience cared about accuracy and had the right to probe.

Perhaps the once-a-year performance appraisals by one's boss are not here to stay. Many companies, in addition to GE, have already made the move away from this approach, including Accenture, Adobe, Deloitte, Gap, Medtronic, and Microsoft. More frequent input from more people on more observable criteria is the future. However, due to its inherently subjective nature, we cannot completely program bias out of our assessment processes. So, how else can we help managers do better?

Conduct Timely Bias Awareness Interventions

When presenting our research on performance management, the first or second question we typically get asked is: "What about the gender or race of the evaluator?" As discussed earlier, this is often less important than people think. Most stereotypes are shared, independent of our own characteristics. As affinity would predict, we once in a while do find that evaluators preferentially treat people who share their demographic characteristics—but given that in-group preferences and stereotypes sometimes contradict each other, the evidence is complex. In some cases, female evaluators have been found to assess other women more leniently and in others more harshly. One possible reason for this appears to be the degree to which female evaluators see other women as competitors rather than cooperators. A woman might prefer a female friend at work but if she feels that the slots for women are scarce, she might appreciate a female superior she can learn from more than a female peer she has to compete with.

One possible avenue for understanding differences across managers is their own experience with performance evaluations. Managers who had bad experiences with performance appraisals evaluated employees differently than those who were happy with how their own performance had been evaluated—which takes us right back to people's identities. In a study by sociologists Emilio Castilla and Aruna Ranganathan, female managers and managers of color, based on their own more negative experiences as employees, evaluated merit much more narrowly than their white male counterparts, who described more positive appraisal experiences. Narrowness was not necessarily superior to the more diffuse approach adopted by white male managers, although it meant focusing on work actions and outcomes more quantitatively. However, it missed the broader perspective of employees' contributions to teams and the work environment. While we can see why female managers might shy away from more subjective criteria given our earlier discussion, such cross-manager differences raise even more red flags about idiosyncrasies not based on an employees' performance. What to do?

We can draw inspiration from seat belt usage, which has thankfully become a norm in many countries. It helps when drivers are reminded that they should wear seat belts, and immediacy is key: when drivers were reminded to buckle up several minutes before they jumped in the car, the intervention lost much of its effectiveness. Intrigued, one law firm we worked with introduced fairness reminders immediately before its promotion committee launched into its annual two-day performance review and promotion retreat. The firm reminded committee members, all senior partners, of how our own experiences and stereotypical assessments can cloud our judgments. Joan Williams tried a similar approach with another firm, finding that a bias workshop led to all employees— women, men, people of color, and white employees—receiving more useful feedback. Better feedback helps everyone, especially those of us who are prone to receive inflated reviews or "white lies": women.

One of the best studies examining the timeliness question found that when teachers in Italy were informed of their unconscious biases (measured earlier in an Implicit Association Test) against immigrant students immediately before grading math exams, increased awareness helped the teachers grade more accurately and overcome their biases. Inspired, we tried a similar approach at Ericsson, the multinational telecommunications and engineering company. In two field experiments, we found that reminding managers of the importance of diversity right when they were about to hire a new employee or recommend a team member for promotion increased the likelihood that they selected members of underrepresented groups.

We do not know whether such awareness interventions have any long-term impacts—likely not—but Ericsson, the Italian schools, and the law firm we worked with only needed the impact to last for a short while. Reminders work because they help focus our attention and make top-of-mind things that we might have forgotten or neglected otherwise, such as wearing a seat belt or wishing a friend a happy birthday. In addition, reminders often carry a normative message that we "should" do something, such as remember to turn off the lights when leaving the office. Some firms use meeting invites to remind employees of desired behaviors. For example, you might have been the recipient of a cue in your calendar reminding you to provide feedback to one colleague at the end of each week.

Reminders work, at least when people are inclined to do the right thing. They help close the intention-action gap. In the Italian study, being reminded of one's unconscious biases was particularly effective for those teachers who were not consciously biased against immigrants, according to a survey. In theory, they wanted to treat immigrant and Italian children equally; in practice, they fell short because of their unconscious biases, and the reminder helped them follow through on their virtuous intentions. Similarly, Ericsson had a long-standing commitment to fairness and the law firm felt that its partners fell into the category of "do-gooders" who wanted to become "good doers," and the reminder helped them do exactly that when making promotion decisions.

Make Performance Assessment and Promotion Less Risky for the Evaluated

When Google noticed that its female employees were less likely to nominate themselves for promotion, one of its heads of engineering sent out an email to all technical employees explicitly inviting women to nominate themselves. But being invited to a party does not mean that it will be safe to show up, so in addition, Google sent managers this reminder: "I wanted to update everyone on our efforts to encourage women to self-nominate for promotion. . . . Any Googler who is ready for promotion should feel encouraged to self-nominate and managers play an important role in ensuring that they feel empowered to do so. . . ." The explicit invitation, coupled with the knowledge that their managers had their backs, lowered the risk of self-promotion and encouraged women to put themselves forward.

Pushing this line of thought one step further, organizations may consider presenting the question differently altogether. Instead of asking employees whether they want to opt in and be considered for promotion, they could tell them that employees with certain qualifications are automatically assumed to be ready for promotion unless they indicate otherwise and literally opt out of the promotion process. An opt-out frame is an even stronger signal that a person is not only invited but, in fact, assumed to join in, decreasing the risk for women even further. Early results suggest that gender gaps in competitive environments such as promotion settings can be attenuated when women are automatically included in the competition.

Economist Katherine Baldiga Coffman investigated the circumstances under which people are willing to put themselves forward. Her work suggests that Google was right to focus on making self-nominations less risky. To examine the relevance of the potential cost involved when asserting oneself, she turned to test-taking. In many multiple-choice tests, people are rewarded with points for correct answers and penalized with point deductions for wrong answers. In fact, until 2015, millions of American students taking one of the most important tests, the SAT, which hugely influenced which college a person would be admitted to, gained a point for correct answers and lost a quarter of a point for wrong answers on the multiple-choice part of the test. Thus, volunteering an answer was risky. Not as risky as applying for a promotion—but with the same outcome: women were less likely than men to take a chance and, when in doubt, preferred leaving the answer box blank and skipping the question (which yielded zero points).

Thankfully, in 2014, the College Board, which administers the SAT, decided to remove penalties for wrong answers on the SAT I test, something Coffman's research had shown to be promising. In laboratory experiments, she was able to close the gender gap in volunteering answers when it was costless to do so. After all, the tests were not designed to penalize those less willing or able to take risk but instead to gauge students' knowledge. In 2015, the policy change was adopted in Chile for its college entrance examination (Prueba de Selección Universitaria), with much success: removing penalties from wrong answers dramatically decreased the gender gap in skipped questions as well as in performance, especially among the best performers.

Unfortunately, we cannot just set the potential risk involved in going after career opportunities to zero, and some attempts at lowering the risk have not worked out as imagined. When more standardized evaluation practices started to be introduced in the 1970s, they were seen as a countermeasure against managerial discretion, arbitrariness, and other non-performance-related considerations that affect promotions and pay. Many companies started to give employees voice by asking them to first self-evaluate and share their self-evaluations with their managers before the latter made up their minds. This practice is still common today. However, if employees fear that performance-attribution bias impacts how their manager reads and interprets their self-assessments, they may hold back. Some may prefer skipping instead of answering.

This might be a wise response. Evaluators often penalize women for being assertive in what they ask for, and female evaluators are no better than their male counterparts. A strategy meant to give employees an opportunity to weigh in on their performance appraisals is not equally accessible to all and may exacerbate gender differences that have nothing to do with performance. So, if playing it right is not possible, should we just stop playing?

This is what the financial services firm we worked with decided to do. In order to make evaluations fair, it no longer shares employee self-evaluations with managers before the managers write their evaluations. In an unusual turn of events, the firm benefited from a technical glitch in its system that did not allow it to follow its standard practice in 2016 and share self-assessments with managers before they made up their minds. This was not a perfect experiment—but close enough for us to take a good look at their performance data before, during, and after the glitch year, and for the firm to learn from it. In a typical nonglitch year, women, and particularly women of color, gave themselves lower ratings, and women of color ended up with the lowest final ratings after managers had weighed in. The glitch year broke this pattern for newly hired employees (to exclude the potential influence of previous year's ratings): women of color were evaluated on par with white male and female employees when self-ratings were not available.

Gender gaps in self-ratings are not uncommon. Reflektive, a company providing employers a software platform to manage their performance evaluation processes, gave economist Lisa Abraham access to the performance data of 170 of its customer companies that represented 15 different industries. While there unfortunately was no data available on race, her analysis confirmed our finding that female employees assessed themselves more harshly than men, and managers had self-assessments available before they chose a rating in 90 percent of cases. It seems our financial services firm was right when it stopped sharing self-assessments. IBM came to the same conclusion based on outreach to its 380,000 employees in 170 countries. It learned that a majority of employees did not think that self-assessments were help-ful, so the company did away with them. By decreasing the gendered risk involved in career advancement, IBM, along with our financial services company and Google, has moved in the right direction—but more can be done. We can also work at equalizing the expected benefits of climbing up the career ladder.

Allocate and Reward Opportunities Fairly

Equalizing the benefits of career progression means increasing the likelihood and the rewards of such advancement for women. At a minimum, we need to make pay equity a reality and overcome performance-reward bias where women and people of color receive lower pay increases for identical performance scores. In addition, we need to make sure positions with higher pay are accessible to women.

Some companies are making progress. Take 1980 as a baseline. There was not a single woman occupying one of the ten highest-ranking roles in a Fortune 100 company. Forty years later, in 2021, 27 percent of these top leadership positions were held by women. The increase was by no means linear but fluctuations are to be expected given the small number of top leaders per company. What is less encouraging is that women rarely won the biggest prizes: in 2021, just 6 percent of CEOs, presidents, and COOs were women. Women tended to be in support functions, which typically meant leading HR, finance, or legal.

For women, moving up often means moving across. A larger share of women than men came to their leadership roles from the outside, something possibly related to women being more concentrated in functional roles where skills are more transferable. After all, HR, ac-counting, and legal standards are pretty comparable across industries. The phenomenon is also due to companies not focusing enough on succession planning such that there are smaller shares of women, and even tinier fractions of women of color, in upper middle management.

As we have mentioned, executive search firms may help by casting the net widely and turning passive candidates into active ones. This does not mean that we can take our eye off the ball when it comes to traditional feeder roles: it tends to be operational and general management roles, ideally with profit and loss responsibility, that fast-track people into the highest tiers.

One possible reason why women did not end up in these high-power, highly paid jobs and instead wound up in support functions is that providing support is widely associated with women. It goes way beyond functional roles. A research team has coined it "non-promotable work": office tasks that need to get done and are valuable to the organization but are not typically factored in as part of performance appraisals and promotion decisions. Taking meeting notes, hosting the speaker series, and overseeing the summer internship program are all helpful for the organization as a whole but not required of any particular individual—nor rewarded for advancement. Evidence from one consulting firm suggests that compared to their male colleagues, women spent around 200 hours more a year, on average, on such dead-end work. Assuming an eight-hour workday, that is about 25 days, or more than a month's worth of work. To cope, the academics who introduced the term "non-promotable"—Linda Babcock, Brenda Peyser, Lise Vesterlund, and Laurie Weingart—formed the No Club, also the title of their subsequent book, to protect themselves from overengaging in this type of office housework.

To make such invisible work count at Harvard Kennedy School, we introduced a workload system whereby faculty earn points for service activities and can be compensated for additional service with, for example, fewer teaching responsibilities. As research is decisive for promotion at Harvard and many other universities, both teaching and service relief matter for a person's productivity. So it is not just about making sure women have access to the "cool roles" that are central to the organization's mission, but also about rewarding and distributing service tasks more fairly.

This is, essentially, a formalized way of turn-taking, something you can introduce in your organization even if you do not formally count or reward contributions to the public good. Students, as we remind ours every year, should apply these insights to their teamwork and make sure promotable and non-promotable tasks are spread evenly. While one study found that in many cases, making room reservations for teams to meet was a woman's job, we cannot think of any reason why our female students would be more adept at this task than their male colleagues. Some have referred to such behaviors as "strategic incompetence," or as one white man describes: "I started to understand some of those behaviors as manipulative, a way of getting others to do work I didn't want to do. When I saw those tendencies in myself, I couldn't unsee them. And I began to see the damage this kind of behavior does to women and people of color—and to the morale, productiveness, and creativity of everyone in a workplace." Parents might take the idea to their next parent-teacher association meeting. Note takers don't have to be women!

A law firm we worked with took these insights to heart. Their data told them that Jamila had been responsible for the summer internship program as well as helping with the onboarding of first-year associates, but had not gotten the same credit as John for bringing in new clients nor benefited from the career support that John had received. Thus the firm introduced a work allocation system where responsibility for non-promotable tasks rotated. It also took a close look at the language managers used to describe the associates they had worked with. Was Jamila more likely to be described using gender-stereotypical communal language that praised her for her support activities and John more likely to be described with agentic descriptors and standout adjectives attesting to his amazingness as a go-getter? Rather than scrutinizing hundreds of pages of feedback by hand, they employed an algorithm similar to the one used to de-bias language in job advertisements. Analytics can also help with performance management.

They did not, however, relegate their judgments to AI. Wouldn't it be tempting to rely on AI-based assessments that can collect and process much more data much faster and more frequently (even continuously with systems monitoring behaviors and outcomes in real time), without being affected by human biases such as order effects and recency bias? Besides, with the data centrally stored, managers could compare across departments and regions, identify potential problems early on, and intervene in a more targeted way. Feedback, too, could be given more frequently and in a more personalized fashion. For some, a leadership development program might be exactly what they need, whereas for others, a skills workshop might be more helpful. Precision (or personalized) medicine, after all, is gaining so much traction because it allows treatment to be optimized based on the particular profile of the patient.

This vision is tempting, but interestingly, not as widespread as one might think. Employers are weighing the benefits of AI against the potential cost of built-in bias. In addition, they also worry about losing human judgment. Machines are not empathetic and cannot take, say, the implications of a personal crisis into account. They don't know about mental health, burnout, or other stress-related symptoms (although some might argue that if we designed the algorithm appropriately, data could be useful in predicting employee well-being). Equally importantly, collecting data from employees at work might feel intrusive (and could potentially be illegal in some jurisdictions) with Big Brother watching us all the time. And finally, neither managers nor employees seem to want to relegate to a machine the power of promotion, or even firing.

This is why Google's then–VP of people analytics, Prasad Setty, shared in 2014 that Google would not rely on a formula to determine its promotions. The people analytics team had the model ready to go and had already tested it—but nobody liked it. "They didn't want to hide behind a black box," Setty said. "They wanted to own the decisions. They didn't want to use a model to do so." If employees at a company like Google who live and breathe data are skeptical, this should give us pause.

The deeper point, though, is that data-driven design does not equal algorithms, and even when we seek help in big data, it does not have to mean giving up on human decision-making. Machines can keep track of KPIs, generate metrics, analyze data, and suggest possible adjustments. They should not replace people but instead help us make better decisions.

* * *

We often use the EAST framework to summarize what more effective performance appraisal processes might look like. The *E* in *EAST* stands for making things easy, the *A* for attractive, the *S* for social, and the *T* for timely:

- **Easy:** Make a performance review plan at the beginning of the year, creating habits and holding time on evaluators' calendars (ideally, a recurring time slot every week, month, or quarter). Use a predesigned questionnaire where evaluators can choose among predetermined feedback options, not an open-ended survey. Ask evaluators to respond to specific, observable criteria (outcomes and behaviors).

- **Attractive:** Hold evaluators accountable by requiring them to provide specific evidence for their assessments. Employ a comply-or-explain approach if evaluators do not respond in time, and send reminders.

- **Social:** Crowdsource assessments by including feedback from supervisors, peers, direct reports, and clients. Collect feedback on the performance appraisal process itself from employees, and share data on how the process is working (such as the share of managers completing their evaluations on time) to create and reinforce social norms.

- **Timely:** Give and ask for frequent feedback. For example, share suggestions right after a meeting where a colleague delivered a presentation. For formal evaluations, collect evidence on performance as it happens. Remind managers of potential pitfalls and desired behaviors immediately before they make formal assessments.

If this reminds you of our discussion of job candidate evaluations, it is not a coincidence. Standardized processes that benefit from the input of a diverse set of people generally help us make better decisions and using the EAST framework makes it more likely that we will actually follow through on our virtuous intentions. Evaluating people is hard, and it is almost impossible to prevent all biases from factoring in. But we can make progress toward leveling the playing field by designing our appraisal processes smartly and making career opportunities equally available to women and men.

---

1. Mitigate against bias in performance ratings
2. Use more and more accurate performance data
3. Conduct timely bias awareness interventions
4. Make performance assessment and promotion less risky for the evaluated
5. Allocate and reward opportunities fairly

PART III

MAKE IT NORMAL: EMBEDDING FAIRNESS

CHAPTER 10

Work Arrangements to Level the Playing Field

A few years ago, a midsize global consulting firm based in the United States wanted to help more women advance into its top ranks, where men made up 90 percent of partners. Over the course of a year, sociology and organizational behavior scholars Irene Padavic, Robin Ely, and Erin Reid supported the firm in uncovering potential root causes and finding solutions to the gender disparity. Their findings and the resulting recommendations were so disconcerting to the firm that the CEO ultimately terminated the project.

What could they possibly have found that was so shocking?

The researchers discovered that women weren't the problem—the firm's culture of overwork was. Instead of women leaving at higher rates than men, as the firm thought was the case, turnover was equivalent for both groups. Instead of conflict between work and life being something only women struggled with, as the leaders surmised, all employees were distressed by the demands for extremely long hours and constant availability—though they disproportionately impacted women's advancement as women were more likely to avail themselves of firm-provided accommodations such as reduced hours, leaves of absence, and internal rather than client-facing projects. When women did so, their careers stalled. Faced with this evidence, the researchers recommended fixing the system of long work hours instead of the women. In their words: "These clearly well-intentioned, otherwise empirically minded professionals rejected out of hand the data and analysis they had requested, maintaining their belief that work-family conflict was primarily a women's problem, that it explained women's lack of success, and that any solution must therefore target women."

Such thinking is pervasive. In a study of more than 6,500 Harvard Business School alumni/ae, a large majority of women and men cited women prioritizing family over work as their top explanation for women's lagging career advancement. Yet men have children too, and have been shown to suffer from work-family conflict—but they pay a much lower price in terms of career outcomes. Somehow the extremely long hours required by high-level jobs are incompatible with women's, but not men's, nonwork lives.

The way out of work-life conflict is not to make women compatible with work—as the consulting firm tried to do—but the reverse. We need to finally embrace the fact that we humans are not "ideal workers" with zero nonwork responsibilities (or someone else on hand to take care of those responsibilities). The COVID-19 pandemic made this more visible than ever. We need and deserve fulfilling work lives *and* fulfilling personal lives, and that requires flexibility. While the idea of flexible work is not new, as we know, design matters. And the way workplace flexibility has traditionally been designed has exacted a high cost from those seeking it—primarily women—in terms of pay, career advancement, and satisfaction.

For career-minded college graduates, the problem is "greedy work," as laid out by labor economist and economic historian Claudia Goldin in her formative book *Career and Family: Women's Century-Long Journey Toward Equity*. Goldin, who won the 2023 Nobel Prize in Economics for her research on gender and work, explains that we have shifted from paying for output in the early twentieth century to now paying for time. Greedy jobs—consulting, law, medicine, tech, finance, and numerous others—expect people to be available for work at all times and are organized so that it is very difficult for one colleague to substitute for another.

This results in people who are willing to work, say, 80 hours a week earning more than twice what someone working 40 hours a week earns. There is a disproportionate reward for working extremely long hours, which are incompatible with many nonwork pursuits. For couples with caregiving responsibilities, greedy work creates a financial incentive for one person (in heterosexual couples, often a man) to go all-in on their career while the other (often a woman) takes the lead on caregiving and works fewer hours. At the consulting firm where cultural expectations included 24/7 availability and constant overwork, this is exactly what happened to women: many of them opted for more flexible work arrangements and paid a high price for this flexibility in terms of lower pay and stymied career progression.

In low-paid frontline jobs, the problem is also related to time, namely, schedule instability. Approximately 17 percent of American employees work in the retail and food service sectors, where schedules can vary unpredictably from day to day and week to week, making it impossible to plan life outside work. Such schedules are associated with many negative consequences for hourly workers in shift-based jobs, including increased work-life conflict, diminished mental health, missed work, and significant material hardship. Worse, unstable schedules can lead to insufficient hours and economic insecurity, making it difficult for employees to scrape together the income needed to support themselves and their families. More generally, low-income earners are the ones hardest hit by the lack of workplace flexibility because their jobs often cannot be done remotely; they are less likely to have access to paid leave for illness or caregiving; and they are more likely to be single parents.

Although these problems are different in many important ways, control over one's time looms large for all employees. While this chapter won't be able to do full justice to the dire working conditions many low-income earners face in the United States and around the world, we recommend the Shift Project, which sheds much-needed light on the importance of work schedule predictability for hourly service workers, as an excellent resource.

When it comes to time management for college-educated employees, a key factor for fair working conditions is something you might not have thought about before: whether work is designed such that employees can serve as substitutes for each other. What happened in pharmacies in the United States over the last half century is an illustrative example. In 1970, 70 percent of pharmacists were owners or employees of independent mom-and-pop pharmacies, and more than 90 percent were men. Female pharmacists made only 67 cents to a male pharmacist's dollar. But the world gradually changed. The industry became more corporate such that today, nearly 90 percent of pharmacists are employees of hospitals or large pharmacy chains (like CVS and Walgreens). Drugs became more standardized and the IT systems used to manage prescriptions more sophisticated. These changes made it easier for pharmacists to substitute for each other. If one person is traveling, sick, or has care responsibilities at home, a coworker can seamlessly step in and get the work done. As a result, there is no discernible flexibility penalty in pharmacy. A pharmacist working 60 hours a week gets paid twice what a colleague working 30 hours a week makes, and long, irregular hours are generally not necessary. Female pharmacists take fewer career breaks compared to women working in finance and law, and around one-third of them work part-time. The gender pay gap has virtually closed, and women now make up the majority of pharmacists.

In pharmacy, this evolution happened organically as a result of broader marketplace changes. But it shows that we *can* redesign our workplaces to be more egalitarian and accessible if we want to. Long, inflexible hours do not have to be a given if employees can easily take over for each other with the aid of smart systems, processes, and technology. Since it worked in pharmacy, the question is why it could not also work in other professions, including law, finance, consulting and others, which today are very much like pharmacy was nearly sixty years ago.

Embracing flexibility is a game-changing opportunity to make work fair and unleash the talents of scores of employees—especially women—whose contributions have previously been limited due to how work has been structured. But reaping the full rewards of this opportunity requires us to go beyond one-off policy changes and reconceptualize work on a more fundamental level, moving from a focus on face-to-face surveillance to a focus on output and measurable results. Making work more flexible can help liberate us from our fixation on *where* people work and for *how long*, and instead focus on what they actually *do*. It is not easy, but it is possible.

WATT Global Media, an Illinois-based marketing firm serving the global agrifood and pet food industries, has done it. In the aftermath of the 2008 financial crisis, the company shifted to a digital-forward strategy and moved to a results-only work environment where employees are evaluated based on performance, not presence. As long as people are accomplishing defined objectives, they are free to work whenever, wherever, and however they choose. As the company states on its website: "Work isn't a place you go, it's something you do." A critical enabler of this culture change was an initial push of training. In workshops, people learned how to turn casual requests ("Could you look into this for me?") into structured negotiations with clear timelines and expectations; how to fend off, and ultimately eliminate, passive-aggressive comments about whether and when they were working; and how not to feel weird running personal errands on a weekday.

Leveling the playing field at work is one side of the coin whose other side is leveling the playing field at home. Claudia Goldin explains for the United States: "We've come to a point in which women's employment is extremely high, and yet there are inequalities. And those inequalities are inequalities that occur within households." Women around the globe still do the majority of unpaid work whether they also engage in paid work or not. Organizational flexibility policies play a role because they can influence our preferences around how to structure our personal lives, as social policy scholar Marc Grau Grau and organizational behavior scholar Hannah Riley Bowles explain: "The workplace is the environment where cultural and organizational norms and prejudices most clearly limit or enhance fathers' childcare and in-home family engagement." Indeed, a study of unmarried and childless Americans aged 18 to 32 found that large majorities of both women and men across education levels preferred an egalitarian relationship structure (where both spouses share work and family tasks equally) provided that they would have access to paid family leave, subsidized childcare, and work-from-home options. But not otherwise.

We strongly support everyone's personal choices about how, where, when, and how much to work, paid or unpaid—and to us, true fairness means that each person can make those decisions unconstrained by organizational policies, societal norms, stereotypes, or systems that push them toward particular choices. Moving flexible work onto a more equal footing with nonflexible work (in terms of pay and career advancement) and tackling the inequities at home (through more equal uptake of leave and more accessible care) will move us in this direction.

In this chapter, we share with you evidence-based ways to level the playing field at work—and, we hope, eventually at home. In many countries, some of these policies are set at the national level and provided to most, if not all, workers. Our focus here is on what organizations can do to either supplement those policies or create a base level of work-life support where they do not exist. These solutions can be useful to you whether you have the power to implement them for a whole organization or your team—and even if your workplace doesn't have these policies yet, in which case we urge you to advocate for their adoption. There has never been a better time: COVID-19 forced us to rethink our norms around how, where, and when work gets done so that everyone—including people with disabilities, those caring for relatives, pet parents, people with long commutes, and those with volunteer duties—can thrive.

Normalize and Support Remote Work

A decade before the COVID-19 pandemic, the world's first randomized controlled trial on remote work—which, for our purposes, means working any portion of time from somewhere other than the office—was conducted in China. Shanghai-based Ctrip, China's largest travel agency, wanted to reduce its office rental costs as well as its annual employee turnover rate of around 50 percent. But many managers worried that working from home would turn into "shirking from home" if employees were liberated from the watchful eyes of their supervisors. The company partnered with economist Nicholas Bloom and colleagues to conduct a nine-month experiment, as part of which Ctrip offered nearly 1,000 workers in its airfare and hotel booking departments the option to work from home four days a week. Managers remained office-based.

The results were prescient. Remote work led to a 13 percent increase in performance, which was driven primarily by taking fewer breaks and sick days and secondarily by being more productive thanks to a quieter and more convenient work environment. Attrition dropped by 50 percent among employees working from home four days a week compared to those working in the office every day. Remote workers also reported higher satisfaction with work.

After the success of the experiment, Ctrip decided to roll out a remote work option to the whole firm while researchers continued to collect data. This second phase revealed that the effects of remote work were even more positive when employees could choose their optimal work arrangements: those who were more successful and productive working from home did so, while those who did their best work in the office (or succumbed to one of the "three great enemies of working from home: the fridge, television, and the bed") stayed there. As a result, performance gains for Ctrip nearly doubled to 22 percent in the second phase.

Like us, you may be impressed with these results. But you may also wonder how they translate into our transformed post-pandemic world. Fortunately, in 2021 and 2022, Ctrip—by then renamed Trip.com after its acquisition of the eponymous company in 2017—conducted another experiment, this time on the effects of hybrid work among 1,612 engineers as well as marketing and finance employees. Participants included both managers and non-managers, nearly all of whom had at least an undergraduate degree. Half had children and two-thirds were men. As before, they were randomized into two groups: one that was allowed to work from home on Wednesdays and Fridays, and one where everyone had to work from the office five days a week.

The results of this six-month experiment add important nuance to our understanding of the benefits and drawbacks of remote work. Having the ability to work from home reduced attrition by 33 percent— especially among women, employees with longer commutes, and those with shorter tenures—and improved employees' self-reported job satisfaction, life satisfaction, and work-life balance. Employees cited flexibility as the most significant benefit, with many shifting when they worked (fewer hours on at-home days and more on in-office days and weekends).

However, there were significant differences between managers and nonmanagers. Nonmanagers were much more likely to actually work from home and to report increased productivity. While non-managers' attrition rates fell, those of managers who were eligible for hybrid work increased slightly compared to their in-office peers. Managing employees remotely is harder, which may be why managers also reported negative impacts on their productivity. Even so, Trip.com ended up rolling out the new remote work policy to the whole company.

Data makes clear that remote work is here to stay. In the United States, the share of days worked from home was 28 percent in June 2023—four times that in 2019. As of 2023, about 30 percent of the total US workforce worked remotely part of the time, while just over 10 percent worked fully remotely and around 60 percent worked fully on-site. Global data paints a similar picture. Full-time workers across 27 countries averaged 1.5 days of remote work per week in 2021–22, though there was significant variation across geographies. Women tend to work remotely slightly more than men, and while all people living with children do so at higher rates, the trend is particularly notable for women with children. In fact, the availability of remote work enabled some mothers of young children who would have otherwise left the labor force to keep working during and after the pandemic.

The biggest determinant of remote work is education. Americans with a high school education or less—the lowest-paid segment of workers that tend to be employed in frontline jobs including retail, travel, cleaning, and food services—worked, on average, 20 percent of all paid workdays from home, whereas those with a graduate degree worked nearly double that (36 percent). A recent analysis of online job ads in the United States confirms that opportunities to work remotely skew toward higher-paid jobs that require more experience, more education, and a full-time commitment.

Employees tend to be more enthusiastic about remote work than employers, naming time saved from commuting and the ability to better balance work and personal life as the greatest benefits. Six in ten employees working fully remotely said they would look for a new job if the ability to work from home was taken away. Across 27 countries, employees value the option to work remotely two or three days a week at an average of 5 percent of pay. As in China, people with longer commutes as well as women and parents of all genders tend to value the remote work option even more highly.

Large-scale remote work is a relatively new phenomenon, but early research suggests that both the upsides and downsides are real.

The question is not whether we should incorporate remote work into our workplaces, but *how* we can structure it to maximize fairness and minimize pitfalls.

One concern is that remote work reduces productivity. Here it is important to distinguish between fully remote and hybrid (some time spent in the office) work arrangements. Based on several studies, the evidence on fully remote work is mixed. Being permanently physically separated from colleagues can make communication, innovation, and creating new connections more difficult. Thus it perhaps is no coincidence that the 10 percent of people working fully remotely are often in administrative roles like IT support, payroll, or benefits administration that can be done independently with limited in-person interaction with others.

With hybrid work, however, the evidence is clearer: productivity either did not change or increased. For example, when US Patent & Trademark Office employees were allowed to work from anywhere four days a week, the number of patents they examined increased by 4.4 percent. And when corporate HR employees of BRAC, the world's largest nongovernmental organization with headquarters in Bangladesh, were randomized to work a varying number of days from home for nine weeks, those who worked in the office between a quarter and half of the time did—and felt—best.

To improve communication and knowledge-sharing in a hybrid environment, leveraging asynchronous communication technologies (such as shared documents, messaging channels, or company-specific internal portals) is essential. For example, online team "huddles" to prepare for meetings or debrief them afterward can mimic the benefits of in-person hallway conversations. At fully remote software company GitLab, employees collectively maintain a working handbook that explains in detail how work gets done. Before meetings, organizers highlight relevant sections so that attendees can get on the same page and share questions and ideas; after meetings, the handbook is updated with new decisions. GitLab's approach is a promising model for all organizations since the democratization of knowledge tends to be a ubiquitous challenge. Fortunately, more solutions are emerging, such as AI-powered technology platform Sugarwork, which helps organizations manage, retain, and share their "hidden" knowledge.

Another concern is that remote work hurts employees' career advancement. Here, many open questions remain. The experiences of software engineers at a US Fortune 500 company illustrate the complexities involved. When the pandemic-induced physical separation made on-the-job learning largely disappear, young engineers under 30 were five times—and female engineers four times—more likely to quit compared to when they were colocated in the office. They missed the mentorship and feedback that previously had propelled their performance. But another group benefited: senior engineers, especially women, whose output increased during remote work since they spent less time advising junior colleagues. The study's authors conclude: "Tension exists between short-term productivity and the long-run development of younger employees, suggesting a hybrid model might be best." It appears that in a hybrid world, working from the office on the same days as senior colleagues can be especially beneficial to junior employees and those who stand to gain from receiving mentorship.

While concerns about lack of support and connection are well founded, organizations have started to design around the social downsides of remote work. Zapier, another fully remote software company, organizes "temporary colocation events" where all colleagues are invited to spend a few days together at the company's expense. Technology company Dropbox launched its Virtual First policy in October 2020, making fully remote work the default for all employees. Existing office spaces became Dropbox Studios, designated for quarterly in-person collaboration and community-building (not solo work). Dropbox also set core work hours, with overlap across time zones to facilitate communication. Recognizing that successful remote work requires the whole company to learn to operate differently, Dropbox developed a Virtual First Toolkit with practical tips and exercises to help teams set goals, define norms, and increase well-being. A company-wide survey two years in showed that 93 percent of respondents felt they could work effectively from home, and only a quarter wished to meet in person more often.

Dropbox made remote work the norm. Even if your organization or team doesn't go that far, to signal that working remotely is truly welcome, offer remote work opportunities on an opt-out as opposed to an opt-in basis: opt-out means flexibility is assumed. And to ensure fairness, track the career outcomes of all employees by work location to ensure that colleagues working remotely are not unfairly penalized.

Default to Flexibility

What if we could shift our image of the ideal worker and reframe flexible work as something that enables thriving, sustainable careers in the long run? Making flexibility the default can help by increasing the number of people who work in different ways. The evidence tells us this can work. In a seminal, pre-pandemic study on the effects of workplace flexibility, researchers from several universities teamed up with the IT division of an American Fortune 500 company to implement an intervention called STAR: "Support. Transform. Achieve. Results." The goal of STAR was to give employees more control over when and where they worked while increasing managers' support for flexible modes of working. The intervention consisted of two complementary approaches: employees were prompted to rethink their daily practices in order to work smarter while managers were trained to support their employees' autonomy around how best to get their work done.

The intervention resulted in a significant improvement in participating employees' work-family balance and in managers' support for combining work and personal life, with the largest benefits for employees who struggled with work-life conflict the most. Work hours did not change, although locations did. With more control over where to work, STAR employees' work-from-home hours nearly doubled, from 10 to 19 per week. Employees also adopted more variable schedules to fit in appointments and personal activities whenever needed.

Indeed, flexibility goes well beyond remote work and means different things to different people and organizations. Even in jobs that require physical on-site presence, employees might have greater flexibility in their choice of hours or shifts, the ability to block off certain hours for focus work or personal activities, or an allocation of administrative tasks they could do from home at the start or end of the day. A nine-month experiment in an Italian multiutility company showed that this type of expansive concept of flexibility can be beneficial for a wide range of organizations. The company, which had a traditional ethos and had never used flexible working practices, discovered that employees who had full flexibility over their hours and place of work once a week were more satisfied with their lives, more able to focus and make decisions, and less stressed than colleagues without such flexibility. In addition, flexible working had similar effects on women and men, with both groups increasing their time spent on household and care activities.

Against this backdrop, it is not surprising that there is strong demand for flexible work among employees. In a 2022 survey, US employees and managers cited schedule flexibility and remote work options as far and away the top two factors they considered— besides salary and benefits—in deciding whether to leave or stay at a firm. Employers, however, tend to underestimate the importance of flexible work to employees, especially as a means to attract talent from diverse backgrounds.

Flexible work is a powerful tool not only to improve employees' health and life satisfaction, but also to specifically support women in the workplace. Evidence from the United Kingdom and Germany indicates that access to flexible arrangements, such as part-time work, allows mothers to keep working more hours after childbirth and to earn more. While women make up nearly three-quarters of part-time workers in the United States, part-time options are a critical enabler of continued attachment to the labor market for people of all genders who wish to—temporarily or permanently—reduce their work hours.

Flexible work options are only helpful in leveling the playing field if employees actually take advantage of them. This is a real concern because data collected across hundreds of US organizations pre-COVID revealed low utilization rates for most flexibility policies, sometimes because employees were simply not aware of their existence. Since flexible work has been stigmatized in the past, employees have been concerned about being sidelined, "mommy-tracked," or held back in their careers if they expressed interest in working flexibly.

To overcome these hurdles, organizations can begin by asking employees about their desired modes of flexibility and then ensure that policies are responsive to those needs and universally available to everyone. In fact, two critical success factors for all flexible work policies that emerged from the STAR experiment in the Fortune 500 company were broad-based implementation and manager support.

A flexible work policy is mere words on paper if supervisors at all levels do not support it in practice. Inconsistency across managers in how flexible work requests are received is one of the most significant barriers to employees asking for flexibility. Organizational behavior scholar Kathleen McGinn explains: "[During the pandemic] Dads were exposed [to family demands]. The shock was real. . . . And yet they feel they don't have a lot of opportunity to create big changes in the household because of the perceived demands of their employers." These demands can be quite explicit: A male contact of Siri's, who works at an investment firm and recently had his first child, was told by his male boss that "while you're entitled to paternity leave and similar things . . . those policies aren't meant for people like you and me but for assistants and those who cannot afford help at home." In this firm and all others, flexible work should not be a request-based special accommodation that only a handful of people take advantage of, but a company-wide practice offered to all employees by default.

Once again, it can be done. Organizations around the globe have successfully transformed their culture around flexible work through simple and often inexpensive nudges. In pre-pandemic Sydney, Australia, the New South Wales government's Behavioural Insights Unit worked with eight organizations to encourage people to shift their work hours and commute to the office outside peak times. Besides a formal policy, the organizations deployed three creative nudges. First, they changed the default hours on employees' Microsoft Outlook calendars from the typical 9-to-5 to a shorter window, making it easier to arrive late or depart early. Second, they used building entry data to show managers that their teams tended to mimic their arrival and departure times; managers were then encouraged to model flexible hours to their teams. Third, they organized a team-based competition to reward off-peak commuting as well as other forms of flexible work, including part-time and hybrid work. All three nudges had lasting positive effects, with off-peak office arrivals and departures increasing substantially.

One intriguing model to consider is a four-day workweek where employees essentially get one paid day off per week while their workload remains the same. In a series of pilot projects ranging from six to twelve months in Canada, Ireland, the UK, and the US, the results were promising. Out of 41 companies that participated in the United States and Canada (nearly half of which were fully remote organizations), none planned to go back to a traditional five-day workweek after the trial. Likewise, 95 percent of employees wanted to continue with a four-day workweek. In keeping with the aim of the trial, the average number of hours worked per week dropped from a baseline of 38 to 33 after 12 months.

While the typical company participating in the pilot had only 11–25 employees, the lessons learned might be useful more generally.

The key to productivity in the compressed week was not cramming five days' worth of work into four, but assessing which tasks were of the highest value—and then cutting other, lower-value activities. Employees reported reducing the number of meetings and spending more time on uninterrupted work. A focus on actual productivity and output, rather than the hours worked, was another success factor. Lastly, as with other flexibility policies, making them organization-wide (rather than available by request) and having leaders model their use was important to shift culture.

One Florida location of American fast-food chain Chick-fil-A went a step further and introduced a three-day workweek where employees could choose to put in all of their weekly full-time hours in just three days. Groups of participating employees work together Monday through Wednesday for two weeks, then switch to Thursday–Saturday for the next two weeks, providing full schedule predictability. A quarter of the location's employees immediately opted in and their feedback was universally positive. The owner of the location also reported higher retention and lower absenteeism among employees on the three-day schedule, as well as increased applications to open positions specifically as a result of the flexible-schedule option.

These examples show that there are numerous ways to redesign work to make it fair by offering more flexibility. The onus is on employers and managers to get creative and find what works in their context.

Make Paid Work Compatible with Other Pursuits

For a truly level playing field over the lifetime of an employee's career, work needs to become more compatible with nonwork pursuits, whether they entail taking care of children, housework, hobbies, personal passion projects, caring for older relatives, or self-care, to mention just a few possibilities. Here we first focus on the compatibility of paid work with different types of caregiving responsibilities, which have been extensively researched and which impact an enormous share of the workforce. Then we expand to the broader implications of the often implicit presumption that every worker has a "backup" at home.

The majority of US adults have children: among those aged 40–49, 84 percent of women have given birth and 77 percent of men have fathered a child. About a quarter of all American adults, and more than half of Americans in their 40s, have a child younger than 18 as well as a living parent over 65, making them members of the "sandwich" generation with both childcare and senior care responsibilities. Nearly 70 percent of these sandwich caregivers do paid work and report substantial financial and emotional challenges. Employers are often clueless about these dynamics, as more than half do not collect data on their employees' caregiving responsibilities and only a quarter think caregiving impacts work performance. More than 80 percent of employees, by contrast, feel that caregiving affects their productivity from time to time.

Making it easier for all people to combine work and caregiving in the long term may be even more consequential than short-term interventions like parental leave or paying for a nanny to accompany a parent on work trips, because caregiving responsibilities tend to occur throughout one's career. Since nearly every person will be impacted at some point, we can no longer treat care obligations as separate from work. Two interventions can be particularly effective at making work and caregiving more compatible: affordable childcare and schedule predictability.

Consider Liuba Grechen Shirley, who had a one-year-old and a three-year-old at home when she left her job as director of operations managing three research institutes at New York University to run for US Congress in New York's 2nd district in 2018. Still on the wait list for daycare, she immediately realized that arranging childcare while campaigning without pay would be a financial challenge. So Grechen Shirley became the first person in more than 240 years of electoral democracy in the United States to petition the Federal Election Commission to allow her to spend campaign funds on childcare expenses. Her request was approved, and dozens of candidates—women as well as men—have since followed in her footsteps. As of 2023, 30 US states have authorized the use of campaign funds for childcare according to Vote Mama Foundation, an organization that Grechen Shirley founded to promote the political participation of mothers.

Around the world, affordable childcare along with early care and education has been found to enable the employment of parents. In countries like the United States that lack large-scale, affordable childcare infrastructure, organizations can make a big difference by stepping in to help. Outdoor clothing retailer Patagonia has offered on-site childcare since 1983. While the company concedes it is expensive, it reports that it recoups nearly all associated costs through reduced turnover, increased employee engagement, and tax refunds. UPS, a global shipping and logistics company, came to a similar conclusion when it started offering emergency on-site childcare during evening shifts as part of a pilot program at a California facility. Four-fifths of eligible hourly shift workers used the service, and retention increased from 69 percent to 96 percent among participating employees. As a result, the pilot was expanded to additional facilities and shifts. Even small companies see the value. Red Rooster Coffee, a roastery in rural Virginia with just over forty employees, has offered subsidized on-site childcare since 2018, when it established its own daycare center (which is also open to locals at market rates). Most of the company's employees have used it.

While likely less powerful, childcare referral programs, where companies help to connect employees with local childcare centers, are associated with women of all races as well as men of color advancing in the workplace. The intersectionality is important because in the US, securing childcare is a greater challenge for Black, Hispanic, and Asian American parents than for their white counterparts. Other ways employers can help with childcare include vouchers and subsidies to help pay for the cost of care; emergency childcare assistance through a partnership with a care provider; internal forums or peer groups for parents to share tips and resources; and discounts on care-related goods and services. These approaches are also promising to help with the increasing demands of senior care.

Besides care assistance, another important way to support employees—especially those in frontline and service sector jobs—is schedule predictability. The challenges brought on by precarious work schedules are particularly dire for parents and caregivers. Three-quarters of service sector employees report that they are expected to be ready to work almost anytime, including outside the normal opening hours of daycare centers, when over a quarter of parents need childcare assistance. Data from the Shift Project shows that American parents working in retail and food services often have to rely on informal childcare arrangements or even leave children without adult supervision due to last-minute shift changes and on-call work. The work-life conflict arising from schedule instability is most acute for single mothers not living with a partner.

While the benefits of more predictable schedules are clear for employees, there is also substantial upside for employers. At global home goods retailer IKEA, schedule stability was strongly associated with retention among US workers: employees who had more consistent start times, more stable hours, and closer to a full-time schedule were more likely to stay at IKEA. Clothing retailer Gap had a similar experience when it ended on-call shifts, provided schedules two weeks in advance, and asked managers to schedule workers at consistent times whenever possible. Nine months later, employees reported being more able to combine work with their personal lives; managers reported increased morale and productivity; and the company saw sales increase by 7 percent and labor productivity rise by 5 percent.

With predictable schedules, employers create working conditions that do not presume a partner or other support system at home. Nearly a quarter of American households are headed up by a single parent who is most likely a woman and/or a person of color. More than half of all US households are dual-earner households where one person works full-time and the other works at least part-time; so are two-thirds of households with children under the age of 18. It is the highest-earning men who are the exception: A whopping 71 percent of men in the top one percent of the US income distribution have a spouse who does not work outside the home; only 16 percent of women in the one percent do. Given that women are less likely than men to have a stay-at-home spouse, the playing field is stacked against them.

But these statistics tell a bigger story: it is no longer reasonable to assume that employees of any gender have a spouse that they can rely on for housework, childcare, and other life tasks. This also applies to organizational policies. If you have ever worked for an organization with an expense policy, you are likely familiar with a scenario where the policy will cover your transportation to a work dinner, the cost of the food and drinks, and perhaps even a night's stay at a nearby hotel if you live far away—but not the cost of a babysitter who would enable you to attend the dinner in the first place, as Caroline Criado Perez details in her excellent book *Invisible Women.*

Beyond policies and working conditions that assume the existence of a partner, many organizations have formal expectations not only of the people they employ, but also of their spouses who are presumed to contribute to the organization on an unpaid basis. One of Siri's friends, whose husband works in college athletics, has managed several cross-state moves with two children in tow while building her own career. Her uncompensated but expected contributions to her husband's employer include organizing tailgates and social events around athletic games; welcoming and settling in the families of newly hired coaches and athletic directors; and creating community through birthday celebrations, food trains, and children's activities. While she enjoys this work, it is not optional: declining to contribute would jeopardize her husband's career. These types of expectations are also common in the military and clergy, as well as in many high-ranking government, private sector, and university positions where the employee's spouse is part of a "two-for-one deal" and often vetted alongside the candidate during the hiring process.

The ball is in leaders' and organizations' court to design fair workplace policies that do not assume the existence of a partner. It's time we move beyond the adage, "Behind every successful executive is a spouse that has the time and wherewithal to manage the household."

Provide Paid, Gender-Neutral, and Nontransferable Parental Leave

In 2013, Josh Levs, then a journalist at CNN, was getting ready to welcome his third child when he came face-to-face with a particularly ubiquitous manifestation of gender inequity at work: his employer's parental leave policy. Time Warner, then CNN's parent company, offered ten weeks of paid leave to birth mothers as well as parents of any gender who adopted a child—but only two weeks to biological fathers. "[The structure] was preventing both men and women from having options. As long as you're pushing men to stay at work, you're pushing women to stay home," said Levs.

He approached Time Warner with a request for equal leave, and after months of radio silence followed by negotiation, finally got his answer when his daughter was born prematurely: no. Levs proceeded to file a gender discrimination complaint with the Equal Employment Opportunity Commission. One year later, Time Warner announced that it was voluntarily changing its leave policies to make them more generous to parents of all genders. A year after that, the EEOC issued guidance clarifying that while leave for "pregnancy, childbirth, or related medical conditions can be limited to women affected by those conditions," any parental leave offered for the purpose of bonding with or taking care of a child "must be provided to similarly situated men and women on the same terms." As Levs, who wrote the book *All In* about his experiences at CNN, explains: "We're a generation that grew up believing that women should have equal opportunities. We're coming to understand that if men do not have equal opportunities to be caregivers, women will not have equal opportunities in the workplace."

We wholeheartedly agree and wish that parents of any gender did not have to work this hard to spend time with their children because the benefits of paid parental leave to children, parents, organizations, and society as a whole are well-known. Consider the case of California, whose first-in-the-nation state-level paid family leave program was introduced in 2004. It currently offers all parents up to eight weeks of leave paid at 60–70 percent of weekly earnings. Across dozens of studies, the introduction of the program has been shown to have positive impacts in many domains, including household income, children's health, and women's labor force participation. An important theme is that those who would have been least able to take unpaid leave (i.e., lower-income and less-educated families, especially single mothers) benefit the most from having access to paid leave.

How leave policies are structured can make or break their effectiveness. Evidence strongly suggests that providing *paid, gender-neutral,* and *nontransferable* parental leave to all employees regardless of their gender, family structure, and how a child comes into their family (i.e., through biological birth, adoption, surrogacy, fostering, or any other way) is the best way to level the playing field. Let us explain why each of these qualifiers is critical.

First, in order to be useful in practical terms, parental leave needs to be *paid*, ideally at the highest wage replacement rate possible. In a survey of nearly 12,000 people across 17 countries, the lack of sufficient replacement pay was the number one reason—cited by 49 percent of women and men—for not taking the full amount of parental leave offered. Replacement pay can be an especially important factor in men's decisions to take leave, since men earn more than women, on average, and therefore stand to lose out on more income if leave is unpaid or poorly paid. In San Francisco, a city ordinance that increased wage replacement rates boosted men's leave-taking more than four times as much as women's.

The overwhelming majority of the world's countries have figured this out and provide at least some parental leave at the national level. As of 2022, 186 countries offered some parental leave for mothers while 122 offered some parental leave for fathers, with significantly longer leaves offered to women across the board. Only 20 countries offered equal paternity leave rights to gay couples and only 42 to adoptive fathers.

The United States is the only high-income country, and one of only six overall, that does not guarantee national paid parental leave.* Only a quarter of American employees have access to paid leave through their employer, with full-time workers more than twice as likely to have access than part-time workers. The lowest-earning workers who most need paid leave are currently least likely to have access to it by a wide margin. There are also major racial disparities, with Black and Hispanic employees having less access to paid leave than white employees. Offering paid parental leave is therefore a powerful tool in companies' toolbox to level the playing field not only for gender, but also for race and socioeconomic background.

Second, positioning parental leave as *gender-neutral* and making it available equally to parents of all genders in all circumstances is not only fair, but also important to change gender stereotypes. When leave conversations and policies focus on women, we perpetuate the descriptive norm that caregiving is primarily a "women's issue"—as well as the prescriptive norm that it should be so. Policies that specify a "primary" and "secondary" caregiver reinforce the notion that care responsibilities are not, cannot, or should not be shared equally when two parents are involved. Gender-neutral parental leave policies can help to de-gender caregiving and make it more socially acceptable

---

* People in the United States technically have access to 12 weeks of unpaid leave to take care of children or family members through the Family and Medical Leave Act (FMLA) enacted in 1993, but only 60 percent of US employees are eligible (due to requirements around employer size and hours worked). Most of them for financial reasons cannot afford to take unpaid time off.

and appealing to men. They also help to put LGBTQ+ parents on the same footing as heterosexual parents.

Encouragingly, gender-neutral leave policies are becoming more common in organizations globally, even in countries that already provide generous national parental leave. Equileap's analysis of nearly 4,000 large public companies in 23 developed markets showed that between 2022 and 2023, the number of companies offering equal leave to both parents nearly doubled to 322 firms—still a small fraction of the total, but progress nonetheless. Some of the world's leading companies in this regard include United Kingdom–based investment company Abrdn, which offers 40 weeks of fully paid parental leave to all of its UK employees, and Swedish growth investment firm Kinnevik, which offers 39 weeks of fully paid leave to all parents globally. Even in the United States, more than 70 percent of firms with fewer than 100 employees in the states of New York and New Jersey supported paid family leave in a 2020 survey, and firms that had experienced it were the most supportive. This is remarkable, as we might have feared that small firms in particular would not be able to manage.

Third, making parental leave *nontransferable* such that each parent has their own use-it-or-lose-it allocation has proven to be a highly effective way to increase men's leave-taking and move households toward a more equal dual-earner, dual-caregiver model. In Quebec, Canada, the "second parent" has had a reserved leave allocation since 2006. More than 80 percent of dads in Quebec took at least some amount of parental leave, compared with around 15 percent of dads in the rest of Canada before a 2019 nationwide policy gave the "second parent" a dedicated allocation of five to eight weeks, depending on the benefit rate. Parents in Quebec also started to contribute more equitably at home (and at work) as a result of fathers taking longer parental leave. The effects of men's increased leave-taking have been similar at UK-based insurance company Aviva, which offers mothers and fathers an equal 52 weeks of leave, half of it at full pay; in

Norway, which launched a four-week paternity leave quota in 1993; and in Sweden, where fathers take just under a third of all parental leave thanks to a "daddy month" of nontransferable, reserved parental leave introduced in 1995.

You may have noticed that we have not said anything yet about the ideal length of parental leave. Generally, maternity leaves of up to a year have positive impacts on lower-income women's employment outcomes, while leaves longer than a year can harm well-educated, higher-income women's careers and earnings. Additional research is required to better understand how health and well-being benefits vary over time, but as of now, leave during the first months of a child's life appears paramount.

The question of how to encourage uptake is especially relevant since we traditionally see sizable gender gaps in parental leave usage—and because women and men cite negative career impacts as a chief concern when deciding how much parental leave to take. Defaults could come in handy here again. Consider defaulting every single employee, regardless of gender, to take the maximum amount of leave (while, of course, allowing them to take less). This sends a strong signal that you not only tolerate, but actually encourage, employees to take advantage of the full leave offered. If some components of leave (or other flexibility policies) are negotiable, be transparent about who can negotiate and what.

Clarifying the administrative processes around going on and returning from parental leave is also important, and formalized "reboarding" programs that help new parents transition back to work are becoming more popular. Law firm Reed Smith organizes gender-neutral seminars advising all prospective parents on the ins and outs of managing their parental leave, such as when to inform their supervisor, how to establish boundaries and determine a reasonable amount of work-related communication while on leave, and what to do with key clients. The firm tracks parental leave usage by gender, which has allowed HR leaders to identify groups where leadership may not have set the most supportive example—and then to work directly with those groups to ensure that company-wide policies are reflected in the day-to-day culture. Reed Smith has also purposefully highlighted people promoted to partner while working part-time to role model the possibility.

Normalizing the culture around leave is especially important for men, since taking parental leave is more counter-stereotypical (and, still today, less common) for them. One barrier standing in the way is pluralistic ignorance, or our misguided beliefs about what other people believe. At Santander bank in the UK, 99 percent of men supported flexible work, but only 65 percent thought that their colleagues would encourage men to work flexibly. Informing men about this gap between their private beliefs and those of others helped to promote more leave-taking: the number of men planning to take parental leave increased by nearly 13 percentage points relative to those colleagues who received no information about other people's beliefs. The results were similar at a second large UK bank, where men's leave intentions increased by 50 percent.

Japan is another example of how offering leave is only one part of the puzzle. Even though Japanese men are entitled to paid, father-specific leave for around 12 months, the cultural norms that discourage men's leave-taking are so strong that only about 6 percent of fathers applied to take any paternity leave in 2018—most for only a few days. Research has demonstrated that like employees in British banks, Japanese men tend to overestimate their peers' negative attitudes toward parental leave and that this pluralistic ignorance is a major factor in their low uptake of paternity leave.

To change norms and dispel perceptions that taking leave harms career advancement, senior employees can lead by example. Meta's CEO Mark Zuckerberg and Reddit's cofounder Alexis Ohanian both took a full parental leave and were vocal about their positive experiences. As Ronak Patel, equities sales trader at Morgan Stanley in

London who took 16 consecutive weeks of parental leave, put it: "The more men that do it, the less of a big deal it becomes." You can make role models more present at any level if you connect employees who are about to go on leave with colleagues who have already returned successfully from their leaves.

To make work—and caregiving—fair, every organization should provide paid, gender-neutral, and nontransferable parental leave while actively encouraging people to take advantage of it. Employees, employers, children, and all of society will benefit as a result.

* * *

Making it easier for everyone to combine the proverbial "work" and "life" through increased flexibility will go a long way toward leveling the playing field at work and making life better for *everyone*—though as long as women shoulder a larger share of responsibilities at home, the absence of flexible work hurts them more than men. Demographic trends, including women leading men in degree attainment at all levels, suggest that women—and specifically women with some caregiving responsibilities—will make up an increasingly large share of the workforce of the future. So if you take one thing away from this chapter, let it be that making work more flexible is an urgent priority to ensure not only fairness, but also access to the full talent pool.

---

1. Normalize and support remote work
2. Default to flexibility
3. Make paid work compatible with other pursuits
4. Provide paid, gender-neutral, and nontransferable parental leave

---

CHAPTER 11

Norms That Create Equal Opportunities

At the conclusion of a workshop held in Tuskegee, Alabama, in 2006, participants were given a piece of paper and asked to do one of two things: list three workshop takeaways or write "Me Too" if they had survived sexual abuse and were seeking help. Many of the women and girls in the audience put down the latter, plus their name, not only signaling that they needed help but declaring that they, too, had experienced what celebrities like Oprah Winfrey, Gabrielle Union, Queen Latifah, and Mary J. Blige had gone through before them. Tarana Burke, the activist who coined the term "Me Too" and who would later become one of *Time* magazine's 100 most influential people and the recipient of many prestigious awards, always started her workshops by sharing these celebrities' stories, and also her own. She wanted to signal to people who had gone through these traumatic experiences that they were not alone. That others—people they looked up to—were survivors too. She wanted to normalize talking about sexual abuse and take away the shame so that women and girls could start healing.

A bit more than ten years later, in 2017, the term went viral when actor and activist Alyssa Milano invited people who had experienced sexual harassment or assault to post #MeToo on social media. Just a few days earlier, *New York Times* investigative reporters Jodi Kantor and Megan Twohey had exposed Hollywood film producer Harvey Weinstein based on allegations of sexual abuse from numerous women stretching back almost three decades, including leading voices like actor and activist Ashley Judd, who had decided to come forward using her name. In a moving 2019 book and 2022 film, *She Said*, Kantor and Twohey report that 82 women followed Judd, accusing Weinstein of a litany of sexual crimes. He was later convicted, with additional lawsuits pending.

The day after Milano's call to action, #MeToo was trending No. 1 on Twitter. In just a few hours, Milano had received 55,000 replies. During the following year, interest in the topic skyrocketed on social as well as mainstream media in the United States and around the world. Film producers in Hollywood started to reach out to more female writers, with female producers and people previously associated with Weinstein driving the change. Based on research by economist Hong Luo and management scholar Laurina Zhang, the likelihood that these producers worked with a woman writer on new movies increased by 35 percent after the #MeToo movement took off. Way beyond Hollywood, to make workplaces safer and fairer, corporations have adjusted their policies and an unprecedented number of bills have been introduced at the federal level and in nearly all states in the US. The same trend is also observable across OECD countries where the number of investigations of and arrests for sexual crimes has gone up substantially.

Much more work needs to be done but Burke, Milano, Judd, Kantor, and Twohey have helped change what we believe to be normal and acceptable. They are norm entrepreneurs. Norm entrepreneurship, a term coined by legal scholar Cass Sunstein to describe how people can change social norms, is on the rise. Social media, for better or worse, is enabling change makers to reach larger audiences in less time and at lower cost than ever before. Norm entrepreneurs have in common that they want to shift human behavior away from what people are currently doing and towards a new equilibrium perceived to be better.

If we want to make our workplaces truly fair, we must learn from these norm entrepreneurs. Moral appeals will not suffice. Anti-harassment training will not do, nor can fairness be achieved by relying on command-and-control approaches or financial incentives alone. We can—and should—try to deter harassment by sanctioning bad behavior, but we cannot create environments where everyone can flourish without a shared understanding of the norms we want to uphold. We can incentivize people to comply with regulations but a compliance frame will not move us beyond what is required by the law. Instead, we need to work on what we want to accept as normal in our workplaces.

Norms are transmitted through symbols and rituals, interactions, and everyday experiences that constantly reinforce the direction that we are heading in. When we include our personal pronouns reflecting our gender identity, for example, we signal our support for colleagues who identify as nonbinary, and, research suggests, the LGBTQ+ community more generally. The pronouns serve as cues for "identity safety" and have been shown to instill positive attitudes about the organization among members of impacted communities. Diversity, equity, and inclusion strategist Lily Zheng recalls how they and a friend decided to introduce themselves by their pronouns in a big meeting: "[After the two of us, the third person] very tentatively tried to introduce themself with their pronouns, then the fourth person did the same thing, and then the fifth person did the same thing. . . . Everyone just sort of did it because it seemed like the right thing to do." Zheng emphasizes that they did not have any formal power, nor did they run the meeting, yet they saw an opportunity to shape norms and create a new micro-culture of including one's pronouns as part of meeting introductions.

Norms are also transmitted by the stories we tell, which is why Kantor and Twohey's reporting was so important. The journalists provided evidence that the phenomenon was not only real but also widespread. Combined with the 55,000 replies that Milano received, they created a critical mass for change. As the two commented in the film *She Said*: "The only way these women are going to go on the record . . . ," Twohey started, ". . . is if they all jump together," Kantor finished. The rising number of responses to #MeToo sent an increasingly credible signal that the women were in fact jumping together, motivating more to join in and speak up. At a Harvard event in the fall of 2022, Judd added: "I've been sexually harassed on set more times than I can count, and I never knew where to go or whom to tell. Now on my union card . . . there is a sexual harassment hotline to call."

The transformation that Tarana Burke was able to ignite is nothing short of astonishing. She and the movement did more than point fingers, which is not necessarily a winning strategy. In fact, this may be one of the reasons why researchers found neither sexual harassment training programs nor general harassment training programs that included racial and other forms of harassment to have much impact. Trainings that focus on legal compliance did not fare any better. Raising awareness alone does not automatically shift prevalent norms, let alone outcomes such as hiring, promotion, or turnover. We hope that they can improve working conditions but have no evidence on this. Unfortunately, people tend to become defensive if they feel like they are accused of being potential culprits. People also overlook rights they theoretically have if they do not feel empowered to actually use them.

Tarana Burke had to learn this the hard way. She did not start out with workshops aimed at destigmatizing survivors' experiences. Rather, she first tried to work with community leaders imploring them to take sexual abuse seriously—but to little avail. She was constantly undermined, being told that these were topics parents or women and girls themselves were responsible for, and that "the issue was in itself a distraction." She also feared that for many, sadly, it was too close to home: "Too many people would have to start examining the ways that they were complicit, the ways that they turned their heads, the ways they built up leaders in our community that they knew were predators," said Burke. This was when she realized that she had to change what people perceived to be acceptable. Neither sexual violence nor looking the other way was.

In this chapter, we will show you how we all can become norm entrepreneurs, in small and in big ways. Norm entrepreneurship typically requires credible messengers: people with courage who through their activism elevate a topic to social consciousness, or people who might already have a megaphone that others are listening to. Sometimes they are peers, sometimes they are grassroots activists, and sometimes they are role models: leaders we trust and look up to, like Tarana Burke and Ashley Judd, who put words to people's experiences and helped them make sense of what was going on. In our workplaces, there are many Burkes and Judds. Perhaps you are one too—and if not, in this chapter we share some things you might consider doing to become one.

Change Perceptions of the Prevalent Norms

People have mastered the art of avoiding information, particularly if it makes them feel bad. We know where not to look, what not to read, which news channels not to listen to, and when to turn off our minds. This is why moral appeals are often ineffective. They remind us that we should eat more veggies and use public transportation to cut down on emissions—but many of us don't want to feel guilty about eating that chocolate chip cookie or driving our car to work.

We cannot always avoid the critical look—and some organizations have figured out how to leverage guilt or even shame for positive ends. Many parents will know the feeling. While our kids will not touch broccoli at home despite our best admonitions, they devour it at summer camp where the norm is to finish off your plate. Our kids have not changed how they feel about eating broccoli but to fit in, they go with the flow. Eventually, after having tried it several times, they may even develop a taste for broccoli and keep up the healthy habit back home. But the change in attitude comes second (if at all), not first. Initially, our kids just want to avoid standing out. They respond to what they believe others would want them to do, which is why affecting these beliefs is such a powerful means to change behavior.

When instituting a "we finish our plates" rule, sometimes accompanied by a competition where the group that produces the least food waste is recognized in some fashion, camps try to establish a social expectation: everyone should chip in as this is not only the right thing to do but will also increase the chances of winning the prize. Given that behavior is observable, kids take their cues from each other. If despite the camp's best efforts hardly anyone finishes their plate, they won't eat their veggies either; if, on the other hand, most everyone returns a clean plate, they will automatically eat their veggies as well. In the latter case, finishing your plate has become the social norm. The kids follow the rule because they believe most of their peers do so and because they believe that most everyone else expects them to do so. As such, the prevalence of the behavior has given it normative appeal. It now is no longer only what we *are* doing but also what we *should be* doing.

This is why campaigns reminding us that most people *are* voting, saving energy, or reusing their towels in hotels have been able to increase turnout, energy conservation, and towel reusage, respectively. These interventions work when we underestimate what others are doing and then adjust our behaviors according to the new information. As we discovered in the previous chapter when we encountered pluralistic ignorance, our beliefs are often miscalibrated. In the United States, for example, beliefs about earnings among married heterosexual couples lag behind the actual state of affairs. In 2022, almost half of wives earned the same as or more than their husbands. Yet, only 3 percent of Americans thought that men would prefer that the wife was the primary earner, and only 7 percent that women would prefer the wife to earn more. The numbers were a bit higher for acceptance of spouses earning the same but way short of the actual share of wives making as much as or more than their husbands.

While we know our own beliefs, without the benefit of observing what others are doing, we tend to have a hard time predicting what the people around us think. Car drivers in the state of Montana, for example, were found to underestimate the fraction of drivers who use seat belts. While 85 percent of Montanans reported buckling up, they estimated that only 60 percent of other drivers in the state would do so. Similarly, in Saudi Arabia, married men substantially underestimated the share of other husbands who supported their wives working outside the home. A large majority—87 percent of Saudi men—reported being supportive but they believed that only 63 percent of their countrymen who also participated in the study would be.

When informed of the true number of supporters of working women, Saudis joined in with the campers who ate their broccoli. Specifically, the Saudi men who were aware that the vast majority of married men were in support of their wives working outside the home were substantially more likely to sign their wives up for a job-matching app for Saudi women compared with those men whose beliefs were not corrected. The increase was exclusively driven by the men who had underestimated the true fraction of supporters: they were 57 percent more likely to sign up their wives. Five months later, significantly more of these women had applied for a job compared to the wives of the men who were not informed of the true number of supporters. Moreover, knowing that working outside the home was more acceptable among other men than the husbands initially thought, more of them wanted their wives to take driving lessons.

Given that based on the Arab Barometer, 89 percent of women in Saudi Arabia are supportive of women's labor force participation, overcoming pluralistic ignorance by providing accurate information on the social norms seems like a win-win—for the women, the men, and the country—and could be the basis for a truly embedded solution to advance fairness. This is the power of social norms: They help us eat our broccoli, wear our seat belts, and make work fair because we want to be part of the club and fear social sanctions if we deviate.

Implicit in this argument is the assumption that we care about the "club." Put differently, not any club will do. The response would likely have been muted if the Saudi men had learned about the beliefs of a random set of men. Psychologists refer to the people whose behavior and beliefs might influence our own as our referents. We typically have something significant in common with our reference group. This commonality could consist of one's nationality, religion, a shared occupation, hobby, favorite sports team, or a social identity such as gender, race, or ethnicity. As you might have noted, all the celebrities Burke referred to in her workshops were Black women—because most of her participants were Black girls. These were the people the girls could identify with, possibly even role models they aspired to emulate.

For Iris's household, the neighbors were the reference group. Her family was part of a large-scale field experiment that included tens of thousands of households across the United States where some received energy reports comparing their electricity consumption to that of their neighbors. At the time, a company called Opower (since acquired by Oracle) collaborated with utility companies to improve their customer interfaces and help all of us save energy. The returns on this investment were huge: at basically no cost (save for a little bit of ink on a piece of paper), households like Iris's ended up consuming 2.5 percent less electricity than households that had not received the comparative information. In a similar study in the US state of Georgia that focused on water usage, the decrease in water consumption of the households that were informed of their neighbors' usage was as large as the effect the water utility saw from price increases of 12 to 15 percent per month. In both cases, savings lasted for several years, persisting well beyond the intervention. Surely, most consumers would prefer the additional ink to the additional cost.

In addition to highlighting that many referents are already engaging in the desired behavior, you can also consider reminding people that many others are starting to engage in the behavior that you are hoping to scale. A company we were working with, for example, wanted to introduce a new norm during hybrid meetings. They had noticed that people who joined virtually often had no chance of participating in the deliberation: once the conversation got going among in-person participants in the room, they struggled to get a word in. So the company wanted every meeting to start with the virtual participants being invited to share their thoughts first. This was a new norm, so the company could not say that most meeting organizers were already doing it. But there were enough team leaders who signed up early to try the approach that the company could say that calling on virtual participants first had become increasingly popular. It was what others like you were starting to do, so you might want to give it a go as well.

At best, exposing people to what the social norm is changes our behavior for good, and we keep eating our broccoli—because we actually have developed a taste for it, or because we feel bad or guilty if we succumb to our inner devil hooked on French fries. In fact, this happened in the above company. Meeting participants saw the benefits of giving everyone a chance to participate and they now give virtual participants the floor automatically. They have internalized the new norm. However, a second-best option is that we privately keep hating broccoli but do not express our sentiments in public—because we feel embarrassed and ashamed if we do, and/or because we fear the disapproval of our peers. And perhaps this is actually what happened in the above company. Maybe employees are annoyed at having to listen to the virtual participants first but keep playing the game for the game's sake. This may well be the best outcome norm entrepreneurs can hope for. It is hard to change deeply rooted beliefs that we have learned and internalized over many years, but we can disrupt their impact on our behaviors.

This has practical relevance too. At the BBC, whose 50:50 The

Equality Project you read about in Chapter 2, "we weren't trying to change anyone—we wanted to give them a tool to change themselves," explained Angela Henshall, who worked on the 50:50 team for many years. Ros Atkins spread 50:50 through word of mouth, strategically targeting influential BBC programs and teams that he knew could serve as role models to get even more teams on board. In a matter of months, there was an increasingly widespread sense that many teams were already succeeding at reaching 50–50 women and men in their content, and that it was "the thing to do." Monitoring representation data was becoming the norm, that is, what was seen as the acceptable and expected way to behave.

Unfortunately, norm entrepreneurship is a double-edged sword. Social norms are a powerful tool, and beliefs can be influenced for better or for worse. Pressure to conform does not always lead to better outcomes. When Iris's older son, at the time a second grader who wanted to comply with the camp norm of finishing his plate to minimize food waste, ate his French toast for breakfast, he got quite sick. He was allergic to egg. And while the hypermasculine Marlboro Man was able to convince men to smoke cigarettes because it was a "manly" thing to do, few of us would declare this a success. Most concerningly, of course, demagogues from across the world have mastered the use of social influence. In fact, much of the early research on the sway of social norms was motivated by the horrors of World War II, with scholars trying to unpack how Adolf Hitler was able to mobilize so many people for evil. He, too, was able to change what many Germans thought to be acceptable.

Norms are a powerful tool in our collective change-making toolbox. But what the tool is used for is up to us to decide. Let's make sure we employ it to make the world better and recognize when norm entrepreneurship is exploited to make it worse.

Identify Credible Norm Messengers

An ideal norm messenger is someone who not only shares the message but also impacts our beliefs about what other people think. Often the leader of the pack is able to do this in a way the lonely wolf can't. This is why the decisions of the US Supreme Court matter. When psychologists Betsy Levy Paluck and Margaret Tankard interviewed Americans before and after the Supreme Court established same-sex marriage as a constitutional right in 2015, they found that people's personal opinions had not shifted. What had changed dramatically in the wake of the ruling was that people believed other Americans' opinions had shifted. They thought that their fellow citizens were more likely to support same-sex marriage after 2015 than before, when all that in fact had happened was a new ruling by the Supreme Court.

Beyond their traditional role in creating a formal system of control, laws can also create, validate, or undermine social norms, something that has been referred to as the "expressive function of the law." As such, laws—say, prohibiting smoking—activate informal systems of control where it is not a police officer who asks a smoker to refrain from lighting up a cigarette but rather another patron in a restaurant.

The degree to which the law serves this role is an empirical question. It depends on whether it broadly captures a latent feeling in the population: something we can imagine others agreeing with even if we ourselves might not. When the German government approved a bylaw restricting heating of public buildings to no more than 19 degrees Celsius (about 66° Fahrenheit) in anticipation of an energy crisis in the winter of 2022–23 due to Russia's war against Ukraine, it might have been aware of the earlier research that took place in the buildings of the OECD in Paris. It showed that going much lower than 19 degrees could be tough. Absent an emergency, setting the heating norm 1°C lower than the typical temperature was tolerated by the OECD employees, but a decrease of 2°C backfired. This was norm entrepreneurship taken a bridge too far.

Time will have to tell whether the US Supreme Court's 2022 decision to overturn *Roe v. Wade*, a constitutional right to abortion that had been in effect for nearly fifty years, will fall into the "too far" category or shift opinions in the longer term. A survey by Pew Research

Center shortly after the decision did not find an immediate response, with a majority of Americans saying that abortion should be legal in all or most cases both before and after the ruling. The survey did not ask what the respondents thought other people might believe, so we do not know how the impact of the 2022 ruling on norms compares to the one in 2015 for same-sex marriage.

Our general message is this: norm entrepreneurship is more likely to work if it broadly meets people where they are, and then moves them just a bit because of their beliefs about what the norm expresses about others' feelings. It tends to work when people do not have strong views about something. Hating broccoli is a pretty strong view, which can likely only be overcome by intense social pressure. And it will likely not stop children from favoring French fries and avoiding broccoli if they can. But banning French fries, we imagine, would also be a bridge too far.

So when you contemplate your own power to shape norms, first assess where people are at. In rural India, for example, simple norm interventions have not been able to increase support for women's labor force participation, which is one of the lowest in the world. Perhaps the norms suggesting women should not work outside the home are just too strong to be overcome by relatively light-touch interventions, or perhaps it did not help that the intervention was led by an employer, a kindergarten provider, keen on increasing the share of female teachers. As it happens, developing a good understanding of your target group's beliefs is also one of the top recommendations when you search for "How to become an influencer" online. Successful influencers on social media know their audience well, and for better or worse, speak to it.

Second, interrogate whether you are the right messenger or whether you have to become more creative in sharing a message you care deeply about. You can take inspiration from *Shuga*, a TV series filmed in Nigeria that questioned the acceptability of domestic violence. It led male viewers, who in an experiment had been exposed to the series eight months earlier, to be more than 20 percent less likely to justify gender-based violence than men in the control group who had not watched the series. Similarly, when soap operas in Brazil started to feature small families, women's fertility preferences were impacted with the strongest effects on poor households. These are valuable reminders that norm entrepreneurship goes well beyond the law. Any message that can credibly express a shared value can serve as a tipping point where we follow the crowd, or more precisely, our perceptions of where the crowd is heading.

New norms also spread in India when cable television became available and exposed rural viewers to ways of life more typical in urban areas. It changed what viewers perceived to be "normal" and decreased the acceptability of beating women and giving sons preferential treatment. More generally, exposure to more gender-inclusive programming, sometimes referred to as edutainment, has been found to have quite sizable impacts on social norms related to gender and beyond. In postgenocide Rwanda, such programming worked even for bitter enemies, the Hutus and the Tutsis. But like in the case of the US Supreme Court, the pathway to change was not personal attitudes but beliefs about what constituted socially acceptable behavior. As Paluck, who led this research, explained: "I may not personally believe in letting my daughter marry someone from the other ethnicity, but I'm going to let her—because that's what we as Rwandans are doing now. So I found that people's behavior changed even when their personal beliefs stayed the same." The programs work not because they introduce something completely unheard-of, but because they exploit latently available notions of right and wrong.

When looking for the equivalent of the Supreme Court or a TV series like *Shuga* for our workplaces, we can learn from the work Paluck did at 56 US middle schools that wanted to decrease bullying and harassment on their campuses. The research team performed a social network analysis to understand the power nodes among the 24,000 students at these schools. Then these power players—students who were central in their respective networks and therefore likely to influence others—

received the *Shuga* equivalent of an antiharassment intervention. They were also asked to share the insights gained with their respective networks. The strategy led to a 30 percent decrease in harassment in the schools that had received the treatment—an astonishing drop, really, based on a relatively low-cost intervention.

We can all become smarter about whom we target with our messages. Are these opinion leaders, people others defer to and who might in fact serve as influencers on the factory floor or in the laboratory? Or just a random sample of employees who have self-selected into a particular program or training? If you do not know who in your organization sits in power nodes, try this instead: find your vegan bodybuilder. Why? Because this is exactly the strategy that the film *The Game Changers* employed. Featuring stuntman and martial artist Jackie Chan; tennis player Novak Djokovic; race car driver Lewis Hamilton; and body builder and actor (and former governor) Arnold Schwarzenegger, among others, the film shows how plant-based diets can go hand in hand with strength, athleticism, and success, dismantling the stereotype that associates eating meat with masculinity.

Research aiming to decrease racist online harassment discovered that white men who had many followers on Twitter were most effective at playing the role of the vegan body builder. They gained credibility precisely because we did not expect them to stand up against racism. Using Twitter bots that spoke out against racist harassment, political scientist Kevin Munger ran an experiment where the bot was identified either as a white or as a Black man and had either many or few followers. When confronted with a message like, "Hey man, just remember that there are real people who are hurt when you harass them with that kind of language," white men decreased their use of racial slurs most when the admonition came from another white guy with many followers. In addition to the message being unexpected given the messenger's characteristics, both of the messenger's attributes are important. We are more likely to listen to someone we feel close to—in this case, an in-group member who shares the same race—and we are more likely to care about what they have to say when we perceive them to be influential.

Credible norm messengers who influence us make information available to us because they are close to us or because we look up to them. When Colin Kaepernick, a football quarterback at the time playing for the San Francisco 49ers, took a knee during a pregame national anthem in 2016, he shone a light on racism in the United States. Inspired, Megan Rapinoe, at the time the captain of the US women's soccer team, did the same at the 2021 Tokyo Olympics alongside her teammates and players from many other teams. They used their voices in the "fight for equality and justice," as the British soccer team's captain, Steph Houghton, posted on Instagram. Kneeling has now become a symbol of antiracism and an act to protest discrimination.

By taking a stance in public, Kaepernick, Rapinoe, Houghton, and their colleagues made themselves vulnerable (and experienced substantial backlash from some groups). A norm entrepreneur's influence derives not only from their status but also from their willingness to take such a risk.

Create Pathways to Change

When universities launch a healthy-eating campaign, it goes without saying that they make fruits and vegetables easily available. For Iris's household, it was helpful that the Opower-induced urge to conserve energy was supported by ready access to energy-efficient lightbulbs and refrigerators. The beauty of replacing a lightbulb, of course, is that it has to be done only once every other year or so. Refrigerators last even longer. The true breakthrough for Iris's household was insulating the roof, a once-in-a-lifetime investment (at least, so she hopes!). But it may well not have happened if it had not been for her husband's insistence. He wanted to be part of the solution.

And so do others. To our initial surprise, given that so many trainings have been shown not to work to change behaviors, antiharassment trainings that focused on managers (instead of all employees) had more success. The researchers suggest that this is because these trainings treated managers as allies: not as a part of the problem but rather as a part of the solution. Instead of blaming some managers and victimizing others, these programs ideally focus on giving managers the tools to identify unwanted behaviors, interrupt them, and prevent bullying and harassment from escalating. In short, they turn managers from "bystanders" into "upstanders," people who speak up and step in. By doing so, these programs overcome a big challenge of traditional trainings, namely a focus on what not to do.

Siri learned this in her first certification course for teaching fitness. Telling people to "not arch your back" doesn't get the job done; asking them to "stand tall and keep your spine long" is much more effective to achieve proper weightlifting form. Highlighting the behaviors we *want* people to pursue—the dos instead of the don'ts—is a winning strategy across the board.

Of course, ideally we would keep the bad stuff from happening by focusing on what we can do to proactively prevent it. This is the goal of bystander interventions, which are increasingly common on school and university campuses and have also been employed by the military and a number of NGOs and firms. More corporations should learn from them. Research suggests that empowering bystanders to speak up and step forward might be one of the most promising pathways to reduce (sexual) violence. Most programs involve learning to recognize the telltale signs of situations that could spiral out of control and developing strategies to intervene before it's too late. Examining the effectiveness of twelve bystander programs, mostly conducted on college campuses by researchers rigorously comparing impacts on those who were part of the program with a control group that was not, yielded encouraging results. Most programs found reductions in harassment and violence and reductions in the acceptance of such behaviors, as well as increases in bystander efficacy. Soldiers who had received bystander training in the US Army, for example, were more likely than their untrained counterparts to report that they had taken action when they saw something bad happen.

Taking action might also include coming forward and reporting. While no organization wants to see an uptick in sexual harassment, we have to learn that, at least initially, an increase in complaints can be a sign that employees trust the process and are comfortable speaking up. In fact, this is exactly what the US Equal Employment Opportunity Commission recommended—but we realize that getting the balance between the preventive stick and the mitigating carrot right is not easy. Ideally we would want to reward managers for empowering members of their teams to come forward but not for sexual harassment taking place.

People are more likely to act when they believe members of their reference group support such an action. Students' beliefs about peers' approval when intervening to prevent, for example, sexual violence or substance misuse on college campuses is therefore a key factor. But while awareness of the norm can help, there still remains a collective action problem where people are holding back in the hope that some-one else will step forward. Sometimes also referred to as "diffusion of responsibility," some student groups at Harvard have tackled this prob-lem head-on and made stepping in a formal responsibility. At every event involving alcohol, there is at least one designated nondrinker whose responsibility is to keep watch and intervene if necessary. The role rotates so that almost every group member experiences this other side of the coin at some point during the academic year.

You could do the same for your meetings and events. Have your colleagues take turns being what you might want to think of as the "norm champion" for the day: the person helping all of us uphold the norms we have agreed on by speaking up and stepping in when we are about to violate them. If not during the meeting, the person can take people aside afterward and share any observations. Maybe the norm champion noted that some people who should have been in the room because of their subject matter expertise were not invited; or that the seating arrangement with some people sitting at the table and others in an outer ring created unnecessary hierarchies and stifled discussion; or that some people were "in the know," possibly having participated in a pre-meeting, and others were not; or that some people's contributions were systematically overlooked, interrupted, or dismissed. It can be hard to notice some of these behaviors in the heat of the moment—but someone tasked with the job can.

The norm champion can move all of us closer to the norms we want to uphold by noticing and speaking up, but also by creating environments that themselves reinforce the norms. Seats can be rearranged, name tags made more gender-inclusive, and meeting protocols adjusted. Phoenix Group, the UK's largest long-term savings and retirement company, has been focused on finding small everyday moments in which work can be made more fair. "One of the moments we identified was coming in to present to the executive committee. You'd open this big door to our boardroom to see a table full of senior leaders with no seat for you. That 'where am I supposed to go' moment was unsettling for people and added to the pressure. We wanted to understand how we could create an environment that enables them to perform at their best," explained talent director Tamar Hughes. "We made a simple change so that every person who comes in to present now has a committee sponsor. The sponsor's job is to reserve a seat for them in the room, welcome them when they arrive, and introduce them to the rest of the leaders. It feels much more inclusive now."

Such changes not only literally affect how we do things but also serve as signals of the type of world we want to live in. They build fairness into our standard operating procedures so that it is easier for us to follow through on an ongoing basis. In many ways, this is not so different from what Megan Rapinoe, the US soccer star, shared when asked what corporate leaders should do to promote inclusion: "One thing is to set the environment first, prior to someone being there. For example, I don't think any NFL owner would say, 'We don't want gay players on our team.' But they don't seem very welcoming. The environment includes the language you use, the training courses you offer, your hiring practices, who you do business with, what your executive suite looks like. All those things signal to people whether they're safe or not. The proactivity of people in the majority is really important."

Let's home in on the language we use for a moment. Sharing gender pronouns ("she," "he," "they," "ze," etc.) has become an important way to acknowledge people's gender identity. The use of the gender-inclusive "they/them" has spread in English, while in Sweden, the gender-neutral pronoun "hen" was introduced into the 2015 Academy Glossary that determines norms for the Swedish language. Research suggests that the use of "hen," together with "hon" (she) and "han" (he), is common now—and it matters. When presented with gender-neutral pronouns, people exhibited less bias against women and LGBTQ+ individuals because the male default became less associated with the human norm. For the English language, the American Psychological Association has published a detailed Inclusive Language Guide (that includes but also goes beyond gender) that you might find helpful.

Arguably, gender inclusion is even harder for gendered languages with feminine and masculine forms of many words. The languages most spoken in the world that are gendered (that is, nouns and pronouns have a gender) include Arabic, French, Hindi, and Spanish. In English, pronouns but not nouns are gendered, while Finnish, Mandarin, Turkish, and many indigenous languages are categorized as gender-neutral or genderless since neither nouns nor pronouns have a marked gender.

Cooperativa Pacífico, a leading financial institution in Peru, tackled language as one of the first frontiers to change norms. The company realized that it often defaulted to the masculine form in internal and external communications with employees, clients, and customers. But then, "We simply went from saying 'hola todos' [the

masculine form] to 'hola todos y todas,'" explained Anthony Miyagusuku, Cooperativa Pacífico's manager of sustainability. It wasn't so
hard and could rather easily be built into formal communications.
"And then we applied the same fairness lens to examine our visuals in
order to, for example, remove stereotypical photos of women around
Mother's Day and men around Father's Day."

Anthony Miyagusuku shows us what it means to be a norm entrepreneur and an ally. Instead of feeling threatened by the new insights,
he became curious and acted on them. As legal scholars Kenji Yoshino
and David Glasgow write in their timely book *Say the Right Thing:
How to Talk about Identity, Diversity, and Justice*, "good allies
exhibit curiosity" as it helps us learn and be vulnerable—and speak
up against bias to advocate for those who are most underappreciated
in our organizations. Much like the use of inclusive language, allyship
can serve as a cue for identity safety and has been shown to increase
Black women's sense of organizational belonging. As a starting point,
we recommend LeanIn.Org's open-access resource for how to become
an ally.

When considering what words to use, we have to guard against
"cheap talk." Words do not automatically serve as credible signals.
In fact, signaling norms credibly is no easy feat—but we can take
inspiration from how Brazilian fishers are signaling norms to each
other. When the fishers and shrimpers go out on their lake in northeastern Brazil, they can use fishing gear that is more or less likely to
preserve the common resource they all depend on. If they use fish-
nets with small mesh sizes and build shrimp traps with small holes,
they are more likely to catch smaller fish and shrimp that have not
yet reached reproductive maturity. The fishers are well aware that
this is a problem: they need these small fish and shrimp to survive
into adulthood and reproduce for their livelihoods to be sustained.

Thankfully, the fishers have found an ingenious solution to what
researchers have referred to as "the tragedy of the commons," where
it is in our individual self-interest to overharvest our fields, overgraze

our pastures, and overfish our lakes and oceans because if we don't do it, someone else will. The solution is nets and traps with larger holes so that the smaller fish and shrimp can escape. It works because hole sizes are observable and thus, fishers can be held accountable for their choices. A big hole is a credible signal that a fisher complies with the norm of not overfishing.

These credible signals that go beyond diversity-washing are what we are after—and transparency can certainly help. Much like the fishers don't want to be caught overfishing by their colleagues and our children don't want to be scolded by their peers when they don't finish their plates, most of us want to be perceived as doing the right thing by our friends, coworkers, and the public. As discussed earlier, things like ESG commitments might not primarily affect our behaviors by providing incentives that are powerful enough for individual executives to change course; rather, they can serve as a signal of the type of organization we want to be, the type of employee we want to attract, and what we consider to be normal.

* * *

Five years after #MeToo went viral, a large majority of Americans believed that the movement had had a substantial impact, importantly by redefining "normality." Women and men now mostly agree on what constitutes sexual harassment, debunking the idea that men just don't know. Women surveyed both before and after #MeToo went viral report lower levels of sexual violence in 2018 than in 2016, something they attribute to the increased scrutiny on the topic. Sharyn Potter, a sociologist studying sexual violence who testified before a US House of Representatives veterans' affairs subcommittee, brings us right back to where we started this chapter: "So many victims blame themselves, so a bystander saying, 'This isn't your fault, you didn't do anything wrong,' is really, really important."

In a Pew Research Center nationally representative survey conducted in the summer of 2022, 70 percent of the respondents believed that "people who commit sexual harassment or assault in the workplace are now more likely to be held responsible." Most also indicated that those who report such experiences were more likely to be believed, and very few, 15 percent, said that false reporting was common. Women were somewhat more likely than men to support the #MeToo movement.

Much more work needs to be done, including to protect those who are most vulnerable, such as low-income and temporary employees as well as gig workers with little or no legal protection. But most everyone agrees that "me too" has turned from a moment into a movement with real impacts on the ground. Beyond its most immediate goal of decreasing sexual and gender-based violence, it can serve as a model of exemplary norm entrepreneurship: shaping what we believe to be acceptable behaviors and making available concrete ways of upholding social norms.

---

1. Change perceptions of the prevalent norms
2. Identify credible norm messengers
3. Create pathways to change

CHAPTER 12

Culture That Fosters Thriving

In April 2019, 300 female high school students gathered at Curtin University in Perth, Western Australia, to listen to some of the country's leading scientists. They included, among others, Katarina Miljkovic, the only Australian participating in NASA's InSight Mission to Mars; Asha Bowen, a pediatric clinician-scientist working to eradicate skin disease in Indigenous children; and Arlie Chapman, an accomplished roboticist at the University of Melbourne. Later in the year, a similar event took place on the country's east coast at the University of New South Wales. Both were part of a program designed to expose high school–aged girls to female role models in science, which was launched in France by L'Oréal, the world's largest cosmetics company, in 2014. Over the past decade, *For Girls in Science* has inspired thousands of budding female scientists around the world. In May 2023, the Centro Criollo de Ciencia y Tecnología del Caribe celebrated the graduation of its first cohort of female high school students participating in a similar, albeit more extensive, program in Puerto Rico.

Remember how you felt when you first "met" Katherine Johnson, Mary Jackson, and Dorothy Vaughan, three brilliant mathematicians who worked as "human computers" for NASA at the Langley Research Center in Virginia during the space race in the 1960s? Perhaps you watched the film *Hidden Figures*, or read the nonfiction book with the same title by Margot Lee Shetterly that inspired the film. The three women—who excelled in counter-stereotypical roles, defied the odds, and surmounted enormous sexism and racism—have inspired many. Jackson became the first female African American engineer at NASA. Vaughan was the space agency's first African American supervisor. And Johnson conducted crucial research on flight trajectories for various space shuttle missions that led her to receive the Presidential Medal of Freedom in 2015. Langley Research Center also named a building in her honor.

In this chapter, we start by examining how we can make work fair by making the counter-stereotypical no longer countercultural. Seeing others who look like we do helps us imagine that we too could be scientists or mathematicians—or anything else we aim for. Within organizations, the sheer fact that there are women in counter-stereotypical roles sends a signal that "people like us" can thrive there.

Role models serve at least three functions. They inspire, suggesting that something that we might have thought was out-of-bounds is actually possible; they allow us to emulate them, showing what successful behaviors look like; and they serve as an indication for what an organization stands for. As such, role models are an important part of organizational culture. They are both a symbol for and shaper of "how we do things around here," a common characterization of corporate culture we also subscribe to.

For culture to become real in an organization, we need to see more. Not only who people are and which roles they occupy but also how they behave and how they are treated. Seeing how much support employees receive to do their jobs, what type of feedback is given to help them grow, and how they are included in meetings (or not) builds a shared understanding of values and expectations. Between 2016 and 2021, about 10 percent of US employees reported experiencing a toxic workplace culture defined as "disrespectful, non-inclusive, unethical, cutthroat, or abusive." Both women and men indicated mistreatment at work but women were about 35 percent more inclined to talk about toxic culture in their Glassdoor reviews than men, a gap that further increased during COVID-19. Based on a meta-analysis of 400 studies, women were more likely to indicate being subject to discrimination and harassment while men reported more abusive supervision and interpersonal conflict. The pattern for employees of color was similar to that for women, but unfortunately, the data was not collected in a manner that allowed the researchers to analyze it intersectionally.

Many argue that to model desired behaviors, leaders are key. While the tone from the top certainly is important, middle managers have emerged as linchpins in the creation of a healthy organizational culture. They have been found to be up to six times more relevant in predicting employee misconduct than company-wide factors, particularly when managers were farther removed from headquarters. Middle managers might be among the most important culture carriers in an organization as employees see them on a regular basis and learn from them about which behaviors are acceptable and which ones are not.

These perceptions are reinforced by "cultural artifacts": the paintings on our walls, the language we use, the stories we tell, the jokes we find acceptable, the dress code we impose, the rituals we observe, the taboos we accept, the occasions we celebrate, the role models we admire, and the people we interact with—or not. All of these are manifestations of our shared identity as employees of an organization and can catalyze or inhibit our success at work.

Interacting with others who differ from us, not in a casual but in a deep way, can help overcome cleavages that divide us, something political scientist Robert Putnam referred to as "bridging social capital." When we interact with members of our own group (with high levels of similarity on one or more core dimensions), "bonding social capital" tends to grow. This may also be happening in affinity or employee resource groups where we get strength and inspiration from others who have similar life experiences.

However, we need to strike a fine balance between sameness and difference, given the context we find ourselves in. Sometimes, same-gender (or other same-identity) interactions are preferable (e.g., exposure to same-identity role models) and sometimes, they are not (e.g., connecting with different-identity teammates and collaborators). And sometimes, unexpected complexities are at play, such as when employees fear same-identity competition more than different-identity competition. Then they might forgo their preference for similarity and opt for difference instead.

As you can tell, designing an environment where everyone can thrive is a tall order—but thankfully, there is quite a bit of evidence on how different strategies have fared thus far. We share it with you here.

Make Role Models Available

You might be surprised by just how much role models matter. Even the relatively low-key exposure to role models that the Australian high schoolers experienced at the *For Girls in Science* event can make a difference. Working with the L'Oréal Foundation, researchers took a close look at a role modeling intervention in France that inspired the program. It consisted of one-hour in-class meetings in high schools where female scientists shared with students, female and male, what their lives as scientists looked like, including addressing gender stereotypes. Half of these scientists were young professionals; the other half were doctoral students and postdoctoral researchers in STEM.

The experiment included about 100 schools and almost 20,000 high schoolers in grades 10 and 12 (the final year when students choose which university program to enroll in) in the Paris region. Half of them were randomly chosen to be exposed to a role model and the other half served as a control group. The exposure to a female scientist did not matter for the tenth graders. However, the impact on twelfth-grade female students was remarkable. The intervention increased the share of women enrolling in undergraduate programs focused on mathematics, physics, computer science, or engineering by between 20 and 28 percent, with the strongest impact on female students who excelled at math. There was no impact on male students.

Women already working in STEM were the most successful role models, perhaps because they could more clearly describe a scientist's career path and stimulate students' aspirations—or because they just exuded a sense of normalcy.

A bit like Tarja Halonen, Finland's first female president, who was elected in 2000. After serving two terms and leaving office in 2012, President Halonen shared the story of visiting a Finnish kindergarten in the mid-2000s and asking the children, all of whom had been born since she took office, what they wanted to be when they grew up. When she asked a little boy if perhaps he would like to be president of Finland one day, he looked confused and replied, "No, because boys can't be president in Finland." In the span of a few years, a new generation of children was growing up with the default assumption that presidents are—and should be—women.

Seeing truly is believing, which is why it is so important to have exposure to a diverse set of role models representative of the world. Project #ShowUs, developed by Dove, the personal care brand owned by Unilever, contains thousands of stock photos of women and nonbinary individuals "to shatter beauty stereotypes by showing us as we are, not as others believe we should be." Similarly, the *This Girl Can* campaign in the United Kingdom and in Australia depicts women "in all shapes and sizes with all abilities and from all backgrounds" to inspire women to do sports.

For role models to be effective, they need to be chosen based on the needs of the people they are meant to inspire. When Southern Methodist University in Dallas decided to recruit alumnae role models to increase the share of women majoring in economics, it got help from economics students themselves. The role models the students identified had graduated with an economics degree a few years earlier, had successful careers in business, worked in various sectors and countries, and were charismatic as well as strong communicators. One thing the role models had in common was that they did not work in jobs stereotypically associated with an economics major and as such, broadened the appeal of the subject. The intervention's impact in Dallas was similarly astounding as in Paris: a short visit by one of these successful and inspiring female economists was able to almost double the likelihood of female students majoring in economics.

People who embody our dreams are able to ever so slightly shift what we thought possible for ourselves. They may also, as psychologist Nilanjana Dasgupta put it, serve as "social vaccines who increase social belonging and inoculate fellow group members' self-concept against stereotypes." Research specifically examining the role model effect found that similarity, desirability, and attainability are key. Same-gender and same-race role models tend to have more impact, particularly in counter-stereotypical domains.

Mentors and advisors are an interesting case in point. Many colleges provide their students with first-year advisors to help them navigate the new academic landscape. Working with the American University of Beirut, a private four-year college in Lebanon, researchers took a look at whether the gender of the advisors influenced the types of majors students chose. Students could not select their advisors but were randomly assigned one. Similar to colleges in the United States, at this university male students have traditionally been almost three times as likely to declare a major in STEM as their female counterparts.

Exposure to a female rather than a male science advisor doubled the likelihood that women enrolled in a STEM field. The gender of the advisor was not significant for male students. The reduction of the gender gap almost completely carried over to graduation rates four years later, as these women tended to stick with their choices. Like in France, having a female role model available had the biggest impact on the most mathematically gifted female students who already had the ability but needed a little nudge to take the plunge into one of the heavily male-dominated STEM fields.

In addition to being similar and desirable, role models should ideally be within reach. This, of course, is not the case with a head of state. President Halonen normalized seeing a woman as a leader of a country, but having a female mayor might be even more behaviorally relevant. Through the Panchayati Raj Act, a 1993 amendment to its constitution reserving a third of village head positions for women, India was able to increase the fraction of women in local government from 5 percent to 40 percent in just a dozen years. Already in 2005, it exceeded its initial goal of 33 percent. With female role models available, female villagers started speaking up more in town hall meetings and were inspired to run for public office themselves. The act even changed what parents thought possible for their daughters: they now wanted them to become politicians. On the heels of this success, in 2023, India reserved a third of the seats in its lower house of parliament and in state legislative assemblies for women.

The same pattern has been found in the private sector. The more available role models are, the more likely they are to have an impact. This might be the reason why members of boards of directors, who tend to be barely visible to employees, do not seem to be as powerful role models as we might have expected. Following the introduction of quotas in Norway in 2003 and in Italy in 2011, gender diversity on corporate boards dramatically increased, but the gender composition of senior management did not follow suit in either country, nor were there any discernible effects on women's labor market outcomes. In contrast, much like mayors who are close to their communities, managers are influential for their employees. Based on data from a US law firm, retention rates of junior talent were highly correlated with their supervisor's demographic characteristics, particularly for members of traditionally underrepresented groups: women and people of color.

The role model effect is surprisingly powerful. To make it work, focus on role models who are similar, whose careers are desirable, and whose positions are attainable. If you are able, be one yourself. Otherwise, point such role models out to your colleagues. Or better yet, promote their visibility throughout your whole team or organization. And increase representation. We need to see to believe.

Make the Workplace Psychologically Safe

For much of the last century, creating a safe working environment meant better protecting employees from physical harm. Offices like the Occupational Health and Safety Administration in the United States have invested heavily in making machines safer through automation and safeguards, appropriate labels and warnings, mats against slippery footing, as well as personal protective equipment (PPE) that many of us who don't ordinarily work in hazardous occupations first encountered during COVID-19.

This was also when we learned that PPE quite literally was not "fit" for women. Based on a 2021 survey conducted in more than 50 countries by Women in Global Health, only a tiny fraction of female healthcare providers had access to properly fitted PPE during the pandemic. Indeed, the report goes into detail on how little PPE has taken women's body shapes (think height, weight, and pregnancy), bodily needs (think menstruation and bathrooms), or culture (think head coverings and dresses in contrast to pants) into account. However, much like Astrid Linder and her team knew what was required to make cars safer for all, these frontline workers who helped keep the pandemic in check knew what they needed. Some of the headlines include sizes that fit women's faces and bodies as well as designs appropriate for different climates, hairstyles, headwear, clothing, and bodily needs.

While we still have much work to do on physical safety, we can learn from the progress made to date to move the needle on "psychological safety," a term coined by organizational behavior scholar Amy Edmondson. It is the "belief that one will not be punished or humiliated for speaking up with ideas, questions, concerns, or mistakes." In most guidelines on physical safety at work, spaces (e.g., buildings, stairways, exterior walkways), equipment (e.g., smoke detectors, hard hats, PPE), and communication (e.g., tone from the top, safety refreshers, and handwashing reminders in bathrooms) rank at the top. We need similar guidelines for psychological safety, and as you will see, addressing various forms of vulnerability is key.

Women, and even more so women of color, are vulnerable because they often are the "onlys" in the room. The lone Latina or Black woman is more likely to stand out, be scrutinized, and be taken for a token representing their whole group—when all they ever wanted was to be taken seriously for the expertise they bring to the table. Meetings are one particularly important moment for psychological safety to come alive. How we conduct them, whom we include, and how we treat each other sends a strong message about the culture we want to uphold. As such, meetings might be one of the most important tools at our disposal to make work fair.

It all starts with who is at the table, and much research has gone into better understanding what a difference it makes for meeting effectiveness. What we know is that just putting a few smart people together in a room is not a winning strategy. To maximize a group's "collective intelligence," we need to go after complementarities between group members. Take the professions required to build a house as an example. When we looked it up, a list of more than twenty entries appeared: carpenters, roofers, architects, electricians, and many more. None of them could do it alone, and none of them could do it by cloning themselves twenty times. In his illuminating book *The Difference*, decision scientist Scott Page makes just that point mathematically. Sometimes, diversity = productivity.

Pushing the argument further, organizational psychologist Anita Williams Woolley and colleagues evaluated the collective intelligence of many groups and found that it was the groups that scored highest on "social sensitivity" that were best able to benefit from diversity. Those that took turns speaking and listening were able to build on each other's arguments. In their research, women were particularly adept at making the whole larger than the sum of its parts and thereby advancing collective intelligence.

Making meetings more fair benefits everyone, but particularly women, as they are more likely to be interrupted, overlooked, or not given credit for their ideas than men—subtle, everyday disrespect and degradations for which psychiatrist Chester Pierce introduced the term "microaggressions" in the 1970s to highlight offensive behaviors experienced by Black people. They manifest themselves in many ways, including in our body language: not being looked at when someone addresses the group (a.k.a. men speaking to each other); rolling eyes or hand gestures as a sign of annoyance; and backs turned to some people as a sign of disengagement and disrespect. Based on audio analysis of meetings and talks with machine learning tools, research now can quite easily document these. Female economists, for example, were less likely to be spoken to in a positive tone and more likely to be interrupted in patronizing or hostile ways when giving talks or conducting seminars.

While it is a leadership failure if microaggressions go unnoticed or unaddressed, leaders cannot carry this water alone. We all are responsible for doing our part to create workplaces and meetings free of microaggressions. If you already have a "devil's advocate" who helps you protect your meetings from groupthink, have them also serve in the role we introduced in the previous chapter: a norm champion who upholds the norms you collectively subscribe to. They can listen carefully, make sure all voices are heard, explicitly question assumptions, and critique conclusions. At Harvard Kennedy School, we refer to them as our "culture ambassadors." If you don't have such a person, design around it: use a timer to give everyone equal airtime and establish the "two-two rule," whereby speakers limit their comments to two minutes and wait for at least two other colleagues to speak before chiming in again.

Of course, microaggressions are not only experienced in meetings. Here is a subtle one that we are sure many of you have encountered: the informal conversations that take place before the official meeting starts and highlight that some of us are "in the know" (e.g., just joining from a different meeting that some continue to talk about); have shared moments of bonding (e.g., in the real or proverbial golf club); and generally have things in common (e.g., a preferred vacation destination).

Women of color, women with disabilities, and LGBTQ+ women are particularly vulnerable to "othering" microaggressions that cast doubt on whether they belong. They differ in more than one dimension from the male, white, able-bodied, heterosexual "norm" in most workplaces, and are also less likely to benefit from micro-sponsorship such as recognition, affirmation, and praise. In fact, this is one of our favorite things to leave people with: to make work fair, become a micro-sponsor! Validate others' ideas and make sure they get credit for them when they are overlooked (or worse, attributed to someone else). Acknowledge everyone's presence by making eye contact and calling people by their preferred names and pronouns. Pass opportunities on to others whenever possible, and praise your colleagues, not in a superficial but in a real way. And help make sure worthy ideas see the light of day.

After years of research, Google discovered that psychological safety was the secret sauce to team effectiveness: "Individuals on teams with higher psychological safety are less likely to leave Google, they're more likely to harness the power of diverse ideas from their teammates, they bring in more revenue, and they're rated as effective twice as often by executives." In her TEDx talk, "Building a Psychologically Safe Workplace," Amy Edmondson explains that making this happen would entail framing work as a learning problem, acknowledging your fallibility, and modeling curiosity. Specifically:

- Focus on information sharing, not judgment and evaluation

- Frame differences as a growth opportunity, not a basis for dispute

- Ask open questions, not closed ones where the answer is predetermined

- Aim for shared ownership, not individual blame

- Be a micro-sponsor, not a micro-aggressor

We warmly encourage you to implement these strategies. Psychologically safe meetings and workplaces are not only more effective, but also more fun.

Provide Support for All

In 2017, Iris wrote an article for the *New York Times* titled "Tackling the Thin File That Can Prevent a Promotion." In a law firm she worked with, partners kept telling her that some associates just had a "thin file" when they came up for promotion. What they meant was that the employee's track record did not contain enough promotable work, important mandates, key clients, or blockbuster deals. The gender (and race) gap in the file turned out to start right out of the gate when partners chose the first-year associates they wanted to work with—and selected people who looked male and pale, just like them. Women and people of color had become victims of "performance-support bias." The sad fact is that some people in our organizations get more support and resources to help them excel from day one.

We also noted that thin files came with less feedback and advice, the kind of support that is often provided by mentors and sponsors. In 2004, the American Economic Association's Committee on the Status of Women in the Economic Profession (CSWEP) launched a mentoring program for early-career female assistant professors. When it was evaluated a few years later, the findings were encouraging: the program had increased the research productivity of the random set of women who had participated in it compared to those who had not. More generally, based on data from 800 US firms over more than 40 years, the presence of mentorship programs was correlated with substantial increases in the shares of Black, Asian American, and Hispanic women and men in management.

Most companies do not evaluate the impact of their mentoring programs. They (you!) should. For some, voluntary programs work best since they attract the people most open to learning. For others, mandatory programs would be better. In a 2019 randomized controlled trial in a call center that directly compared compulsory to voluntary mentoring, those who needed the mentoring most were the ones most likely to opt out. This is particularly surprising as in this case, the focus was on productivity, and mentors helped employees improve their skills to be more productive and make more money. While it is not entirely clear why the lower-performing workers who would have benefited were the least likely to avail themselves of the offered help, the pattern is reminiscent of other findings. For example, based on the Illinois Workplace Wellness Study, it is the less healthy who choose not to participate in wellness programs.

What experts agree on is that, once again, design is key. Based on an extensive review by psychologist Tammy Allen, a mentoring program has a higher chance of success if it is supported by top management; mentors are carefully selected and matched with their mentees; the mentoring partners establish a clear understanding (possibly, a contract) outlining the terms of engagement, number of interactions, and types of support; and program evaluation is built in to institute accountability and continuous learning.

We also know that advice is better than feedback, and mentors are uniquely positioned to offer it since the type of input employees receive in performance appraisals is mostly evaluative and can lead many people to just shut down. We know the feeling. Teaching evaluations by students can be harsh, and the temptation to just gloss over them is huge. But when executive education participants in a program Iris chaired shared what they thought about the faculty's teaching, they were more likely to provide helpful input that could be used to improve the learning of future cohorts when framed as "advice" instead of "feedback." For example, one participant who was asked for advice wrote: "I loved the cases. But I would have preferred concentrating more time on learning specific tools that would help improve the XXX skills of the participants." So helpful!

In contrast, a participant in the feedback condition stated: "This faculty's content and style of teaching was not satisfactory." Gee, thanks. Feedback tends to be backward-looking and evaluative, whereas advice is more likely to be forward-looking and as such more change-oriented, something shown to be useful not only in class-rooms but also in boardrooms. After all, we cannot modify the past but we can improve the future. So next time you find yourself asking for or giving feedback, ask for or give advice instead.

Finally, the more a mentor can serve as a sponsor, the better. While anyone can be a mentor and offer help and advice, a sponsor is some-one more senior than you who can influence your career advancement in concrete ways. Sponsors are so powerful precisely because they can channel opportunities your way; make critical introductions and bring you along to places you wouldn't have been invited to otherwise; and be your advocate in rooms that you are not in.

When sponsors actively endorse their protégé(e)s and put their own social and political capital on the line to vouch for them, they send an additional signal of competence, particularly in counter-stereotypical areas. As mentioned earlier, job referrals tend to make the biggest dif-ference for candidates who might otherwise have to contend with bias in hiring or promotion. However, in many cases it still is the stereo-typical person who gets the endorsements. Sociologist Emilio Castilla found that white men received more endorsements when applying to a US business school than women and people of color. One of the most powerful things you can do to make your workplace more fair is to find someone you can support, mentor, and/or sponsor: a more junior person, the newest hire, a peer—or a more senior person in what some have referred to as "reverse mentoring."

A culture of support comes down to providing advice equitably, giving everyone equal opportunities to build their "file," and provid-ing access to mentors and sponsors.

Create Opportunities for Deep Contact Across Difference

In 1996, the US Supreme Court ruled that the Virginia Military Institute had to admit women as cadets. The share of women in the military has slowly risen during the past half century and now stands at about 15 percent in the United States, a fraction similar to other OECD countries such as France and Norway. Women's integration into our armed forces represents an interesting case study of the relevance of interpersonal contact between women and men in a heavily male-dominated environment where gender stereotypes loom large.

To better understand these dynamics, a group of researchers collaborated with the Norwegian military and ran an experiment during boot camp. They randomly assigned female recruits to some squads but kept others all-male so that they had a control group to compare with. Being in a squad means working and living together for eight weeks under sometimes grueling conditions. The research found that men in mixed teams performed just as well and were just as satisfied as those in all-male teams. What is more, after this intense exposure to female colleagues, men's attitudes started to shift. Compared to the control group, male soldiers in mixed teams were substantially more likely to report that mixed teams performed as well or better than same-gender teams. Following boot camp, they were also more likely to select military occupations with a higher share of women. Alas, the effects of increased contact did not last. After military service, men's gender attitudes fell right back to those of the control group that had not been exposed to female colleagues.

In fact, documented positive long-term impacts of intergroup contact on behavior are rare. They are more likely to occur in situations of deep and sustained contact, such as among college roommates who live together with people different from them or colleagues who work together towards a shared goal over a long period. Playing sports is illustrative. Political scientist Salma Mousa worked with Iraqis displaced by ISIS (the Islamic State of Iraq and Syria) and randomly assigned Christians to either play soccer on mixed teams with Muslims or, in the control group, on all-Christian teams. The Christian players in the mixed teams were more likely to exhibit tolerant behaviors toward Muslims compared to the control group. These behaviors included registering for a mixed team the following season; training with Muslims six months after the intervention; and voting for a non-teammate Muslim to receive a sportsmanship award. Similar positive effects of sports practice were found in other parts of the world, including for intercaste relations in India when Indian men were randomly assigned either to mixed-caste or same-caste cricket teams.

In contrast, casual contact doesn't seem to help and can even lead to backlash. For example, when Boston commuters saw a larger share of people of a different ethnic origin on their train, they felt worse about that group. Similarly, in Afghanistan, casual interethnic contact heightened group differences and increased in-group identification.

What to do? In 1954, when Gordon Allport first proposed the contact hypothesis suggesting that interpersonal contact between members of different groups could decrease prejudice, he set a high bar for its success: equal status between the different groups, intergroup cooperation, common goals, and societal and institutional support. While it is unlikely for this set of conditions to occur in concert, one thing is clear: for intergroup contact to have the desired effects, we need to embed it into our organizations. While limited exposure to a same-gender (or race) role model can inspire us, exposure to an opposite-gender (or race) individual is more likely to impact us positively if the contact is deep and sustained. We purposely wrote "individual" here as we suspect that one of the benefits of intensive contact is that we get to know the person beyond the group and realize that differences within groups can sometimes be greater than between groups.

Connecting to the individual might well be the most important takeaway here, and in organizations, middle managers can again be helpful. When a large retail chain's CEO told managers to "do what they can" to decrease turnover, the likelihood that employees quit declined by about a quarter. As it turns out, these managers increased time spent with employees.

Novartis, one of the world's largest pharmaceutical companies, headquartered in Switzerland, ran a related experiment. In the fall of 2021, the managers of over 1,000 teams (consisting of about 7,000 employees in total) were encouraged to have more one-on-one meetings with their team members, and in one of the treatment conditions, were specifically advised to discuss their employees' needs and aspirations. The nudge worked. Managers ended up meeting more often with their team members than in the control condition, where they were just informed that a study on meetings was taking place.

While we do not know what was discussed in the meetings, employees were more likely to report being supported by their manager and considering their manager a role model. Being invited to share their needs increased how strongly employees agreed with two standard measures of psychological safety: "Different perspectives are valued in my team" and "I feel safe sharing feedback with my colleagues." You should try it. If you are uncertain about how to best conduct your one-on-one meetings, you may want to check out a guide created by Culture Amp (included in the endnotes).

Assess Culture

Many companies describe the principles and values they uphold—their corporate culture—on their website. However, when researchers tried to see whether any of these proclamations were correlated with measures of company performance (short- and long-term), they could not detect any significant relationship at all. Perhaps culture does not matter for performance in the end? Or perhaps what companies say is less relevant than what employees experience?

To solve the puzzle around culture and performance, economist Luigi Guiso and colleagues examined the Great Place to Work Institute's survey data on how employees in about 1,000 US companies perceived their company's values. Homing in on one of the most popular values described on company web pages—integrity—the researchers found that when employees rated firms high on integrity, they indeed were more profitable. While there was no way to establish a causal link, this certainly suggests that integrity and profitability can go hand in hand.

We can also apply natural language processing (NLP) tools to the massive amounts of text reviews available on companies' cultures. They allow researchers to identify cultural attributes distinctive to particular companies. While such analyses are gaining in popularity, often based on Glassdoor data, it is not entirely clear how representative the data is. Some have argued that Glassdoor reviews tend to be rather polarized, with employees either loving or hating their companies, while others have suggested that this is not the case. Be that as it may, companies care because Glassdoor provides an additional entry point for job seekers to learn more about a company's culture than what they can find on public web pages or through word of mouth.

Companies are up against a lot. Not only might employee reviews not be representative or accurate, but the true state of affairs is difficult to establish. Culture has proven to be hard to measure. Already in 2009, 70 different culture diagnostic instruments were in use. Since then, many more have been developed. Some argue that culture is about something an organization *is* and others that it is something an organization *has*. We focus on culture reflecting what people *do*.

The measurement of inclusion as a key aspect of culture suffers from the same assessment challenges, starting with how to define the concept so that we know what to measure. According to one definition, inclusion consists of seven key dimensions: "fair treatment, integrating differences, decision-making, psychological safety, trust, belonging, and diversity." Many consulting firms in the space have developed their own assessment methodologies. For example, UK-based Included provides an inclusion diagnostic focused on behavioral questions, and Culture Amp offers its clients employee engagement surveys benchmarked against other employers in the same industry.

We are always intrigued by assessment tools that allow us to compare and calibrate, not just across firms but also across topics employees care about. In the typical survey, we rarely learn about this. Employees likely respond that more of everything—role models, support, contact with their managers, mentorship, etc.—is just better, which of course is true. But it's not necessarily doable. It would be rather helpful if organizations could assess what employees value most and spend their resources accordingly.

Wegmans, the US supermarket chain, tackled this exact question when it tried to assess what types of health benefits employees cared most about. To get a better sense of how people felt about different options, they were surveyed about various packages that forced them to make realistic trade-offs (e.g., a lower deductible but higher premium versus a higher deductible but lower premium). Through this analysis, Wegmans learned what its employees really valued and could target every dollar spent on healthcare to yield the highest benefits.

* * *

You can do this too. Whichever tool you use to assess culture, we urge you to go beyond simple measurement. Data is absolutely critical for diagnosing what is broken and evaluating which of the fixes work—but it can also help you optimize your interventions. Ask your employees about the relative importance they assign to the different ways in which a culture can be made healthier. Would having a sponsor be more impactful than meetings where you never get interrupted again? If you ran such an analysis with us right now, you would learn that we are most intrigued by the powerful impact role models can have as a low-cost, high-benefit intervention. In addition, building psychological safety, which is not easy but feels like a must in our increasingly diverse world, is just good management practice. Providing support for all is something that will require resources but can be done, including by each and every one of us when we act as micro-sponsors. Be one!

1. Make role models available
2. Make the workplace psychologically safe
3. Provide support for all
4. Create opportunities for deep contact across difference
5. Assess culture

Change for Good

"Our hearts and minds were always in the right place. But things really changed when it went from a 'should do' to being part of the process."

The "it" John Iino is talking about is fairness. Iino, the recently retired director of global diversity, equity, and inclusion at law firm Reed Smith, joined the Pittsburgh-based company more than twenty years ago as a lawyer. "We were always intentional about looking at the demographics and the gender split of our promotion classes and thinking about these things at a high level," recounted Iino. But their best intentions hadn't always translated into results. Like many people and organizations that care about fairness, Reed Smith was stuck in what Ros Atkins at the BBC termed a "constant state of trying."

The firm's state of trying morphed into action when Iino started asking for detailed data on the workforce. In 2017, the company rolled out scorecards that tracked the gender, race, and sexual orientation of all lawyers by office and practice group; the following year, they added a client-level scorecard tracking the composition of client teams. Every practice group leader, office managing partner, and department head received their own personal scorecard and was compared to a benchmark as well as ranked against other practices and offices. This allowed

Reed Smith to examine hidden hurdles in their systems—and it made fairness count.

Between 2018 and 2022, Reed Smith's senior management team went from 43 percent to 50 percent women, and the share of women among office managing partners increased from 22 to 37 percent. In 2023, women made up over 40 percent of partner promotions, and 40 percent of lateral partner hires firmwide were diverse (defined by Reed Smith as people that identify as having a disability, or being ethnically diverse, LGBTQ+, Black, or a military veteran). These numbers are transparently shared with the world through annual reports.

Iino's team also dove into analyzing the systems and processes that drove the numbers. They identified time use as a key lever for increasing fairness across the business since, as Iino noted, "with attorneys, it all comes down to billable hours." The team also tackled succession planning after Dana Alvaré, sociologist and Reed Smith's senior global gender equity advisor, identified it as a hot spot of potential bias. In order to create a more open and thoughtful process, leaders were asked for the names of three individuals who could succeed them every year, allowing Reed Smith to assess if bias may have crept into the transition process.

Fundamentally, Reed Smith's leaders realized that in order to achieve real results and level the playing field, they had to make fairness an inextricable part of their everyday work of managing clients, hiring and promoting lawyers, and setting goals for the firm. They could not rely purely on individuals' good intentions but had to turn it into systemic practice to make fairness stick.

While the firm has been helped by a robust internal DEI team, the true testament of how fairness has become built into its culture is that another 140 people are formally spending part of their time in leadership roles working to advance fairness—and *all* employees can contribute as part of their core work (billable hours). "We chose our slogan, 'All Rise,' to reflect the fact that this work is everyone's responsibility and for everyone's benefit," explained John Iino. "It permeates all aspects of our organization." In the words of our book, it makes fairness normal.

As we shared with you at the outset of our quest, to make work fair, you need to build fairness into everything you do. Throughout this book, we have discovered numerous concrete ways to make (your) work fair, whether you are a summer intern or the CEO. While no *one* of the strategies we have discussed will fix unfairness overnight, implementing any of them will be a step in the right direction. And many small steps can add up to giant leaps, with real results.

Maria Klawe and the computer science department she oversaw proved this at Harvey Mudd College, a science and engineering–focused liberal arts college in California. When Klawe arrived on Harvey Mudd's campus as its first female president in 2006, only 10 percent of computer science majors were women. Four years later, the share of female computer science students had quadrupled, and in 2018, the graduating class included an all-time high of 56 percent women among its computer science degree recipients (compared to the US national average of 20 percent). As of 2023, the student body was 49 percent women; the share of Black students had increased from less than one percent when Klawe arrived to more than 15 percent; and Hispanic students made up roughly a quarter of the college.

Klawe and the computer science (CS) department followed the same data-driven playbook we have shared with you to achieve these results. They started by diagnosing the problem and built on previous research suggesting that women "do not find CS interesting, believe they will not do well in CS, and feel uncomfortable in the computing culture," as Maria Klawe summarized. The department redesigned its introductory course to make it more accessible to all students, even those without any programming experience, and changed classroom culture to make it easier for everyone to contribute while promoting more collaboration and "micro-tutoring" between students. To expose women to role models, Harvey Mudd started sponsoring first-year female students in all fields to attend the Grace Hopper Celebration of Women in Computing conference. And to break stereotypes and boost students' confidence in their ability to do the work of a computer scientist, faculty created paid summer research projects for students early on in their CS journey. The projects turned out to be especially impactful in encouraging women to major in CS.

Klawe supported these departmental efforts by allocating resources and directing a broader push across the college to redesign recruitment materials and showcase more diverse role models in imagery across campus. Klawe also spearheaded the diversification of Harvey Mudd's faculty, increasing the proportion of female professors to 40 percent and appointing women to chair departments.

Any single one of these actions would likely have moved the needle, even though it is hard to know exactly how much. But when implemented together as a holistic, systemic approach to increase women's presence on campus, they created a sea change—one that has become a model for the US government's efforts to make STEM accessible to all, as Klawe shared at a White House conference in 2022.

Effective solutions that have been proven to yield real results are the heart of our book. But applying them to your work and selecting the actions that are best suited to achieve your particular goals will be up to you. Whatever you do, we urge you to A/B test and measure the effects of your actions whenever possible, as so many of the people and organizations we have encountered have done. This truly is the only way for us to continue expanding our knowledge base on what works and what doesn't—and to move us toward a new paradigm of evidence-based fairness.

If you encounter resistance or skepticism in your quest to make work fair, you are not alone. But just like the many norm entrepreneurs you have encountered in our book—managers, public servants, journalists, entrepreneurs, actors, CEOs, activists, engineers, heads of state, consultants, military personnel, sports stars, artists, civil society members, lawyers, board members, mayors, first responders, pharmacists, researchers, teachers, students, doctors, governors, nurses, astronauts, university presidents, scientists, and DEI leaders—you can continue to make progress if you channel your energies where they are most likely to make a difference. In her wonderful book *The Person You Mean to Be*, psychologist Dolly Chugh reminds us of the 20/60/20 rule: Roughly 20 percent of people will be enthusiastically with you and another 20 percent staunchly against you no matter what. The 60 percent group in the middle is where you have a lot of opportunity to shape social norms and influence people's behavior.

You can start by using the evidence in this book to question the status quo of how work is done and shift the burden of proof to those who are most supportive of current practices. If your colleagues love whiteboarding exercises in hiring, can they demonstrate that this public act is better at predicting future performance than a less stressful work sample test—and can they guarantee it does not negatively impact traditionally underrepresented applicants? Or if leaders resist counting and rewarding service to the organization, can they justify how punishing people who provide public goods that benefit all will lead to better results?

Change can be activated at any level, and what matters is that *you* now know what to do. Our ardent hope is that you will share this roadmap with the people around you. Bring key recommendations to your manager. Be a visible micro-sponsor and speak up next time a colleague gets interrupted in a meeting. Find a way to measure an aspect of fairness that is relevant to your work and share the results with your team. Be vocal about why you will ask all interviewees the same standard set of questions going forward. Or organize a book club to brainstorm how you can implement these solutions in your organization.

To make change for good, we have to keep at it. The price of not persisting is simply too high—for each of us, companies and govern-ments, and societies across the globe. Unfair work keeps the right people from doing the right job the right way in the right positions. That's what we call a market failure in economics. So let's not keep failing. We can get this right. You—yes, *you*—can be the change agent to make work fair, for good.

We can't wait to see what you will do!

ACKNOWLEDGMENTS

We are immensely grateful to the large group of loved ones, friends, colleagues, and publishing industry experts who have supported us in bringing this book to you. It has been a joy to experience this journey with all of them.

Thank you to the individuals and organizations whose work (and, in some cases, data) we have been able to feature in this book. You inspire us and give us hope that making work fair is indeed possible. Special thanks to all the people who gave us their time in interviews.

Our fabulous agents, Celeste Fine and Sarah Passick, were instrumental in bringing this book to life and helping us navigate the maze of publishing. Thank you for your support, commitment, and guidance. And thank you to the whole team at Park & Fine Literary and Media, especially John Maas, Melissa Rodman, and Mia Vitale, for enthusiastically embracing our vision of this book from day one.

We have been extremely fortunate to have Hollis Heimbouch as our editor and publisher at Harper Business. She has shared our passion from the moment we met and has been an incomparable thought partner and advocate at every stage of the process. We are truly grateful. We also want to sincerely thank Kirby Sandmeyer and the whole team at Harper Business. We have so appreciated the opportunity to work with you all.

We also thank Barbara Henricks and Betsy de Jesu at Cave Henricks Communications for their terrific publicity support; the AuthorBytes team for the wonderful design of the book website; and Howard Zaharoff and Jason Gish for providing essential legal assistance.

Many friends and fellow authors provided invaluable counsel, help, and encouragement as we navigated the complicated process of publishing a book. We are enormously appreciative of your wisdom: Colleen Ammerman, Christie Hunter Arscott, Dolly Chugh, Adam Grant, Elaine Lin Hering, Justin Krasner, Thomas LeBien, Robert Livingston, Tania Luna, Katy Milkman, Michael Norton, Ellen Gordon Reeves, Todd Rogers, Lise Vesterlund, and Elizabeth Weingarten.

We thank all the people who were exceptionally generous in reading drafts of this book and providing most insightful advice: Anisha Asundi, Ros Atkins, Dominik Bohnet Zürcher, Matt Breitfelder, Anna Burgess, Steve Dry, James Elfer, Kate Glazebrook, Sharad Goel, James Heighington, Lisa Kirby, Rebecca Lee, Elizabeth Linos, Vanessa Liu, Robert Livingston, Kathleen McGinn, Courtney Munnings, Annie McNerney, Frida Polli, Nicole Carter Quinn, Rachel Rosenberg, Erica Santoni, Caren Ulrich Stacy, and Judith Williams, as well as Lisa Damon, Christy Kiely, and Laura Maechtlen, who reviewed select sections. We are immensely grateful for your comments, all of which made this book better. Thank you also to Sarah Wald for her wise counsel and to everyone who served as a sounding board for the title.

Our ongoing work to advance gender equity in the workplace has been greatly shaped and supported by our world-class colleagues at the Women and Public Policy Program at Harvard Kennedy School. Our heartfelt thanks go to Anisha Asundi, Laura Botero, Hannah Riley Bowles, Anna Burgess, Kelsey Heroux, Hayley Murks-Abdikadirova, Moira Notarstefano, Katie Omberg, Nicole Carter Quinn, Hanna Rassouli, and Ruth Reyes. A very special thank-you to Lexi Serino and Sophia Gustafson for their exceptional assistance with more things than we can count.

We are also grateful to all of the interns and research assistants who have worked with us on research related to gender equity over the last several years: Alycia Cary, Xialene Chang, Iris Chen, Mayumi

Cornejo, Sophia Gustafson, Amy Huang, Sidnee Klein, Joy Wang, and Giulia Zaratti.

Our community at Harvard is a constant source of inspiration. We feel privileged to learn from the students in our degree and executive education programs, including the Young Global Leaders of the World Economic Forum, as well as our doctoral students, colleagues, advisees, research fellows, and seminar speakers. We thank you for shaping our thinking.

We are thrilled to have had the opportunity to work with many amazing collaborators on gender-related projects. Our profound thanks to Cansin Arslan, Max Bazerman, John Beshears, Hannah Riley Bowles, Hui-Yih Chai, Edward Chang, Oriane Georgeac, Fiona Greig, Oliver Hauser, Kessely Hong, Erika Kirgios, Deborah Kolb, Ariella Kristal, Kim Louw, Kathleen McGinn, Maliheh Paryavi, Jessica Porter, Aneeta Rattan, Farzad Saidi, Alexandra van Geen, Richard Zeckhauser, and the wonderful MoreThanNow team of James Elfer, Guusje Lindemann, and Katryn Wright.

We have much benefited from the conversations we have had over the years with the many fantastic members of the gender-focused organizations we are or have been affiliated with: Applied, chaired by Kate Glazebrook; Diversity Lab, led by Caren Ulrich Stacy; EDGE, led by Aniela Unguresan; the FTSE Women Leaders Review, led by Denise Wilson and Vivienne Artz; the G7 Gender Equality Advisory Council, chaired by Sarah Sands; genEquality, led by Sherry Hakimi; Generation CEO; the Global Agenda Council on Women's Empowerment of the World Economic Forum, led by Saadia Zahidi; the Global Institute for Women's Leadership at King's College London, chaired by the Hon. Julia Gillard AC; the MBA for Women Foundation, chaired by Mirjam Staub-Bisang; the Müller-Möhl Foundation, chaired by Carolina Müller-Möhl; Paradigm for Parity; the Snap Inc. Catalyze Tech Working Group, led by Oona King; the UK Government Equalities Office; the United Nations Advisory Group on the Gender Equality Acceleration Plan, led by Deputy Secretary-General Amina J. Mohammed; We Shape Tech with Petra Ehmann; and Women in Banking and Finance, led by Anna Lane.

We gratefully acknowledge the support of Abigail Disney, Janice Bryant Howroyd, Pivotal Ventures, the Radcliffe Institute, David Rubenstein, the Women and Public Policy Program, and the Women's Leadership Board at Harvard Kennedy School. Your generosity has enabled us to bring our ideas to the world, and we are most appreciative.

Iris wishes to thank her parents, Ruth and Paul, and her sister Brigitte and her family for their kindness and support. It is such a blessing to be surrounded by so much love. Finally, Iris's gratitude goes to her wonderful husband, Michael, and their two children, Dominik and Luca, for their love, inspiration, and support. You each made the book better in so many ways. Thank you for who you are and for the wisdom and happiness you bring to our world every day!

Siri wishes to thank her beloved JP, who is not only the most incredible husband, but also a phenomenal line editor, intellectual partner, and cheerleader. She feels blessed beyond measure to be his wife. Siri is also forever grateful to her dear parents, Laura and Jukkis Uotila, for the love and unconditional support they have always given her in all of her endeavors. Thank you for making this book possible in all the small and big ways!

NOTES

Introduction: Design for Fairness

ix   Astrid Linder developed the first female crash test dummy: Astrid Linder et al., "EvaRID—Anthropometric and Biomechanical Specification of a Finite Element Dummy Model of an Average Female for Rear Impact Testing," conference paper, 22nd International Technical Conference on the Enhanced Safety of Vehicles, Washington, D.C., June 13–16, 2011, https://www.academia.edu/80188345/EvaRID_Anthropometric_and_Biomechanical_Specification_of_a_Finite_Element_Dummy_Model_of_an_Average_Female_for_Rear_Impact_Testing.

ix   another ten are severely injured: Astrid Linder, "Eva, the Female Crash Test Dummy," 2018, video filmed at TEDxKTHWomen 2018, 0:41, https://www.ted.com/talks/astrid_linder_eva_the_female_crash_test_dummy.

ix   women are more likely to be injured: Alyssa Ryan et al., "The Impact of Sex on Motor Vehicle Crash Injury Outcomes," *Journal of Transportation Safety & Security* 14, no. 5 (2022): 818–42, https://doi.org/10.1080/19439962.2020.1834478.

ix   Astrid Linder aims, in her own words: Unni Eikeseth and Randi Lillealtern, "Gender Equality for Crash Test Dummies, Too," *ScienceNordic*, January 24, 2013, https://sciencenordic.com/cars-and-traffic-crash-test-dummies-forskningno/gender-equality-for-crash-test-dummies-too/1381623.

x   Women are not only lighter and shorter: Astrid Linder and Mats Y. Svensson, "Road Safety: The Average Male as a Norm in Vehicle Occupant Crash Safety Assessment," *Interdisciplinary Science Reviews* 44, no. 2 (2019): 140–53, https://doi.org/10.1080/03080188.2019.1603870.

x   keep men meaningfully safer than women: Patrick M. Carter et al., "Comparing the Effects of Age, BMI and Gender on Severe Injury (AIS 3+) in Motor-vehicle Crashes," *Accident Analysis & Prevention* 72 (2014): 146–60, https://doi.org/10.1016/j.aap.2014.05.024.

x   regulations around the world continue to specify: Astrid Linder and Wanna Svedberg, "Review of Average Sized Male and Female Occupant Models in European Regulatory Safety Assessment Tests and European Laws: Gaps and Bridging Suggestions," *Accident Analysis and Prevention* 127 (2019): 156–62, https://doi.org/10.1016/j.aap.2019.02.030.

x   developed two female crash test dummies: Astrid Linder, Kristian Holmqvist, and Mats Y. Svensson, "Average Male and Female Virtual Dummy Model (BioRID and EvaRID) Simulations with Two Seat Concepts in the Euro NCAP Low Severity Rear Impact Test Configuration," *Accident Analysis & Prevention* 114 (2018): 62–70, https://doi.org/10.1016/j.aap.2017.05.029.

x   Government Accountability Office recommended: United States Government Accountability Office, "Vehicle Safety: DOT Should Take Additional Actions to Improve the Information Obtained from Crash Test Dummies," Report to Congressional Committees (GAO-23-13-105595), March 2023, https://www.gao.gov/assets/gao-23-105595.pdf.

xii   crucial for how well they fare as adults: "Opportunity Atlas Data Tool," United States Census Bureau, accessed April 12, 2024, https://www.census.gov/programs-surveys/ces/data/analysis-visualization-tools/opportunity-atlas.html.

xii   women in India: Lori Beaman et al., "Powerful Women: Does Exposure Reduce

Bias?," *Quarterly Journal of Economics* 124, no. 4 (2009): 1497–1540, https://doi
.org/10.1162/qjec.2009.124.4.1497.

xii girls in France: Thomas Breda et al., "How Effective Are Female Role Models in
Steering Girls Towards STEM? Evidence from French High Schools," *Economic Journal*
133, no. 653 (2023): 1773–1809, https://doi.org/10.1093/ej/uead019.

xii a 40 percent quota for men: Ursina Schaede and Ville Mankki, "Quota Vs Quality?
Long-Term Gains from an Unusual Gender Quota," CESifo Working Paper Series 9811,
CESifo, Munich, 2022, https://doi.org/10.2139/ssrn.4150133.

xii more at risk in collisions: "Inclusive Crash Test Dummies: Rethinking Standards
and Reference Models," Gendered Innovations in Science, Health & Medicine, Engineering, and Environment, accessed July 25, 2023, https://genderedinnovations.stanford.edu
/case-studies/crash.html#tabs-1.

xiv "details, facts, and analysis": Ruth Umoh, "JPMorgan's Jamie Dimon Talks DEI: 'I'm a
Full-Throated, Red-Blooded, Patriotic, Unwoke, Capitalist CEO,'" Yahoo! Finance, January 24,
2024, https://finance.yahoo.com/news/jpmorgan-jamie-dimon-talks-dei-132700973.html.

xiv faculty use an application called Teachly: "Teachly," Teachly, accessed October 7,
2023, https://teachly.me/.

xv "Our approach to inclusion marketing": Sandy Saputo, "How Rihanna's Fenty
Beauty Delivered 'Beauty for All'—and a Wake-up Call to the Industry," Think with Google, June 2019, https://www.thinkwithgoogle.com/future-of-marketing/management
-and-culture/diversity-and-inclusion/-fenty-beauty-inclusive-advertising/.

xv In Colombia, the country's largest brewery, Bavaria: Laura Luque, interview with Siri
Chilazi, June 23, 2023.

xvi In a massive nationwide experiment: Patrick Kline, Evan K. Rose, and Christopher
R. Walters, "Systemic Discrimination Among Large U.S. Employers," *Quarterly Journal of
Economics* 137, no. 4 (2022): 1963–2036, https://doi.org/10.1093/qje/qjac024.

xviii 2020 US Census only asked if people are female or male: Eric Schmid, "The 2020
Census Is Underway, but Nonbinary and Gender-Nonconforming Respondents Feel
Counted Out," St. Louis Public Radio, March 17, 2020, https://news.stlpublicradio.org
/politics-issues/2020-03-17/the-2020-census-is-underway-but-nonbinary-and-gender
-nonconforming-respondents-feel-counted-out.

xviii Census Bureau introduced questions about gender identity: Thom File and Jason-
Harold Lee, "Phase 3.2 of Census Bureau Survey Questions Now Include SOGI, Child Tax
Credit, COVID Vaccination of Children," United States Census Bureau, August 5, 2021,
https://www.census.gov/library/stories/2021/08/household-pulse-survey-updates-sex
-question-now-asks-sexual-orientation-and-gender-identity.html.

xviii as Richard V. Reeves outlines: Richard V. Reeves, *Of Boys and Men: Why the Modern
Male Is Struggling, Why It Matters, and What to Do About It* (Washington, DC: Brookings
Institution Press, 2022), 151.

Chapter 1: The Myths We Need to Debunk

1 "my experience with diversity, equity, and inclusion in the workplace": Caroline Fong,
"MLD-310: Reflection Assignment 1," February 6, 2023.

1 humans tend to gravitate toward framing problems: Nick Chater and George Loe-
wenstein, "The i-frame and the s-frame: How Focusing on Individual-Level Solutions
Has Led Behavioral Public Policy Astray," *Behavioral and Brain Sciences* (2022): 1–60,
https://doi.org/10.1017/S0140525X22002023.

2 "When society points": Jae Yun Kim, Gráinne M. Fitzsimons, and Aaron C. Kay,
"Lean in Messages Increase Attributions of Women's Responsibility for Gender Inequality," *Journal of Personality and Social Psychology* 115, no. 6 (2018): 974–1001, https://doi
.org/10.1037/pspa0000129.

4 recruiters reported: Judd B. Kessler, Corinne Low, and Colin D. Sullivan, "Incentivized Resume Rating: Eliciting Employer Preferences Without Deception," *American
Economic Review* 109, no. 11 (2019): 3713–44, https://doi.org/10.1257/aer.20181714.

6 "Children need their mothers": Siri Chilazi, Iris Bohnet, and Anisha Asundi, *Advancing Gender Equality in Venture Capital* (Cambridge, MA: Women and Public Policy
Program, 2019), https://projects.iq.harvard.edu/wappp/files/wappp/files/gender_and
_culture_in_vc_literature_review_final.pdf.

6 "Women shouldn't be deployed": Vandana Sharma, Jennifer Scott, and Carlued Leon, *Applying Behavioral Design Innovations to Address Gender Bias Among Humanitarian Practitioners and Organizations in Ethiopia: Pilot Report*, 2022.

6 "I don't like women": Rachel Louise Ensign, "The Rich and Famous Love This Banker, Even If She's a Little Mean to Them," *Wall Street Journal*, September 10, 2023, https://www.wsj.com/finance/banking/the-rich-and-famous-love-this-banker-even-if -shes-a-little-mean-to-them-14bca59a.

6 women and men by and large hold: Curtis D. Hardin and Mahzarin R. Banaji, "The Nature of Implicit Prejudice: Implications for Personal and Public Policy," in *The Behavioral Foundations of Public Policy*, ed. Eldar Shafir (Princeton, NJ: Princeton University Press, 2013), 13–31, https://doi.org/10.2307/j.ctv550cbm.

7 Canadian study of nearly 40 million outpatient referrals: Fahima Dossa et al., "Sex Differences in the Pattern of Patient Referrals to Male and Female Surgeons," *JAMA Surgery* 157, no. 2 (2022): 95–103, https://doi.org/10.1001/jamasurg.2021.5784.

7 By age six: Lin Bian, Sarah-Jane Leslie, and Andrei Cimpian, "Gender Stereotypes About Intellectual Ability Emerge Early and Influence Children's Interests," *Science* 355, no. 6323 (2017): 389–91, https://doi.org/10.1126/science.aah6524.

7 in Italian middle schools: Michela Carlana, "Implicit Stereotypes: Evidence from Teachers' Gender Bias," *Quarterly Journal of Economics* 134, no. 3 (2019): 1163–1224, https://doi.org/10.1093/qje/qjz008.

8 In grocery stores: Alexandra C. Feldberg, "The Task Bind: Explaining Gender Differences in Managerial Tasks and Performance," *Administrative Science Quarterly* 67, no. 4 (2022): 1049–92, https://doi.org/10.1177/00018392221124607.

8 In medicine: M. Teresa Cardador, Patrick L. Hill, and Arghavan Salles, "Unpacking the Status-Leveling Burden for Women in Male-Dominated Occupations," *Administrative Science Quarterly* 67, no. 1 (2022): 237–84, https://doi.org/10.1177/00018392211038505.

8 meta-analyses synthesizing evidence: Elizabeth Levy Paluck et al., "Prejudice Reduction: Progress and Challenges," *Annual Review of Psychology* 72, no. 1 (2021): 533–60, https://doi.org/10.1146/annurev-psych-071620-030619. See also Katerina Bezrukova et al., "A Meta-analytical Integration of over 40 years of Research on Diversity Training Evaluation," *Psychological Bulletin* 142, no. 11 (2016): 1227–74, https://doi.org/10.1037/bul0000067.

9 accurately identify the gender of a white man: Joy Buolamwini and Timnit Gebru, "Gender Shades: Intersectional Accuracy Disparities in Commercial Gender Classification," *Proceedings of Machine Learning Research* 81 (2018): 1–15, https://proceedings.mlr .press/v81/buolamwini18a/buolamwini18a.pdf.

9 the policy that gives women: Simon Usborne, "'It Was Seen as Weird': Why Are So Few Men Taking Shared Parental Leave?," *Guardian*, October 5, 2019, https:// www.theguardian.com/lifeandstyle/2019/oct/05/shared-parental-leave-seen-as-weird -paternity-leave-in-decline.

9 hiring practices used in nearly 1,500 German companies: Doris Weichselbaumer, "Multiple Discrimination Against Female Immigrants Wearing Headscarves," *ILR Review* 73, no. 3 (2020): 600–27, https://doi.org/10.1177/0019793919875707.

10 defense in possible lawsuits: Lauren B. Edelman et al., "When Organizations Rule: Judicial Deference to Institutionalized Employment Structures," *American Journal of Sociology* 117, no. 3 (2011): 888–954, https://doi.org/10.1086/661984.

10 more than 40 years of personnel and administrative data: Frank Dobbin and Alexandra Kalev, *Getting to Diversity: What Works and What Doesn't* (Cambridge, MA: Harvard University Press, 2022), 19–20, 24–25.

10 measured the effects of a voluntary one-hour online module: Edward H. Chang et al., "The Mixed Effects of Online Diversity Training," *Proceedings of the National Academy of Sciences* 116, no. 16 (2019): 7778–83, https://doi.org/10.1073/pnas.1816076116.

11 showed both significant reductions in unconscious bias: Patricia G. Devine et al., "Long-Term Reduction in Implicit Race Bias: A Prejudice Habit-Breaking Intervention," *Journal of Experimental Social Psychology* 48, no. 6 (2012): 1267–78, https://doi .org/10.1016/j.jesp.2012.06.003. See also Patrick S. Forscher et al., "Breaking the Prejudice Habit: Mechanisms, Timecourse, and Longevity," *Journal of Experimental Social Psychology* 72 (2017): 133–46, https://doi.org/10.1016/j.jesp.2017.04.009.

12 hired more new female faculty: Patricia G. Devine, "A Gender Bias Habit-Breaking

Intervention Led to Increased Hiring of Female Faculty in STEMM Departments," *Journal of Experimental Social Psychology* 73 (2017): 211–15, https://doi.org/10.1016/j .jesp.2017.07.002.

12 gender bias in academia: A recent extensive review of the evidence on gender differences in academia for tenure-track women and men suggests a nuanced picture: gender gaps in teaching ratings and salaries in favor of men and in hiring in favor of women, and no gender differences in grant funding, journal acceptances, and letters of recommendation. See Stephen J. Ceci, Shulamit Kahn, and Wendy M. Williams, "Exploring Gender Bias in Six Key Domains of Academic Science: An Adversarial Collaboration," *Psychological Science in the Public Interest* 24, no. 1 (2023): 15–73, https://doi .org/10.1177/15291006231163179.

12 increased their ability to detect subtle expressions of sexism: Jessica L. Cundiff et al., "Testing an Intervention for Recognizing and Reporting Subtle Gender Bias in Promotion and Tenure Decisions," *Journal of Higher Education* 89, no. 5 (2018): 611–36, https://doi .org/10.1080/00221546.2018.1437665.

12 "integrate principles for inclusion and diversity": "Written Ministerial Statement on Unconscious Bias Training," Cabinet Office, UK Government, December 17, 2020, https://www.gov.uk/government/news/written-ministerial-statement-on-unconscious -bias-training.

13 "Diversity training, in general terms, is wildly overvalued": James Elfer, "One of our academic friends just emailed me with a question: Why are people so attached to the idea of diversity training when structural/nudge changes are more effective?," LinkedIn post, October 2022, https://www.linkedin.com/posts/jameselfer_one-of-our-academic-friends -just-emailed-activity-6991335171056631808—_hp?.

13 when people feel pressured to exhibit less of it: Lisa Legault, Jennifer N. Gutsell, and Michael Inzlicht, "Ironic Effects of Antiprejudice Messages: How Motivational Interventions Can Reduce (but Also Increase) Prejudice," *Psychological Science* 22, no. 12 (2011): 1472–77, https://doi.org/10.1177/0956797611427918.

13 "morally licensed": Irene Blanken, Niels van de Ven, and Marcel Zeelenberg, "A Meta-Analytic Review of Moral Licensing," *Personality and Social Psychology Bulletin* 41, no. 4 (2015): 540–58, https://doi.org/10.1177/0146167215572134.

13 window-dressing effect: Cheryl R. Kaiser et al., "Presumed Fair: Ironic Effects of Organizational Diversity Structures," *Journal of Personality and Social Psychology* 104, no. 3 (2013): 504–19, https://doi.org/10.1037/a0030838.

13 perceive organizations to be fairer when they offer diversity training: Laura M. Brady et al., "It's Fair for Us: Diversity Structures Cause Women to Legitimize Discrimination," *Journal of Experimental Social Psychology* 57 (2015): 100–10, https://doi.org/10.1016/j .jesp.2014.11.010.

14 what has happened in many organizations: Te-Ping Chen and Lauren Weber, "The Rise and Fall of the Chief Diversity Officer," *Wall Street Journal*, July 21, 2023, https:// www.wsj.com/articles/chief-diversity-officer-cdo-business-corporations-e110a82f.

15 Ericsson: Edward Chang et al., "Why You Should Start A/B Testing Your DEI Initiatives," *Harvard Business Review*, April 18, 2023, https://hbr.org/2023/04/why-you -should-start-a-b-testing-your-dei-initiatives.

16 Employee resource groups: Theresa M. Welbourne, Skylar Rolf, and Steven Schlachter, "The Case for Employee Resource Groups: A Review and Social Identity Theory-Based Research Agenda," *Personnel Review* 46, no. 8 (2017): 1816–34, https://doi.org/10.1108 /PR-01-2016-0004.

16 evidence we have: Lumumba Seegars, "Sanctioned Radicals: A Comparative Study of Gender and Race Employee Resource Groups in Tech" (PhD diss., Harvard University, 2021), https://dash.harvard.edu/handle/1/37368349. See also Gregory R. Beaver, "Individual Outcomes of Employee Resource Group Membership" (PhD diss., University of Minnesota, 2018), https://conservancy.umn.edu/handle/11299/201079.

16 presence of ERGs is linked: Frank Dobbin and Alexandra Kalev, *Getting to Diversity*, 106–8.

16 a 2022 McKinsey & Company report: Natacha Catalino et al., "Effective Employee Resource Groups Are Key to Inclusion at Work. Here's How to Get Them Right," McKinsey & Company, December 7, 2022, https://www.mckinsey.com/capabilities/people-and

-organizational-performance/our-insights/effective-employee-resource-groups-are-key
-to-inclusion-at-work-heres-how-to-get-them-right.

17 "strategically impact business": Judi C. Casey, "Employee Resource Groups: A Strategic Business Resource for Today's Workplace," Boston College Center for Work & Family, 2021, https://www.bc.edu/content/dam/files/centers/cwf/research/publications3
/executivebriefingseries-2/ExecutiveBriefing_EmployeeResourceGroups.pdf.

17 "The actual job of delivering real progress": Kelsey Butler, "Big Tech Layoffs Are
Hitting Diversity and Inclusion Jobs Hard," Bloomberg, January 24, 2023, https://
www.bloomberg.com/news/articles/2023-01-24/tech-layoffs-are-hitting-diversity-and
-inclusion-jobs-hard.

18 program for gifted students: David Card and Laura Giuliano, "Universal Screening
Increases the Representation of Low-Income and Minority Students in Gifted Education,"
Proceedings of the National Academy of Sciences 113, no. 48 (2016): 13678–83, https://
doi.org/10.1073/pnas.1605043113.

20 do not benefit from all the best people available: Muriel Niederle, Carmit Segal,
and Lise Vesterlund, "How Costly Is Diversity? Affirmative Action in Light of Gender
Differences in Competitiveness," *Management Science* 59, no. 1 (2013): 1–16, https://doi
.org/10.1287/mnsc.1120.1602.

20 ECB introduced gender targets: Laura Hospido, Luc Laeven, and Ana Lamo. "The
Gender Promotion Gap: Evidence from Central Banking," *Review of Economics and Statistics* 104, no. 5 (2022): 981–96, https://doi.org/10.1162/rest_a_00988.

20 Women tended to outperform men: Nava Ashraf et al., "Gender and the Misalloca-
tion of Labor Across Countries," working paper, 2023, https://navaashraf.com/wp-content
/uploads/2023/09/abmq_misallocation.pdf.

21 "mythical-fixed-pie mindset": Max H. Bazerman, "The Mind of the Negotiator:
The Mythical Fixed Pie," *Negotiation* 1, no. 1 (2003), https://www.hbs.edu/faculty/Pages
/item.aspx?num=16100.

21 research suggests that our zero-sum beliefs can be limiting: Anna Stefaniak, Robyn
K. Mallett, and Michael J. A. Wohl, "Zero-Sum Beliefs Shape Advantaged Allies' Support
for Collective Action," *European Journal of Social Psychology* 50, no. 6 (2020): 1259–75,
https://doi.org/10.1002/ejsp.2674.

21 men's zero-sum thinking increased: Sophie L. Kuchynka et al., "Zero-Sum Thinking and the Masculinity Contest: Perceived Intergroup Competition and Workplace
Gender Bias," *Journal of Social Issues* 74, no. 3 (2018): 529–50, https://doi.org/10.1111
/josi.12281.

21 zero-sum beliefs about gender at work: Joelle C. Ruthig et al., "When Women's Gains
Equal Men's Losses: Predicting a Zero-Sum Perspective of Gender Status," *Sex Roles* 76
(2017): 17–26, https://doi.org/10.1007/s11199-016-0651-9.

22 Up to 40 percent of economic growth: Chang-Tai Hsieh et al., "The Allocation of
Talent and U.S. Economic Growth," *Econometrica* 87, no. 5 (2019): 1439–74, https://doi
.org/10.3982/ECTA11427.

22 "It's an economic necessity": Sarah Chaney Cambon and Sabrina Siddiqui, "Help Wanted:
Women to Fix America's Infrastructure," *Wall Street Journal*, September 7, 2023, https://
www.wsj.com/us-news/help-wanted-women-to-fix-americas-infrastructure-f7671df6.

22 prohibits discrimination on the basis of disability: "Introduction to the Americans
with Disabilities Act," US Department of Justice Civil Rights Division, accessed August 7,
2023, https://www.ada.gov/topics/intro-to-ada/.

22 4 percent of the US adult population: "Morbidity and Mortality Weekly Report:
Prevalence of Mobility and Self-Care Disability—United States, 1990," Centers for Disease
Control and Prevention, last reviewed May 2, 2001, https://www.cdc.gov/mmwr/preview
/mmwrhtml/00021988.htm.

22 share has grown to more than 12 percent: "Disability Impacts All of Us," National
Center on Birth Defects and Developmental Disabilities, Centers for Disease Control and
Prevention, last reviewed May 15, 2023, https://www.cdc.gov/ncbddd/disabilityandhealth
/infographic-disability-impacts-all.html.

22 positive impact fairness has on cooperation: Eric S. Dickson, Sanford C. Gordon, and
Gregory A. Huber, "Identifying Legitimacy: Experimental Evidence on Compliance with
Authority," *Science Advances* 8, no. 7 (2022), https://doi.org/10.1126/sciadv.abj7377.

22 many more desirable outcomes: Ernst Fehr, Lorenz Goette, and Christian Zehnder, "A Behavioral Account of the Labor Market: The Role of Fairness Concerns," *Annual Review of Economics* 1 (2009): 355–84, https://doi.org/10.1146/annurev.economics .050708.143217. See also E. Allan Lind and Tom R. Tyler, *The Social Psychology of Procedural Justice* (New York: Plenum Press, 1988).

23 business case sends the message: Robin J. Ely and David A. Thomas, "Getting Serious About Diversity: Enough Already with the Business Case," *Harvard Business Review*, November–December 2020, https://hbr.org/2020/11/getting-serious-about-diversity -enough-already-with-the-business-case.

23 the business case can be counterproductive: Oriane A. M. Georgeac and Aneeta Rattan, "The Business Case for Diversity Backfires: Detrimental Effects of Organizations' Instrumental Diversity Rhetoric for Underrepresented Group Members' Sense of Belonging," *Journal of Personality and Social Psychology* 124, no. 1 (2023): 69–108, https://doi .org/10.1037/pspi0000394.

23 "Don't justify your commitment to diversity": Oriane Georgeac and Aneeta Rattan, "Stop Making the Business Case for Diversity," *Harvard Business Review*, June 15, 2022, https://hbr.org/2022/06/stop-making-the-business-case-for-diversity.

24 "He asked each of us": *RBG*, directed by Julie Cohen and Betsy West, featuring Ruth Bader Ginsburg (Storyville Films, 2018), 16:09, https://www.amazon.com/RBG-Ruth -Bader-Ginsburg/dp/B07CT8KKRZ.

24 constitute 30 percent of the population: Women Donors Network, *System Failure: What the 2020 Primary Elections Revealed About Our Democracy*, May 2021, https:// wholeads.us/research/system-failure-2020-primary-elections/.

24 "To make progress in achieving gender equality": Sonia K. Kang and Sarah Kaplan, "Working Toward Gender Diversity and Inclusion in Medicine: Myths and Solutions," *Lancet* 393, no. 10171 (2019): 579–86, https://doi.org/10.1016/S0140-6736(18)33138-6.

25 risks involved in *not* tackling unfairness: Joan C. Williams and Jamie Dolkas, "Keeping Diversity Metrics While Controlling for Legal Risk: The Risks of Diversity Data Are Changing," Center for WorkLife Law, 2022, https://biasinterrupters.org/wp-content /uploads/2022/12/Keeping-Diversity-Metrics-While-Controlling-for-Legal-Risk-1.pdf.

26 Pinterest knows this: Douglas Wigdor, "Trial Lawyer David Lowe Reflects On His Historic $22.5 Million Gender Discrimination Settlement With Pinterest," *Forbes*, December 21, 2020, https://www.forbes.com/sites/douglaswigdor/2020/12/21 /trial-lawyer-david-lowe-reflects-on-his-historic-225-million-gender-discrimination -settlement-with-pinterest/.

26 "protected classes": "3. Who is protected from employment discrimination?," US Equal Opportunity Employment Commission, accessed January 18, 2024, https://www .eeoc.gov/employers/small-business/3-who-protected-employment-discrimination.

26 equal opportunity and antidiscrimination executive orders: "Executive Order 11246—Equal Employment Opportunity," US Department of Labor, Office of Federal Contract Compliance Programs, accessed October 15, 2023, https://www.dol.gov/ofccp /regs/compliance/ca_11246.htm.

26 research has found AAP goals to be effective: Fidan Ana Kurtulus, "The Impact of Affirmative Action on the Employment of Minorities and Women: A Longitudinal Analysis Using Three Decades of EEO-1 Filings," *Journal of Policy Analysis and Management* 35, no. 1 (2016): 34–66, https://doi.org/10.1002/pam.21881.

Chapter 2: Data as an Engine for Change

31 BBC journalist Ros Atkins: Siri Chilazi, Aneeta Rattan, and Oriane Georgeac, "Ros Atkins and the 50:50 Project at the BBC (A)," London Business School Case CS-20-00 -010 (London: London Business School Publishing, 2020), https://publishing.london .edu/cases/ros-atkins-and-the-5050-project-at-the-bbc-a/.

33 "We have managed to keep it going": "50:50 The Equality Project," BBC, accessed June 21, 2023, https://www.bbc.co.uk/5050.

34 "Data is like an X-ray:" Oona King, "How to Move an Industry: Behind the Scenes of the ACT Report," Women and Public Policy Program virtual seminar, Cambridge, MA, April 17, 2023.

34 his eponymous book: John Doerr, *Measure What Matters: How Google, Bono, and the Gates Foundation Rock the World with OKRs* (New York: Portfolio/Penguin, 2018).

34 study looking at 179 American publicly traded companies: Erik Brynjolfsson, Lorin M. Hitt, and Heekyung Hellen Kim, "Strength in Numbers: How Does Data-Driven Decisionmaking Affect Firm Performance?," working paper, 2011, https://dx.doi.org/10.2139/ssrn.1819486.

34 examined more than 10,000 performance evaluations: David A. Garvin, "How Google Sold Its Engineers on Management," *Harvard Business Review*, December 2013, https://hbr.org/2013/12/how-google-sold-its-engineers-on-management.

35 In the documentary *This Changes Everything*, Davis recalls: *This Changes Everything*, directed by Tom Donahue, featuring Geena Davis (Creative Chaos Ventures, 2018), 55:05, https://www.amazon.com/This-Changes-Everything-Geena-Davis/dp/B07VBHTCRH.

36 the one hundred top-grossing family films: Chris Colin, "How Sexist Is Hollywood? Check Out Geena Davis's Spreadsheet," *New York Times*, May 25, 2023, https://www.nytimes.com/2023/05/25/business/geena-davis-hollywood-sexism-gender.html.

36 Male characters continue to outnumber female ones: "What's the Issue?," Geena Davis Institute on Gender in Media, accessed June 21, 2023, https://seejane.org/about-us/whats-the-issue/.

36 MaLisa Foundation, established in 2016, found for German films: Elizabeth Prommer, Julia Stüwe, and Juliane Wegner conducted the research on "Diversity in German Film" and Christine Linke and Ruth Kasdorf on "Portrayal of Gender-Based Violence on German TV." See "When We Offer a Distorted View of Violence Against Women, We Are Part of the Problem," MaLisa Foundation, November 22, 2021, https://malisastiftung.org/en/wenn-wir-gewalt-gegen-frauen-verzerrt-darstellen-sind-wir-teil-des-problems/.

39 research suggests they don't: Emilio J. Castilla, "Gender, Race, and Meritocracy in Organizational Careers," *American Journal of Sociology* 113, no. 6 (2008): 1479–1526, https://doi.org/10.1086/588738.

40 sample size is large enough to protect people's identities: Latanya Sweeney, "Simple Demographics Often Identify People Uniquely," Data Privacy Working Paper 3, Carnegie Mellon University, Pittsburgh, 2000, https://dataprivacylab.org/projects/identifiability/paper1.pdf.

40 Kimberlé Crenshaw coined the term "intersectionality": Kimberlé Crenshaw, "Demarginalizing the Intersection of Race and Sex: A Black Feminist Critique of Antidiscrimination Doctrine, Feminist Theory, and Antiracist Politics [1989]," in *Feminist Legal Theory: Readings in Law and Gender*, ed. Katharine T. Bartlett and Rosanne Kennedy (New York: Routledge, 2018), 57–80, https://doi.org/10.4324/9780429500480-5.

40 American women earned: Rakesh Kochhar, "The Enduring Grip of the Gender Pay Gap," Pew Research Center, March 1, 2023, https://www.pewresearch.org/social-trends/2023/03/01/the-enduring-grip-of-the-gender-pay-gap/.

40 pay gap also varied substantially among different groups of Asian Americans: Chabeli Carrazana and Jasmine Mithani, "Why the Wage Gap Differs Among Asian-American Women," The 19th News, April 5, 2023, https://19thnews.org/2023/04/aapi-womens-equal-pay-day-wage-gap-ethnicity/.

40 straight women earn less than lesbian or bisexual women: M. V. Lee Badgett, Christopher S. Carpenter, and Dario Sansone, "LGBTQ Economics," *Journal of Economic Perspectives* 35, no. 2 (2021): 141–70, https://doi.org/10.1257/jep.35.2.141.

41 50:50 The Equality Project started by focusing: Siri Chilazi, Aneeta Rattan, and Oriane Georgeac, "Ros Atkins and the 50:50 Project at the BBC (C)," London Business School Case CS-23-03-008 (London: London Business School Publishing, 2024), https://publishing.london.edu/cases/ros-atkins-and-the-5050-project-at-the-bbc-c/.

42 MoreThanNow conducted with Transport for London: James Elfer, "How We Talk Matters Part 2," MoreThanNow, July 23, 2019, https://www.morethannow.co.uk/single-post/2019/7/8/how-we-talk-matters-part-2.

43 data from Google's annual employee pulse survey: James Heighington, "Corporate Diversity Reports: Solving the Right Problem with the Wrong Data with James Heighington," Women and Public Policy Program virtual seminar, March 27, 2023, 7:40, https://www.youtube.com/watch?v=xXn7T0KFJjs.

43 the resulting Action to Catalyze Tech (ACT) Report: The report recommends collecting self-reported demographic data on the following categories in the United States: race/ethnicity (with an ability to select multiple options), gender, LGBTQ+ identification, disability, veteran status, socioeconomic status (using household income, community college attendance, first-generation college status, or Pell Grant receipt as a proxy), and caregiving/parental/family responsibilities. The Tech Accountability Coalition, the successor organization to the ACT Report, has created an Equity Framework with common standards regarding terms, data collection, and progress sharing for the tech industry. See Catalyze Tech Working Group, *The ACT Report: Action to Catalyze Tech, A Paradigm Shift for DEI* (Aspen Institute and Snap Inc., October 2021), https://actreport.com. See also "Tech Accountability Coalition," Aspen Institute, accessed January 11, 2024, https://www.aspeninstitute.org/programs/tech-accountability-coalition/.

43 Police & Nurses Limited: "How P&N Group Uses Diversity Demographics to Make Data-Informed Employee Experience Strategies," Culture Amp, accessed June 23, 2023, https://www.cultureamp.com/case-studies/pn-group.

44 1.6 percent of adults identified: Anna Brown, "About 5% of Young Adults in the U.S. Say Their Gender Is Different from Their Sex Assigned at Birth," Pew Research Center, June 7, 2022, https://www.pewresearch.org/short-reads/2022/06/07/about-5-of-young-adults-in-the-u-s-say-their-gender-is-different-from-their-sex-assigned-at-birth/.

44 nonbinary or transgender in the United States: Fortunately, additional evidence on the workplace experiences of gender diverse individuals is emerging from nationally representative samples. One showed that the general population tends to underestimate the level of support for transgender people in the workplace when in fact three-quarters of Americans support nondiscrimination protections. See Billur Aksoy, Christopher S. Carpenter, and Dario Sansone, "Understanding Labor Market Discrimination Against Transgender People: Evidence from a Double List Experiment and a Survey," working paper, 2022, https://doi.org/10.48550/arXiv.2209.02335.

44 the United Nations: United Nations, "Gender Equality in the Right to Privacy—an Essential for All," press release, March 5, 2020, https://www.ohchr.org/en/press-releases/2020/03/gender-equality-right-privacy-essential-all.

44 track and report both actual, raw numbers: Iris Bohnet and Siri Chilazi, "Overcoming the Small-N Problem," in *What Works? Evidence-Based Ideas to Increase Diversity, Equity, and Inclusion in the Workplace*, ed. David Pedulla (Amherst: University of Massachusetts, 2020), 38–44, https://www.umass.edu/employmentequity/overcoming-small-n-problem.

45 Laura Morgan Roberts and Melissa Thomas-Hunt potently note: Laura Morgan Roberts and Melissa Thomas-Hunt, "Data-Driven Approaches to Diversity, Equity and Inclusion," *People + Strategy Journal*, 2022, https://www.shrm.org/executive/resources/people-strategy-journal/winter2022/pages/feature-approach-dei-data-morgan-roberts.aspx.

45 women made up only 8 percent: Chad M. Topaz et al., "Diversity of Artists in Major U.S. Museums," *PLOS One* 14, no. 3 (2019), https://doi.org/10.1371/journal.pone.0212852.

45 "At first, I didn't believe in the premise of the show": Nonie Gadsden, interview with Siri Chilazi, September 11, 2023.

46 explained the logic: Chilazi, Rattan, and Georgeac, "Ros Atkins and the 50:50 Project at the BBC (A)."

46 a scientifically evaluated measurement tool: Laura Mascarell Espuny and Severin Klingler, "Evaluation of Ringier's Equal Voice Factor," Media Technology Center, ETH Zurich, January 27, 2022.

47 Equal Voice shows progress: "EqualVoice Factor Mid-Year Review 2023: All Titles Increased Their Body Score in Print," Ringier, September 19, 2023, https://www.ringier.com/equalvoice-factor-mid-year-review-2023-all-titles-increased-their-body-score-in-print/.

47 pyramid diagram: Siri Chilazi and Iris Bohnet, "How to Best Use Data to Meet Your DE&I Goals," *Harvard Business Review*, December 3, 2020, https://hbr.org/2020/12/how-to-best-use-data-to-meet-your-dei-goals.

47 Traffic light labeling: Michael Hallsworth and Elspeth Kirkman, *Behavioral Insights* (Cambridge, MA: MIT Press, 2020), 11.

47 first in a lineup of drink choices: Kelly Ann Schmidtke et al., "Menu Positions In-

fluence Soft Drink Selection at Touchscreen Kiosks," *Psychology & Marketing* 36 (2019): 964–70, https://doi.org/10.1002/mar.21248.

47   expressing a vehicle's fuel efficiency: Jack B. Soll, Katherine L. Milkman, and John W. Payne, "A User's Guide to Debiasing," in *The Wiley Blackwell Handbook of Judgment and Decision Making*, ed. Gideon Keren and George Wu (Chichester: John Wiley & Sons, 2015), 924–51, https://doi.org/10.1002/9781118468333.ch33.

48   Social comparisons: Leon Festinger, "A Theory of Social Comparison Processes," *Human Relations* 7, no. 2 (1954): 117–40, https://doi.org/10.1177/001872675400700202. See also Abraham P. Buunk and Frederick X. Gibbons, "Social Comparison: The End of a Theory and the Emergence of a Field," *Organizational Behavior and Human Decision Processes* 102, no. 1 (2007): 3–21, https://doi.org/10.1016/j.obhdp.2006.09.007.

49   Jamie Dimon drove this point home: Ruth Umoh, "JPMorgan's Jamie Dimon Talks DEI: 'I'm a Full-Throated, Red-Blooded, Patriotic, Unwoke, Capitalist CEO,'" Yahoo! Finance, January 24, 2024, https://finance.yahoo.com/news/jpmorgan-jamie-dimon-talks-dei-132700973.html.

50   "We strive to judge progress through data": John C. Miller, April Kelly-Drummond, and Fasika Melaku-Peterson, "Inside Denny's Decades-Long DEI Journey," *Harvard Business Review*, September 13, 2021, https://hbr.org/2021/09/inside-dennys-decades-long-dei-journey.

50   specifically new mothers: Iris Bohnet, *What Works: Gender Equality by Design* (Cambridge, MA: Harvard University Press, 2016), 105.

51   "structured approach": David Anderson, Margrét V. Bjarnadóttir, and David Gaddis Ross, "A Better Way for Companies to Address Pay Gaps," *Harvard Business Review*, February 2, 2024, https://hbr.org/2024/02/a-better-way-for-companies-to-address-pay-gaps. See also David Anderson, Margrét Vilborg Bjarnadóttir, and David Gaddis Ross, "Bridging the Gap: Applying Analytics to Address Gender Pay Inequity," *Production and Operations Management* 32, no. 6 (2023): 1846–64, https://doi.org/10.1111/poms.13944.

51   starting in 2024—all of the EU: "Directive (EU) 2022/2464 of the European Parliament and of the Council of 14 December 2022 amending Regulation (EU) No 537/2014, Directive 2004/109/EC, Directive 2006/43/EC and Directive 2013/34/EU, as regards corporate sustainability reporting (Text with EEA relevance)," 2022, *Official Journal* L322, 15–80, https://data.europa.eu/eli/dir/2022/2464/oj.

52   Research suggests that the tool is working: Giannina Vaccaro, "Using Econometrics to Reduce Gender Discrimination: Evidence from a Difference-in-Discontinuity Design," working paper, IZA Institute of Labor Economics, Bonn, 2017, https://conference.iza.org/conference_files/Gender_2018/vaccaro_g23998.pdf.

52   "women must complete one additional degree": Wendy Chun-Hoon, "5 Fast Facts: The Gender Wage Gap," US Department of Labor Blog, March 14, 2023, https://blog.dol.gov/2023/03/14/5-fast-facts-the-gender-wage-gap.

52   Google found and implemented: Iris Bohnet, *What Works*, 105.

52   SMEs can make work fair: Key Appointments UK, "How to Embrace Diversity, Equity and Inclusion in Your SME Recruitment Strategy," LinkedIn, March 8, 2023, https://www.linkedin.com/pulse/how-embrace-diversity-equity-inclusion-your-sme/.

53   the percentage of women at the company: Gwen Houston, "Global Diversity & Inclusion Update—Sharing Our Latest Workforce Numbers," Microsoft, November 23, 2015, https://blogs.microsoft.com/blog/2015/11/23/global-diversity-inclusion-update-sharing-our-latest-workforce-numbers/.

54   the following year, when Microsoft shared: Gwen Houston, "Global Diversity & Inclusion Update at Microsoft: Deepening Our Commitment," Microsoft, November 17, 2016, https://blogs.microsoft.com/blog/2016/11/17/global-diversity-inclusion-update-microsoft-deepening-commitment/.

54   by 2022, women made up 32.7 percent: Microsoft, *Global Diversity & Inclusion Report 2022*, 2022, https://www.microsoft.com/en-us/diversity/inside-microsoft/annual-report.

54   disparate impact: While relevant across geographies, "disparate impact" is a technical term in the United States. See "Title VI Legal Manual, Section VII—Proving Discrimination: Disparate Impact," US Department of Justice, Civil Rights Division, accessed January 18, 2024, https://www.justice.gov/crt/fcs/T6Manual7.

54 company assessed potential negative consequences: Ania G. Wieckowski, "Overcoming Today's DEI Leadership Challenges," *Harvard Business Review*, September 14, 2023, https://hbr.org/2023/09/overcoming-todays-dei-leadership-challenges.

54 early data from a wave of US tech industry layoffs: Linda Calvin et al., *System Upgrade: Rebooting Corporate Policies for Impact*, Reboot Representation and McKinsey & Company, 2023, https://www.rebootrepresentation.org/2023-report/.

55 study of more than 300 US firms: Alexandra Kalev, "How You Downsize Is Who You Downsize: Biased Formalization, Accountability, and Managerial Diversity," *American Sociological Review* 79, no. 1 (2014): 109–35, https://doi.org/10.1177/0003122413518553.

55 "It's a totally different conversation when you have the data": Daniella Foster, interview with Siri Chilazi, December 5, 2022.

Chapter 3: Goals That Promote Desirable Behavior

56 "At this lunch, I realized that everybody was stuck": Helena Morrissey, interview with Iris Bohnet, November 28, 2016.

57 Among the ten recommendations: John Beshears, Iris Bohnet, and Jenny Sanford, "Increasing Gender Diversity in the Boardroom: The United Kingdom in 2011 (A)," Harvard Business School Case 918-08-006 (Boston: Harvard Business School, 2017), https://www.hbs.edu/faculty/Pages/item.aspx?num=53381.

58 the Hampton-Alexander Review: Hampton-Alexander Review, *Improving Gender Balance—5 Year Summary Report*, February 2021, https://ftsewomenleaders.com/wp-content/uploads/2021/03/Hampton-Alexander-Review-Report-2020_web.pdf.

58 the goal "appeared ambitious and stretching": FTSE Women Leaders Review, *Achieving Gender Balance*, February 2022, https://ftsewomenleaders.com/wp-content/uploads/2022/05/2021_FTSE-Women-Leaders-Review_Final-Reportv1_WA.pdf.

58 As of 2024: FTSE Women Leaders Review, *Achieving Gender Balance*, February 2024, https://ftsewomenleaders.com/wp-content/uploads/2024/04/ftse-women-leaders-report-final-april-2024.pdf.

58 Progress in diversifying senior executive roles: Aaron Page et al., "Regulation and the Trickle-down Effect of Women in Leadership Roles," *Leadership Quarterly* (2023), https://doi.org/10.1016/j.leaqua.2023.101721.

59 30% Club has grown into a global movement: "What Is the 30% Club?," 30% Club, accessed October 14, 2023, https://30percentclub.org/what-is-the-30-club/.

59 "One of the fascinating changes in organizations": Iris Bohnet and Siri Chilazi, *Goals and Targets for Diversity, Equity, and Inclusion: A High Leverage Point to Advance Gender Equality in the U.S. Tech Industry* (Cambridge, MA: Women and Public Policy Program, 2020), https://www.hks.harvard.edu/centers/wappp/publications/goals-and-targets-diversity-equity-and-inclusion-high-leverage-point.

59 research over more than five decades: Tracy Epton, Sinead Currie, and Christopher J. Armitage, "Unique Effects of Setting Goals on Behavior Change: Systematic Review and Meta-Analysis," *Journal of Consulting and Clinical Psychology* 85, no. 12 (2017): 1182–98, https://doi.org/10.1037/ccp0000260. See also Edwin A. Locke and Gary P. Latham, "Building a Practically Useful Theory of Goal Setting and Task Motivation," *American Psychologist* 57, no. 9 (2002): 705–17, https://doi.org/10.1037/0003-066X.57.9.705.

60 only 16 percent of Fortune 100 companies: Erika L. Kirgios, Ike M. Silver, and Edward H. Chang, "Concrete Diversity Goals Attract Minorities, but Managers Resist Using Them" (unpublished manuscript, 2022).

60 Airbnb: "An Update on Diversity and Belonging Progress at Airbnb," Airbnb, September 15, 2022, https://news.airbnb.com/an-update-on-diversity-and-belonging-progress-at-airbnb/.

60 PwC: PwC, *Earning Trust Through Equity and Sustainability: FY22 Purpose and Inclusion Report*, 2022, https://www.pwc.com/us/en/about-us/purpose-and-values/assets/fy22-pwc-purpose-report-full-report.pdf.

60 Snap Inc.: "Our 2025 Goals," Snap Inc., accessed January 25, 2024, https://diversity.snap.com/exec-summary/2025-goals.

60 Starbucks: "Inclusion & Diversity," Starbucks Stories & News, updated September 2023, https://stories.starbucks.com/stories/inclusion-diversity/.

60   The Home Depot: The Home Depot, *2022 ESG Report: Doing Our Part*, 2022, https://
      corporate.homedepot.com/sites/default/files/2022-10/2022_ESG_Report_final_4.pdf.

60   Xerox: Xerox, *Global Diversity, Inclusion, and Belonging Report*, 2023, https://
      www.xerox.com/downloads/usa/en/g/global-diversity-inclusion.pdf.

60   companies that set diversity goals: Alexandra Kalev and Frank Dobbin, "How Com-
      panies Should Set—and Report—DEI Goals," *Harvard Business Review*, September 29,
      2022, https://hbr.org/2022/09/how-companies-should-set-and-report-dei-goals.

61   Approximately 120 countries have some form of legislative gender quota: Cesi Cruz
      and Bea Rivera, "Measuring the Impact of Gender Quotas on Political Institutions," Inter-
      American Development Bank, June 2, 2021, https://blogs.iadb.org/ideas-matter/en
      /measuring-the-impact-of-gender-quotas-on-political-institutions/.

61   In Rwanda, a new 2003 constitution: Andrea Guariso, Bert Ingelaere, and Mari-
      jke Verpoorten, "When Ethnicity Beats Gender: Quotas and Political Representation in
      Rwanda and Burundi," *Development and Change* 49, no. 6 (2018): 1361–91, https://doi
      .org/10.1111/dech.12451.

61   more than 60 percent female legislators: Emma Batha and Lin Taylor, "Women
      in Parliament: Which Countries Are Making Progress?," *Context*, September 22, 2023,
      https://www.context.news/socioeconomic-inclusion/women-in-parliament-which
      -countries-are-making-progress.

61   a law that became effective in 2017: "France Backs Gender Quotas in Corporate
      Top Management," *RFI*, December 16, 2021, https://www.rfi.fr/en/france-backs-gender
      -quotas-in-corporate-top-management.

61   quota in the highly male-dominated French Club Championship: José De Sousa and
      Muriel Niederle, "Trickle-Down Effects of Affirmative Action: A Case Study in France,"
      NBER Working Paper Series 30367, National Bureau of Economic Research, Cambridge,
      MA, 2022, https://doi.org/10.3386/w30367.

61   in India, quotas have long been used: "Why India Needs a New Debate on Caste
      Quotas," BBC, August 29, 2015, https://www.bbc.com/news/world-asia-india-34082770.

62   fairness goals are increasingly endorsed in Europe: Aniela Unguresan, "How Com-
      panies Can Adapt to Europe's Evolving DEI Policies," *Forbes*, October 6, 2023, https://
      www.forbes.com/sites/forbesbusinesscouncil/2023/10/06/how-companies-can-adapt
      -to-europes-evolving-dei-policies/.

62   Accenture published a series of goals: Ellyn Shook, "How to Set—and Meet—
      Your Company's Diversity Goals," *Harvard Business Review*, June 21, 2021, https://hbr
      .org/2021/06/how-to-set-and-meet-your-companys-diversity-goals.

63   This effect was observed in retirement savings: John Beshears et al., "The Effect of
      Providing Peer Information on Retirement Savings Decisions," *Journal of Finance* 70, no.
      3 (2015): 1161–1201, https://doi.org/10.1111/jofi.12258.

63   less likely to remain committed to the goals: Jennifer Whelan and Robert Wood, *Tar-
      gets and Quotas for Women in Leadership: A Global Review of Policy, Practice, and Psycho-
      logical Research* (Melbourne: Centre for Ethical Leadership, Melbourne Business School,
      2012), https://www.uq.edu.au/about/files/6045/targets_and_quotas_report_2012.pdf.

64   Amazon, for example . . . reported in 2021: Beth Galetti, "Diversity, Equity, and
      Inclusion," Amazon, June 10, 2021, https://www.aboutamazon.com/news/workplace
      /diversity-equity-and-inclusion.

64   The Coca-Cola Company benchmarks itself: The Coca-Cola Company, *2022 Busi-
      ness & Sustainability Report*, 2020, https://www.coca-colacompany.com/content/dam
      /company/us/en/reports/coca-cola-business-sustainability-report-2022.pdf.

64   on average, ten board members: EY Center for Board Matters, *Corporate Gov-
      ernance by the Numbers*, September 30, 2023, https://assets.ey.com/content/dam
      /ey-sites/ey-com/en_us/topics/board-matters/ey-corporate-governance-by-the
      -numbers-september-2023.pdf.

65   "twokenism" phenomenon: Edward H. Chang et al., "Diversity Thresholds: How So-
      cial Norms, Visibility, and Scrutiny Relate to Group Composition," *Academy of Manage-
      ment Journal* 62, no. 1 (2019): 144–71, https://doi.org/10.5465/amj.2017.0440.

65   increase the proportion of women in management positions: "Diversity, Equity, and
      Inclusion," Adidas, accessed July 6, 2023, https://report.adidas-group.com/2021/en
      /group-management-report-our-company/our-people/diversity-equity-and-inclusion.html.

65 goal of gender proportionality: Siri Chilazi, Iris Bohnet, and Oliver Hauser, "Achieving Gender Balance at All Levels of Your Company," *Harvard Business Review*, November 30, 2021, https://hbr.org/2021/11/achieving-gender-balance-at-all-levels -of-your-company. While the proportionality principle can theoretically be used to promote equal opportunity for any group, it is particularly well suited to contexts where the main challenge is not the talent pool but rather how organizations develop and support the talent they already have. In contexts where the current representation of a particular group is extremely low, applying proportionality across levels and over time would yield scant progress and other approaches (such as increased external hiring) may be needed.

66 In 2020, CBS introduced targets: Peter White, "CBS Sets Diversity Targets for Reality Casts; 50% of Talent Must Be BIPOC & Commits 25% of Unscripted Development Budget to BIPOC Creatives," Deadline, November 9, 2020, https://deadline.com/2020/11/cbs-diversity-targets-reality-casts-bipoc-commits-unscripted -development-budget-1234611548/.

66 $1 billion investment in two new funds: Leslie Shribman and Courtney Power, "TPG Announces Inaugural TPG NEXT Fund to Invest in Underrepresented Alternative Asset Managers," BusinessWire, January 10, 2023, https://www.businesswire.com/news /home/20230109005934/en/TPG-Announces-Inaugural-TPG-NEXT-Fund-to-Invest -in-Underrepresented-Alternative-Asset-Managers.

66 directing its money to younger private equity managers: Dawn Lim, "Calpers Makes $1 Billion Bet on Small Funds as New CIO Reshapes Pension," Bloomberg, January 10, 2023, https://www.bloomberg.com/news/articles/2023-01-10/calpers-makes-1-billion -bet-on-up-and-coming-firms-as-new-cio-reshapes-pension.

67 Both types of goals can be effective: Eric Barends, Barbara Janssen, and Cedric Velghe, *Rapid Evidence Assessment of the Research Literature on the effect of Goal Setting on Workplace Performance* (London: Chartered Institute of Personnel and Development, 2016), https://www.cipd.org/globalassets/media/knowledge/knowledge-hub/reports /rapid-evidence-assessment-of-the-research-literature-on-the-effect-of-goal-setting-on -workplace-performance_tcm18-16903.pdf.

67 Novartis implemented "guidelines": Novartis, *Novartis US Equal Employment Opportunity/Diversity & Inclusion Report 2021*, 2021, https://www.novartis.com/us-en /sites/novartis_us/files/2022-03/nvs-eeo-di-report-2021_0.pdf.

68 Rooney Rule: Gus Garcia-Roberts, "The Failed NFL Diversity 'Rule' Corporate America Loves," *Washington Post*, October 4, 2022, https://www.washingtonpost.com /sports/interactive/2022/rooney-rule-nfl-black-coaches/.

68 nonwhite candidate was about 20 percent more likely to be hired: Cynthia DuBois, "The Impact of 'Soft' Affirmative Action Policies on Minority Hiring in Executive Leadership: The Case of the NFL's Rooney Rule," *American Law and Economics Review* 18, no. 1 (2016): 208–33, https://doi.org/10.1093/aler/ahv019.

68 By 2013 there were only three Black coaches left: Garcia-Roberts, "The Failed NFL Diversity 'Rule' Corporate America Loves."

69 In the four years up to and including 2022: Washington Post Staff, "Key Findings from 'Black Out,' the Post's Series on Black NFL Coaches," *Washington Post*, September 21, 2022, https://www.washingtonpost.com/sports/interactive/2022/takeaways-black -out-nfl/.

69 a Black coach was significantly more likely to be selected: Stefanie K. Johnson, "What Amazon's Board Was Getting Wrong About Diversity and Hiring," *Harvard Business Review*, May 14, 2018, https://hbr.org/2018/05/what-amazons-board-is-getting-wrong -about-diversity-and-hiring.

69 tokenism is more severe: Rosabeth Moss Kanter, "Some Effects of Proportions on Group Life: Skewed Sex Ratios and Responses to Token Women," *American Journal of Sociology* 82, no. 5 (1977): 965–90, https://doi.org/10.1086/226425.

69 evaluated a three-person finalist pool: Stefanie K. Johnson, David R. Hekman, and Elsa T. Chan, "If There's Only One Woman in Your Candidate Pool, There's Statistically No Chance She'll Be Hired," *Harvard Business Review*, April 26, 2016, https://hbr .org/2016/04/if-theres-only-one-woman-in-your-candidate-pool-theres-statistically-no -chance-shell-be-hired.

69   NFL took these learnings to heart and announced: Garcia-Roberts, "The Failed NFL Diversity 'Rule' Corporate America Loves."

69   variations of the Rooney Rule have spread: Garcia-Roberts.

70   *New York Times* have reported: Emily Flitter, "At Wells Fargo, a Quest to Increase Diversity Leads to Fake Job Interviews," *New York Times*, May 19, 2022, https://www.nytimes.com/2022/05/19/business/wells-fargo-fake-interviews.html.

70   The Mansfield Rule directs voluntarily participating entities: "Mansfield Rule," Diversity Lab, accessed July 6, 2023, https://www.diversitylab.com/pilot-projects/mansfield-overview/.

71   The goal has been expanded in scope: John Iino, Jim Sandman, and Caren Ulrich Stacy, "Diversifying Leadership: How the Mansfield Rule Is Driving Change," Bloomberg Law, June 17, 2022, https://news.bloomberglaw.com/us-law-week/diversifying-leadership-how-the-mansfield-rule-is-helping.

71   one component of a more holistic approach: John Iino, Jim Sandman, and Caren Ulrich Stacy, "Diversifying Leadership: How the Mansfield Rule Is Driving Change."

71   worked in concert to shine a light: John Beshears, Iris Bohnet, and Jenny Sanford, "Increasing Gender Diversity in the Boardroom: The United Kingdom in 2011 (A and B)," Harvard Business School Case 918–08-006 and 918–08-007 (Boston: Harvard Business School, 2017), https://www.hbs.edu/faculty/Pages/item.aspx?num=53381.

72   can lead to backlash, unintended negative consequences, or false progress: Rebecca Temkin and Taimi Itembu, "The Unintended Consequences of Diversity & Inclusion Initiatives: Lisa Leslie's Recent Work & Ideas for Putting her Framework to Use," WAPPP Wire, January 29, 2020, https://wapppwire.blogspot.com/2020/01/the-unintended-consequences-of_29.html.

73   In a series of laboratory experiments: Maliheh Paryavi, Iris Bohnet, and Alexandra van Geen, "Descriptive Norms and Gender Diversity: Reactance from Men," *Journal of Behavioral Public Administration* 2, no. 1 (2019): 1–16, https://doi.org/10.30636/jbpa.21.51.

73   "appeared less threatening and helped garner support": Rohini Anand, *Leading Global Diversity, Equity, and Inclusion: A Guide for Systemic Change in Multinational Organizations* (Oakland: Berrett-Koehler, 2021), 143.

73   "we haven't lowered the bar for women": Siri Chilazi, Anisha Asundi, and Iris Bohnet, *Advancing Gender Equality in Venture Capital* (Cambridge, MA: Women and Public Policy Program, Harvard Kennedy School, 2019), https://wappp.hks.harvard.edu/venture-capital-and-entrepreneurship.

73   women became targets of sabotage by their peers: Andreas Leibbrandt, Liang Choon Wang, and Cordelia Foo, "Gender Quotas, Competitions, and Peer Review: Experimental Evidence on the Backlash Against Women," *Management Science* 64, no. 8 (2018): 3501–16, https://doi.org/10.1287/mnsc.2017.2772.

74   In French chess clubs: De Sousa and Niederle, "Trickle-Down Effects of Affirmative Action."

74   In an academic workplace, this could entail tracking: De Sousa and Niederle.

74   female faculty were not institutionally set up for success: Courtney Humphries, "Measuring Up," *MIT Technology Review*, August 16, 2017, https://www.technologyreview.com/2017/08/16/149744/measuring-up/.

74   performance-support bias: Janice Fanning Madden, "Performance-Support Bias and the Gender Pay Gap Among Stockbrokers," *Gender & Society* 26, no. 3 (2012): 488–518, https://doi.org/10.1177/0891243212438546.

74   watch out for tunnel vision: Robert Gibbons, "Incentives in Organizations," *Journal of Economic Perspectives* 12, no. 4 (1998): 115–32, https://doi.org/10.1257/jep.12.4.115.

75   Thinking through where, when, and how: Todd Rogers et al., "Beyond Good Intentions: Prompting People to Make Plans Improves Follow-through on Important Tasks," *Behavioral Science & Policy* 1, no. 2 (2015): 33–41, https://doi.org/10.1177/237946151500100205.

75   Accenture's top five hundred leaders globally: Shook, "How to Set—and Meet—Your Company's Diversity Goals."

75   Bayer also uses integrated scorecards: "Statutory Targets for the Proportion of Women in Senior Management Positions," Bayer, accessed August 10, 2022, https://www.bayer.com/en/inclusion-diversity/women-management-positions.

76   One paper on goal attainment: Aneesh Rai et al., "A Field Experiment on Subgoal Framing to Boost Volunteering: The Trade-Off Between Goal Granularity and Flexibility," *Journal of Applied Psychology* 108, no. 4 (2023): 621–34, https://doi.org/10.1037/apl0001040.

76   prospect of being asked to explain or justify: Iris Bohnet, *What Works: Gender Equality by Design* (Cambridge, MA: Harvard University Press, 2016), 272–73, 283.

76   more likely to achieve organization-wide goals: Alexandra Kalev, Frank Dobbin, and Erin Kelly, "Best Practices or Best Guesses? Assessing the Efficacy of Corporate Affirmative Action and Diversity Policies," *American Sociological Review* 71, no. 4 (2006): 589–617, https://doi.org/10.1177/000312240607100404.

77   social accountability: Jennifer S. Lerner and Philip E. Tetlock, "Accounting for the Effects of Accountability," *Psychological Bulletin* 125, no. 2 (1999): 255–75, https://doi.org/10.1037/0033-2909.125.2.255.

77   breaking long or complicated tasks into bite-sized pieces: Bohnet and Chilazi, *Goals and Targets for Diversity, Equity, and Inclusion.*

77   Unilever did exactly this in 2010: "Nine Ways We're Making Unilever a More Gender-Balanced Business," Unilever, March 3, 2020, https://www.unilever.com/news/news-search/2020/nine-ways-we-are-making-unilever-a-more-gender-balanced-business/.

78   when managers personally participate: Frank Dobbin, Daniel Schrage, and Alexandra Kalev, "Rage Against the Iron Cage: The Varied Effects of Bureaucratic Personnel Reforms on Diversity," *American Sociological Review* 80, no. 5 (2015): 1014–44, https://doi.org/10.1177/0003122415596416.

78   Travel company Expedia: Expedia Group, *Inclusion & Diversity Report 2022*, 2022, https://s202.q4cdn.com/757635260/files/doc_downloads/2023/06/Expedia-Group-ID-Report-2022.pdf.

78   consumer goods giant Johnson & Johnson: Johnson & Johnson, *We All Belong: 2022 Diversity, Equity & Inclusion Impact Review*, 2022, https://belong.jnj.com/2022/_assets/downloads/johnson-johnson-diversity-equity-inclusion-impact-review-2022.pdf.

78   among marathon runners: Aaron M. Sackett et al., "Harnessing Optimism: How Eliciting Goals Improves Performance," working paper, 2014, https://dx.doi.org/10.2139/ssrn.2544020.

78   economics students: Max van Lent and Michiel Souverijn, "Goal Setting and Raising the Bar: A Field Experiment," *Journal of Behavioral and Experimental Economics* 87 (2020), https://doi.org/10.1016/j.socec.2020.101570.

Chapter 4: Incentives to Drive Results

80   the "Massport Model": Robert Livingston and Laura Winig, "The Massport Model: Integrating Diversity and Inclusion into Public-Private Partnerships," Harvard Kennedy School Case 2153.0 (Cambridge, MA: Harvard Kennedy School Case Program, March 2019), https://case.hks.harvard.edu/the-massport-model-integrating-diversity-and-inclusion-into-public-private-partnerships/.

81   Boston mayor Michelle Wu was joined: Alexi Cohan, "Boston-Area Mayors Sign Compact to Improve Diversity in Real Estate Projects," GBH, May 11, 2023, https://www.wgbh.org/news/local-news/2023/05/11/boston-area-mayors-sign-compact-to-improve-diversity-in-real-estate-projects.

82   achievement of goals related to workplace fairness: Alexis Krivkovich et al., *Women in the Workplace 2022*, McKinsey & Company and LeanIn.Org, 2022, https://wiw-report.s3.amazonaws.com/Women_in_the_Workplace_2022.pdf.

82   Mastercard, for example, introduced new performance metrics: Michael Miebach, "Sharing Accountability and Success: Why We're Linking Employee Compensation to ESG Goals," Mastercard Newsroom, April 19, 2022, https://www.mastercard.com/news/perspectives/2022/esg-goals-and-employee-compensation/.

82   "Tying DEI": Randall Tucker, "Mastercard's Chief Inclusion Officer on the Critical Role of DEI (and 3 Keys to Getting It Right)," *Fortune*, June 20, 2022, https://fortune.com/2022/06/20/diversity-equity-inclusion-juneteenth-pride-month-mastercard/.

82   ties 7 percent of all employee bonuses: Yoree Koh, "Intel Hits an Internal Goal for Workforce Diversity," *Wall Street Journal*, October 29, 2018, https://www.wsj.com/articles/intel-hits-a-novel-diversity-target-it-calls-full-representation-1540818005.

82   ESG metric makes up 10 percent: Verizon, *Environment, Social and Governance (ESG) Report 2021*, 2021, https://www.verizon.com/about/sites/default/files/Verizon-2021-ESG-Report.pdf.

82   publicly specified what that metric entails: Marguerite Ward and Maddy Simpson, "Here's the Plan Verizon Uses to Tie Executives' Pay to Diversity and Inclusion Goals—and How Other Companies like Mastercard and Chipotle Are Following Suit," Business Insider, March 24, 2021, https://www.businessinsider.com/companies-tying-executive-bonuses-meeting-diversity-esg-goals-2020-11.

82   Other companies that have tied: Emily Glazer and Theo Francis, "CEO Pay Increasingly Tied to Diversity Goals," *Wall Street Journal*, June 2, 2021, https://www.wsj.com/articles/ceos-pledged-to-increase-diversity-now-boards-are-holding-them-to-it-11622626380.

83   large textile firms in India: Nicholas Bloom et al., "Does Management Matter? Evidence from India," *Quarterly Journal of Economics* 128, no. 1 (2013): 1–51, https://doi.org/10.1093/qje/qjs044.

83   These intertemporal choice problems: Keith Marzilli Ericson and David Laibson, "Intertemporal Choice," in *Handbook of Behavioral Economics: Applications and Foundations 1*, eds. B. Douglas Bernheim, Stefano DellaVigna, and David Laibson, vol. 2 (Amsterdam: North-Holland, 2019), 1–67, https://doi.org/10.1016/bs.hesbe.2018.12.001.

83   coined the term "status quo bias": William Samuelson and Richard Zeckhauser, "Status Quo Bias in Decision Making," *Journal of Risk and Uncertainty* 1, no. 1 (1988): 7–59, https://doi.org/10.1007/BF00055564.

84   they were substantially more inclined: Bloom et al., "Does Management Matter?," 1–51.

84   "Womenomics," a term coined by Kathy Matsui and colleagues: "'Womenomics' Reveals the Power of the Purse in Japan," Goldman Sachs, April 2019, https://www.goldmansachs.com/our-firm/history/moments/1999-womenomics.html.

84   Womenomics did not have a transformative impact: Mark Crawford, "Abe's Womenomics Policy, 2013–2020: Tokenism, Gradualism, or Failed Strategy?," *Asia-Pacific Journal* 19, no. 4 (2021), https://apjjf.org/2021/4/crawford.

84   Japan ranked 104th in the World Bank's survey: "Japan Drops to 104th in Gender Disparity Rank in World Bank Survey," *Kyodo News*, March 2, 2023, https://english.kyodonews.net/news/2023/03/8c3d6ae8b92a-japan-drops-to-104th-in-gender-disparity-rank-in-world-bank-survey.html.

85   123rd in the World Economic Forum's Economic Participation and Opportunity Index: World Economic Forum, *Global Gender Gap Report 2023*, June 2023, https://www3.weforum.org/docs/WEF_GGGR_2023.pdf.

85   GDP boost provided by women's increased participation: Antoinette M. Sayeh, Alejandro Badel, and Rishi Goyal, "Countries That Close Gender Gaps See Substantial Growth Returns," *IMF Blog*, September 27, 2023, https://www.imf.org/en/Blogs/Articles/2023/09/27/countries-that-close-gender-gaps-see-substantial-growth-returns.

85   GDP per capita would also increase: Chang-Tai Hsieh et al., "The Allocation of Talent and U.S. Economic Growth," *Econometrica* 87, no. 5 (2019): 1439–74, https://doi.org/10.3982/ECTA11427.

85   benefits of working for pay also abound: Erin K. Fletcher, Rohini Pande, and Charity Troyer Moore, "Women and Work in India: Descriptive Evidence and a Review of Potential Policies," HKS Faculty Research Working Paper Series RWP18–08-004, Harvard Kennedy School, Cambridge, MA, 2017, https://www.hks.harvard.edu/publications/women-and-work-india-descriptive-evidence-and-review-potential-policies.

86   80 percent of about 5,000 surveyed organizations: Payscale, *2023 Compensation Best Practices Report*, 2023, https://www.payscale.com/research-and-insights/cbpr/.

86   about a quarter used: John Borneman, Jennifer Teefey, and Matthew Mazzoni, "ESG + Incentives 2022 Report," Harvard Law School Forum on Corporate Governance, August 22, 2022, https://corpgov.law.harvard.edu/2022/08/22/esg-incentives-2022-report/.

87   "shape the story your incentives tell": Uri Gneezy, *Mixed Signals: How Incentives Really Work* (New Haven, CT: Yale University Press, 2023), 112.

87   In an actual car shopping experiment: Gneezy, 112.

87   human brain organizes financial activities in different buckets: Richard H. Thaler,

"Mental Accounting Matters," *Journal of Behavioral Decision-Making* 12, no. 3 (1999): 183–206, https://doi.org/10.1002/(SICI)1099-0771(199909)12:3%3C183::AID -BDM318%3E3.0.CO;2-F.

88 Xylem Inc.: Borneman, Teefey, and Mazzoni, "ESG + Incentives 2022 Report."

88 "non-financial performance measures": Kristen Sullivan and Maureen Bujno, "Incorporating ESG Measures into Executive Compensation Plans," Harvard Law School Forum on Corporate Governance, May 24, 2021, https://corpgov.law.harvard.edu/2021/05/24 /incorporating-esg-measures-into-executive-compensation-plans/.

88 famous 1979 paper: Daniel Kahneman and Amos Tversky, "Prospect Theory: An Analysis of Decision under Risk," *Econometrica* 47, no. 2 (1979): 263–91, https://doi .org/10.2307/1914185.

89 impact on morale and motivation: Truman F. Bewley, *Why Wages Don't Fall During a Recession* (Cambridge, MA: Harvard University Press, 1999).

89 field experiment with a Chinese high-tech firm: Tanjim Hossain and John A. List, "The Behavioralist Visits the Factory: Increasing Productivity Using Simple Framing Manipulations," *Management Science* 58, no. 12 (2012): 2151–67, https://doi.org/10.1287 /mnsc.1120.1544.

89 HP did in 2017: Monidipa Fouzder, "Be More Diverse or We'll Withhold 10% of Your Fees, IT Giant Tells Firms," *Law Society Gazette*, February 15, 2017, https://www .lawgazette.co.uk/practice/be-more-diverse-or-well-withhold-10-of-your-fees-it-giant -tells-firms/5059833.article.

90 Rivera said in 2020: Ruiqi Chen, "HP Legal Chief Rivera: Demand Diversity, Law Firms Will Listen," Bloomberg Law, October 13, 2020, https://news.bloomberglaw.com /business-and-practice/hp-legal-chief-rivera-demand-diversity-law-firms-will-listen.

90 more likely to be hired: Emilio J. Castilla, "Social Networks and Employee Performance in a Call Center," *American Journal of Sociology* 110, no. 5 (2005): 1243–83, https://doi.org/10.1086/427319.

90 can make all the difference: Jennifer Merluzzi and Adina Sterling, "Lasting Effects? Referrals and Career Mobility of Demographic Groups in Organizations," *Industrial & Labor Relations Review* 70, no. 1 (2017): 105–31, https://doi.org/10.1177/0019793916669507.

90 offering twice the referral reward: Cat Zakrzewski, "Intel Doubles Up on Hiring Women and Minorities," *Wall Street Journal*, August 3, 2015, https://www.wsj.com /articles/BL-DGB-42906.

90 Accenture and Pinterest: Alexandra Carter, "3 Examples of Great Diversity Employee Referral Programs," *Ongig*, September 12, 2021, https://blog.ongig.com/diversity -and-inclusion/diversity-employee-referral-programs/.

90 Pinterest reported a dramatic increase: Michelle Quinn, "Quinn: Pinterest's Diversity Experiments," *Mercury News*, August 11, 2016, https://www.mercurynews .com/2016/01/29/quinn-pinterests-diversity-experiments/.

91 "present bias": David Laibson, "Golden Eggs and Hyperbolic Discounting," *Quarterly Journal of Economics* 112, no. 2 (1997): 443–78, https://doi .org/10.1162/003355397555253.

91 experiment to raise young children's immunization rates in India: Abhijit Vinayak Banerjee et al., "Improving Immunisation Coverage in Rural India: Clustered Randomised Controlled Evaluation of Immunisation Campaigns with and without Incentives," *BMJ* 340, no. 7759 (2010), https://doi.org/10.1136/bmj.c2220.

91 "temptation bundling": Katherine L. Milkman, Julia A. Minson, and Kevin G. M. Volpp, "Holding the Hunger Games Hostage at the Gym: An Evaluation of Temptation Bundling," *Management Science* 60, no. 2 (2014): 283–99, https://doi.org/10.1287/mnsc.2013.1784.

91 Another evidence-based example: Erika L. Kirgios et al., "Teaching Temptation Bundling to Boost Exercise: A Field Experiment," *Organizational Behavior and Human Decision Processes* 161 (2020): 20–35, https://doi.org/10.1016/j.obhdp.2020.09.003.

92 they were asked to stuff campaign mailings: Jeffrey Carpenter and Erick Gong, "Motivating Agents: How Much Does the Mission Matter?," *Journal of Labor Economics* 34, no. 1 (2016): 211–36, https://doi.org/10.1086/682345.

92 there are cases where they don't: Bruno S. Frey, *Not Just for the Money: An Economic Theory of Personal Motivation* (Cheltenham: Edward Elgar, 1997).

92   something daycare centers in Israel had to learn: Uri Gneezy and Aldo Rustichini, "A Fine Is a Price," *Journal of Legal Studies* 29, no. 1 (2000): 1–17, https://doi.org/10.1086/468061.

93   textile factory in China: Sherry Jueyu Wu and Elizabeth Levy Paluck, "Designing Nudges for the Context: Golden Coin Decals Nudge Workplace Behavior in China," *Organizational Behavior and Human Decision Processes* 163 (2021): 43–50, https://doi.org/10.1016/j.obhdp.2018.10.002.

93   survey by the Hoover Institute and partners: Stephen H. Haber et al., *2022 Survey of Investors, Retirement Savings, and ESG*, Corporate Governance Research Initiative, Stanford Rock Center for Corporate Governance, November 2022, https://www.gsb.stanford.edu/faculty-research/publications/2022-survey-investors-retirement-savings-esg.

93   Deloitte Global Human Capital Trends surveys: Steve Hatfield and Lauren Kirby, "Taking Bold Action for Equitable Outcomes," *Deloitte Insights*, January 9, 2023, https://www2.deloitte.com/us/en/insights/focus/human-capital-trends/2023/diversity-equity-inclusion-belonging.html.

94   An extensive review of the literature: Lea Cassar and Stephan Meier, "Nonmonetary Incentives and the Implications of Work as a Source of Meaning," *Journal of Economic Perspectives* 32, no. 3 (2018): 215–38, https://doi.org/10.1257/jep.32.3.215.

94   voted more than 1,500 times: Blackrock, *Investment Stewardship Annual Report*, September 2020, https://www.blackrock.com/corporate/literature/publication/blk-annual-stewardship-report-exec-summary-2020.pdf.

94   expanded its diversity expectations: Larry Fink and Rob Kapito, "Our Actions to Advance Racial Equity and Inclusion," BlackRock, June 22, 2020, https://www.blackrock.com/corporate/about-us/social-impact/advancing-racial-equity.

94   films must meet specific representation benchmarks: "Representation and Inclusion Standards," Academy of Motion Picture Arts and Sciences, accessed June 5, 2024, https://www.oscars.org/awards/representation-and-inclusion-standards.

94   Similar standards are already in place: Brian Lowry, "The Oscars Make Inclusion a Requirement for Best Picture Consideration Beginning in 2024," CNN, September 8, 2020, https://www.cnn.com/2020/09/08/entertainment/oscars-rules-changes/index.html.

96   two-thirds of full-time workers: Women's Bureau, US Department of Labor, *Issue Brief: Understanding the Gender Wage Gap*, March 2023, https://www.dol.gov/sites/dolgov/files/WB/equalpay/WB_issuebrief-undstg-wage-gap-v1.pdf.

96   less likely to receive variable pay: Jason Sockin and Michael Sockin, "A Pay Scale of Their Own: Gender Differences in Variable Pay," working paper, 2019, https://doi.org/10.2139/ssrn.3512598.

96   the old-age poverty rate: OECD, *Pensions at a Glance 2023*, December 13, 2023, https://www.oecd.org/publications/oecd-pensions-at-a-glance-19991363.htm.

96   definition of equal pay: "Equal Pay for Work of Equal Value," Equal Pay International Coalition, last modified July 25, 2018, https://www.equalpayinternationalcoalition.org/equal-pay/.

96   janitors, who are mostly men, make on average 15 percent more: "Median weekly Earnings of Full-time Wage and Salary Workers by Detailed Occupation and Sex (2022)," US Department of Labor, Bureau of Labor Statistics, last modified January 25, 2023, https://www.bls.gov/cps/aa2022/cpsaat39.htm.

96   studies examining the US labor market: Asaf Levanon, Paula England, and Paul Allison, "Occupational Feminization and Pay: Assessing Causal Dynamics Using 1950–2000 U.S. Census Data," *Social Forces* 88, no. 2 (2009): 865–91, https://doi.org/10.1353/sof.0.0264. See also Jorgen Harris, "Do Wages Fall When Women Enter an Occupation?," *Labour Economics* 74 (2022), https://doi.org/10.1016/j.labeco.2021.102102.

96   recreation workers: Claire Cain Miller, "As Women Take Over a Male-Dominated Field, the Pay Drops," *New York Times*, March 18, 2016, https://www.nytimes.com/2016/03/20/upshot/as-women-take-over-a-male-dominated-field-the-pay-drops.html.

97   job classification systems are common: Rose Khattar, "Promoting Equal Pay for

Work of Equal Value," in *Pay Transparency Tools to Close the Gender Wage Gap* (France: Organisation for Economic Co-operation and Development, 2021), https://www.oecd-ilibrary.org/sites/7a2d25c5-en/index.html?itemId=/content/component/7a2d25c5-en.

97   guidelines for employers: Marie-Thérèse Chicha, *Promoting Equity: Gender-Neutral Job Evaluation for Equal Pay: A Step-by-Step Guide* (Geneva: International Labour Office, 2008), https://www.ilo.org/declaration/info/publications/eliminationofdiscrimination/WCMS_122372/lang—en/index.htm.

97   Employees who feel that they are underpaid compared to their peers: Marianna Baggio and Ginevra Marandola, "Employees' Reaction to Gender Pay Transparency: An Online Experiment," *Economic Policy* 38, no. 113 (2023): 161–88, https://doi.org/10.1093/epolic/eiac066.

97   Evidence from Denmark: Morten Bennedsen et al., "Do Firms Respond to Gender Pay Gap Transparency?," *Journal of Finance* 77, no. 4 (2022): 2051–91, https://doi.org/10.1111/jofi.13136.

97   tend to punish the "second earner": OECD Social Policy Division, "PF1.4: Neutrality of Tax-Benefit Systems," OECD Family Database, August 11, 2016, https://www.oecd.org/els/soc/PF1_4_Neutrality_of_tax_benefit_systems.pdf.

97   the degree to which gender considerations are included in tax codes: OECD, *Joining Forces for Gender Equality: What Is Holding Us Back?* (Paris: OECD Publishing, 2023), https://doi.org/10.1787/67d48024-en.

98   highest gender differences in part-time work: "Share of Women Working Part-Time Higher than Men," Eurostat, March 3, 2023, https://ec.europa.eu/eurostat/web/products-eurostat-news/w/EDN-20230303-1.

98   estimated how many more hours women would work: Alexander Bick and Nicola Fuchs-Schündeln, "Quantifying the Disincentive Effects of Joint Taxation on Married Women's Labor Supply," *American Economic Review* 107, no. 5 (2017): 100–4, https://doi.org/10.1257/aer.p20171063.

98   This is exactly what happened in Sweden: Håkan Selin, "The Rise in Female Employment and the Role of Tax Incentives: An Empirical Analysis of the Swedish Individual Tax Reform of 1971," *International Tax and Public Finance* 21, no. 5 (2014): 894–922, https://doi.org/10.1007/s10797-013-9283-y.

99   introduction of the Earned Income Tax Credit: Jacob Bastian, "The Rise of Working Mothers and the 1975 Earned Income Tax Credit," *American Economic Journal: Economic Policy* 12, no. 3 (2020): 44–75, https://doi.org/10.1257/pol.20180039.

Chapter 5: Transparency for Accountability

100   A decade later, she was thoroughly fed up: Mia Perdomo, interview with Siri Chilazi, March 28, 2023.

101   PAR digs into voluntarily participating companies' data: "Ranking PAR," Aequales, accessed April 11, 2024, https://aequales.com/rankingpar/.

101   Cofounders Perdomo and de la Piedra explain: Mia Perdomo, email to Siri Chilazi, November 3, 2023.

102   The data painted a bleak picture: Siri Chilazi and Iris Bohnet, "How to Best Use Data to Meet Your DE&I Goals," *Harvard Business Review*, December 3, 2020, https://hbr.org/2020/12/how-to-best-use-data-to-meet-your-dei-goals.

102   disclosure requirements have spurred innovation and progress: Iris Bohnet, *What Works: Gender Equality by Design* (Cambridge, MA: Harvard University Press, 2016), 266.

102   first corporate responsibility report in 2002: Intel, *Global Citizenship Report 2001: Vision & Values*, 2002, https://csrreportbuilder.intel.com/PDFfiles/archived_reports/Intel%202001%20CSR%20Report.pdf.

102   that number stood at 25.9 percent: "Diversity and Inclusion are Key to Innovation," Intel, accessed July 9, 2023, https://www.intel.com/content/www/us/en/diversity/diversity-at-intel.html.

103   Intel's current goal is to reach 40 percent women: Dawn Jones, "A Year of Uniting the Industry and Further Embedding D+I," Intel, May 12, 2022, https://www.intel.com/content/www/us/en/newsroom/opinion/a-year-of-uniting-industry-and-embedding-d-plus-i.html#gs.285mis.

103   "Publishing data became the 'end' instead of the 'means'": Catalyze Tech Working

Group, *The ACT Report: Action to Catalyze Tech, A Paradigm Shift for DEI*, Aspen Institute and Snap Inc., October 2021, https://actreport.com/.

103 research examining disclosures: Atinuke O. Adediran, "Disclosing Corporate Diversity," *Virginia Law Review* 109, no. 2 (2023): 307–72, https://virginialawreview.org/wp-content/uploads/2023/04/Adediran_Book.pdf.

104 "Sunlight is said to be the best of disinfectants": Louis D. Brandeis, *Other People's Money: and How the Bankers Use It* (New York: F. A. Stokes, 1914), 92.

104 more likely to repay their debts: Ricardo Perez-Truglia and Ugo Troiano, "Shaming Tax Delinquents," *Journal of Public Economics* 167 (2018): 120–37, https://doi.org/10.1016/j.jpubeco.2018.09.008.

104 business owners reported on average 3 percent higher incomes: Erlend E. Bø, Joel Slemrod, and Thor O. Thoresen, "Taxes on the Internet: Deterrence Effects of Public Disclosure," *American Economic Journal: Economic Policy* 7, no. 1 (2015): 36–62, https://dx.doi.org/10.1257/pol.20130330.

104 umpires made fewer racially biased calls: Christopher A. Parsons et al., "Strike Three: Discrimination, Incentives, and Evaluation," *American Economic Review* 101, no. 4 (2011): 1410–35, https://doi.org/10.1257/aer.101.4.1410.

105 diversity-related disclosures have become a fixture of the reports: Atinuke O. Adediran, "Disclosing Corporate Diversity."

105 more than three-quarters of Russell 1000 companies: "JUST Jobs Scorecard Shows Room for Companies to Lead on Job Quality Disclosure, With Established Leaders Outperforming Peers," JUST Capital, March 13, 2023, https://justcapital.com/news/just-jobs-scorecard-shows-room-for-companies-to-lead-on-job-quality/.

105 Corporate Sustainability Reporting Directive (CSDR): "Corporate Sustainability Reporting," European Commission, accessed January 25, 2024, https://finance.ec.europa.eu/capital-markets-union-and-financial-markets/company-reporting-and-auditing/company-reporting/corporate-sustainability-reporting_en.

105 directive will reach about 50,000 companies: "How Will EU CSRD Change DE&I Management and Reporting?," EDGE, November 20, 2023, https://www.edge-cert.org/article/eu-csrd-changes-dei-management-and-reporting/.

105 Examining major US technology and financial firms: David P. Daniels et al., "Do Investors Value Workforce Gender Diversity?," *Organization Science* (forthcoming), https://papers.ssrn.com/sol3/papers.cfm?abstract_id=4825030.

106 In a recent experiment: Maya Balakrishnan, Jimin Nam, and Ryan W. Buell, "Differentiating on Diversity: How Disclosing Workforce Diversity Influences Consumer Choice," *Production and Operations Management* (2024), https://doi.org/10.1177/10591478241239934.

106 refrigerants in grocery stores made up a larger share: Nigel Topping, "How Does Sustainability Disclosure Drive Behavior Change?," *Journal of Applied Corporate Finance* 24 (2012): 45–48, https://doi.org/10.1111/j.1745-6622.2012.00377.x.

106 meta-analysis examining the effects of goal setting: Tracy Epton, Sinead Currie, and Christopher J. Armitage, "Unique Effects of Setting Goals on Behavior Change: Systematic Review and Meta-Analysis," *Journal of Consulting and Clinical Psychology* 85, no. 12 (2017): 1182–98, https://doi.org/10.1037/ccp0000260.

106 "While we had set internal representation goals for many years": Ellyn Shook, "How to Set—and Meet—Your Company's Diversity Goals," *Harvard Business Review*, June 21, 2021, https://hbr.org/2021/06/how-to-set-and-meet-your-companys-diversity-goals.

107 experiment with nearly 3,000 female employees: Katryn Wright, Guusje Lindemann, and James Elfer, "Women in Leadership—An Experiment at Ericsson," MoreThanNow, April 24, 2023, https://www.morethannow.co.uk/single-post/2023/3/31/women-in-leadership-an-experiment-at-ericsson.

107 numerical, forward-looking targets: Wei Cai et al., "Diversity Targets," working paper, 2022, https://dx.doi.org/10.2139/ssrn.4301472.

107 Snap Inc. tracks its performance: Snap Inc., *Diversity Annual Report 2022*, 2022, https://assets.ctfassets.net/kql3ubzzanzk/2cQsbIyDTVGUjkD9SYiNqV/3b99da49a3675d6e0902949e6b351796/Snap_DAR-2022_English.pdf?lang=en-US.

108 trade secrets: Jamillah Bowman Williams, "Diversity as a Trade Secret," *Georgetown Law Journal* 107, no. 6 (2019): 1685–1732, https://www.law.georgetown.edu

/georgetown-law-journal/wp-content/uploads/sites/26/2019/07/Diversity-as-a-Trade
-Secret.pdf.

108 US research universities voluntarily came together: Williams, "Diversity as a Trade
Secret."

108 "diversity musical chairs": Catalyze Tech Working Group, *The ACT Report*.

109 analysis of nearly 1,500 clinical trials: Alexandra Z. Sosinsky et al., "Enrollment of
Female Participants in United States Drug and Device Phase 1–3 Clinical Trials Between
2016 and 2019," *Contemporary Clinical Trials* 115 (2022), https://doi.org/10.1016/j
.cct.2022.106718.

109 when clinical trials aren't racially representative: Marcella Alsan et al., "Representation and Extrapolation: Evidence from Clinical Trials," *Quarterly Journal of Economics*
139, no. 1 (2024): 575–635, https://doi.org/10.1093/qje/qjad036.

109 analysis of its 213 clinical trials: Melinda Rottas et al., "Demographic Diversity of
Participants in Pfizer Sponsored Clinical Trials in the United States," *Contemporary Clinical Trials* 106 (2021), https://doi.org/10.1016/j.cct.2021.106421.

109 Pfizer is working to build fairness: "Diversity in Our Clinical Trials," Pfizer, accessed
June 21, 2023, https://www.pfizer.com/science/clinical-trials/diversity.

110 speak up more on counter-stereotypical topics: Jana Gallus and Emma Heikensten,
"Awards and the Gender Gap in Knowledge Contributions in STEM," *AEA Papers and
Proceedings* 110 (2020): 241–44, https://doi.org/10.1257/pandp.20201042.

110 cannot be assumed to be the social norm: Carly D. Robinson et al., "The Demotivating Effect (and Unintended Message) of Awards," *Organizational Behavior and Human
Decision Processes* 163 (2021): 51–64, https://doi.org/10.1016/j.obhdp.2019.03.006.

110 Switzerland-based EDGE: "EDGE Empower," EDGE, accessed June 25, 2023,
https://www.edgeempower.com.

111 Equileap is a Netherlands-based, independent data provider: "The Leading Provider of
Gender Equality Data & Insights," Equileap, accessed June 21, 2023, https://equileap.com.

111 JUST Capital, an independent US nonprofit: JUST Capital, "The JUST Jobs Scorecard," accessed June 26, 2023, https://justcapital.com/the-just-jobs-scorecard/.

111 Women's Empowerment Principles Gender Gap Analysis Tool: "The Women's Empowerment Principles Gender Gap Analysis Tool," UN Women and UN Global Compact,
accessed July 5, 2023, https://www.weps.org/resource/weps-gender-gap-analysis-tool.

111 BlendScore focuses: "About BlendScore," Blendscore, accessed June 21, 2023,
https://www.blendscore.co.

111 Genentech's then–CEO, Art Levinson, gave a pivotal presentation: Cynthia Burks,
"How One Biotech Company Narrowed the Gender Gap in Its Top Ranks," *Harvard
Business Review*, June 2, 2021, https://hbr.org/2021/06/how-one-biotech-company
-narrowed-the-gender-gap-in-its-top-ranks.

113 "At the BBC, organizing the annual 50:50 Challenge month": Ros Atkins, interview
with Siri Chilazi, June 28, 2023.

113 Iris and her coauthor, Richard Zeckhauser, ran a simple experiment: Iris Bohnet
and Richard Zeckhauser, "Social Comparisons in Ultimatum Bargaining," *Scandinavian Journal of Economics* 106, no. 3 (2004): 495–510, https://doi.org/10.1111/j.0347
-0520.2004.00376.x.

114 The US Women's National Soccer Team: Christine L. Exley et al., "Negotiating for
Equal Pay: The U.S. Women's National Soccer Team (A)," Harvard Business School Case
920–00-029 (Boston: Harvard Business School, December 2019), https://www.hbs.edu
/faculty/Pages/item.aspx?num=57451. See also Christine L. Exley et al., "Negotiating for
Equal Pay: The U.S. Women's National Soccer Team (B)," Harvard Business School Case
920-030 (Boston: Harvard Business School, December 2019), https://www.hbs.edu
/faculty/Pages/item.aspx?num=57454.

115 "We very much believe it is our responsibility": Andrew Das, "U.S. Women's Soccer Team Sues U.S. Soccer for Gender Discrimination," *New York Times*, March 8, 2019,
https://www.nytimes.com/2019/03/08/sports/womens-soccer-team-lawsuit-gender
-discrimination.html.

115 "a tacit admission": Andrew Das, "U.S. Soccer and Women's Players Agree to Settle
Equal Pay Lawsuit."

115 substantially increased the prize money: Nancy Armour, "FIFA Boosts Prize Money for Women's World Cup. All Players Get $30,000, Winners $270,000," *USA Today*, June 9, 2023, https://www.usatoday.com/story/sports/soccer/2023/06/09/fifa-prize-money -increase-womens-world-cup-narrows-gap-with-men-equity/70303993007/.

115 In 2023, the European Union introduced: "Pay Transparency in the EU," Council of the European Union, last reviewed May 2, 2023, https://www.consilium.europa.eu/en /policies/pay-transparency/.

116 eighteen different policies that steer pay transparency: Zoe Cullen, "Is Pay Transparency Good?," *Journal of Economic Perspectives* 38, no. 1 (2024): 153–80, http://doi .org/10.1257/jep.38.1.153.

116 President Barack Obama signed an executive order: "Executive Order—Non-Retaliation for Disclosure of Compensation Information," White House Office of the Press Secretary, last modified April 8, 2014, https://obamawhitehouse.archives.gov/the-press -office/2014/04/08/executive-order-non-retaliation-disclosure-compensation-information.

116 interprets its mandate: "Your Right to Discuss Wages," National Labor Relations Board, accessed July 19, 2023 https://www.nlrb.gov/about-nlrb/rights-we-protect/your -rights/your-rights-to-discuss-wages.

116 As a result, the gender pay gap decreased: Morten Bennedsen, Birthe Larsen, and Jiayi Wei, "Gender Wage Transparency and the Gender Pay Gap: A Survey," *Journal of Economic Surveys*, 2023, https://doi.org/10.1111/joes.12545.

116 university faculty members' salaries were disclosed: Michael Baker et al., "Pay Transparency and the Gender Gap," *American Economic Journal: Applied Economics* 15, no. 2 (2023): 157–83, https://doi.org/10.1257/app.20210141.

117 transparency helped decrease pay gaps between women and men: Jack Blundell, "Wage Responses to Gender Pay Gap Reporting Requirements," Discussion Paper 1750, Centre for Economic Performance, London, 2021, https://cep.lse.ac.uk/pubs/download /dp1750.pdf.

117 workers in an Indian manufacturing plant: Emily Breza, Supreet Kaur, and Yogita Shamdasani, "The Morale Effects of Pay Inequality," *Quarterly Journal of Economics* 133, no. 2 (2018): 611–63, https://doi.org/10.1093/qje/qjx041.

117 after government employees' salaries were published: David Card et al., "Inequality at Work: The Effect of Peer Salaries on Job Satisfaction," *American Economic Review* 102, no. 6 (2012): 2981–3003, https://doi.org/10.1257/aer.102.6.2981.

117 salary history bans: Amy Dalrymple, "Issue Brief: Equal Pay in the United States," Women's Bureau, US Department of Labor, March 2023, https://www.dol.gov/sites /dolgov/files/WB/equalpay/508_WB_issuebrief-equal-pay_03142023.pdf.

117 have decreased pay gaps by increasing the pay of women: Sourav Sinha, "US Salary History Bans—Strategic Disclosure by Job Applicants and the Gender Pay Gap," working paper, Yale University, New Haven, CT, 2022, https://doi.org/10.48550 /arXiv.2202.03602.

118 In Austria: Wolfgang Frimmel et al., "Mandatory Wage Posting, Bargaining and the Gender Wage Gap," Johannes Kepler University of Linz, Department of Economics Working Paper 2202, Linz, 2022, https://www.economics.jku.at/papers/2022 /wp2202.pdf.

118 Slovakia, where employers are expected: Samuel Skoda, "Directing Job Search in Practice: Mandating Pay Information in Job Ads," working paper, University of Zurich, Zurich, 2022, https://samuelskoda.github.io/skoda_jmp.pdf.

118 mandated that expected salary be included: David Arnold, Simon Quach, and Bledi Taska, "The Impact of Pay Transparency in Job Postings on the Labor Market," working paper, 2022, https://dx.doi.org/10.2139/ssrn.4186234.

118 2020 study examining teachers' pay negotiations in Wisconsin: Barbara Biasi and Heather Sarsons, "Information, Confidence, and the Gender Gap in Bargaining," *AEA Papers and Proceedings* 111 (2021): 174–78, https://doi.org/10.1257/pandp.20211019.

118 decreasing ambiguity in pay negotiations: Hannah Riley Bowles, Linda Babcock, and Kathleen L. McGinn, "Constraints and Triggers: Situational Mechanics of Gender in Negotiation," *Journal of Personality and Social Psychology* 89, no. 6 (2005): 951–65, https://doi.org/10.1037/0022-3514.89.6.951.

119　we accurately anticipate social backlash: Hannah Riley Bowles, Linda Babcock, and Lei Lai, "Social Incentives for Gender Differences in the Propensity to Initiate Negotiations: Sometimes It Does Hurt to Ask," *Organizational Behavior and Human Decision Processes* 103, no. 1 (2007): 84–103, https://doi.org/10.1016/j.obhdp.2006.09.001.

119　female job seekers received the same number of offers: Nina Roussille, "The Role of the Ask Gap in Gender Pay Inequality," *Quarterly Journal of Economics* (2024), https://doi.org/10.1093/qje/qjae004.

119　women were more likely to apply: Andreas Leibbrandt and John A. List, "Do Women Avoid Salary Negotiations? Evidence from a Large-Scale Natural Field Experiment," *Management Science* 61, no. 9 (2015): 2016–24, https://doi.org/10.1287/mnsc.2014.1994.

119　A recent experiment with experienced MBA students: Julia B. Bear et al., "Gender, Pay Transparency, and Competitiveness: Why Salary Information Sometimes, but Not Always, Mitigates Gender Gaps in Salary Negotiations," *Group Decision and Negotiation* 32 (2023): 1143–63, https://doi.org/10.1007/s10726-023-09837-x.

119　research suggests that the gender gap in salary negotiations is closing: Laura Kray, Jessica Kennedy, and Margaret Lee, "Now, Women Do Ask: A Call to Update Beliefs About the Gender Pay Gap," *Academy of Management Discoveries* 10, no. 1 (2023), https://doi.org/10.5465/amd.2022.0021.

120　Arjuna publishes an annual scorecard: Natasha Lamb and Michael Passoff, "Racial and Gender Pay Scorecard—Sixth Edition," Arjuna Capital and Proxy Impact, March 2023, https://static1.squarespace.com/static/5bc65db67d0c9102cca54b74/t/640f22770d7c0634287c57c3/1678713464204/Racial+and+Gender+Pay+Scorecard+2023.pdf.

120　"I think one of the reasons we've been so successful": Matt O'Brien, "Insider Q&A: Arjuna Capital's Natasha Lamb," AP News, December 20, 2021, https://apnews.com/article/climate-technology-business-environment-bill-gates-a6f11eb17bb9fa2459309f43d688b0a8.

120　the pay of new hires rapidly converged: Zoe B. Cullen, Shengwu Li, and Ricardo Perez-Truglia, "What's My Employee Worth? The Effects of Salary Benchmarking," NBER Working Paper 30570, National Bureau of Economic Research, Cambridge, MA, 2022, https://doi.org/10.3386/w30570.

Chapter 6: Talent Attraction to Cast a Wide Net

125　the FDNY was keen to attract: Anthony Barrows et al., *Behavioral Design Teams: A Model for Integrating Behavioral Design in City Government*, ideas42, 2018, https://givingcompass.org/article/behavioral-design-teams-model-integrating-nudges-city-government.

126　deterred by administrative hassles: S. L. Reeves, "Caught Up in Red Tape: Bureaucratic Hassles Undermine Sense of Belonging in College among First Generation Students" (PhD diss., University of Texas at Austin, 2015), https://hdl.handle.net/2152/32082.

126　government support programs like college financial aid: Eric P. Bettinger et al., "The Role of Application Assistance and Information in College Decisions: Results from the H&R Block FAFSA Experiment," *Quarterly Journal of Economics* 127, no. 3 (2012): 1205–42, https://doi.org/10.1093/qje/qjs017.

126　among Black candidates: Barrows et al., *Behavioral Design Teams*.

126　women tend to underestimate their abilities: Christine L. Exley and Judd B. Kessler, "The Gender Gap in Self-Promotion," *Quarterly Journal of Economics* 137, no. 3 (2022): 1345–81, https://doi.org/10.1093/qje/qjac003.

127　Recruiters did not adjust: Raviv Murciano-Goroff, "Missing Women in Tech: The Labor Market for Highly Skilled Software Engineers," *Management Science* 68, no. 5 (2021): 3262–81, https://doi.org/10.1287/mnsc.2021.4077.

127　believe that they were "good enough": Leonie Nicks et al., *Gender Differences in Response to Requirements in Job Adverts*, UK Government Equalities Office and the Behavioural Insights Team, March 2022, https://www.bi.team/wp-content/uploads/2022/03/Gender-differences-in-response-to-requirements-in-job-adverts-March-2022.pdf.

127　currently employed production supervisors: Joseph B. Fuller and Manjari Raman, *Dismissed by Degrees* (Cambridge, MA: Accenture, Grads of Life, Harvard Business

School, October 2017), https://www.hbs.edu/managing-the-future-of-work/Documents /dismissed-by-degrees.pdf.

127 stronger focus on specific skills: Joseph B. Fuller et al., *The Emerging Degree Reset*, Burning Glass Institute, 2022, https://static1.squarespace.com/static/6197797102be715f55c0e0a1 /t/6202bda7f1ceee7b0e9b7e2f/1644346798760/The+Emerging+Degree+Reset +%2822.02%29Final.pdf.

127 the less ambiguous the situation is: Hannah Riley Bowles, Linda Babcock, and Kathleen L. McGinn, "Constraints and Triggers: Situational Mechanics of Gender in Negotiation," *Journal of Personality and Social Psychology* 89, no. 6 (2005): 951–65, https://doi .org/10.1037/0022-3514.89.6.951.

128 they had not put themselves forward initially: Jennifer L. Lawless and L. Fox Richard, *It Still Takes a Candidate: Why Women Don't Run for Office* (New York: Cambridge University Press, 2010).

128 they are not wanted: Raina A. Brands and Isabel Fernandez-Mateo, "Leaning Out: How Negative Recruitment Experiences Shape Women's Decisions to Compete for Executive Roles," *Administrative Science Quarterly* 62, no. 3 (2017): 405–42, https://doi .org/10.1177/0001839216682728.

129 ran an experiment: Iris Bohnet et al., "Closing the Gender Gap in Re-applications for Senior Roles," working paper, 2023.

129 "understand my worth": Linda Calvin et al., *System Upgrade: Rebooting Corporate Policies for Impact*, Reboot Representation and McKinsey & Company, 2023, https:// www.rebootrepresentation.org/2023-report/.

129 Partnering with Upwork: Katherine B. Coffman, Manuela Collis, and Leena Kulkarni, "Whether to Apply," *Management Science* (2023), https://doi.org/10.1287 /mnsc.2023.4907.

131 conducted with the ride-sharing company Uber: Lisa Abraham, Johannes Hallermeier, and Alison Stein, "Words Matter: Experimental Evidence from Job Applications," working paper, 2023, https://drive.google.com/file/d/1mOl_P9ezjGY0Dfo1Bzus47yfCUY8LyYf/view.

132 hypercompetitive compensation schemes: Jeffrey A. Flory, Andreas Leibbrandt, and John A. List, "Do Competitive Workplaces Deter Female Workers? A Large-Scale Natural Field Experiment on Job Entry Decisions," *Review of Economic Studies* 82, no. 1 (2015): 122–55, https://doi.org/10.1093/restud/rdu030.

132 opaque salary negotiations: Andreas Leibbrandt and John A. List, "Do Women Avoid Salary Negotiations? Evidence from a Large-Scale Natural Field Experiment," *Management Science* 61, no. 9 (2015): 2016–24, https://doi.org/10.1287/mnsc.2014.1994.

132 throw your hat in the ring: Laura K. Gee, "The More You Know: Information Effects on Job Application Rates in a Large Field Experiment," *Management Science* 65, no. 5 (2019): 2077–94, https://doi.org/10.1287/mnsc.2017.2994.

132 women who applied by 11 percent: James Heighington, "Corporate Diversity Reports: Solving the Right Problem with the Wrong Data with James Heighington," Women and Public Policy Program virtual seminar, March 27, 2023, 6:38, https://www.youtube .com/watch?v=xXn7T0KFJjs.

133 "social sciences": "2022 Postings," American Statistical Association Committee on Minorities in Statistics, accessed September 25, 2023, https://community.amstat.org /cmis/opportunities/2022.

133 Health sector employers in Zambia: Nava Ashraf et al., "Losing Prosociality in the Quest for Talent? Sorting, Selection, and Productivity in the Delivery of Public Services," *American Economic Review* 110, no. 5 (2020): 1355–94, https://doi.org/10.1257 /aer.20180326.

133 police forces in the United States: Elizabeth Linos, "More Than Public Service: A Field Experiment on Job Advertisements and Diversity in the Police," *Journal of Public Administration Research and Theory* 28, no. 1 (2018): 67–85, https://doi.org/10.1093 /jopart/mux032.

133 peek behind the curtain: Isabel Fernandez-Mateo and Roberto M. Fernandez, "Bending the Pipeline? Executive Search and Gender Inequality in Hiring for Top Management Jobs," *Management Science* 62, no. 12 (2016): 3636–55, https://doi.org/10.1287 /mnsc.2015.2315.

134 number of job seekers who apply: Rachel Rosenberg, email message to Iris Bohnet, November 21, 2023.

135 Human Rights Watch issued a special report: Human Rights Watch, *"Only Men Need Apply": Gender Discrimination in Job Advertising in China*, April 2018, https://www.hrw.org/sites/default/files/report_pdf/china0418_web.pdf.

135 "'beautiful girls' as coworkers": "China: Job Ads Discriminate Against Women," Human Rights Watch, April 23, 2018, https://www.hrw.org/news/2018/04/23/china-job-ads-discriminate-against-women.

135 "dedicated teachers": Afra R. Chowdhury et al., "Reflections of Employers' Gender Preferences in Job Ads in India: An Analysis of Online Job Portal Data," Policy Research Working Paper 8379, World Bank Group, Washington, DC, 2018, https://doi.org/10.1596/1813-9450-8379.

136 what a difference the change made: Peter Kuhn, Kailing Shen, and Shuo Zhang, "Gender-Targeted Job Ads in the Recruitment Process: Facts from a Chinese Job Board," *Journal of Development Economics* 147 (2020), https://doi.org/10.1016/j.jdeveco.2020.102531. See also Peter J. Kuhn and Kailing Shen, "What Happens When Employers Can No Longer Discriminate in Job Ads?," *American Economic Review* 113, no. 4 (2023): 1013–48, http://doi.org/10.1257/aer.20211127.

137 low-cost investment with a potentially high return: Lucia Del Carpio and Thomas Fujiwara, "Do Gender-Neutral Job Ads Promote Diversity? Experimental Evidence from Latin America's Tech Sector," NBER Working Paper Series 31314, National Bureau of Economic Research, Cambridge, MA, 2023, https://doi.org/10.3386/w31314.

137 be . . . more appealing to women: Danielle Gaucher, Justin Friesen, and Aaron C. Kay, "Evidence That Gendered Wording in Job Advertisements Exists and Sustains Gender Inequality," *Journal of Personality and Social Psychology* 101, no. 1 (2011): 109–28, https://doi.org/10.1037/a0022530.

137 broaden the applicant pool: Joyce He and Sonia Kang, "Identities Between the Lines: Re-Aligning Gender and Professional Identities in Job Advertisements," *Academy of Management Annual Meeting Proceedings*, 2022, https://doi.org/10.5465/AMBPP.2022.10415abstract.

137 fill open roles five days faster: "T-Mobile Rejects the Tradeoff between Hiring Quickly and Hiring Diversely with the Help of Textio," Textio, accessed December 14, 2023, https://explore.textio.com/case-study-t-mobile.

138 resonate with men but not women: Jessica Nordell, "How Slack Got Ahead in Diversity," *Atlantic*, April 26, 2018, https://www.theatlantic.com/technology/archive/2018/04/how-slack-got-ahead-in-diversity/558806/.

138 free gender decoder: "Finding Subtle Bias in Job Ads," Gender Decoder, accessed December 14, 2023, https://gender-decoder.katmatfield.com/.

138 earliest papers on the topic: Gaucher, Friesen, and Kay, "Evidence That Gendered Wording in Job Advertisements Exists and Sustains Gender Inequality."

138 evidence-based cheat sheet: "De-Biasing Job Advertisements," Engendering Success in STEM, 2020, https://successinstem.ca/wp-content/uploads/2020/10/De-Biasing-Job-Advertisements.pdf.

138 among founders, employees, and investors: Mihwa Seong and Simon C. Parker, "Does Gendered Wording in Job Advertisements Deter Women from Joining Start-Ups? A Replication and Extension of Gaucher, Friesen, and Kay (2011)," *Strategic Entrepreneurship Journal* (2023), https://doi.org/10.1002/sej.1489.

138 in some of the more established firms: Emilio J. Castilla and Hye Jin Rho, "The Gendering of Job Postings in the Online Recruitment Process," *Management Science* 69, no. 11 (2023): 6912–39, https://doi.org/10.1287/mnsc.2023.4674.

139 training program targeted women only: Lucía Del Carpio and Maria Guadalupe, "More Women in Tech? Evidence from a Field Experiment Addressing Social Identity," *Management Science* 68, no. 5 (2022): 3196–3218, https://doi.org/10.1287/mnsc.2021.4035.

139 is not a viable (let alone ethical) strategy: Erin Dowell and Marlette Jackson, "'Woke-Washing' Your Company Won't Cut It," *Harvard Business Review*, July 27, 2020, https://hbr.org/2020/07/woke-washing-your-company-wont-cut-it. See also Vern Howard and Forbes Technology Council, "The Dangers of 'Diversity Washing' and What to Do

Instead," *Forbes*, November 30, 2020, https://www.forbes.com/sites/forbestechcouncil/2020/11/30/the-dangers-of-diversity-washing-and-what-to-do-instead/.

139 evidence-based fairness cues work: Leigh S. Wilton et al., "Show Don't Tell: Diversity Dishonesty Harms Racial/Ethnic Minorities at Work," *Personality & Social Psychology Bulletin* 46, no. 8 (2020): 1171–85, https://doi.org/10.1177/0146167219897149.

139 when the messaging is perceived as insincere: Kathryn M. Kroeper, Heidi E. Williams, and Mary C. Murphy, "Counterfeit Diversity: How Strategically Misrepresenting Gender Diversity Dampens Organizations' Perceived Sincerity and Elevates Women's Identity Threat Concerns," *Journal of Personality and Social Psychology* 122, no. 3 (2022): 399–426, https://doi.org/10.1037/pspi0000348.

140 the very people they want to support: Lisa M. Leslie, David M. Mayer, and David A. Kravitz, "The Stigma of Affirmative Action: A Stereotyping-Based Theory and Meta-Analytic Test of the Consequences for Performance," *Academy of Management Journal* 57, no. 4 (2014): 964–89, https://doi.org/10.5465/amj.2011.0940.

140 possibly well-intended EEO statement: Andreas Leibbrandt and John A. List, "Do Equal Employment Opportunity Statements Backfire? Evidence from a Natural Field Experiment on Job-Entry Decisions," NBER Working Paper Series 25035, National Bureau of Economic Research, Cambridge, MA, 2018, https://doi.org/10.3386/w25035.

140 A Canadian study: Sonia K. Kang et al., "Whitened Résumés: Race and Self-Presentation in the Labor Market," *Administrative Science Quarterly* 61, no. 3 (2016): 469–502, https://doi.org/10.1177/0001839216639577.

140 A study that gives us hope: Jeffrey A. Flory et al., "Increasing Workplace Diversity: Evidence from a Recruiting Experiment at a Fortune 500 Company," *Journal of Human Resources* 56, no. 1 (2021): 73–92, https://doi.org/10.3368/jhr.56.1.0518-9489R1.

141 number of jobs advertised as flexible increased by 20 percent: Kristina Londakova et al., "'Double Nudge' Encourages Employers to Offer Flexibility, in Turn Boosting Job Application Rates," Behavioural Insights Team, May 29, 2020, https://www.bi.team/blogs/double-nudge-encourages-employers-to-offer-flexibility-in-turn-boosting-job-application-rates/.

141 follow-up trial in the UK found similar results: Kristina Londakova et al., "BIT's Biggest Trial So Far Encourages More Flexible Jobs and Applications," Behavioural Insights Team, March 4, 2021, https://www.bi.team/blogs/bits-biggest-trial-so-far-encourages-more-flexible-jobs-and-applications/.

141 advertising jobs as flexible by default: Behavioural Insights Team and Employment and Social Development Canada, *How to Improve Workplace Equity–Evidence-Based Actions for Employers*, 2023, https://www.bi.team/wp-content/uploads/2023/03/How-to-Improve-Workplace-Equity.pdf.

142 "excellence in careers outside academia": "2022 Postings," American Statistical Association Committee on Minorities in Statistics.

142 organizations that truly value diversity can succeed: Robin J. Ely and David A. Thomas, "Getting Serious About Diversity: Enough Already with the Business Case," *Harvard Business Review*, November–December 2020, https://hbr.org/2020/11/getting-serious-about-diversity-enough-already-with-the-business-case.

142 living wages across the country's states and districts: Chris Kolmar, "This Is How Much a Living Wage Is in Each State," Zippia, 2017, https://research.zippia.com/living-wage.html.

142 based on the number of malpractice lawsuits: Chris Kolmar, "This Interactive Map Shows Which States Sue Doctors the Most," Zippia, 2016, https://research.zippia.com/states-that-sue.html.

142 in a 2021 experiment: Jung Ho Choi et al., "Do Jobseekers Value Diversity Information? Evidence from a Field Experiment and Human Capital Disclosures," *Journal of Accounting Research* 61, no. 3 (2023): 695–735, https://doi.org/10.1111/1475-679X.12474.

143 setting public diversity goals: Erika L. Kirgios, Ike M. Silver, and Edward H. Chang, "Concrete Diversity Targets Can Increase Applications from Historically Marginalized Candidates," working paper, 2023.

144 with and without affirmative action in Colombia: Marcela Ibañez and Gerhard Riener, "Sorting Through Affirmative Action: Three Field Experiments in Colombia," *Journal of Labor Economics* 36, no. 2 (2018): 437–78, https://doi.org/10.1086/694469.

144 laboratory experiments in Austria: Loukas Balafoutas and Matthias Sutter, "Affirmative Action Policies Promote Women and Do Not Harm Efficiency in the Laboratory," *Science* 335, no. 6068 (2012): 579–82, https://doi.org/10.1126/science.1211180.

144 and the United States: Muriel Niederle, Carmit Segal, and Lise Vesterlund, "How Costly Is Diversity? Affirmative Action in Light of Gender Differences in Competitiveness," *Management Science* 59, no. 1 (2013): 1–16, https://doi.org/10.1287/mnsc.1120.1602.

144 hiring managers are often reluctant: Summer R. Jackson, "(Not) Paying for Diversity: Repugnant Market Concerns Associated with Transactional Approaches to Diversity Recruitment," *Administrative Science Quarterly* 68, no. 3 (2023): 824–66, https://doi.org/10.1177/00018392231183649.

Chapter 7: Applicant Screening for Accuracy

146 spend less than ten seconds: "Ladders Updates Popular Recruiter Eye-Tracking Study with New Key Insights on How Job Seekers Can Improve Their Resumes," PR Newswire, November 6, 2018, https://www.prnewswire.com/news-releases/ladders-updates-popular-recruiter-eye-tracking-study-with-new-key-insights-on-how-job-seekers-can-improve-their-resumes-300744217.html.

146 the first 124 resumes: "12 Things Recruiters Look at First When Going Through Job Applications," *Forbes*, June 17, 2020, https://www.forbes.com/sites/forbeshumanresourcescouncil/2020/06/17/12-things-recruiters-look-at-first-when-going-through-job-applications/.

146 Swiss recruitment platform Job-Room: Dominik Hangartner et al., "Monitoring Hiring Discrimination Through Online Recruitment Platforms," *Nature* 589, no. 7843 (2021): 572–76, https//doi.org/10.1038/s41586-020-03136-0.

147 audit or correspondence experiments: Almost half of audit studies have focused on race/ethnicity or national origin and a quarter of the studies on gender. The remainder examined other candidate characteristics such as age, or the impact of specific pieces of information provided, such as whether or not the applicant was a parent. In addition to gender dynamics, this large set of studies has documented substantial evidence of differential treatment of otherwise identical applicants based on age, disability, marital status, physical appearance, race/ethnicity, sexual orientation, national origin, religion, and wealth. See Louis Lippens et al., "The State of Hiring Discrimination: A Meta-analysis of (Almost) All Recent Correspondence Experiments," *European Economic Review* 151, no. 104315 (2023), https://doi.org/10.1016/j.euroecorev.2022.104315. See also David Neumark, "Experimental Research on Labor Market Discrimination," *Journal of Economic Literature* 56, no. 3 (2018): 799–866, https://doi.org/10.1257/jel.20161309.

147 still going strong in most cases: Lincoln Quillian et al., "Meta-analysis of Field Experiments Shows No Change in Racial Discrimination in Hiring Over Time," *Proceedings of the National Academy of Sciences* 114, no. 41 (2017): 10870–75, https://doi.org/10.1073/pnas.1706255114.

147 France was the only country: Lincoln Quillian and John J. Lee, "Trends in Racial and Ethnic Discrimination in Hiring in Six Western Countries," *Proceedings of the National Academy of Sciences* 120, no. 6 (2023), https://doi.org/10.1073/pnas.2212875120.

147 men applying to jobs in female-dominated occupations: Michael Schaerer et al., "On the Trajectory of Discrimination: A Meta-Analysis and Forecasting Survey Capturing 44 Years of Field Experiments on Gender and Hiring Decisions," *Organizational Behavior and Human Decision Processes* 179 (2023), https://doi.org/10.1016/j.obhdp.2023.104280.

148 applicants' sexual orientation or gender identity: M. V. Lee Badgett, Christopher S. Carpenter, and Dario Sansone, "LGBTQ Economics," *Journal of Economic Perspectives* 35, no. 2 (2021): 141–70, https://doi.org/10.1257/jep.35.2.141.

148 transgender people: "U.S. Transgender Survey," National Center for Transgender Equality, accessed December 14, 2023, https://transequality.org/issues/us-transgender-survey. See also Billur Aksoy, Christopher S. Carpenter, and Dario Sansone, "Understanding Labor Market Discrimination Against Transgender People: Evidence from a Double List Experiment and a Survey," *Management Science* (2024), https://doi.org/10.1287/mnsc.2023.02567.

148 protections are less well-known: Billur Aksoy, Christopher S. Carpenter, and Dario Sansone, "Knowledge About Federal Employment Nondiscrimination Protections on the

Basis of Sexual Orientation," *AEA Papers and Proceedings* 113 (2023): 541–45, https://doi .org/10.1257/pandp.20231054.

148 race and gender discrimination report cards: Patrick M. Kline, Evan K. Rose, and Christopher R. Walters, "A Discrimination Report Card," NBER Working Paper Series 32313, National Bureau of Economic Research, Cambridge, MA, 2024, https://doi .org/10.3386/w32313.

148 is rather tenuous: Chad H. Van Iddekinge et al., "A Meta-analysis of the Criterion-Related Validity of Prehire Work Experience," *Personnel Psychology* 72, no. 4 (2019): 571–98, https://doi.org/10.1111/peps.12335. See also Frank L. Schmidt and John E. Hunter, "The Validity and Utility of Selection Methods in Personnel Psychology: Practical and Theoretical Implications of 85 Years of Research Findings," *Psychological Bulletin* 124, no. 2 (1998): 262–74, https://doi.org/10.1037/0033-2909.124.2.262.

149 the same kind of attention as their male counterparts: Tristan L. Botelho and Mabel Abraham, "Pursuing Quality: How Search Costs and Uncertainty Magnify Gender-based Double Standards in a Multistage Evaluation Process," *Administrative Science Quarterly* 62, no. 4 (2017): 698–730, https://doi.org/10.1177/0001839217694358.

149 focused on STEM fields was taken seriously: J. Aislinn Bohren et al., "The Dynamics of Discrimination: Theory and Evidence," *American Economic Review* 109, no. 10 (2019): 3395–3436, https://doi.org/10.1257/aer.20171829.

149 if they did not make this additional information available: Christine L. Exley et al., "The Transparency Gap," working paper, 2022.

149 they were not considered to belong: Natasha Quadlin, "The Mark of a Woman's Record: Gender and Academic Performance in Hiring," *American Sociological Review* 83, no. 2 (2018): 331–60, https://doi.org/10.1177/0003122418762291.

149 traits also stereotypically associated with femininity: Madeline E. Heilman, "Description and Prescription: How Gender Stereotypes Prevent Women's Ascent Up the Organizational Ladder," *Journal of Social Issues* 57, no. 4 (2001): 657–74, https://doi .org/10.1111/0022-4537.00234. See also Amy J. C. Cuddy, Susan T. Fiske, and Peter Glick, "Warmth and Competence as Universal Dimensions of Social Perception: The Stereotype Content Model and the BIAS Map," *Advances in Experimental Social Psychology* 40 (2008): 61–149, https://doi.org/10.1016/S0065-2601(07)00002-0.

150 "you do not end up with diversity": Siri Chilazi, Anisha Asundi, and Iris Bohnet, "Venture Capitalists Are Using the Wrong Tools to Improve Gender Diversity," *Behavioral Scientist*, March 12, 2019, https://behavioralscientist.org/venture-capitalists-are-using -the-wrong-tools-to-improve-gender-diversity/.

150 "identity-based impression-management": Joyce C. He and Sonia K. Kang, "Covering in Cover Letters: Gender and Self-Presentation in Job Applications," *Academy of Management Journal* 64, no. 4 (2021): 1097–1126, https://doi.org/10.5465/AMJ.2018.1280.

150 "whitened résumés": Sonia K. Kang et al., "Whitened Résumés: Race and Self-Presentation in the Labor Market," *Administrative Science Quarterly* 61, no. 3 (2016): 469–502, https://doi.org/10.1177/0001839216639577.

150 recruitment platform, Applied: "The Ethical Recruitment Software That Predicts the Best Hire," Applied, accessed September 20, 2023, https://www.beapplied.com/.

151 using such "unusual" words as "women" on their résumés: Jeffrey Dastin, "Amazon Scraps Secret AI Recruiting Tool That Showed Bias Against Women," Reuters, October 10, 2018, https://www.reuters.com/article/us-amazon-com-jobs-automation -insight/amazon-scraps-secret-ai-recruiting-tool-that-showed-bias-against-women -idUSKCN1MK08G.

151 promise to fix one of its products: Alistair Barr, "Google Mistakenly Tags Black People as 'Gorillas,' Showing Limits of Algorithms," *Wall Street Journal*, July 1, 2015, https:// www.wsj.com/articles/BL-DGB-42522.

151 was accused of gender discrimination: Neil Vigdor, "Apple Card Investigated After Gender Discrimination Complaints," *New York Times*, November 10, 2019, https://www .nytimes.com/2019/11/10/business/Apple-credit-card-investigation.html.

151 there was no evidence of algorithmic bias: Ian Carlos Campbell, "The Apple Card Doesn't Actually Discriminate against Women, Investigators Say," The Verge, March 23, 2021, https://www.theverge.com/2021/3/23/22347127/goldman-sachs-apple-card-no -gender-discrimination.

151 World Economic Forum's Global Gender Gap Index: World Economic Forum, *Global Gender Gap Report 2020*, December 16, 2019, https://www.weforum.org/reports /gender-gap-2020-report-100-years-pay-equality/.

152 reinforcing the way we all are using the product: Madalina Vlasceanu and David M. Amodio, "Propagation of Societal Gender Inequality by Internet Search Algorithms," *Proceedings of the National Academy of Sciences* 119, no. 29 (2022), https://doi.org/10.1073 /pnas.2204529119.

152 a quarter demonstrating both gender and racial bias: Center for Equity, Gender and Leadership, *Mitigating Bias in Artificial Intelligence* (Berkeley Haas School of Business, 2023), https://haas.berkeley.edu/equity/resources/playbooks/mitigating-bias-in-ai/.

152 "the magnification of certain biases can be mitigated": Ayanna Howard, "Real Talk: Intersectionality and AI," *MIT Sloan Management Review*, August 24, 2021, https:// sloanreview.mit.edu/article/real-talk-intersectionality-and-ai/.

152 all now lead efforts: Buolamwini's and Noble's books, *Unmasking AI: My Mission to Protect What Is Human in a World of Machines* (New York: Random House, 2023) and *Algorithms of Oppression: How Search Engines Reinforce Racism* (New York: New York University Press, 2018) provide us with key insights on intersectional bias in AI. Chowdhury's NGO, Humane Intelligence (https://www.humane-intelligence.org/), uses crowdsourcing to detect problems in AI systems. Gangadharan, cofounder of Our Data Bodies (https://www.odbproject.org/), examines how AI affects vulnerable populations who tend to be even more overwhelmed and further marginalized by the onslaught of technology. Gebru founded the independent, community-based Distributed AI Research Institute (https://www.dair-institute.org/). Noble founded the Center on Race & Digital Justice (https://www.raceanddigitaljustice.org/), focused on civil and human rights and the role of regulation. See also Lorena O'Neil, "These Women Tried to Warn Us About AI," *Rolling Stone*, August 12, 2023, https://www.rollingstone.com/culture/culture-features /women-warnings-ai-danger-risk-before-chatgpt-1234804367/.

154 Research by political psychologist Jon Krosnick: Bo MacInnis et al., "Candidate Name Order Effects in New Hampshire: Evidence from Primaries and from General Elections with Party Column Ballots," *PloS One* 16, no. 3 (2021), https://doi.org/10.1371 /journal.pone.0248049.

154 application they had seen immediately before: Kate Glazebrook and Janna Ter Meer, "Hiring, Honeybees and Human Decision-making," Medium, June 29, 2017, https:// medium.com/finding-needles-in-haystacks/hiring-honeybees-and-human-decision -making-33f3a9d76763.

154 assumed to be less committed to the job: Stefan Eriksson and Dan-Olaf Rooth, "Do Employers Use Unemployment as a Sorting Criterion When Hiring? Evidence from a Field Experiment," *American Economic Review* 104, no. 3 (2014): 1014–39, https://doi .org/10.1257/aer.104.3.1014.

155 additional motherhood (and, in some cases, fatherhood) penalty: Shelley Correll et al., "Getting a Job: Is There a Motherhood Penalty?," *American Journal of Sociology* 112, no. 5 (2007): 1297–1338, https://doi.org/10.1086/511799. See also David S. Pedulla, "Penalized or Protected? Gender and the Consequences of Nonstandard and Mismatched Employment Histories," *American Sociological Review* 81, no. 2 (2016): 262–89, https:// doi.org/10.1177/0003122416630982.

155 parents who discontinued work: Katherine Weisshaar, "From Opt Out to Blocked Out: The Challenges for Labor Market Re-entry after Family-Related Employment Lapses," *American Sociological Review* 83, no. 1 (2018): 34–60, https://doi .org/10.1177/0003122417752355.

155 more patient and resilient: Nahla Davies, "Taking a Career Hiatus Is Now Perfectly Okay," *Fast Company*, May 23, 2022, https://www.fastcompany.com/90753552/taking -a-career-hiatus-is-now-perfectly-okay.

155 such skills are increasingly in demand: David J. Deming, "The Growing Importance of Social Skills in the Labor Market," *Quarterly Journal of Economics* 132, no. 4 (2017): 1593–1640, https://doi.org/10.1093/qje/qjx022.

155 "returnship" programs: Tom Ragland, "The Return of Returnships," Harrison-Rush, accessed September 20, 2023, https://harrisonrush.com/the-return-of-returnships/.

155 ways of framing work experience on résumés: Ariella S. Kristal et al., "Reducing Dis-

crimination Against Job Seekers with and Without Employment Gaps," *Nature Human Behaviour* 7 (2023): 211–18, https://doi.org/10.1038/s41562-022-01485-6.

156 around 85 percent of check-writing investors: "All Raise x Crunchbase VC Check-writer Dashboard," All Raise, accessed January 9, 2024, https://allraise.org/all-raise-x-crunchbase-vc-checkwriter-dashboard.

156 2 percent of venture funding goes to female founders: Dominic-Madori Davis, "Women-Founded Startups Raised 1.9% of All VC Funds in 2022, a Drop from 2021," TechCrunch, January 18, 2023, https://techcrunch.com/2023/01/18/women-founded-startups-raised-1-9-of-all-vc-funds-in-2022-a-drop-from-2021/.

156 Azolla Ventures redacted names: Michael Campos, Lauren Hartle, and Amy Duffuor, "Should VCs and Startups Add Blind Review to Their Hiring Toolkit?," *MCJ Collective Newsletter*, January 2, 2022, https://myclimatejourney.substack.com/p/should-vcs-and-startups-add-blind.

157 It erased differences in callback rates: Ulf Rinne, "Anonymous Job Applications and Hiring Discrimination," *IZA World of Labor*, 2018, https://doi.org/10.15185/izawol.48.v2.

158 climbed at least sevenfold since: Claudia Goldin and Cecilia Rouse, "Orchestrating Impartiality: The Impact of 'Blind' Auditions on Female Musicians," *American Economic Review* 90, no. 4 (2000): 715–41, https://doi.org/10.1257/aer.90.4.715.

158 Anonymization did not work for applicants of color: Daisy Auger-Domínguez, *Inclusion Revolution: The Essential Guide to Dismantling Racial Inequity in the Workplace* (New York: Seal Press, 2022), 86.

159 support such anonymization: Nihar B. Shah, "The Role of Author Identities in Peer Review," *PLOS ONE* 18, no. 6 (2023): 1–15, https://doi.org/10.1371/journal.pone.0286206.

159 shown to be a Nobel laureate: Jürgen Huber et al., "Nobel and Novice: Author Prominence Affects Peer Review," *Proceedings of the National Academy of Sciences* 119, no. 41 (2022), https://doi.org/10.1073/pnas.2205779119.

159 had not been given access to Hubble before: Dalmeet Singh Chawla, "Record Number of First-Time Observers Get Hubble Telescope Time," *Nature*, November 25, 2021, https://www.nature.com/articles/d41586-021-03538-8.

159 not a representative sample of all French firms: Luc Behaghel et al., "Unintended Effects of Anonymous Résumés," *American Economic Journal: Applied Economics* 7, no. 3 (2015): 1–27, https://doi.org/10.1257/app.20140185.

161 "at least not in the short term": Ashley Whillans and Jeff Polzer, "Applied: Using Behavioral Science to Debias Hiring (A and B)," Harvard Business School Case 9-99-921-01-046 and 9-99-921-01-047 (Boston: Harvard Business School, 2021), https://www.hbs.edu/faculty/Pages/item.aspx?num=59779.

161 Iris has served on the board of Applied: Iris first learned about Applied when Kate contacted her in 2015. Impressed by the data-driven approach and the use of behavioral insights, she then became an advisor. When Applied, which was first conceived while Kate and her cofounder, Theo Fellgett, worked at the UK Behavioural Insights Team (BIT), spun out of BIT, she joined the board of directors for a couple of years.

161 more impartial hiring practices in the Brazilian public sector: Tatiana Mocanu, "Designing Gender Equity: Evidence from Hiring Practices and Committees," working paper, 2023, https://tatianamocanu.github.io/jm/mocanu_jmp_hiring.pdf.

162 criminal justice: David Arnold et al., "Measuring Racial Discrimination in Algorithms," *AEA Papers and Proceedings* 111 (2021): 49–54, https://doi.org/10.1257/pandp.20211080.

162 healthcare: Ziad Obermeyer et al., "Dissecting Racial Bias in an Algorithm Used to Manage the Health of Populations," *Science* 366, no. 6464 (2019): 447–53, https://doi.org/10.1126/science.aax2342.

162 finance: Robert Bartlett et al., "Consumer-Lending Discrimination in the FinTech Era," *Journal of Financial Economics* 143, no. 1 (2022): 30–56, https://doi.org/10.1016/j.jfineco.2021.05.047.

162 advertising: Latanya Sweeney, "Discrimination in Online Ad Delivery," *Communications of the ACM* 56, no. 5 (2013): 44–54, https://doi.org/10.48550/arxiv.1301.6822.

162 including hiring: Jon Kleinberg et al., "Discrimination in the Age of Algorithms," *Journal of Legal Analysis* 10 (2018): 113–74, https://doi.org/10.1093/jla/laz001.

162 The EEOC's list of issues: "The Americans with Disabilities Act and the Use of Software, Algorithms, and Artificial Intelligence to Assess Job Applicants and Employees," US Equal Employment Opportunity Commission, accessed December 14, 2023, https://www.eeoc.gov/laws/guidance/americans-disabilities-act-and-use-software-algorithms-and-artificial-intelligence.

163 applicants' credit scores have been used: Kristle Cortés et al., "The Unintended Consequences of Employer Credit Check Bans for Labor Markets," *Review of Economics and Statistics* 104, no. 5 (2022): 997–1009, https://doi.org/10.1162/rest_a_01019.

164 no longer help optimize performance today: Tobias Baer and Vishnu Kamalnath, "Controlling Machine-Learning Algorithms and Their Biases," McKinsey & Company, November 10, 2017, https://www.mckinsey.com/capabilities/risk-and-resilience/our-insights/controlling-machine-learning-algorithms-and-their-biases.

164 increased misinformation and polarization: See, for example, "Disinformation," Harvard Kennedy School Shorenstein Center on Media, Politics, and Public Policy, accessed January 9, 2024, https://shorensteincenter.org/research-initiatives/disinformation/.

165 dramatically increased the number of Black patients: Ziad Obermeyer et al., "Dissecting Racial Bias in an Algorithm Used to Manage the Health of Populations," *Science* 366, no. 6464 (2019): 447–53, https://doi.org/10.1126/science.aax2342.

165 ethical frameworks for artificial intelligence: Anna Jobin et al., "The Global Landscape of AI Ethics Guidelines," *Nature Machine Intelligence* 1, no. 9 (2019): 389–99, https://doi.org/10.1038/s42256-019-0088-2. Transparency requirements are also at the core of European Union Artificial Intelligence Act of December 9, 2023. It is the first legislation on AI by a major regulator anywhere and applies to all AI systems that touch the single European market independent of where the providers are located. See "EU AI Act: First Regulation on Artificial Intelligence," European Parliament, last updated December 19, 2023, https://www.europarl.europa.eu/topics/en/article/20230601STO93804/eu-ai-act-first-regulation-on-artificial-intelligence.

165 algorithmic audit: Christo Wilson et al., "Building and Auditing Fair Algorithms: A Case Study in Candidate Screening," *Proceedings of the 2021 ACM Conference on Fairness, Accountability, and Transparency* (2021): 666–77, https://doi.org/10.1145/3442188.3445928.

166 "archaic system that doesn't predict job fit": Frida Polli, "How AI Will Make Our Workplaces Fair with Diversity Tech Stack," *Forbes*, May 10, 2018, https://www.forbes.com/sites/fridapolli/2018/05/10/diversity-tech-stack-how-ai-will-make-our-workplace-fair/.

166 substantial gains in the diversity of interviewed candidates: Richard Feloni, "Consumer-Goods Giant Unilever Has Been Hiring Employees Using Brain Games and Artificial Intelligence—and It's a Huge Success," Business Insider, June 28, 2017, https://www.businessinsider.com/unilever-artificial-intelligence-hiring-process-2017-6.

166 historical training sets: Bo Cowgill et al., "Biased Programmers? Or Biased Data? A Field Experiment in Operationalizing AI Ethics," *Proceedings of the 21st ACM Conference on Economics and Computation* (2020): 679–81, https://dx.doi.org/10.2139/ssrn.3615404.

168 no differential impact based on job seekers' identity: Uniform Guidelines on Employee Selection Procedure (1978); 43 FR __ (August 25, 1978), https://www.govinfo.gov/content/pkg/CFR-2011-title29-vol4/xml/CFR-2011-title29-vol4-part1607.xml.

168 input variables correlated with the outcome: To comply with US law, pymetrics only does this recalibrating of the algorithm prior to deployment (and/or when a recruitment cycle is over and a new one is to begin).

169 nontraditional hires were more productive: Bo Cowgill, "Bias and Productivity in Humans and Algorithms: Theory and Evidence from Resume Screening," working paper, Columbia Business School, 2018.

169 "assessing risk": Sharad Goel et al., "The Accuracy, Equity, and Jurisprudence of Criminal Risk Assessment," in *Research Handbook on Big Data Law*, ed. Roland Vogl (Northampton, MA: Edward Elgar, 2021), 9–28, https://doi.org/10.4337/9781788972826.00007.

169 "the algorithm is a force for racial equity": Jon Kleinberg et al., "Human Decisions and Machine Predictions," *Quarterly Journal of Economics* 133, no. 1 (2018): 237–93, https://doi.org/10.1093/qje/qjx032.

169   increase profits: Will Dobbie and Jae Song, "Debt Relief and Debtor Outcomes: Measuring the Effects of Consumer Bankruptcy Protection," *American Economic Review* 105, no. 3 (2015): 1272–1311, https://doi.org/10.1257/aer.20130612.

169   Many vendors argue: Manish Raghavan et al., "Mitigating Bias in Algorithmic Hiring," *Proceedings of the 2020 Conference on Fairness, Accountability, and Transparency* (2020): 469–81, https://dl.acm.org/doi/10.1145/3351095.3372828.

Chapter 8: Hiring the Best Person for the Job

172   Rometty and coauthors suggest: Colleen Ammerman, Boris Groysberg, and Ginni Rometty, "The New-Collar Workforce," *Harvard Business Review*, March–April 2023, https://hbr.org/2023/03/the-new-collar-workforce.

173   OneTen Coalition: "Hire Skills for Higher Returns," OneTen, accessed December 20, 2023, https://oneten.org.

173   at least ten states: Amanda Winters, "Governors Leading on Skills-Based Hiring to Open Opportunity Pathways," National Governors Association, June 1, 2023, https://www.nga.org/news/commentary/governors-leading-on-skills-based-hiring-to-open-opportunity-pathways/.

173   Massachusetts governor Maura Healey: "Executive Order 627 of January 25, 2024, Instituting Skills-Based Hiring Practices," Office of the Governor, Commonwealth of Massachusetts, https://www.mass.gov/doc/skilled-based-eo/download.

173   A recent McKinsey & Company article: Bryan Hancock et al., "Taking a Skills-Based Approach to Building the future Workforce," McKinsey & Company, November 15, 2022, https://www.mckinsey.com/capabilities/people-and-organizational-performance/our-insights/taking-a-skills-based-approach-to-building-the-future-workforce.

173   "'make a lot more use' of skills-based hiring": Jane Thier, "Condoleezza Rice, Who Holds 3 Degrees, Says America Needs to 'Make a Lot More Use' of Skills-Based Hiring," *Fortune*, June 23, 2023, https://fortune.com/2023/06/23/condoleezza-rice-skills-based-hiring/.

174   hire the best people through interviews: Lauren A. Rivera, "Hiring as Cultural Matching: The Case of Elite Professional Service Firms," *American Sociological Review* 77, no. 6 (2012): 999–1022, https://doi.org/10.1177/0003122412463213.

175   white job candidates were 150 percent more likely to receive an offer: Lincoln Quillian, John J. Lee, and Mariana Oliver, "Evidence from Field Experiments in Hiring Shows Substantial Additional Racial Discrimination after the Callback," *Social Forces* 99, no. 2 (2020): 732–59, https://doi.org/10.1093/sf/soaa026.

175   Investors favored pitches delivered by men: Alison Wood Brooks et al., "Investors Prefer Entrepreneurial Ventures Pitched by Attractive Men," *Proceedings of the National Academy of Sciences* 111, no. 12 (2014): 4427–31, https://doi.org/10.1073/pnas.1321202111.

175   unconscious bias flourishes: Jason Dana, Robyn Dawes, and Nathanial Peterson, "Belief in the Unstructured Interview: The Persistence of an Illusion," *Judgment and Decision Making* 8, no. 5 (2013): 512–20, https://doi.org/10.1017/S1930297500003612.

175   research on federal district court judges: Alma Cohen and Crystal S. Yang, "Judicial Politics and Sentencing Decisions," *American Economic Journal: Economic Policy* 11, no. 1 (2019): 160–91, https://doi.org/10.1257/pol.20170329.

175   decision aids and decision rules: Nathan R. Kuncel et al., "Mechanical Versus Clinical Data Combination in Selection and Admissions Decisions: A Meta-Analysis," *Journal of Applied Psychology* 98, no. 6 (2013): 1060–72, https://doi.org/10.1037/a0034156.

176   Apgar score: "Apgar Score," in *A.D.A.M. Medical Encyclopedia*, last modified October 22, 2022, https://medlineplus.gov/ency/article/003402.htm.

176   matchmaking in the dating world: Faith Hill, "The New Old Dating Trend," *Atlantic*, August 11, 2023, https://www.theatlantic.com/family/archive/2023/08/matchmaking-dating-app-era/674989/.

177   Qualtrics, the global cloud software company: Mandy Wheadon, email message to Iris Bohnet, March 29, 2023.

177   *Women in the Workplace* report: Rachel Thomas et al., *Women in the Workplace 2021*, McKinsey & Company and LeanIn.Org, 2021, https://wiw-report.s3.amazonaws.com/Women_in_the_Workplace_2021.pdf.

177 evidence-based guidelines for structured interviews: Behavioural Insights Team, *How to Run Structured Interviews*, 2021, https://www.bi.team/wp-content/uploads/2021/07/BIT_How_to_improve_gender_equality_guide_RSI.pdf.

177 more predictive of future performance: Frank L. Schmidt and John E. Hunter, "The Validity and Utility of Selection Methods in Personnel Psychology: Practical and Theoretical Implications of 85 Years of Research Findings," *Psychological Bulletin* 124, no. 2 (1998): 262–74, https://doi.org/10.1037/0033-2909.124.2.262.

178 Iris and her coauthors found: Iris Bohnet, Alexandra van Geen, and Max Bazerman, "When Performance Trumps Gender Bias: Joint vs. Separate Evaluation," *Management Science* 62, no. 5 (2016): 1225–34, https://doi.org/10.1287/mnsc.2015.2186.

179 "We don't work in a vacuum": Elizabeth Gibney, "What the Nobels Are—and Aren't—Doing to Encourage Diversity," *Nature*, September 28, 2018, https://www.nature.com/articles/d41586-018-06879-z.

179 "isolated choice effect": Edward H. Chang et al., "The Isolated Choice Effect and Its Implications for Gender Diversity in Organizations," *Management Science* 66, no. 6 (2020): 2752–61, https://doi.org/10.1287/mnsc.2019.3533.

179 Atul Gawande describes: Atul Gawande, *The Checklist Manifesto: How to Get Things Right* (New York: Metropolitan Books, 2010).

180 built the Equity Sequence®: "Equity Sequence: So Much More than DEI Training," Tidal Equality, accessed December 20, 2023, https://www.tidalequality.com/equity-sequence.

180 The program shifted: "Healthcare and Higher Ed: University of Manitoba's Physician Assistant Program," Tidal Equality, accessed July 25, 2023, https://www.tidalequality.com/case-snapshots/healthcase-and-higher-ed-university-of-manitobas-physician-assistant-program.

181 diversity on the selection committee: Manuel F. Bagues and Berta Esteve-Volart, "Can Gender Parity Break the Glass Ceiling? Evidence from a Repeated Randomized Experiment," *Review of Economic Studies* 77, no. 4 (2010): 1301–28, https://doi.org/10.1111/j.1467-937X.2009.00601.x.

181 groupthink: Cass R. Sunstein and Reid Hastie, *Wiser: Getting Beyond Groupthink to Make Groups Smarter* (Boston: Harvard Business School Press, 2014).

182 de-biasing techniques: McKinsey & Company, "Behavioral Science in Business: Nudging, Debiasing, and Managing the Irrational Mind," February 27, 2018, https://www.mckinsey.com/capabilities/people-and-organizational-performance/our-insights/behavioral-science-in-business-nudging-debiasing-and-managing-the-irrational-mind.

182 "advocating equal opportunities": "About Us," Chef:innensache, accessed January 10, 2024, https://chefinnensache.de/en/about-us/.

182 senior executive explained: Alan Tart, interview with Siri Chilazi, June 29, 2023.

183 Cisco chose its CEO, Chuck Robbins: Boris Groysberg et al., "Cisco Systems: In Search of the Next CEO," Harvard Business School Case 416–06-027 (Boston: Harvard Business School, 2015), https://www.hbs.edu/faculty/Pages/item.aspx?num=50131.

184 candidate's high competence: Amanda J. Koch, Susan D. D'Mello, and Paul R. Sackett, "A Meta-Analysis of Gender Stereotypes and Bias in Experimental Simulations of Employment Decision Making," *Journal of Applied Psychology* 100, no. 1 (2015): 128–61, https://doi.org/10.1037/a0036734.

184 stereotype threat: Claude M. Steele and Joshua Aronson, "Stereotype Threat and the Intellectual Test Performance of African Americans," *Journal of Personality and Social Psychology* 69, no. 5 (1995): 797–811, https://doi.org/10.1037/0022-3514.69.5.797.

184 example of disparate impact: Iris Bohnet, Ashley C. Craig, and Clémentine van Effenterre, "Can More Objective Performance Information Overcome Gender Differences in Interview Evaluations?," working paper, Harvard Kennedy School, Cambridge, MA, 2019.

185 This stress-inducing test: Andrew P. Allen et al., "The Trier Social Stress Test: Principles and Practice," *Neurobiology of Stress* 6 (2017): 113–26, https://doi.org/10.1016/j.ynstr.2016.11.001.

185 in the private setting: Mahnaz Behroozi et al., "Does Stress Impact Technical Interview Performance?," in *Proceedings of the 28th ACM Joint Meeting on European Software Engineering Conference and Symposium on the Foundations of Software Engineering* (New York: Association for Computing Machinery, 2020), 481–92, https://doi.org/10.1145/3368089.3409712.

186 stereotype threat in the former and bias in the latter: Abdelrahman Amer, Ashley C. Craig,

and Clémentine Van Effenterre, "Does Better Information Reduce Gender Discrimination in the Technology Industry?," working paper, 2023, https://ashleycraig.com/files/ACV.pdf.

186 unencumbered by what they look like: Jessica Nordell, "How Slack Got Ahead in Diversity," *Atlantic*, April 26, 2018, https://www.theatlantic.com/technology/archive /2018/04/how-slack-got-ahead-in-diversity/558806/.

186 advises caution: Atta Tarki and Tino Sanandaji, "What Top Consulting Firms Get Wrong About Hiring," *Harvard Business Review*, January 14, 2020, https://hbr .org/2020/01/what-top-consulting-firms-gets-wrong-about-hiring.

186 call case interviews "worthless": Laszlo Bock, *Work Rules! Insights from Inside Google That Will Transform How You Live and Lead* (New York: Twelve, 2015), 89.

187 had struggled in case-based assessments: Tarki and Sanandaji, "What Top Consulting Firms Get Wrong About Hiring."

187 together with the unstructured interview rank at the bottom: Sample bias is a concern in this literature as researchers typically only have access to those people who made it through the hiring process successfully, and in some cases do not even have data available that was collected during the selection process but instead only later, after these candidates were already employed. See Frank L. Schmidt and John E. Hunter, "The Validity and Utility of Selection Methods in Personnel Psychology: Practical and Theoretical Implications of 85 Years of Research Findings," *Psychological Bulletin* 124, no. 2 (1998): 262–74, https://doi.org/10.1037/0033-2909.124.2.262. See also Paul R. Sackett et al., "Revisiting Meta-Analytic Estimates of Validity in Personnel Selection: Addressing Systematic Overcorrection for Restriction of Range," *Journal of Applied Psychology* 107, no. 11 (2022): 2040–68, https://doi.org/10.1037/apl0000994.

187 tested how 700 applicants fared: Joe Caccavale, "Does Anonymous Recruitment Work? Everything You Need to Know," Applied, November 15, 2021, https://www.beapplied .com/post/anonymous-recruitment.

188 Based on a 2023 LinkedIn report: LinkedIn Economic Graph, "Skills-First: Reimagining the Labor Market and Breaking Down Barriers," 2023, https://economicgraph. linkedin.com/content/dam/me/economicgraph/en-us/PDF/skills-first-report-2023.pdf.

188 sample questions shared by Applied: "Work Samples Cheatsheet," Applied, accessed January 10, 2024, https://www.beapplied.com/applied-work-sample-cheatsheet.

188 guidelines from the UK's Behavioural Insights Team: Behavioural Insights Team, *How to Use Skill-Based Assessment Tasks*, 2021, https://www.bi.team/wp-content/uploads /2021/07/BIT_How_to_improve_gender_equality_guide-SBAT.pdf.

188 improvement in prediction was greater than 50 percent: Kuncel et al., "Mechanical Versus Clinical Data Combination in Selection and Admissions Decisions."

189 relatively standardized data entry jobs: Mitchell Hoffman, Lisa B. Kahn, and Danielle Li, "Discretion in Hiring," *Quarterly Journal of Economics* 133, no. 2 (2018): 765–800, https://doi.org/10.1093/qje/qjx042.

190 best candidates within each demographic subgroup: David H. Autor and David Scarborough, "Does Job Testing Harm Minority Workers? Evidence from Retail Establishments," *Quarterly Journal of Economics* 123, no. 1 (2008): 219–77, https://doi .org/10.1162/qjec.2008.123.1.219.

191 some say in the final outcome: Berkeley J. Dietvorst, Joseph P. Simmons, and Cade Massey, "Overcoming Algorithm Aversion: People Will Use Imperfect Algorithms If They Can (Even Slightly) Modify Them," *Management Science* 64, no. 3 (2018): 1155–70, https://doi.org/10.1287/mnsc.2016.2643.

192 algorithms to match supply and demand: Alvin E. Roth, *Who Gets What—and Why: The New Economics of Matchmaking and Market Design* (Boston: Houghton Mifflin Harcourt, 2015), 8.

192 allocates all seats in medicine and related subjects: Rustamdjan Hakimov and Dorothea Kübler, "Experiments on Centralized School Choice and College Admissions: A Survey," *Experimental Economics* 24, no. 2 (2021): 434–88, https://doi.org/10.1007/s10683 -020-09667-7.

Chapter 9: Career Advancement That Works for All

194 "inspect any statistically significant demographic differences": Beth Galetti, "Diversity, Equity, and Inclusion," Amazon, June 10, 2021, https://www.aboutamazon.com /news/workplace/diversity-equity-and-inclusion.

194 "potential" for career advancement: Alan M. Benson, Danielle Li, and Kelly Shue, "Potential and the Gender Promotion Gap," *Academy of Management Proceedings*, no. 1 (2023), https://doi.org/10.5465/AMPROC.2023.19580abstract.

194 gender and race dynamics colluded: Iris Bohnet, Ariella Kristal, and Oliver Hauser, "Can Gender and Race Dynamics in Performance Appraisals Be Disrupted? The Case of Social Influence," working paper, 2023, https://scholar.harvard.edu/files/iris_bohnet /files/performance_appraisals.11.19.21-full.pdf.

194 gender gap in career advancement: Anders Frederiksen, Fabian Lange, and Ben Kriechel, "Subjective Performance Evaluations and Employee Careers," *Journal of Economic Behavior & Organization* 134 (2017): 408–29, https://doi.org/10.1016/j .jebo.2016.12.016.

195 how lenient one's manager is: Anders Frederiksen, Lisa B. Kahn, and Fabian Lange, "Supervisors and Performance Management Systems," *Journal of Political Economy* 128, no. 6 (2020): 2123–87, https://doi.org/10.1086/705715.

195 rely on the wrong indicators: Alan Benson et al., "Promotions and the Peter Principle," *Quarterly Journal of Economics* 134, no. 4 (2019): 2085–2134, https://doi.org/10.1093 /qje/qjz022.

195 male students in France and the Netherlands: Anne Boring, "Gender Biases in Student Evaluations of Teaching," *Journal of Public Economics* 145 (2017): 27–41, https:// doi.org/10.1016/j.jpubeco.2016.11.006.

195 An online teaching experiment conducted in the US: Friederike Mengel, Jan Sauermann, and Ulf Zölitz, "Gender Bias in Teaching Evaluations," *Journal of the European Economic Association* 17, no. 2 (2019): 535–66, https://doi.org/10.1093/jeea/jvx057.

195 Backlash against women in positions of authority: Tyler G. Okimoto and Victoria L. Brescoll, "The Price of Power: Power Seeking and Backlash Against Female Politicians," *Personality & Social Psychology Bulletin* 36, no. 7 (2010): 923–36, https://doi .org/10.1177/0146167210371949. See also Laurie A. Rudman et al., "Status Incongruity and Backlash Effects: Defending the Gender Hierarchy Motivates Prejudice Against Female Leaders," *Journal of Experimental Social Psychology* 48, no.1 (2012): 165–79, https://doi.org/10.1016/j.jesp.2011.10.008.

196 nor do we attribute equally: Shelley J. Correll et al., "Inside the Black Box of Organizational Life: The Gendered Language of Performance Assessment," *American Sociological Review* 85, no. 6 (2020): 1022–50, https://doi.org/10.1177/0003122420962080.

197 female researchers received less credit: Heather Sarsons et al., "Gender Differences in Recognition for Group Work," *Journal of Political Economy* 129, no. 1 (2021): 101–47, https://doi.org/10.1086/711401.

197 Based on US Medicare data: Heather Sarsons, "Interpreting Signals in the Labor Market: Evidence from Medical Referrals," working paper, 2017, https://scholar.harvard. edu/sarsons/publications/interpreting-signals-evidence-medical-referrals.

197 viewed as equal: Joan C. Williams et al., "How One Company Worked to Root Out Bias from Performance Reviews," *Harvard Business Review*, April 21, 2021, https://hbr .org/2021/04/how-one-company-worked-to-root-out-bias-from-performance-reviews.

197 female financial advisors: Mark Egan, Gregor Matvos, and Amit Seru, "When Harry Fired Sally: The Double Standard in Punishing Misconduct," *Journal of Political Economy* 130, no. 5 (2022): 1184–1248, https://doi.org/10.1086/718964.

198 gender gaps in involuntary turnover: Rachel Landsman, "Gender Differences in Executive Departure," working paper, 2019, https://economicsdept.blogs.bucknell.edu /files/2019/11/Exec_Departure.pdf.

198 pay decreases: Stefania Albanesi, Claudia Olivetti, and María José Prados, "Gender and Dynamic Agency: Theory and Evidence on the Compensation of Top Executives," in *Gender in the Labor Market*, eds. Solomon W. Polachek, Konstantinos Tatsiramos, and Klaus F. Zimmermann (Bingley, UK: Emerald Group, 2015), 1–59, https://doi .org/10.1108/S0147-912120150000042001.

198 In Ethiopia, employees: Shibiru Ayalew, Shanthi Manian, and Ketki Sheth, "Discrimination from Below: Experimental Evidence from Ethiopia," *Journal of Development Economics* 151 (2021), https://doi.org/10.1016/j.jdeveco.2021.102653.

198 In Malawi, farmers: Ariel BenYishay et al., "Gender Gaps in Technology Diffusion," *Journal of Development Economics* 143 (2020), https://doi.org/10.1016/j.jdeveco.2019.102380.

198 And in India, people: Lata Gangadharan et al., "Social Identity and Governance: The Behavioral Response to Female Leaders," *European Economic Review 90* (2016): 302–25, https://doi.org/10.1016/j.euroecorev.2016.01.003.

198 In the US, temporary workers: Martin Abel, "Do Workers Discriminate Against Female Bosses?," *Journal of Human Resources* 58, no. 6 (2023), https://doi.org/10.3368/jhr.1120-11318R3.

199 expect women to simply be nicer: Natasha Quadlin, "The Mark of a Woman's Record: Gender and Academic Performance in Hiring," *American Sociological Review* 83, no. 2 (2018): 331–60, https://doi.org/10.1177/0003122418762291.

199 lead to a vicious cycle: Clément Bosquet, Pierre-Philippe Combes, and Cecilia García-Peñalosa, "Gender and Promotions: Evidence from Academic Economists in France," *Scandinavian Journal of Economics* 121, no. 3 (2019): 1020–53, https://doi.org/10.1111/sjoe.12300.

199 One of the largest manufacturing firms in Europe: Ingrid Haegele, "The Broken Rung: Gender and the Leadership Gap," working paper, 2023.

199 *Women in the Workplace* reports: Alexis Krivkovich et al., *Women in the Workplace 2022*, McKinsey & Company and LeanIn.Org, 2022, https://wiw-report.s3.amazonaws.com/Women_in_the_Workplace_2022.pdf.

199 Based on the 2023 report: Rachel Thomas et al., *Women in the Workplace 2023*, McKinsey & Company and LeanIn.Org, 2023, https://sgff-media.s3.amazonaws.com/sgff_r1eHetbDYb/Women+in+the+Workplace+2023_+Designed+Report.pdf.

200 larger shares of white coworkers: Elizabeth Linos, Sanaz Mobasseri, and Nina Roussille, "Asymmetric Peer Effects at Work: The Effect of White Coworkers on Black Women's Careers," HKS Faculty Research Working Paper Series RWP23-03-031, Harvard Kennedy School, Cambridge, MA, 2023, https://www.hks.harvard.edu/publications/asymmetric-peer-effects-work-effect-white-coworkers-black-womens-careers.

200 relative numbers matter on teams: Rosabeth Moss Kanter, "Some Effects of Proportions on Group Life: Skewed Sex Ratios and Responses to Token Women," *American Journal of Sociology* 82, no. 5 (1977): 965–90, https://doi.org/10.1086/226425.

200 Black women are doubly disadvantaged: Ashleigh Shelby Rosette and Robert W. Livingston, "Failure Is Not an Option for Black Women: Effects of Organizational Performance on Leaders with Single Versus Dual-Subordinate Identities," *Journal of Experimental Social Psychology* 48, no. 5 (2012): 1162–67, https://doi.org/10.1016/j.jesp.2012.05.002.

201 a 10-point rating scale: Lauren A. Rivera and András Tilcsik, "Scaling Down Inequality: Rating Scales, Gender Bias, and the Architecture of Evaluation," *American Sociological Review* 84, no. 2 (2019): 248–74, https://doi.org/10.1177/0003122419833601.

201 "scrutinize women and their performance": Susie Allen, "Numeric Performance Reviews Can Be Biased Against Women," Kellogg Insight, August 1, 2019, https://insight.kellogg.northwestern.edu/article/gender-bias-performance-reviews-ratings-scale#.

202 wait a half century to be awarded the prize: "All Nobel Prizes in Physics," The Nobel Prize, accessed January 10, 2024, https://www.nobelprize.org/prizes/lists/all-nobel-prizes-in-physics/.

202 "shifting standards": Monica Biernat, Melvin Manis, and Thomas E. Nelson, "Stereotypes and Standards of Judgment," *Journal of Personality and Social Psychology* 60, no. 4 (1991): 485–99, https://doi.org/10.1037/0022-3514.60.4.485.

203 male lawyers billing more hours to clients: Ghazala Azmat and Rosa Ferrer, "Gender Gaps in Performance: Evidence from Young Lawyers," *Journal of Political Economy* 125, no. 5 (2017): 1306–55, https://doi.org/10.1086/693686.

203 male real estate agents listing more homes: Philip Seagraves and Paul Gallimore, "The Gender Gap in Real Estate Sales: Negotiation Skill or Agent Selection?," *Real Estate Economics* 41, no. 3 (2013): 600–31, https://doi.org/10.1111/reec.12006.

203 male physicians seeing more patients: Karen Bloor, Nick Freemantle, and Alan Maynard, "Gender and Variation in Activity Rates of Hospital Consultants," *Journal of the Royal Society of Medicine* 101, no. 1 (2008): 27–33, https://doi.org/10.1258/jrsm.2007.070424.

203 male academics writing more papers: Stephen J. Ceci et al., "Women in Academic Science: A Changing Landscape," *Psychological Science in the Public Interest* 15, no. 3 (2014): 75–141, https://doi.org/10.1177/1529100614541236.

204 fewer ethical violations: Patricia W. Hatamyar and Kevin M. Simmons, "Are Women More Ethical Lawyers? An Empirical Study," *Florida State University Law Review* 31, no. 4 (2004), https://ir.law.fsu.edu/lr/vol31/iss4/2.

204 fewer but higher-priced homes: Sean P. Salter et al., "Broker Beauty and Boon: A Study of Physical Attractiveness and Its Effect on Real Estate Brokers' Income and Productivity," *Applied Financial Economics* 22, no. 10 (2012): 811–25, https://doi.org/10.1080/09603107.2011.627211.

204 less likely to die or be readmitted to the hospital: Yusuke Tsugawa et al., "Comparison of Hospital Mortality and Readmission Rates for Medicare Patients Treated by Male vs Female Physicians," *JAMA Internal Medicine* 177, no. 2 (2016): 206–13, https://doi.org/10.1001/jamainternmed.2016.7875.

204 write more clearly: Erin Hengel, "Publishing While Female: Are Women Held to Higher Standards? Evidence from Peer Review," *Economic Journal* 132, no. 648 (2022): 2951–91, https://doi.org/10.1093/ej/ueac032.

204 frequent check-ins enabled by an app: "How Does GE Do Performance Management Today?," PerformYard, June 14, 2021, https://www.performyard.com/articles/how-does-ge-do-performance-management-today.

204 "empower and inspire" rather than "command and control": Leonardo Baldassarre and Brian Finken, "GE's Real-Time Performance Development," *Harvard Business Review*, August 12, 2015, https://hbr.org/2015/08/ges-real-time-performance-development.

204 contributions to specific projects: "3 Approaches to Performance Management: Google, Betterment and IBM," PerformYard, May 3, 2021, https://www.performyard.com/articles/3-unique-approaches-to-performance-management-google-betterment-and-ibm.

205 more specific feedback prompts: Paola Cecchi-Dimeglio, "How Gender Bias Corrupts Performance Reviews, and What to Do About It," *Harvard Business Review*, April 12, 2017, https://hbr.org/2017/04/how-gender-bias-corrupts-performance-reviews-and-what-to-do-about-it.

205 N=1 rarely is the optimal sample size: Lori Nishiura Mackenzie et al., "Why Most Performance Evaluations Are Biased, and How to Fix Them," *Harvard Business Review*, January 11, 2019, https://hbr.org/2019/01/why-most-performance-evaluations-are-biased-and-how-to-fix-them.

206 had the right to probe: Jennifer S. Lerner and Philip E. Tetlock, "Accounting for the Effects of Accountability," *Psychological Bulletin* 125, no. 2 (1999): 255–75, https://doi.org/10.1037/0033-2909.125.2.255.

206 move away from this approach: Lillian Cunningham and Jena McGregor, "Why Big Business Is Falling Out of Love with the Annual Performance Review," *Washington Post*, August 17, 2015, https://www.washingtonpost.com/news/on-leadership/wp/2015/08/17/why-big-business-is-falling-out-of-love-with-annual-performance-reviews/.

206 more harshly: Manuel F. Bagues and Berta Esteve-Volart, "Can Gender Parity Break the Glass Ceiling? Evidence from a Repeated Randomized Experiment," *Review of Economic Studies* 77, no. 4 (2010): 1301–28, https://doi.org/10.1111/j.1467-937X.2009.00601.x.

206 she has to compete with: Kathleen L. McGinn and Katherine L. Milkman, "Looking Up and Looking Out: Career Mobility Effects of Demographic Similarity Among Professionals," *Organization Science* 24, no. 4 (2013): 1041–60, https://doi.org/10.1287/orsc.1120.0778.

207 even more red flags: Emilio J. Castilla and Aruna Ranganathan, "The Production of Merit: How Managers Understand and Apply Merit in the Workplace," *Organization Science* 31, no. 4 (2020): 909–35, https://doi.org/10.1287/orsc.2019.1335.

207 immediacy is key: John Austin, Sigurdur Oli Sigurdsson, and Yonata Shpak Rubin, "An Examination of the Effects of Delayed Versus Immediate Prompts on Safety Belt Use," *Environment and Behavior* 38, no. 1 (2006): 140–49, https://doi.org/10.1177/0013916505276744.

207 more useful feedback: Williams et al., "How One Company Worked to Root Out Bias from Performance Reviews."

207 receive inflated reviews: Lily Jampol and Vivian Zayas, "Gendered White Lies: Women Are Given Inflated Performance Feedback Compared with Men," *Personality & Social Psychology Bulletin* 47, no. 1 (2021): 57–69, https://doi.org/10.1177/0146167220916622.

208 overcome their biases: Alberto Alesina et al., "Revealing Stereotypes: Evidence from Immigrants in Schools," *American Economic Review* (forthcoming), https://www.aeaweb .org/articles?id=10.1257/aer.20191184.

208 selected members of underrepresented groups: Edward Chang et al., "Incorporating DEI into Decision-Making," *Harvard Business Review*, September 1, 2023, https://hbr .org/2023/09/incorporating-dei-into-decision-making.

208 Reminders work: Christina Gravert, "9 Reminders: Their Value and Hidden Cost," in *Behavioral Science in the Wild*, eds. Nina Mažar and Dilip Soman (Toronto: University of Toronto Press, 2022), 120–32, https://doi.org/10.3138/9781487527525-011.

209 put themselves forward: Laszlo Bock, *Work Rules! Insights from Inside Google That Will Transform How You Live and Lead* (New York: Twelve, 2015), 175.

209 automatically included in the competition: Joyce C. He, Sonia K. Kang, and Nicola Lacetera, "Opt-Out Choice Framing Attenuates Gender Differences in the Decision to Compete in the Laboratory and in the Field," *Proceedings of the National Academy of Sciences* 118, no. 42 (2021), https://doi.org/10.1073/pnas.2108337118.

210 millions of American students: Katherine B. Coffman, "Gender Differences in Willingness to Guess," *Management Science* 60, no. 2 (2014): 434–48, https://doi.org/10.1287 /mnsc.2013.1776.

210 policy change was adopted in Chile: Katherine B. Coffman and David Klinowski, "The Impact of Penalties for Wrong Answers on the Gender Gap in Test Scores," *Proceedings of the National Academy of Sciences* 117, no. 16 (2020): 8794–8803, https://doi .org/10.1073/pnas.1920945117.

211 opportunity to weigh in on their performance appraisals: Hannah Riley Bowles, Linda Babcock, and Lei Lai, "Social Incentives for Gender Differences in the Propensity to Initiate Negotiations: Sometimes It Does Hurt to Ask," *Organizational Behavior and Human Decision Processes* 103, no. 1 (2007): 84–103, https://doi.org/10.1016/j .obhdp.2006.09.001.

211 female employees assessed themselves more harshly than men: Lisa Abraham, "The Gender Gap in Performance Reviews," *Journal of Economic Behavior & Organization* 214 (2023): 459–92, https://doi.org/10.1016/j.jebo.2023.07.039.

212 moved in the right direction: "3 Approaches to Performance Management: Google, Betterment and IBM."

212 overcome performance-reward bias: Emilio J. Castilla, "Gender, Race, and Meritocracy in Organizational Careers," *American Journal of Sociology* 113, no. 6 (2008): 1479–1526, https://doi.org/10.1086/588738.

212 Women tended to be in support functions: Monika Hamori et al., "Women Are Stalling Out on the Way to the Top," *MIT Sloan Management Review*, August 31, 2022, https://sloanreview.mit.edu/article/women-are-stalling-out-on-the-way-to-the-top/.

213 office housework: Linda Babcock et al., *The No Club: Putting a Stop to Women's Dead-End Work* (New York: Simon & Schuster, 2022), 3.

213 distributing service tasks: Iris Bohnet, *What Works: Gender Equality by Design* (Cambridge, MA: Harvard University Press, 2016), 197.

214 making room reservations for teams: Pınar Doğan, "Gender Differences in Volunteer's Dilemma: Evidence from Teamwork among Graduate Students," *Journal of Behavioral and Experimental Economics* 84 (2020), https://doi.org/10.1016/j .socec.2019.101488.

214 "everyone in a workplace": Emma Hinchliffe and Kinsey Crowley, "Why Men Weaponize Strategic Incompetence—and How One Man Learned to Stop," *Fortune*, January 31, 2023, https://fortune.com/2023/01/31/why-men-weaponize-strategic-incompetence -and-how-one-man-learned-to-stop/.

215 Precision (or personalized) medicine: Gustavo Rosa Gameiro et al., "Precision Medicine: Changing the Way We Think about Healthcare," *Clinics* 73 (2018), https://doi .org/10.6061/clinics/2017/e723.

215 "They didn't want to use a model to do so": Jillian D'Onfro, "Google Wrote an Equation for Deciding Which Engineers Should Get Promoted—Here's Why It Failed," Business Insider, November 20, 2014, https://www.businessinsider.com/google -promotion-equation-2014-11.

216 EAST framework: Owain Service et al., *EAST: Four Simple Ways to Apply Behavioural*

Insights, Behavioural Insights Team, 2014, https://www.bi.team/wp-content/uploads/2015/07/BIT-Publication-EAST_FA_WEB.pdf.

Chapter 10: Work Arrangements to Level the Playing Field

221 Their findings and the resulting recommendations: Irene Padavic, Robin J. Ely, and Erin M. Reid, "Explaining the Persistence of Gender Inequality: The Work-Family Narrative as a Social Defense against the 24/7 Work Culture," *Administrative Science Quarterly* 61, no. 1 (2020): 1–51, https://doi.org/10.1177/0001839219832310.

222 study of more than 6,500 Harvard Business School alumni/ae: Robin J. Ely et al., *Life & Leadership After HBS*, Harvard Business School, May 2015, https://www.hbs.edu/women50/docs/L_and_L_Survey_2Findings_13final.pdf.

222 suffer from work-family conflict: Erin M. Reid, "Embracing, Passing, Revealing, and the Ideal Worker Image: How People Navigate Expected and Experienced Professional Identities," *Organization Science* 26 (2015): 997–1017, https://doi.org/10.1287/orsc.2015.0975.

222 shifted from paying for output: Claudia Goldin, *Career and Family: Women's Century-Long Journey Toward Equity* (Princeton, NJ: Princeton University Press, 2021), 9–10.

223 schedule instability: Sigrid Luhr, Daniel Schneider, and Kristen Harknett, "Parenting Without Predictability: Precarious Schedules, Parental Strain, and Work-Life Conflict," *Russell Sage Foundation Journal of the Social Sciences* 8, no. 5 (2022): 24–44, https://doi.org/10.7758/RSF.2022.8.5.02.

223 low-income earners are the ones hardest hit: Claudia Goldin, "Understanding the Economic Impact of COVID-19 on Women," *Brookings Papers on Economic Activity*, no. 1 (2022): 65–139, doi.org/10.1353/eca.2022.0019.

224 we recommend the Shift Project: "The Shift Project," Shift Project, accessed January 11, 2024, https://shift.hks.harvard.edu/.

224 What happened in pharmacies: Claudia Goldin, *Career and Family*, 188, 190–192.

225 results-only work environment: "Our Company," Watt Global Media, accessed October 2, 2023, https://www.wattglobalmedia.com/about-us/our-company/.

225 initial push of training: Cal Newport, "How to Achieve Sustainable Remote Work," *New Yorker*, July 9, 2021, https://www.newyorker.com/culture/cultural-comment/how-to-achieve-sustainable-remote-work.

225 "We've come to a point": Christy DeSmith, "'Those Inequalities Are Inequalities That Occur Within Households,'" *Harvard Gazette*, October 9, 2023, https://news.harvard.edu/gazette/story/2023/10/harvard-claudia-goldin-recognized-with-nobel-in-economic-sciences/.

226 the majority of unpaid work: José Ignacio Giménez-Nadal and José Alberto Molina, "The Gender Gap in Time Allocation," *IZA World of Labor*, 2022, https://doi.org/10.15185/izawol.497.

226 "The workplace is the environment": Marc Grau Grau and Hannah Riley Bowles, "Launching a Cross-disciplinary and Cross-national Conversation on Engaged Fatherhood," in *Engaged Fatherhood for Men, Families, and Gender Equality: Healthcare, Social Policy, and Work Perspectives*, eds. Marc Grau Grau, Mireia las Heras Maestro, and Hannah Riley Bowles (Cham, Switzerland: Springer, 2022), 8, https://doi.org/10.1007/978-3-030-75645-1.

226 preferred an egalitarian relationship structure: David S. Pedulla and Sarah Thébaud, "Can We Finish the Revolution? Gender, Work-Family Ideals, and Institutional Constraint," *American Sociological Review* 80, no. 1 (2015): 116–39, https://doi.org/10.1177/0003122414564008.

227 the world's first randomized controlled trial on remote work: Nicholas Bloom et al., "Does Working from Home Work? Evidence from a Chinese Experiment," *Quarterly Journal of Economics* 130, no. 1 (2015): 165–218, https://doi.org/10.1093/qje/qju032.

228 "three great enemies of working from home": Nicholas Bloom, "Go Ahead, Tell Your Boss You Are Working from Home," filmed May 22, 2017 at TEDxStanford 2017, video, 12:40, https://www.youtube.com/watch?v=oiUyyZPIHyY.

228 conducted another experiment: Nicholas Bloom, Ruobing Han, and James Liang, "How Hybrid Working From Home Works Out," NBER Working Paper Series 30292, National Bureau of Economic Research, Cambridge, MA, 2022, https://doi.org/10.3386/w30292.

229 share of days worked from home: José María Barrero, Nicholas Bloom, and Steven J. Davis, "The Evolution of Work from Home," *Journal of Economic Perspectives* 37, no. 4 (2023): 23–50, https://doi.org/10.1257/jep.37.4.23.

229 workers across 27 countries averaged 1.5 days of remote work: Cevat Giray Aksoy et al., "Working from Home Around the World," NBER Working Paper Series 30446, National Bureau of Economic Research, Cambridge, MA, 2022, https://doi.org/10.3386/w30446.

229 Women tend to work remotely slightly more: José María Barrero, Nicholas Bloom, and Steven J. Davis, "The Evolution of Work from Home."

229 enabled some mothers of young children: Goldin, "Understanding the Economic Impact of COVID-19 on Women."

229 20 percent of all paid workdays from home: Barrero, Bloom, and Davis, "The Evolution of Work from Home."

229 analysis of online job ads: Stephen Hansen et al., "Remote Work Across Jobs, Companies, and Space," NBER Working Paper Series 31007, National Bureau of Economic Research, Cambridge, MA, 2023, https://doi.org/10.3386/w31007.

229 greatest benefits: Cevat Giray Aksoy et al., "Time Savings When Working from Home," *AEA Papers and Proceedings* 113 (2023): 597–603, https://doi.org/10.1257/pandp.20231013.

229 they would look for a new job: "Hybrid Work," Gallup, accessed September 15, 2023, https://www.gallup.com/401384/indicator-hybrid-work.aspx.

229 value the option to work remotely: Aksoy et al., "Working from Home Around the World."

230 Based on several studies: Barrero, Bloom, and Davis, "The Evolution of Work from Home."

230 productivity either did not change or increased: Barrero, Bloom, and Davis.

230 number of patents they examined: Prithwiraj Choudhury, Cirrus Foroughi, and Barbara Zepp Larson, "Work-from-Anywhere: The Productivity Effects of Geographic Flexibility," *Strategic Management Journal* 42, no. 4 (2021): 655–83, https://doi.org/10.1002/smj.3251.

230 randomized to work a varying number of days: Prithwiraj Choudhury et al., "Is Hybrid Work the Best of Both Worlds? Evidence from a Field Experiment," Harvard Business School Working Paper 22–02–063, Harvard Business School, Boston, MA, 2022, https://dx.doi.org/10.2139/ssrn.4068741.

230 online team "huddles": Ashley Whillans, Leslie Perlow, and Aurora Turek, "Experimenting During the Shift to Virtual Team Work: Learnings from How Teams Adapted Their Activities During the COVID-19 Pandemic," *Information and Organization* 31, no. 1 (2021), https://doi.org/10.1016/j.infoandorg.2021.100343.

230 working handbook: Prithwiraj Choudhury, "Our Work-from-Anywhere Future," *Harvard Business Review*, November–December 2020, https://hbr.org/2020/11/our-work-from-anywhere-future.

231 software engineers at a US Fortune 500 company: Natalia Emanuel, Emma Harrington, and Amanda Pallais, "The Power of Proximity to Coworkers," working paper, Federal Reserve Bank of New York, New York, 2023, https://nataliaemanuel.github.io/ne_website/EHP_Power_of_Proximity.pdf.

231 concerns about lack of support and connection are well founded: Kim Parker, "About a Third of U.S. Workers Who Can Work from Home Now Do So All the Time," Pew Research Center, March 30, 2023, https://www.pewresearch.org/short-reads/2023/03/30/about-a-third-of-us-workers-who-can-work-from-home-do-so-all-the-time/.

231 organizes "temporary colocation events": Carmina Ravanera, Kim de Laat, and Sarah Kaplan, *The Future of Work: Will Remote Work Help or Hinder the Pursuit of Equality?* (Toronto: Institute for Gender and the Economy, Rotman School of Management, November 7, 2022), https://www.gendereconomy.org/wp-content/uploads/2022/11/FutureofWork_GATE.pdf.

231 launched its Virtual First policy: "Dropbox goes Virtual First," Dropbox, October 13, 2020, https://blog.dropbox.com/topics/company/dropbox-goes-virtual-first.

232 company-wide survey: Hannah Markell-Goldstein, "What We've Learned from Our First-Ever Life in Virtual First Survey," Dropbox, February 22, 2023, https://blog

.dropbox.com/topics/company/what-weve-learned-from-our-firstever-life-in-virtual
-first-survey.

232 intervention called STAR: Erin L. Kelly et al., "Changing Work and Work-Family Conflict: Evidence from the Work, Family, and Health Network," *American Sociological Review* 79, no. 3 (2014): 485–516, https://doi.org/10.1177/0003122414531435.

233 experiment in an Italian multiutility company: Marta Angelici and Paola Profeta, "Smart Working: Work Flexibility Without Constraints," *Management Science* (2023), https://doi.org/10.1287/mnsc.2023.4767.

233 US employees and managers cited: Humanyze, *The Current State of Employee Retention*, 2022, https://humanyze.com/wp-content/uploads/2022/04/State-of-Employee -Retention-Spring-2022-Report.pdf.

233 underestimate the importance of flexible work: Rachel Thomas et al., *Women in the Workplace 2023*, McKinsey & Company and LeanIn.Org, 2023, https://sgff-media.s3 .amazonaws.com/sgff_r1eHetbDYb/Women+in+the+Workplace+2023_+Designed +Report.pdf.

233 United Kingdom: Heejung Chung and Mariska van der Horst, "Women's Employment Patterns After Childbirth and the Perceived Access to and Use of Flexitime and Teleworking," *Human Relations* 71, no. 1 (2018): 47–72, https://doi .org/10.1177/0018726717713828.

233 Germany: Laura Antonia Langner, "Flexible Men and Successful Women: The Effects of Flexible Working Hours on German Couples' Wages," *Work, Employment and Society* 32, no. 4 (2018): 687–706, https://doi.org/10.1177/0950017017708161.

234 three-quarters of part-time workers in the United States: Joseph B. Fuller et al., *Hidden Workers: Part-Time Potential*, Harvard Business School's Project on Managing the Future of Work, 2023, https://www.hbs.edu/ris/Publication%20Files/Hidden%20Workers— Part%20Time%20Potential%2003.13.23_1d2717e8-471e-49b6-915e-07d67fb827e5.pdf.

234 employees were simply not aware of their existence: Joseph B. Fuller and Manjari Raman, *The Caring Company*, HBS Project on Managing the Future of Work, 2019, https:// www.hbs.edu/managing-the-future-of-work/Documents/The_Caring_Company.pdf.

234 flexible work has been stigmatized in the past: Lindsey Trimble O'Connor and Erin A. Cech, "Not Just a Mothers' Problem," *Sociological Perspectives* 61, no. 5 (2018): 808–29, https://doi.org/10.1177/0731121418768235.

234 one of the most significant barriers: Laura Jones, *Women's Progression in the Workplace*, Government Equalities Office, October 2019, https://www.gov.uk/government /publications/womens-progression-in-the-workplace.

234 "perceived demands of their employers": Kara Baskin, "Working Moms Are Mostly Thriving Again. Can We Finally Achieve Gender Parity?," *Harvard Business School Working Knowledge*, September 14, 2023, https://hbswk.hbs.edu/item/working-moms-are -mostly-thriving-again-can-we-finally-achieve-gender-parity.

235 Behavioural Insights Unit worked with eight organizations: Cindy Wiryakusuma et al., "How We Nudged Employees to Embrace Flexible Work," *Harvard Business Review*, November 3, 2017, https://hbr.org/2017/11/how-we-nudged-employees-to-embrace- flexible-work.

235 series of pilot projects: 4 Day Week Global, *The 4 Day Week: 12 Months On—with New US and Canadian Research*, July 2023, https://www.4dayweek.com/long-term -pilot-report-2023.

236 Employees reported: Sean Smith, "Moving Four-ward?," *BC News*, December 2022, https://www.bc.edu/bc-web/bcnews/nation-world-society/sociology/-study-pilots-four -day-work-week.html.

236 important to shift culture: Ashley Whillans and Charlotte Lockhart, "A Guide to Implementing the 4-Day Workweek," *Harvard Business Review*, September 28, 2021, https://hbr.org/2021/09/a-guide-to-implementing-the-4-day-workweek.

236 three-day workweek: Bill Murphy Jr., "Chick-fil-A Just Introduced a 3-Day Workweek, and People Think It's the Best Idea Ever," *Inc.*, October 29, 2022, https://www.inc .com/bill-murphy-jr/chick-fil-a-just-introduced-a-3-day-work-week-people-think-its -best-idea-ever.html.

237 84 percent of women: Gladys M. Martinez and Kimberly Daniels, *Fertility of Men and Women Aged 15–49 in the United States: National Survey of Family Growth, 2015–*

2019, National Center for Health Statistics, Report no. 179, January 10, 2023, https://dx.doi.org/10.15620/cdc:122080.

237 "sandwich" generation: Juliana Menasce Horowitz, "More Than Half of Americans in Their 40s Are 'Sandwiched' Between an Aging Parent and Their Own Children," Pew Research Center, April 8, 2022, https://www.pewresearch.org/short-reads/2022/04/08/more-than-half-of-americans-in-their-40s-are-sandwiched-between-an-aging-parent-and-their-own-children/.

237 report substantial financial and emotional challenges: Lianlian Lei, Amanda N. Leggett, and Donovan T. Maust, "A National Profile of Sandwich Generation Caregivers Providing Care to Both Older Adults and Children," *Journal of the American Geriatrics Society* 71, no. 3 (2023): 799–809, https://doi.org/10.1111/jgs.18138.

237 more than half do not collect data: Fuller and Raman, *The Caring Company*.

237 Grechen Shirley became the first person: Ekaterina Pechenkina, "Political 'Mamas' Have a Child Care Problem," *Politico*, March 3, 2023, https://www.politico.com/newsletters/women-rule/2023/03/03/political-mamas-have-a-childcare-problem-00085404.

238 As of 2023, 30 US states have authorized: "Campaign Funds for Childcare," Vote Mama Foundation, accessed January 7, 2024, https://www.votemamafoundation.org/cfccstates.

238 enable the employment of parents: Taryn W. Morrissey, "Child Care and Parent Labor Force Participation: A Review of the Research Literature," *Review of Economics of the Household* 15, no. 1 (2017): 1–24, https://doi.org/10.1007/s11150-016-9331-3.

238 Patagonia has offered on-site childcare: Alexandra Kalev and Frank Dobbin, "The Surprising Benefits of Work/Life Support," *Harvard Business Review*, September–October 2022, https://hbr.org/2022/09/the-surprising-benefits-of-work-life-support.

238 started offering emergency on-site childcare: "Atlanta Mayor Andre Dickens Joins UPS CEO Carol B. Tomé at the 2023 UPS Impact Summit," UPS, October 17, 2023, https://about.ups.com/us/en/newsroom/press-releases/our-strategy/2023-ups-impact-summit.html.

238 has offered subsidized on-site childcare: Harriet Torry and Esther Fung, "What One Employer Found When It Started Providing Child Care," *Wall Street Journal*, April 7, 2024, https://www.wsj.com/economy/jobs/child-care-ups-benefits-777c632a.

238 childcare referral programs: Frank Dobbin and Alexandra Kalev, *Getting to Diversity: What Works and What Doesn't* (Cambridge, MA: Harvard University Press, 2022), 146–48.

239 Three-quarters of service sector employees: Linda Smith and Victoria Owens, *The Illusion of Parent Choice: Lessons Learned from BPC's Parent Survey Series*, Bipartisan Policy Center, 2023, https://bipartisanpolicy.org/download/?file=/wp-content/uploads/2023/05/BPC_ECI-Parent-Report_R04.pdf.

239 Data from the Shift Project: Kristen Harknett, Daniel Schneider, and Sigrid Luhr, "Who Cares If Parents have Unpredictable Work Schedules? Just-in-Time Work Schedules and Child Care Arrangements," *Social Problems* 69, no. 1 (2022): 164–83, https://doi.org/10.1093/socpro/spaa020.

239 conflict arising from schedule instability is most acute: Luhr, Schneider, and Harknett, "Parenting Without Predictability."

239 schedule stability was strongly associated: Kristen Harknett, Jeremy Mopsick, and Clem Aeppli, "The Ripple Effects of Job Quality: From Worker Retention to Children's School Success—Schedule Stability and Employee Retention at Ikea," panel paper, Association for Public Policy Analysis & Management research conference, Atlanta, GA, November 11, 2023, https://appam.confex.com/appam/2023/meetingapp.cgi/Paper/50037.

239 ended on-call shifts: Kalev and Dobbin, "The Surprising Benefits of Work/Life Support."

239 headed up by a single parent: A single mother leads 41 percent of Black families, 25 percent of Hispanic families, 13 percent of white families, and 11 percent of Asian American families. See Kalev and Dobbin, "The Surprising Benefits of Work/Life Support."

239 More than half of all US households are dual-earner households: Julie Sullivan, "Comparing Characteristics and Selected Expenditures of Dual- and Single-Income Households with Children," *Monthly Labor Review*, US Bureau of Labor Statistics, September 2020, https://doi.org/10.21916/mlr.2020.19.

240 women are less likely than men to have a stay-at-home spouse: Jill E. Yavorsky, Lisa

A. Keister, and Yue Qian, "Gender in the One Percent," *Contexts* 19, no. 1 (2020): 12–17, https://doi.org/10.1177/1536504220902196.

240 scenario where the policy will cover: Caroline Criado Perez, *Invisible Women* (New York: Abrams Press, 2019), 90.

240 many organizations have formal expectations: Hanna Papanek, "Men, Women, and Work: Reflections on the Two-Person Career," *American Journal of Sociology* 78, no. 4 (1973): 852–72, https://doi.org/10.1086/225406.

240 These types of expectations are also common: Amy Diehl and Leanne M. Dzubinski, *Glass Walls: Shattering the Six Gender Bias Barriers Still Holding Women Back at Work* (Lanham, MD: Rowman & Littlefield, 2023), 30–31.

241 "Behind every successful executive": Orianna Rosa Royle, "Meet the Dads Choosing Caring for Kids over Careers: 'Men Are Starting to Realize That Missing Crucial Morning Time and Bedtime Adds Up,'" *Fortune*, August 24, 2023, https://fortune .com/2023/08/24/stay-at-home-dads-choosing-caregiving-over-breadwinning.

241 "[The structure] was preventing both men and women": Brigid Schulte, "CNN Journalist Josh Levs Forced His Employer to Give New Dads More Time off. Now He Wants Others to Speak Up, Too," *Washington Post*, June 15, 2015, https://www.washingtonpost.com /news/inspired-life/wp/2015/06/15/as-a-new-father-cnn-journalist-josh-levs-forced -his-employer-to-give-dads-more-time-off-now-he-wants-others-to-speak-up-too/.

241 EEOC issued guidance: US Equal Employment Opportunity Commission, "Enforcement Guidance on Pregnancy Discrimination and Related Issues," EEOC Notice 915.003, June 25, 2015, https://www.eeoc.gov/laws/guidance/enforcement-guidance-pregnancy -discrimination-and-related-issues.

241 "We're a generation": Jason Rosario and Kate Murphy, "How a CNN Journalist Fought for Better Paid Paternity Leave—and Won," Yahoo!News, April 24, 2019, https:// www.yahoo.com/video/how-cnn-journalist-fought-for-better-paid-paternity-leave-and -won-130000964.html.

242 household income: Alexandra Boyle Stanczyk, "Does Paid Family Leave Improve Household Economic Security Following a Birth? Evidence from California," *Social Service Review* 93, no. 2 (2019): 262–304, https://doi.org/10.1086/703138.

242 children's health: Shirlee Lichtman-Sadot and Neryvia Pillay Bell, "Child Health in Elementary School Following California's Paid Family Leave Program," *Journal of Policy Analysis and Management* 36, no. 4 (2017): 790–827, https://doi.org/10.1002 /pam.22012.

242 women's labor force participation: Maya Rossin-Slater, Christopher J. Ruhm, and Jane Waldfogel, "The Effects of California's Paid Family Leave Program on Mothers' Leave-Taking and Subsequent Labor Market Outcomes," *Journal of Policy Analysis and Management* 32, no. 2 (2013): 224–45, https://doi.org/10.1002/pam.21676.

242 benefit the most from having access to paid leave: Stanczyk, "Does Paid Family Leave Improve Household Economic Security Following a Birth?"

242 lack of sufficient replacement pay: Nikki van der Gaag et al., "State of the World's Fathers 2023: Centering Care in a World in Crisis," Equimundo, Washington, DC, 2023, https://www.equimundo.org/resources/state-of-the-worlds-fathers-2023.

242 boosted men's leave-taking: William H. Dow, Julia M. Goodman, and Holly Stewart, *San Francisco's Paid Parental Leave Ordinance: The First Six Months*, November 2017, https://www.populationsciences.berkeley.edu/sites/default/files/SF%20Paid %20Parental%20Leave%20-%20UC%20Berkeley%20issue%20brief%201.pdf.

243 186 countries offered some parental leave: van der Gaag et al., "State of the World's Fathers 2023."

243 United States is the only high-income country: Claire Cain Miller, "The World 'Has Found a Way to Do This': The U.S. Lags on Paid Leave," *New York Times*, October 25, 2021, https://www.nytimes.com/2021/10/25/upshot/paid-leave-democrats.html.

243 lowest-earning workers who most need paid leave: Amanda Lenhart, Haley Swenson, and Brigid Schulte, *Lifting the Barriers to Paid Family and Medical Leave for Men in the United States*, New America, December 4, 2019, https://www.newamerica.org/better -life-lab/reports/lifting-barriers-paid-family-and-medical-leave-men-united-states/.

243 major racial disparities: Julia M. Goodman and Daniel Schneider, "Racial/Ethnic and Gender Inequities in the Sufficiency of Paid Leave During the COVID-19 Pandemic:

Evidence from the Service Sector," *American Journal of Industrial Medicine* (2023): 1–10, https://doi.org/10.1002/ajim.23533.

243 caregiving is primarily a "women's issue": Ivona Hideg et al., "Supporting Women During Motherhood and Caregiving Necessary, but Not Sufficient: The Need for Men to Become Equal Partners in Childcare," *Industrial and Organizational Psychology* 16, no. 2 (2023): 215–20, doi.org/10.1017/iop.2023.12.

244 number of companies offering equal leave to both parents: Equileap, *Gender Equality Global Report & Ranking, 2023 Edition*, 2023, https://equileap.com/wp-content /uploads/2023/03/Equileap_Global_Report_2023.pdf.

244 more than 70 percent of firms: Ann P. Bartel et al., "Support for Paid Family Leave Among Small Employers Increases During the COVID-19 Pandemic," *Socius* 7 (2021), https://doi.org/10.1177/23780231211061959.

244 "second parent" has had a reserved leave allocation: Ivona Hideg, "New Parental-Leave Benefit Inches Us Ever Closer Toward Gender Equality," *Globe and Mail*, March 29, 2019, https://www.theglobeandmail.com/opinion/article-new-parental-leave-benefit -inches-us-ever-closer-toward-gender/.

244 contribute more equitably at home: Ankita Patnaik, "Reserving Time for Daddy: The Consequences of Fathers' Quotas," *Journal of Labor Economics* 37, no. 4 (2019): 1009–59, https://doi.org/10.1086/703115.

244 Aviva, which offers mothers and fathers: Simon Usborne, "'It Was Seen as Weird': Why Are So Few Men Taking Shared Parental Leave?," *Guardian*, October 5, 2019, https://www.theguardian.com/lifeandstyle/2019/oct/05/shared-parental-leave-seen-as -weird-paternity-leave-in-decline.

245 Norway, which launched a four-week paternity leave quota: Sara Cools, Jon H. Fiva, and Lars J. Kirkebøen, "Causal Effects of Paternity Leave on Children and Parents," *Scandinavian Journal of Economics* 117, no. 3 (2015): 801–28, https://doi.org/10.1111/sjoe.12113.

245 Sweden, where fathers take just under a third: "In Sweden, It's Possible to Combine Career with Family Life. Here's Why," Sweden/Sverige, November 10, 2022, https://sweden .se/life/society/work-life-balance.

245 Generally, maternity leaves of up to a year: Claudia Olivetti and Barbara Petrongolo, "The Economic Consequences of Family Policies: Lessons from a Century of Legislation in High-Income Countries," *Journal of Economic Perspectives* 31, no. 1 (2017): 205–30, https://doi.org/10.1257/jep.31.1.205.

245 leave during the first months of a child's life: Ann P. Bartel et al., "The Impacts of Paid Family and Medical Leave on Worker Health, Family Well-Being, and Employer Outcomes," *Annual Review of Public Health* 44, no. 1 (2023): 429–43, https://doi .org/10.1146/annurev-publhealth-071521-025257.

245 women and men cite negative career impacts: Brad Harrington, Tina Lawler McHugh, and Jennifer Sabatini Fraone, *Expanded Paid Parental Leave: Measuring the Impact of Leave on Work & Family*, Boston College Center for Work & Family, 2019, https:// www.bc.edu/content/dam/files/centers/cwf/research/publications/researchreports /Expanded%20Paid%20Parental%20Leave-%20Study%20Findings%20FINAL %2010-31-19.pdf.

245 be transparent about who can negotiate and what: Hannah Riley Bowles, Bobbi Thomason, and Inmaculada Macias-Alonso, "When Gender Matters in Organizational Negotiations," *Annual Review of Organizational Psychology and Organizational Behavior* 9 (2022): 199–223, https://doi.org/10.1146/annurev-orgpsych-012420-055523.

245 "reboarding" programs: Tara Weiss, "Returning from Parental Leave Can Be Stressful. How Some Employers Aim to Fix That," *Wall Street Journal*, January 26, 2024, https://www.wsj.com/lifestyle/careers/parental-leave-return-stress-331969e4.

245 Law firm Reed Smith: John Iino and Dana Alvaré, interview with Siri Chilazi, May 22, 2023.

246 At Santander bank in the UK: Shoshana Davidson et al., "Supporting Men to Take Longer Parental Leave and Work Flexibly," Behavioural Insights Team, June 2021, https:// www.bi.team/wp-content/uploads/2021/06/PI-dual-trial-report-080621-for-upload.pdf.

246 Japanese men are entitled to paid, father-specific leave: Marianne Bertrand, "Gender in the Twenty-First Century," *AEA Papers and Proceedings* 110 (2020): 1–24, https://doi .org/10.1257/pandp.20201126.

246 Japanese men tend to overestimate: Takeru Miyajima and Hiroyuki Yamaguchi, "I Want to but I Won't: Pluralistic Ignorance Inhibits Intentions to Take Paternity Leave in Japan," *Frontiers in Psychology* 8 (2017), https://doi.org/10.3389/fpsyg.2017.01508.

246 both took a full parental leave: Kalev and Dobbin, "The Surprising Benefits of Work/Life Support."

247 "The more men that do it": Emma Jacobs, "Paternity Leave in Finance: 'The More Men Do It, the Less of a Big Deal It Becomes,'" *Financial Times*, September 24, 2023, https://www.ft.com/content/1d0357e5-6f44-47de-867a-9e6772a59da8.

Chapter 11: Norms That Create Equal Opportunities

248 women and girls could start healing: Anjani Datla and Robert Wilkinson, "Leading with Empathy: Tarana Burke and the Making of the Me Too Movement," Harvard Kennedy School Case 2197.0 (Cambridge, MA: Harvard Kennedy School Case Program, 2020), https://case.hks.harvard.edu/leading-with-empathy-tarana-burke-and-the-making-of-the-me-too-movement/.

249 exposed Hollywood film producer Harvey Weinstein: Jodi Kantor and Megan Twohey, "Harvey Weinstein Paid Off Sexual Harassment Accusers for Decades," *New York Times*, October 5, 2017, https://www.nytimes.com/2017/10/05/us/harvey-weinstein-harassment-allegations.html.

249 In a moving 2019 book: Jodi Kantor and Megan Twohey, *She Said: Breaking the Sexual Harassment Story That Helped Ignite a Movement* (New York: Penguin Press, 2019).

249 and 2022 film: *She Said*, directed by Maria Schrader (Annapurna Pictures and Plan B Entertainment, 2022), https://www.amazon.com/She-Said-Carey-Mulligan/dp/B0B8M326TT.

249 in the United States and around the world: Jodi Kantor and Megan Twohey, "How to Measure the Impact of #MeToo?," *New York Times*, October 3, 2023, https://www.nytimes.com/interactive/2022/10/03/us/me-too-five-years.html.

249 Film producers in Hollywood: Hong Luo and Laurina Zhang, "Scandal, Social Movement, and Change: Evidence From #MeToo in Hollywood," *Management Science* 68, no. 2 (2022): 1278–96, https://doi.org/10.1287/mnsc.2021.3982.

249 corporations have adjusted their policies: Rachel S. Arnow-Richman, James Hicks, and Steven Davidoff Solomon, "Do Social Movements Spur Corporate Change? The Rise of 'MeToo Termination Rights' in CEO Contracts," *Indiana Law Journal* 98, no. 1 (2022): 125–75, https://dx.doi.org/10.2139/ssrn.3787232.

249 an unprecedented number of bills: Jamillah Bowman Williams, Lisa Singh, and Naomi Mezey, "MeToo as Catalyst: A Glimpse in to 21st Century Activism," *University of Chicago Legal Forum* (2019), https://scholarship.law.georgetown.edu/facpub/2217/.

249 arrests for sexual crimes: Ro'ee Levy and Martin Mattsson, "The Effects of Social Movements: Evidence from #MeToo," working paper, 2023, https://doi.org/10.2139/ssrn.3496903.

249 change social norms: Cass R. Sunstein, "Social Norms and Social Roles," *Columbia Law Review* 96, no. 4 (1996): 903–68, https://doi.org/10.2307/1123430.

250 "identity safety": India R. Johnson et al., "What's in a Pronoun: Exploring Gender Pronouns as an Organizational Identity-Safety Cue Among Sexual and Gender Minorities," *Journal of Experimental Social Psychology* 97 (2021), https://doi.org/10.1016/j.jesp.2021.104194.

250 part of meeting introductions: Amy Gallo and Amy Bernstein (Hosts), "How to Push for Policy Changes at Your Company," November 21, 2022, in *Women at Work*, Harvard Business Review podcast (Season 8, Episode 6), 15:00, https://hbr.org/podcast/2022/11/how-to-push-for-policy-changes-at-your-company.

251 "if they all jump together": *She Said*, directed by Maria Schrader.

251 "a sexual harassment hotline to call": Julia A. Maciejak, Rysa Tahilramani, and Tess C. Wayland, "New York Times Reporter Jodi Kantor, Actress Ashley Judd Discuss the #MeToo Movement at Harvard IOP," *Harvard Crimson*, November 11, 2022, https://www.thecrimson.com/article/2022/11/11/kantor-judd-metoo-iop/.

251 Trainings that focus on legal compliance: Frank Dobbin and Alexandra Kalev, *Getting to Diversity: What Works and What Doesn't* (Cambridge, MA: Harvard University Press, 2022), 20–21.

251 hiring, promotion, or turnover: Ayushi Narayan, "The Limits of Using Grievance Procedures to Combat Workplace Discrimination," *Industrial Relations* 63, no. 1 (2024): 26–42, https://doi.org/10.1111/irel.12335.

252 change what people perceived to be acceptable: Datla and Wilkinson, "Leading with Empathy."

252 many of us don't want to feel guilty: Kate Sweeny et al., "Information Avoidance: Who, What, When, and Why," *Review of General Psychology* 14, no. 4 (2010): 340–53, https://doi.org/10.1037/a0021288.

253 most people *are* voting: Alan S. Gerber and Todd Rogers, "Descriptive Social Norms and Motivation to Vote: Everybody's Voting and so Should You," *Journal of Politics* 71, no. 1 (2009): 178–91, https://doi.org/10.1017/S0022381608090117.

253 saving energy: Hunt Allcott, "Social Norms and Energy Conservation," *Journal of Public Economics* 95, no. 9 (2011): 1082–95, https://doi.org/10.1016/j.jpubeco.2011.03.003.

253 reusing their towels in hotels: Noah J. Goldstein, Robert B. Cialdini, and Vladas Griskevicius, "A Room with a Viewpoint: Using Social Norms to Motivate Environmental Conservation in Hotels," *Journal of Consumer Research* 35, no. 3 (2008): 472–82, https://doi.org/10.1086/586910.

253 beliefs about earnings among married heterosexual couples: Richard Fry et al., "In a Growing Share of U.S. Marriages, Husbands and Wives Earn About the Same," Pew Research Center, April 13, 2023, https://www.pewresearch.org/social-trends/2023/04/13/in-a-growing-share-of-u-s-marriages-husbands-and-wives-earn-about-the-same/.

254 other drivers in the state would do so: Dale T. Miller and Deborah A. Prentice, "Changing Norms to Change Behavior," *Annual Review of Psychology* 67 (2016): 339–61, https://doi.org/10.1146/annurev-psych-010814-015013.

254 wives working outside the home: Leonardo Bursztyn et al., "Misperceived Social Norms: Women Working Outside the Home in Saudi Arabia," *American Economic Review* 110, no. 10 (2020): 2997–3029, https://doi.org/10.1257/aer.20180975.

255 help all of us save energy: Hunt Allcott and Todd Rogers, "The Short-Run and Long-Run Effects of Behavioral Interventions: Experimental Evidence from Energy Conservation," *American Economic Review* 104, no. 10 (2014): 3003–37, https://doi.org/10.1257/aer.104.10.3003.

255 prefer the additional ink to the additional cost: Paul J. Ferraro and Michael K. Price, "Using Nonpecuniary Strategies to Influence Behavior: Evidence from a Large-Scale Field Experiment," *Review of Economics and Statistics* 95, no. 1 (2013): 64–73, https://doi.org/10.1162/REST_a_00344.

257 expected way to behave: Aneeta Rattan et al., "Tackling the Underrepresentation of Women in Media," *Harvard Business Review*, June 6, 2019, https://hbr.org/2019/06/tackling-the-underrepresentation-of-women-in-media.

258 a new ruling by the Supreme Court: Margaret E. Tankard and Elizabeth Levy Paluck, "The Effect of a Supreme Court Decision Regarding Gay Marriage on Social Norms and Personal Attitudes," *Psychological Science* 28, no. 9 (2017): 1334–44, https://doi.org/10.1177/0956797617709594.

258 another patron in a restaurant: Cass R. Sunstein, "On the Expressive Function of Law," *University of Pennsylvania Law Review* 144, no. 5 (1996): 2021–53, https://doi.org/10.2307/3312647.

258 German government approved a bylaw restricting heating: Kate Connolly, "German Government Approved a Bylaw Restricting Heating," *Guardian*, August 24, 2022, https://www.theguardian.com/world/2022/aug/24/germany-approves-limit-on-heating-public-buildings-to-save-energy.

258 a bridge too far: Zachary Brown et al., "Testing the Effect of Defaults on the Thermostat Settings of OECD Employees," *Energy Economics* 39 (2013): 128–34, https://doi.org/10.1016/j.eneco.2013.04.011.

259 for same-sex marriage: "Majority of Public Disapproves of Supreme Court's Decision to Overturn Roe v. Wade," Pew Research Center, July 6, 2022, https://www.pewresearch.org/politics/2022/07/06/majority-of-public-disapproves-of-supreme-courts-decision-to-overturn-roe-v-wade/.

259 increasing the share of female teachers: Joshua T. Dean and Seema Jayachandran,

"Changing Family Attitudes to Promote Female Employment," *AEA Papers and Proceedings* 109 (2019): 138–42, https://doi.org/10.1257/pandp.20191074.

259 "How to become an influencer" online: Werner Geyser, "How to Become an Influencer: 7 Easy Steps to Becoming a Social Media Influencer Today," Influencer Marketing Hub, January 30, 2024, https://influencermarketinghub.com/how-to-become-an-influencer/.

259 take inspiration from *Shuga*: Abhijit Banerjee, Eliana La Ferrara, and Victor Orozco, "Entertainment, Education, and Attitudes Toward Domestic Violence," *AEA Papers and Proceedings* 109 (2019): 133–37, https://doi.org/10.1257/pandp.20191073.

260 soap operas in Brazil started to feature small families: Eliana La Ferrara, Alberto Chong, and Suzanne Duryea, "Soap Operas and Fertility: Evidence from Brazil," *American Economic Journal: Applied Economics* 4, no. 4 (2012): 1–31, https://doi.org/10.1257/app.4.4.1.

260 cable television became available: Robert Jensen and Emily Oster, "The Power of TV: Cable Television and Women's Status in India," *Quarterly Journal of Economics* 124, no. 3 (2009): 1057–94, https://doi.org/10.1162/qjec.2009.124.3.1057.

260 "personal beliefs stayed the same": Maanvi Singh, "'Genius Grant' Winner Used a Soap Opera to Prove a Point About Prejudice," NPR, October 11, 2017, https://www.npr.org/sections/goatsandsoda/2017/10/11/556869077/genius-grant-winner-used-a-soap-opera-to-prove-a-point-about-prejudice.

260 at 56 US middle schools: Elizabeth Levy Paluck, Hana Shepherd, and Peter M. Aronow, "Changing Climates of Conflict: A Social Network Experiment in 56 Schools," *Proceedings of the National Academy of Sciences* 113, no. 3 (2016): 566–571, https://doi.org/10.1073/pnas.1514483113.

261 stereotype that associates eating meat with masculinity: *The Game Changers*, directed by Louie Psihoyos (Joseph Pace and James Wilks, 2018), https://gamechangersmovie.com/.

261 political scientist Kevin Munger ran an experiment: Kevin Munger, "Tweetment Effects on the Tweeted: Experimentally Reducing Racist Harassment," *Political Behavior* 39, no. 3 (2017): 629–49, https://doi.org/10.1007/s11109-016-9373-5.

262 he shone a light on racism in the United States: "Colin Kaepernick Takes a Knee for National Anthem," ABC News, September 2, 2016, YouTube video, https://www.youtube.com/watch?v=bBdoDOXMWkg.

262 Kneeling has now become a symbol of antiracism: "Women Soccer Players Take a Knee in Protest of Racism at Tokyo Olympics," Associated Press, July 22, 2021, https://www.today.com/news/megan-rapinoe-alex-morgan-soccer-players-take-knee-protest-tokyo-t226302.

262 antiharassment trainings that focused on managers: Dobbin and Kalev, *Getting to Diversity*, 25–32.

263 effectiveness of twelve bystander programs: Samuel C. Bell, Ann L. Coker, and Emily R. Clear, "Bystander Program Effectiveness: A Review of the Evidence in Educational Settings (2007–2018)," in *Handbook of Sexual Assault and Sexual Assault Prevention*, eds. William T. O'Donohue and Paul A. Schewe (Cham, Switzerland: Springer, 2019), 433–50, https://doi.org/10.1007/978-3-030-23645-8_26.

263 bystander training in the US Army: Sharyn J. Potter and Mary M. Moynihan, "Bringing in the Bystander In-Person Prevention Program to a US Military Installation: Results from a Pilot Study," *Military Medicine* 176, no. 8 (2011): 870–75, https://doi.org/10.7205/MILMED-D-10-00483.

264 what the US Equal Employment Opportunity Commission recommended: Claire Cain Miller, "Sexual Harassment Training Doesn't Work. But Some Things Do," *New York Times*, December 11, 2017, https://www.nytimes.com/2017/12/11/upshot/sexual-harassment-workplace-prevention-effective.html.

264 peers' approval when intervening: Lindsay M. Orchowski et al., "Bystander Intervention Among College Men: The Role of Alcohol and Correlates of Sexual Aggression," *Journal of Interpersonal Violence* 31, no. 17 (2016): 2824–46, https://doi.org/10.1177/0886260515581904.

264 "diffusion of responsibility": John M. Darley and Bibb Latane, "Bystander Intervention in Emergencies: Diffusion of Responsibility," *Journal of Personality and Social Psychology* 8, no. 4 (1968): 377–83, https://doi.org/10.1037/h0025589.

265 "coming in to present to the executive committee": Tamar Hughes, interview with Siri Chilazi, January 25, 2024.

266 "The proactivity of people in the majority is really important": Alison Beard, "Life's Work: An Interview with Megan Rapinoe," *Harvard Business Review*, July–August 2020, https://hbr.org/2020/07/lifes-work-an-interview-with-megan-rapinoe.

266 gender-inclusive "they/them" has spread in English: "Singular 'They,'" Merriam-Webster, accessed January 4, 2024, https://www.merriam-webster.com/wordplay /singular-nonbinary-they.

266 less associated with the human norm: Margit Tavits and Efrén O. Pérez, "Language Influences Mass Opinion Toward Gender and LGBT Equality," *Proceedings of the National Academy of Sciences* 116, no. 34 (2019): 16781–86, https://doi.org/10.1073 /pnas.1908156116.

266 detailed Inclusive Language Guide: "Inclusive Language Guide," American Psychological Association, accessed January 4, 2024, https://www.apa.org/about/apa/equity -diversity-inclusion/language-guidelines.

266 neither nouns nor pronouns have a marked gender: Nayantara Dutta, "The Subtle Ways Language Shapes Us," BBC, October 6, 2020, https://www.bbc.com/culture /article/20201006-are-some-languages-more-sexist-than-others.

267 remove stereotypical photos: Anthony Miyagusuku, interview with Siri Chilazi, May 15, 2023.

267 "good allies exhibit curiosity": Kenji Yoshino and David Glasgow, *Say the Right Thing: How to Talk about Identity, Diversity, and Justice* (New York: Atria Books, 2023), 65.

267 Black women's sense of organizational belonging: India R. Johnson and Evava S. Pietri, "An Ally You Say? Endorsing White Women as Allies to Encourage Perceptions of Allyship and Organizational Identity-Safety among Black Women," *Group Processes & Intergroup Relations* 25, no. 2 (2022): 453–73, https://doi.org/10.1177/1368430220975482.

267 open-access resource for how to become an ally: "Allyship at Work," LeanIn.Org, accessed August 31, 2023, https://leanin.org/allyship-at-work.

267 Brazilian fishers are signaling norms to each other: Ernst Fehr and Andreas Leibbrandt, "A Field Study on Cooperativeness and Impatience in the Tragedy of the Commons," *Journal of Public Economics* 95, no. 9 (2011): 1144–55, https://doi.org/10.1016/j .jpubeco.2011.05.013.

268 debunking the idea that men just don't know: Stefanie K. Johnson et al., "Has Sexual Harassment at Work Decreased Since #MeToo?," *Harvard Business Review*, July 18, 2019, https://hbr.org/2019/07/has-sexual-harassment-at-work-decreased-since-metoo.

268 increased scrutiny on the topic: Ksenia Keplinger et al., "Women at Work: Changes in Sexual Harassment Between September 2016 and September 2018," *PloS One* 14, no. 7 (2019), https://doi.org/10.1371/journal.pone.0218313.

268 "is really, really important": Miller, "Sexual Harassment Training Doesn't Work. But Some Things Do."

269 70 percent of the respondents believed: Anna Brown, "More Than Twice as Many Americans Support Than Oppose the #MeToo Movement," Pew Research Center, September 29, 2022, https://www.pewresearch.org/social-trends/2022/09/29/more-than-twice -as-many-americans-support-than-oppose-the-metoo-movement/.

Chapter 12: Culture That Fosters Thriving

270 country's leading scientists: Lucien Wilkinson, "Perth Hosts Forum to Inspire the Next Generation of Female Researchers," Curtin University, April 2, 2019, https:// research.curtin.edu.au/news/perth-hosts-forum-to-inspire-the-next-generation-of -female-researchers/?type=media.

270 inspired thousands of budding female scientists around the world: "L'Oréal Australia Presents Girls in Science Forum 2019," UNSW Sydney, accessed August 23, 2023, https:// www.events.unsw.edu.au/event/loreal-australia-presents-girls-science-forum-2019.

270 similar, albeit more extensive, program in Puerto Rico: "L'Oréal for Girls in Science Puerto Rico Program Graduates 20 High School Students," News Is my Business, May 10, 2023, https://newsismybusiness.com/loreal-for-girls-in-science-puerto-rico-program -graduates-20-high-school-students/.

271 inspired the film: Margot Lee Shetterly, *Hidden Figures: The American Dream and the Untold Story of the Black Women Mathematicians Who Helped Win the Space Race* (New York: William Morrow, 2016). See also Maya Wei-Haas, "The True Story of 'Hidden Figures,' the Forgotten Women Who Helped Win the Space Race," *Smithsonian Magazine*, September 8, 2016, https://www.smithsonianmag.com/history/forgotten-black-women-mathematicians-who-helped-win-wars-and-send-astronauts-space-180960393/.

271 a toxic workplace culture: Donald Sull and Charles Sull, "The Toxic Culture Gap Shows Companies Are Failing Women," *MIT Sloan Management Review*, March 14, 2023, https://sloanreview.mit.edu/article/the-toxic-culture-gap-shows-companies-are-failing-women/.

272 The pattern for employees of color: Mallory A. McCord et al., "A Meta-Analysis of Sex and Race Differences in Perceived Workplace Mistreatment," *Journal of Applied Psychology* 103, no. 2 (2018): 137–63, https://doi.org/10.1037/apl0000250.

272 "bridging social capital": Robert D. Putnam, *Bowling Alone: The Collapse and Revival of American Community* (New York: Simon & Schuster, 2020).

273 opt for difference instead: Erika L. Kirgios, Edward H. Chang, and Katherine L. Milkman, "Going It Alone: Competition Increases the Attractiveness of Minority Status," *Organizational Behavior and Human Decision Processes* 161 (2020): 20–33, https://doi.org/10.1016/j.obhdp.2020.03.009.

274 they just exuded a sense of normalcy: Thomas Breda et al., "How Effective Are Female Role Models in Steering Girls Towards STEM? Evidence from French High Schools," *Economic Journal* 133, no. 653 (2023): 1773–1809, https://doi.org/10.1093/ej/uead019.

274 "boys can't be president in Finland": Adrian Lewis, "30th Anniversary of the CEDAW Committee," *Global Justice Center Blog*, June 27, 2016, https://www.globaljusticecenter.net/30th-anniversary-of-the-cedaw-committee/.

274 "not as others believe we should be": "Breaking Down Narrow Beauty Stereotypes," Dove, accessed August 23, 2023, https://www.dove.com/us/en/stories/about-dove/breaking-down-narrow-beauty-stereotypes.html.

274 *This Girl Can* campaign in the United Kingdom: "This Girl Can," This Girl Can UK, accessed August 23, 2023, https://www.thisgirlcan.co.uk/.

274 in Australia: "This Girl Can—Victoria," This Girl Can AU, accessed August 23, 2023, https://thisgirlcan.com.au/.

275 female students majoring in economics: Catherine Porter and Danila Serra, "Gender Differences in the Choice of Major: The Importance of Female Role Models," *American Economic Journal: Applied Economics* 12, no. 3 (2020): 226–54, https://doi.org/10.1257/app.20180426.

275 "self-concept against stereotypes": Nilanjana Dasgupta, "Ingroup Experts and Peers as Social Vaccines Who Inoculate the Self-Concept: The Stereotype Inoculation Model," *Psychological Inquiry* 22, no. 4 (2011): 231–46, https://doi.org/10.1080/1047840X.2011.607313.

275 similarity, desirability, and attainability are key: Thekla Morgenroth, Michelle K. Ryan, and Kim Peters, "The Motivational Theory of Role Modeling: How Role Models Influence Role Aspirants' Goals," *Review of General Psychology* 19, no. 4 (2015): 465–83, https://doi.org/10.1037/gpr0000059.

275 the types of majors students chose: Serena Canaan and Pierre Mouganie, "The Impact of Advisor Gender on Female Students' STEM Enrollment and Persistence," *Journal of Human Resources* 58, no. 2 (2023): 593–632, https://doi.org/10.3368/jhr.58.4.0320-10796R2. Similar effects were found for same-gender peer advisors in the US: "Female (but not male) mentors protected women's belonging in engineering, self-efficacy, motivation, retention in engineering majors, and post college engineering aspirations." See Tara C. Dennehy and Nilanjana Dasgupta, "Female Peer Mentors Early in College Increase Women's Positive Academic Experiences and Retention in Engineering," *Proceedings of the National Academy of Sciences* 114, no. 23 (2017): 5964–69, https://doi.org/10.1073/pnas.1613117114.

276 inspired to run for public office themselves: Lori Beaman et al., "Powerful Women: Does Exposure Reduce Bias?," *Quarterly Journal of Economics* 124, no. 4 (2009): 1497–1540, https://academic.oup.com/qje/article-abstract/124/4/1497/1917190.

276 they now wanted them to become politicians: Lori Beaman et al., "Female Leadership Raises Aspirations and Educational Attainment for Girls: A Policy Experiment in India," *Science* 335, no. 6068 (2012): 582–86, https://doi.org/10.1126/science.1212382.

276 in 2023, India reserved a third: Rhea Mogul, "India Agrees to Reserve a Third of Parliament Seats for Women. But the Change Could Still Take years," CNN, September 21, 2023, https://www.cnn.com/2023/09/21/india/india-women-parliament-bill-intl-hnk/index.html.

276 in Norway in 2003: Marianne Bertrand et al., "Breaking the Glass Ceiling? The Effect of Board Quotas on Female Labour Market Outcomes in Norway," *Review of Economic Studies* 86, no. 1 (2019): 191–239, https://doi.org/10.1093/restud/rdy032.

276 in Italy in 2011: Agata Maida and Andrea Weber, "Female Leadership and Gender Gap Within Firms: Evidence from an Italian Board Reform," *Industrial & Labor Relations Review* 75, no. 2 (2022): 488–515, https://doi.org/10.1177/0019793920961995.

276 Based on data from a US law firm: Kathleen L. McGinn and Katherine L. Milkman, "Looking Up and Looking Out: Career Mobility Effects of Demographic Similarity Among Professionals," *Organization Science* 24, no. 4 (2013): 1041–60, https://doi.org/10.1287/orsc.1120.0778.

277 creating a safe working environment: Jeremy M. Beus et al., "Safety Climate and Injuries: An Examination of Theoretical and Empirical Relationships," *Journal of Applied Psychology* 95, no. 4 (2010): 713–27, https://doi.org/10.1037/a0019164.

277 PPE quite literally was not "fit" for women: Rachel Thompson et al., *Fit for Women? Safe and Decent PPE for Women Health and Care Workers*, Women in Global Health, 2021, https://womeningh.org/wp-content/uploads/2022/11/WGH-Fit-for-Women-report-2021.pdf.

277 "with ideas, questions, concerns, or mistakes": Amy C. Edmondson and Mark Mortensen, "What Psychological Safety Looks Like in a Hybrid Workplace," *Harvard Business Review*, April 19, 2021, https://hbr.org/2021/04/what-psychological-safety-looks-like-in-a-hybrid-workplace.

277 guidelines on physical safety at work: "How to Create a Safe Working Environment," Simplified Safety, accessed August 31, 2023, https://simplifiedsafety.com/blog/how-to-create-a-safe-working-environment/.

278 diversity = productivity: Scott E. Page, *The Difference: How the Power of Diversity Creates Better Groups, Firms, Schools, and Societies* (Princeton, NJ: Princeton University Press, 2007).

278 advance collective intelligence: Anita Williams Woolley et al., "Evidence for a Collective Intelligence Factor in the Performance of Human Groups," *Science* 330, no. 6004 (2010): 686–88, https://doi.org/10.1126/science.1193147.

279 "microaggressions" in the 1970s: Chester M. Pierce et al., "An Experiment in Racism: TV Commercials," *Education and Urban Society* 10, no. 1 (1977): 61–87, https://doi.org/10.1177/001312457701000105.

279 less likely to be spoken to in a positive tone: Amy Handlan and Haoyu Sheng, "Gender and Tone in Recorded Economics Presentations: Audio Analysis with Machine Learning," working paper, 2023, https://dx.doi.org/10.2139/ssrn.4316513.

279 more likely to be interrupted in patronizing or hostile ways: Pascaline Dupas et al., "Gender and the Dynamics of Economics Seminars," NBER Working Paper Series 28494, National Bureau of Economic Research, Cambridge, MA, 2021, https://doi.org/10.3386/w28494.

279 At Harvard Kennedy School: "Culture Ambassadors Network," Harvard Kennedy School, accessed September 19, 2023, https://www.hks.harvard.edu/more/about/diversity-equity-and-anti-racism/culture-ambassadors-network.

279 "two-two rule": Kenji Yoshino and David Glasgow, *Say the Right Thing: How to Talk About Identity, Diversity, and Justice* (New York: Atria Books, 2023), 145.

280 worthy ideas see the light of day: Laura Morgan Roberts, Megan Grayson, and Brook Dennard Rosser, "An Antidote to Microaggressions? Microvalidations," *Harvard Business Review*, May 15, 2023, https://hbr.org/2023/05/an-antidote-to-microaggressions-microvalidations.

280 "rated as effective twice as often by executives": Charles Duhigg, "What Google Learned from Its Quest to Build the Perfect Team," *New York Times Magazine*, February

25, 2016, https://www.nytimes.com/2016/02/28/magazine/what-google-learned-from -its-quest-to-build-the-perfect-team.html.

280 modeling curiosity: Amy Edmondson, "Building a Psychologically Safe Workplace," filmed April 12, 2014 at TEDxHGSE, video, https://www.youtube.com/watch?v =LhoLuui9gX8&ab_channel=TEDxTalks.

281 Iris wrote an article: Iris Bohnet, "Tackling 'the Thin File' That Can Prevent a Promo- tion," *New York Times*, October 3, 2017, https://www.nytimes.com/2017/10/03/business /women-minority-promotion.html.

281 victims of "performance-support bias": Janice Fanning Madden, "Performance- Support Bias and the Gender Pay Gap Among Stockbrokers," *Gender & Society* 26, no. 3 (2012): 488–518, https://doi.org/10.1177/0891243212438546.

281 mentoring program for early-career female assistant professors: Donna K. Ginther et al., "Can Mentoring Help Female Assistant Professors in Economics? An Evaluation by Randomized Trial," *AEA Papers and Proceedings* 110 (2020): 205–9, https://doi. org/10.1257/pandp.20201121.

281 presence of mentorship programs: Frank Dobbin and Alexandra Kalev, *Getting to Diversity: What Works and What Doesn't* (Cambridge, MA: Harvard University Press, 2022), 92–93.

282 randomized controlled trial in a call center: Jason Sandvik et al., "Should Workplace Programs Be Voluntary or Mandatory? Evidence from a Field Experiment on Mentor- ship," NBER Working Paper Series 29148, National Bureau of Economic Research, Cam- bridge, MA, 2021, https://doi.org/10.3386/w29148.

282 Illinois Workplace Wellness Study: Damon Jones, David Molitor, and Julian Reif, "What Do Workplace Wellness Programs Do? Evidence from the Illinois Workplace Wellness Study," *Quarterly Journal of Economics* 134, no. 4 (2019): 1747–91, https://doi .org/10.1093/qje/qjz023.

282 accountability and continuous learning: Tammy D. Allen et al., "Taking Stock of Two Relational Aspects of Organizational Life: Tracing the History and Shaping the Future of Socialization and Mentoring Research," *Journal of Applied Psychology* 102, no. 3 (2017): 324–37, https://doi.org/10.1037/apl0000086.

283 we can improve the future: Jaewon Yoon et al., "Why Asking for Advice Is More Effective Than Asking for Feedback," *Harvard Business Review*, September 20, 2019, https://hbr.org/2019/09/why-asking-for-advice-is-more-effective-than-asking-for -feedback.

283 a sponsor is someone: Herminia Ibarra, "How to do Sponsorship Right," *Harvard Business Review*, November–December 2022, https://hbr.org/2022/11/how-to-do -sponsorship-right.

283 white men received more endorsements: Emilio J. Castilla, "Gender, Race, and Net- work Advantage in Organizations," *Organization Science* 33, no. 6 (2022): 2085–2540, https://doi.org/10.1287/orsc.2021.1534.

283 "reverse mentoring": Patrice Gordon, *Reverse Mentoring: Removing Barriers and Building Belonging in the Workplace* (New York: Hachette, 2022).

284 admit women as cadets: United States v. Virginia, 518 U.S. 515 (1996).

284 not been exposed to female colleagues: Gordon B. Dahl, Andreas Kotsadam, and Dan-Olof Rooth, "Does Integration Change Gender Attitudes? The Effect of Randomly Assigning Women to Traditionally Male Teams," *Quarterly Journal of Economics* 136, no. 2 (2021): 987–1030, https://doi.org/10.1093/qje/qjaa047.

284 impacts of intergroup contact on behavior are rare: Elizabeth Levy Paluck, Seth A. Green, and Donald P. Green, "The Contact Hypothesis Re-Evaluated," *Behavioural Public Policy* 3, no. 2 (2019): 129–58, https://doi.org/10.1017/bpp.2018.25.

284 among college roommates: Johanne Boisjoly et al., "Empathy or Antipathy? The Im- pact of Diversity," *American Economic Review* 96, no. 5 (2006): 1890–1905, https://doi .org/10.1257/aer.96.5.1890.

285 receive a sportsmanship award: Salma Mousa, "Building Social Cohesion Between Christians and Muslims Through Soccer in Post-ISIS Iraq," *Science* 369, no. 6505 (2020): 866–70, https://doi.org/10.1126/science.abb3153.

285 mixed-caste or same-caste cricket teams: Matt Lowe, "Types of Contact: A Field Ex-

periment on Collaborative and Adversarial Caste Integration," *American Economic Review* 111, no. 6 (2021): 1807–44, https://doi.org/10.1257/AER.20191780.

285 Boston commuters saw: Ryan D. Enos, "Causal Effect of Intergroup Contact on Exclusionary Attitudes," *Proceedings of the National Academy of Sciences* 111, no. 10 (2014): 3699–3704, https://doi.org/10.1073/pnas.1317670111.

285 in Afghanistan, casual interethnic contact: Luke N. Condra and Sera Linardi, "Casual Contact and Ethnic Bias: Experimental Evidence from Afghanistan," *Journal of Politics* 81, no. 3 (2019): 1028–42, https://doi.org/10.1086/703380.

285 differences within groups can sometimes be greater than between groups: Abdelatif Er-rafiy and Markus Brauer, "Modifying Perceived Variability: Four Laboratory and Field Experiments Show the Effectiveness of a Ready-to-Be-Used Prejudice Intervention," *Journal of Applied Social Psychology* 43, no. 4 (2013): 840–53, https://doi.org/10.1111/jasp.12010.

286 increased time spent with employees: Guido Friebel, Matthias Heinz, and Nikolay Zubanov, "Middle Managers, Personnel Turnover, and Performance: A Long-Term Field Experiment in a Retail Chain," *Management Science* 68, no. 1 (2022): 211–29, https://doi.org/10.1287/mnsc.2020.3905.

286 encouraged to have more one-on-one meetings: Silvia Castro, Florian Engelmaier, and Maria Guadalupe, "Fostering Psychological Safety in Teams: Evidence from an RCT," working paper, 2022, https://dx.doi.org/10.2139/ssrn.4141538.

286 guide created by Culture Amp: Lyssa Test, "One-on-One Meeting Template: How to Lead Effective Meetings," Culture Amp, July 12, 2023, https://www.cultureamp.com/blog/one-on-one-meeting-template.

287 integrity and profitability can go hand in hand: Luigi Guiso, Paola Sapienza, and Luigi Zingales, "The Value of Corporate Culture," *Journal of Financial Economics* 117, no. 1 (2015): 60–76, https://doi.org/10.1016/j.jfineco.2014.05.010.

287 through word of mouth: Arianna Marchetti, "Taking Cultural Heterogeneity Seriously: The Distinct Forms of Cultural Distinctiveness in Organizations," working paper, 2020, https://dx.doi.org/10.2139/ssrn.3712842.

287 70 different culture diagnostic instruments were in use: Jennifer A. Chatman and Charles A. O'Reilly, "Paradigm Lost: Reinvigorating the Study of Organizational Culture," *Research in Organizational Behavior* 36 (2016): 199–224, https://doi.org/10.1016/j.riob.2016.11.004.

287 inclusion consists of seven key dimensions: Lauren Romansky et al., "How to Measure Inclusion in the Workplace," *Harvard Business Review*, May 27, 2021, https://hbr.org/2021/05/how-to-measure-inclusion-in-the-workplace.

288 inclusion diagnostic focused on behavioral questions: "Inclusion Diagnostic—Measure Inclusion, Not Just Diversity," Included, accessed January 4, 2024, https://included.com/inclusion-diagnostic/.

288 employee engagement surveys benchmarked against other employers in the same industry: Lexi Croswell, "20 Employee Engagement Survey Questions You Should Ask," Culture Amp, November 10, 2017, https://www.cultureamp.com/blog/employee-engagement-survey-questions.

288 every dollar spent on healthcare to yield the highest benefits: "Member Success Story—Wegmans: Understanding How Employees Value Their Benefits," CEB Workforce Surveys, 2015, https://studylib.net/doc/8077549/view-case-study.

Conclusion: Change for Good

291 "Our hearts and minds were always in the right place": Dana Alvaré and John Iino, interview with Siri Chilazi, May 22, 2023.

291 Ros Atkins at the BBC termed a "constant state of trying": Chilazi, Rattan, and Georgeac, "Ros Atkins and the 50:50 Project at the BBC (A)."

292 Between 2018 and 2022: Reed Smith, *Diversity, Equity & Inclusion Annual Report 2022*, 2022, https://dei.reedsmith.com/articulate/vwv9xKhlLmsQ6awFJlLV#n5hHaptSVKmacArSb4fyIqlKKC0wvgbkXrr8zezoS1Y.

293 When Klawe arrived on Harvey Mudd's campus: Laura Winig and Robert Livingston, "Harvey Mudd College: Promoting Women in Computer Science through Inclusive Education," Harvard Kennedy School Case 2225.0 (Cambridge, MA: Harvard Ken-

nedy School Case Program, 2021), https://case.hks.harvard.edu/harvey-mudd-college
-promoting-women-in-computer-science-through-inclusive-education/.

293 compared to the US national average of 20 percent: National Girls Collaborative
Project, "The State of Girls and Women in STEM," infographic, March 2023, https://
ngcproject.org/resources/state-girls-and-women-stem.

293 student body was 49 percent women: "Fast Facts: Harvey Mudd College," Harvey
Mudd College, accessed January 20, 2024, https://www.hmc.edu/about/facts/.

293 share of Black students had increased: "White House Summit on Equity and Excellence in STEMM," The White House, streamed live on December 12, 2022, YouTube video,
1:13:33, https://www.youtube.com/watch?v=6l4ynrYnUTg&ab_channel=TheWhiteHouse.

293 Maria Klawe summarized: Maria Klawe, "Increasing Female Participation in Computing: The Harvey Mudd College Story," *Computer* 46, no. 3 (2013): 56–8, https://doi
.org/10.1109/MC.2013.4.

294 Klawe shared at a White House conference in 2022: "White House Summit on Eq-
uity and Excellence in STEMM," The White House, streamed live on December 12, 2022,
YouTube video, 1:08:24, https://www.youtube.com/watch?v=6l4ynrYnUTg&ab_channel
=TheWhiteHouse.

295 20/60/20 rule: Dolly Chugh, *The Person You Mean to Be: How Good People Fight
Bias* (New York: Harper Business, 2018), 211.

INDEX

ABOUT THE AUTHORS

Iris Bohnet

Iris Bohnet is the Albert Pratt Professor of Business and Government and the co-director of the Women and Public Policy Program at Harvard Kennedy School. She is a behavioral economist and the author of the award-winning book *What Works: Gender Equality by Design*.

Iris advises companies and governments on gender equity around the world. She was appointed to the Gender Equality Advisory Council of the G7 in 2021 and named one of the Most Influential Academics in Government and one of the most Influential People in Gender Policy by Apolitical. She regularly speaks on gender equity, including at World Economic Forum meetings, the Aspen Institute, the New York Times New Rules Summit, the Financial Times Women at the Top conference, and Grace Hopper.

Iris's work has been featured in media outlets worldwide, including the *Atlantic*, the BBC, CNN, *Bloomberg News*, the *Economist*, the *Financial Times*, *Harvard Business Review*, the *New York Times*, the *Wall Street Journal*, and the *Washington Post*. Her academic work has been published in the top-ranked peer-reviewed journals of her profession.

Iris received her doctorate in Economics from the University of Zurich, Switzerland, and has received several awards and honorary degrees. She and her family live in Newton, Massachusetts.

Siri Chilazi

Siri Chilazi is a researcher at the Women and Public Policy Program at Harvard Kennedy School and an internationally recognized expert in advancing women and promoting gender equity in organizations.

As an academic researcher, Siri specializes in identifying practical approaches to close gender gaps at work by de-biasing structures and designing fairer processes. As an advisor and speaker, she collaborates with organizations, including start-ups, large multinational companies, top professional services firms, governments, nonprofits, and academic institutions, to advance gender equity through evidence-based insights.

Siri's work regularly appears in leading media outlets including the BBC, *Fast Company*, *Forbes*, *Harvard Business Review*, and the *New York Times*. She has spoken on gender equity at hundreds of large events, including the American College of Surgeons annual meeting, the Women's Forum Global Meeting, and the DEI Innovation Summit.

Siri has an MBA from Harvard Business School, a master's in public policy from Harvard Kennedy School, and a BA in chemistry and physics from Harvard College. In addition to her academic career, she is an award-winning fitness instructor, presenter, and educator. Siri is married and lives in Boston, Massachusetts.